CCNA Voice

Official Exam Certification Guide

Jeremy Cioara, CCIE No. 11727

Michael J. Cavanaugh, CCIE No. 4516

Kris A. Krake, CCIE No. 10229

Cisco Press

800 East 96th Street

Indianapolis, IN 46240

CCNA Voice Official Exam Certification Guide

Jeremy Cioara, CCIE No. 11727; Michael J. Cavanaugh, CCIE No. 4516; Kris A. Krake, CCIE No. 10229

Copyright© 2009 Cisco Systems, Inc.

Cisco Press logo is a trademark of Cisco Systems, Inc.

Published by:
Cisco Press
800 East 96th Street
Indianapolis, IN 46240 USA

Printed in the United States of America

First Printing October 2008

Library of Congress Cataloging-in-Publication Data:

Cioara, Jeremy.
  CCNA Voice official exam certification guide / Jeremy Cioara, Michael J. Cavanaugh, Kris
A. Krake.

     p. cm.

    ISBN 987-158720-2070 (hbk: CD-ROM) 1. Internet
telephony—Examinations—Study guides. I. Cavanaugh, Michael J. II. Krake, Kris A. III.
Title.

    TK5105.8865.C56 2008
    004.69'5076—dc22

                2008040351

ISBN-13: 978-1-58720-207-0

ISBN-10: 1-58720-207-7

Warning and Disclaimer

This book is designed to provide information about the 640-460 Implementing Cisco IOS Unified Communications (IIUC) certification exam. Every effort has been made to make this book as complete and as accurate as possible, but no warranty or fitness is implied.

The information is provided on an "as is" basis. The authors, Cisco Press, and Cisco Systems, Inc., shall have neither liability nor responsibility to any person or entity with respect to any loss or damages arising from the information contained in this book or from the use of the discs or programs that may accompany it.

The opinions expressed in this book belong to the authors and are not necessarily those of Cisco Systems, Inc.

Trademark Acknowledgments

All terms mentioned in this book that are known to be trademarks or service marks have been appropriately capitalized. Cisco Press or Cisco Systems, Inc., cannot attest to the accuracy of this information. Use of a term in this book should not be regarded as affecting the validity of any trademark or service mark.

Corporate and Government Sales

The publisher offers excellent discounts on this book when ordered in quantity for bulk purchases or special sales, which may include electronic versions and/or custom covers and content particular to your business, training goals, marketing focus, and branding interests. For more information, please contact:

U.S. Corporate and Government Sales
1-800-382-3419   corpsales@pearsontechgroup.com

For sales outside the United States please contact:
International Sales
international@pearsoned.com

Feedback Information

At Cisco Press, our goal is to create in-depth technical books of the highest quality and value. Each book is crafted with care and precision, undergoing rigorous development that involves the unique expertise of members from the professional technical community.

Readers' feedback is a natural continuation of this process. If you have any comments regarding how we could improve the quality of this book, or otherwise alter it to better suit your needs, you can contact us through e-mail at feedback@ciscopress.com. Please make sure to include the book title and ISBN in your message.

We greatly appreciate your assistance.

Publisher: Paul Boger

Associate Publisher: Dave Dusthimer

Cisco Representative: Anthony Wolfenden

Cisco Press Program Manager: Jeff Brady

Executive Editor: Brett Bartow

Managing Editor: Patrick Kanouse

Development Editor: Dayna Isley

Senior Project Editor: Tonya Simpson

Copy Editor: Bill McManus

Technical Editors: Alex Hannah, Michael Valentine

Editorial Assistant: Vanessa Evans

Book Designer: Louisa Adair

Composition: Mark Shirar

Indexer: WordWise Publishing Services

Proofreader: Kathy Ruiz

CISCO.

Americas Headquarters	Asia Pacific Headquarters	Europe Headquarters
Cisco Systems, Inc.	Cisco Systems, Inc.	Cisco Systems International BV
170 West Tasman Drive	168 Robinson Road	Haarlerbergpark
San Jose, CA 95134-1706	#28-01 Capital Tower	Haarlerbergweg 13-19
USA	Singapore 068912	1101 CH Amsterdam
www.cisco.com	www.cisco.com	The Netherlands
Tel: 408 526-4000	Tel: +65 6317 7777	www-europe.cisco.com
800 553-NETS (6387)	Fax: +65 6317 7799	Tel: +31 0 800 020 0791
Fax: 408 527-0883		Fax: +31 0 20 357 1100

Cisco has more than 200 offices worldwide. Addresses, phone numbers, and fax numbers are listed on the Cisco Website at **www.cisco.com/go/offices.**

©2007 Cisco Systems, Inc. All rights reserved. CCVP, the Cisco logo, and the Cisco Square Bridge logo are trademarks of Cisco Systems, Inc.; Changing the Way We Work, Live, Play, and Learn is a service mark of Cisco Systems, Inc.; and Access Registrar, Aironet, BPX, Catalyst, CCDA, CCDP, CCIE, CCIP, CCNA, CCNP, CCSP, Cisco, the Cisco Certified Internetwork Expert logo, Cisco IOS, Cisco Press, Cisco Systems, Cisco Systems Capital, the Cisco Systems logo, Cisco Unity, Enterprise/Solver, EtherChannel, EtherFast, EtherSwitch, Fast Step, Follow Me Browsing, FormShare, GigaDrive, GigaStack, HomeLink, Internet Quotient, IOS, IP/TV, iQ Expertise, the iQ logo, iQ Net Readiness Scorecard, iQuick Study, LightStream, Linksys, MeetingPlace, MGX, Networking Academy, Network Registrar, Packet, PIX, ProConnect, RateMUX, ScriptShare, SlideCast, SMARTnet, StackWise, The Fastest Way to Increase Your Internet Quotient, and TransPath are registered trademarks of Cisco Systems, Inc. and/or its affiliates in the United States and certain other countries.

All other trademarks mentioned in this document or Website are the property of their respective owners. The use of the word partner does not imply a partnership relationship between Cisco and any other company. (0609R)

About the Authors

Jeremy D. Cioara, CCIE No. 11727, works in many facets of the Cisco networking realm. As an author, he has written multiple books for Cisco Press and Exam Cram. As an instructor, he teaches at Interface Technical Training (http://www.interfacett. com) in Phoenix, Arizona. Likewise, Jeremy has recorded many E-Learning titles at CBTNuggets (http://www.cbtnuggets.com). Finally, Jeremy is the CIO of AdTEC Networks and works as a network consultant focusing on Cisco network and Voice over IP (VoIP) implementations. Jeremy also runs the Cisco Blog (http://www.ciscoblog.com) in his "free time." Thankfully, he is married to the Certified Best Wife in the World (CBWW), who helps him manage his time and priorities and prevents him from getting an enormous Cisco logo tattooed across his chest.

Michael J. Cavanaugh, CCIE No. 4516 (Routing & Switching, Voice) and MCSE +Messaging, has been in the networking industry for more than 22 years. His employment with companies such as Wachovia, General Electric, Cisco Systems, Inc., BellSouth Communication Systems, and AT&T Communication Systems has allowed him to stay at the forefront of technology and hold leading-edge certifications. He has spent the last eight years focused on Cisco Unified Communications design, professional services, consulting, and support. Michael's passion is learning the practical applications of new technologies and sharing knowledge with fellow engineers.

Kris A. Krake, CCIE No. 10229 (Routing & Switching, Voice), is a Unified Communications Systems Engineer for Cisco Systems. Kris has consulted in the networking arena for more than 13 years and has spent over half of that time focused on Unified Communications. His employment with an Internet service provider and companies such as Aegon USA, BellSouth Communication Systems, and Cisco Systems has given him the opportunity to design, implement, and support a vast array of networks and telecommunications systems that range in size from small business to the globally reaching systems of the Fortune 50.

About the Technical Reviewers

Alex Hannah is a Cisco Certified Systems Instructor for Global Knowledge USA, specializing and teaching the Advanced IP Communications product line. He is president of Hannah Technologies, LLC, a Richmond, Virginia–based Cisco consulting firm specializing in Cisco Advanced IP Communications and application development using Microsoft technologies. He holds a bachelor's degree in Information Systems from Virginia Commonwealth University. He is a CCIE Voice candidate with certifications including CCSI No. 32072, CCVP, UCCX, and CCNA. In his spare time, you can find Alex on his boat wakeboarding with his lovely girlfriend, Amy, and friends.

Michael Valentine has 13 years of experience in the IT field, specializing in network design and installation. Currently he is a Cisco trainer with Skyline Advanced Technology Services and specializes in Cisco Unified Communications, CCNA, and CCNP classes. His accessible, humorous, and effective teaching style has demystified Cisco for hundreds of students since he began teaching in 2002. Mike holds a Bachelor of Arts degree from the University of British Columbia, currently holds the MCSE: Security, CCNA, CCDA, CCNP, CCVP, CCSI No. 31461, C|EH, and CTP certifications and has completed the CCIE written exam. Mike was on the development team for the Cisco Unified Communications Architecture and Design official courseware and is currently developing custom Unified Communications courseware for Skyline. Mike is the coauthor of *CCNA Exam Cram (Exam 640-802)*, Third Edition (Que, January 2008) and has served as technical editor and contributor on several Cisco Press titles.

Dedications

From Jeremy D. Cioara:

I would like to dedicate this book to my darling wife, Susan, who tirelessly works to bring our marriage closer together and closer to God. Her humility, wisdom, loving, and passionate heart makes her shine brighter than anyone I know.

From Michael J. Cavanaugh:

I would like to dedicate this book to my parents, **Paul and Shari K**ottage, for their love, support, and encouragement throughout the years.

From Kris A. Krake:

I would like to dedicate this book to my grandfat**her, Cyrus A. Krake, w**hose life modeled a passion for excellence, continuous learning, **and professional develop**ment.

Acknowledgments

Jeremy D. Cioara: Many thanks to Brett Bartow for all he does in organizing this project. Brett, you're a stud; thanks for your patience and "gentle reminders" that chapters are missing. Thanks also to Dayna Isley...actually, you readers should be thanking her; without her, this book would be full of typos, grammatical errors, and statements like, "Ya'll no how the ol' IOS works, eh?" Dayna, you're a superstar!

Thanks are due as well to my coauthors, Kris and Michael, for without them, this book would be rather short. I'd also like to thank Wendell Odom, who had to step away from this book project. I just met Wendell in person at Cisco Live 2008. What a stellar guy! I've never had anyone offer to ship me a Cisco 2801 router just to help out. Actually, Wendell...if you really don't need that router....

Thanks are always due Jesus Christ, who continues to bless my work tremendously. Without Christ in my life, there'd be no point. And of course, thanks to my wife and daughter and Baby Cioara #2 (that'd be BC #2 for short, who will be born by the time you're reading this). I can't think of a day that's gone by where I haven't smiled at the blessings you are! See? It just happened again. I'm smiling just writing this!

Michael J. Cavanaugh: I would like to thank Brett Bartow and Wendell Odom for giving me the opportunity to participate in the writing of this book.

Thanks to my coauthors, Kris Krake and Jeremy Cioara, for their tireless efforts in making this book a reality. A special thank you goes out to Jeremy for stepping in at the last minute to take a lead role in this publication.

I would like to give special recognition to Dayna Isley, Christopher Cleveland, and all the good people at Cisco Press, for keeping this publication on track.

Finally, I would like to thank my wife, KC, and my daughter, Caitlin, for keeping the fires burning at the home front, allowing me to concentrate on "after hours" writing.

Kris A. Krake: First, I would like to thank Brett Bartow, Dayna Isley, and Christopher Cleveland for your willingness to take on a first-time author. I am truly grateful for the guidance, coaching, and patience you showed me through the publication process.

Thank you to my long-time friends Wendell Odom and coauthor Michael Cavanaugh. Thank you for giving me the opportunity to work with you. I consider it a tremendous honor to be associated in any way with a project you have worked on.

A special thanks goes to my coauthor Jeremy Cioara. Your ability and willingness to step into this project and take its lead role is greatly appreciated. Finally, I would like to thank my wife, Carol, and children, Korie, Kaitlyn, and Conner. Your loving sacrifice of our time and the extra work you did as a family allowed me the opportunity to pursue this dream. You are why "It's good to be a Krake!"

Contents at a Glance

Contents

Icons Used in This Book

 Communication Server

 PC

 PC with Software

 Sun Workstation

 Macintosh

 Terminal

 ISDN/Frame Relay Switch

 Token Ring

 Laptop

 File Server

 Web Server

 Ciscoworks Workstation

 ATM Switch

 Modem

 Gateway

 Access Server

 IBM Mainframe

 Front End Processor

 Cluster Controller

 Multilayer Switch

 Printer

 Router

 Bridge

 Hub

DSU/CSU

FDDI

 Catalyst Switch

Network Cloud

Line: Ethernet

Line: Serial

Line: Switched Serial

 Phone

IP Phone

 Repeater

 PBX Switch

 File Server

 Cisco Unified Communications 500 Series for Small Business

 Cisco Unity Express

Cisco Unified Communication Manager

 Voice-Enabled Router

 Voice-Enabled Workgroup Switch

 Legacy PBX

Multilayer Switch without Text

Unified Personal Communicator (UPC)

Command Syntax Conventions

The conventions used to present command syntax in this book are the same conventions used in the IOS Command Reference. The Command Reference describes these conventions as follows:

- **Boldface** indicates commands and keywords that are entered literally as shown. In actual configuration examples and output (not general command syntax), boldface indicates commands that are manually input by the user (such as a **show** command).

- *Italics* indicate arguments for which you supply actual values.

- Vertical bars (|) separate alternative, mutually exclusive elements.

- Square brackets [ ] indicate optional elements.

- Braces { } indicate a required choice.

- Braces within brackets [{ }] indicate a required choice within an optional element.

Foreword

CCNA Voice Official Exam Certification Guide is an excellent self-study resource for the Cisco IIUC (640-460) exam. Passing the IIUC exam validates the knowledge and skills required to successfully deploy Cisco VoIP technologies. Gaining certification in Cisco technology is key to the continuing educational development of today's networking professional. Through certification programs, Cisco validates the skills and expertise required to effectively manage the modern enterprise network.

Cisco Press exam certification guides and preparation materials offer exceptional—and flexible—access to the knowledge and information required to stay current in your field of expertise or to gain new skills. Whether used as a supplement to more traditional training or as a primary source of learning, these materials offer users the information and knowledge validation required to gain new understanding and proficiencies. Developed in conjunction with the Cisco certifications and training team, Cisco Press books are the only self-study books authorized by Cisco, and they offer students a series of exam practice tools and resource materials to help ensure that learners fully grasp the concepts and information presented.

Additional authorized Cisco instructor-led courses, e-learning, labs, and simulations are available exclusively from Cisco Learning Solutions Partners worldwide. To learn more, visit http://www.cisco.com/go/training.

I hope that you find these materials to be an enriching and useful part of your exam preparation.

Erik Ullanderson
Manager, Global Certifications
Learning@Cisco
May 2008

Introduction

Welcome to the world of CCNA Voice! As technology continues to evolve, the realm of voice, which was traditionally kept completely separate from data, has now begun to merge with the data network. This brings together two different worlds of people: data technicians—historically accustomed to working with routers, switches, servers, and the like—and voice technicians, historically accustomed to working with PBX systems, digital handsets, and trunk lines. Regardless of your background, one of the primary goals of the new CCNA Voice certification is to bridge these two worlds together.

In June 2008, Cisco announced new CCNA specialties, including CCNA Security, CCNA Wireless, and CCNA Voice. These certifications, released 10 years after the initial CCNA, represent Cisco's growth into new and emerging industries. Certification candidates can now specialize in specific areas of study. Figure I.1 shows the basic organization of the certifications and exams used to achieve your CCNA Voice certification.

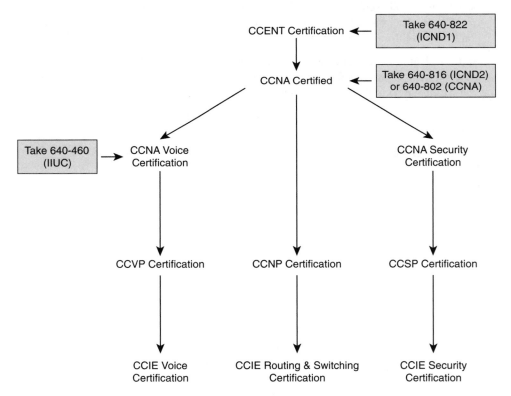

Figure I.1   *Cisco Certifications and CCNA Voice Certification Path*

As you can see from Figure I.1, a traditional CCNA certification is a prerequisite before you venture into the CCNA Voice certification. As of June 2009, the CCNA Voice certification will become a prerequisite before you are able to pursue the Cisco Certified Voice Professional (CCVP) certification.

Goals and Methods

The most important and somewhat obvious goal of this book is to help you pass the Implementing Cisco IOS Unified Communications (IIUC) exam (640-460). In fact, if the primary objective of this book were different, then the book's title would be misleading. The methods used in this book to help you pass the IIUC exam are designed to also make you much more knowledgeable about how to do your job.

This book uses several key methodologies to help you discover the exam topics that you need to review in more depth, to help you fully understand and remember those details, and to help you prove to yourself that you have retained your knowledge of those topics. So, this book does not try to help you pass by memorization, but helps you truly learn and understand the topics. The CCNA Voice exam is the foundation for many of the Cisco professional certifications, and it would be a disservice to you if this book did not help you truly learn the material. Therefore, this book will help you pass the CCNA Voice exam by using the following methods:

- Helping you discover which test topics you have not mastered

- Providing explanations and information to fill in your knowledge gaps

- Supplying exercises and scenarios that enhance your ability to recall and deduce the answers to test questions

- Providing practice exercises on the topics and the testing process via test questions on the CD-ROM.

In addition, this book uses quite a different style from typical certification-preparation books. The newer Cisco certification exams have adopted a style of testing that essentially says, "If you don't know how to do it, you won't pass this exam." This means that most of the questions on the certification exam will require you to deduce the answer through reasoning or configuration rather than just memorizing facts, figures, or syntax from a book. To accommodate this newer testing style, the authors have written this book as a "real world" explanation of Cisco VoIP topics. Most concepts are explained using real-world examples rather than showing tables full of syntax options and explanations, which are freely available on Cisco.com. As you read through this book, you will definitely get a feeling of, "This is how I can *do* this," which is exactly what you need for the newer Cisco exams.

Who Should Read This Book?

The purpose of this book is twofold. The primary purpose is to tremendously increase your chances of passing the CCNA Voice certification exam. The secondary purpose is to provide the information necessary to deploy a VoIP solution using Cisco Unified Communication Manager Express (CME) or the Smart Business Communications System (SBCS). Cisco's new exam approach provides an avenue to write the book with both a real-world and certification-study approach at the same time. As you read through this book and study the configuration examples and exam tips, you will have a true sense of understanding how you could deploy a VoIP system, while at the same time feeling equipped to pass the CCNA Voice certification exam.

Strategies for Exam Preparation

Strategies for exam preparation will vary depending on your existing skills, knowledge, and equipment available. Of course, the ideal exam preparation would consist of building a small voice lab with a Cisco Unified Communications Manager Express 2801 Integrated Services Router and Cisco Unity Express capabilities, a switch, and a few IP phones, which you could then use to work through the configurations as you read through this book. However, not everyone has access to this equipment, so the next best step you can take is to read through the chapters in this book, jotting notes down with key concepts or configurations on a separate notepad. Each chapter begins with a "Do I Know This Already?" quiz designed to give you a good idea of the chapter's content and your current understanding of it. In some cases, you might already know most of or all the information covered in a given chapter.

After you have read through the book, have a look at the current exam objectives for the CCNA Voice exam listed on Cisco.com (http://www.cisco.com/certification). If there are any areas shown in the certification exam outline that you would still like to study, find those sections in the book and review them.

When you feel confident in your skills, attempt the practice exam included on the CD with this book. As you work through the practice exam, note the areas where you lack confidence and review those concepts or configurations in the book. After you have reviewed the areas, work through the practice exam a second time and rate your skills. Keep in mind that the more you work through the practice exam, the more familiar the questions will become, so the practice exam will become a less accurate judge of your skills.

After you have worked through the practice exam a second time and feel confident with your skills, schedule the real IIUC (640-460) exam through Vue (http://www.vue.com). You should typically take the exam within a week from when you consider yourself ready to take the exam, so that the information is fresh in your mind.

Keep in mind that Cisco exams are very difficult. Even if you have a solid grasp of the information, there are many other factors that play into the testing environment (stress, time constraints, and so on). If you pass the exam on the first attempt, fantastic! If not, know that this happens commonly. The next time you attempt the exam, you will have a major advantage: you have experienced the exam first-hand. Although future exams may have different questions, the topics and general "feel" of the exam will remain the same. Take some time to study areas from the book where you felt weak on the exam. Retaking the exam the same or following day from your first attempt is a little aggressive; instead, schedule to retake it within a week, while you are still familiar with the content.

640-460 IIUC Exam Topics

Table I.1 lists the exam topics for the 640-460 IIUC exam. This table also lists the book parts in which each exam topic is covered.

Table I.1 *640-460 IIUC Exam Topics*

Chapter Where Topic Is Covered	Exam Topic
Describe the components of the Cisco Unified Communications Architecture	
Chapter 2	Describe the function of the infrastructure in a UC environment
Chapter 2	Describe the function of endpoints in a UC environment
Chapter 2	Describe the function of the call processing agent in a UC environment
Chapter 2	Describe the function of messaging in a UC environment
Chapter 2	Describe the function of auto attendants and IVRs in a UC environment
Chapter 2	Describe the function of contact center in a UC environment
Chapter 2	Describe the applications available in the UC environment, including Mobility, Presence, and Telepresence
Chapter 2	Describe how the Unified Communications components work together to create the Cisco Unified Communications Architecture
Describe PSTN components and technologies	
Chapter 1	Describe the services provided by the PSTN
Chapter 1	Describe time division and statistical multiplexing
Chapter 1	Describe supervisory, informational, and address signaling
Chapter 1	Describe numbering plans
Chapter 1	Describe analog circuits
Chapter 1	Describe digital voice circuits
Chapter 1	Describe PBX, trunk lines, key-systems, and tie lines
Describe VoIP components and technologies	
Chapter 7	Describe the process of voice packetization
Chapter 7	Describe RTP and RTCP
Chapter 7	Describe the function of and differences between codecs
Chapter 7	Describe H.323, MGCP, SIP, and SCCP signaling protocols

continues

Table I.1   *640-460 IIUC Exam Topics   continued*

Chapter Where Topic Is Covered	Exam Topic
Describe and configure gateways, voice ports, and dial peers to connect to the PSTN and service provider networks	
Chapter 8	Describe the function and application of a dial plan
Chapter 8	Describe the function and application of voice Gateways
Chapter 8	Describe the function and application of voice ports in a Gateway
Chapter 8	Describe the function and operation of call-legs
Chapter 8	Describe and configure voice dial peers
Chapter 8	Describe the differences between PSTN and Internet Telephony Service Provider circuits
Describe and configure a Cisco network to support VoIP	
Chapter 3	Describe the purpose of VLANs in a VoIP environment
Chapter 3	Describe the environmental considerations to support VoIP
Chapter 3	Configure switched infrastructure to support voice and data VLANs
Chapter 3	Describe the purpose and operation of PoE
Chapter 8	Identify the factors that impact voice quality
Chapter 8	Describe how QoS addresses voice quality issues
Chapter 8	Identify where QoS is deployed in the UC infrastructure
Implement UC500 using Cisco Configuration Assistant	
Chapter 11	Describe the function and operation of Cisco Configuration Assistant
Chapter 12	Configure UC500 device parameters
Chapter 12	Configure UC500 network parameters
Chapter 12	Configure UC500 dial plan and voicemail parameters
Chapter 12	Configure UC500 SIP trunk parameters
Chapter 12	Configure UC500 voice system features
Chapter 12	Configure UC500 user parameters

Table I.1 *640-460 IIUC Exam Topics*

Chapter Where Topic Is Covered	Exam Topic
Implement Cisco Unified Communications Manager Express to support endpoints using CLI	
Chapter 4	Describe the appropriate software components needed to support endpoints
Chapter 3	Describe the requirements and correct settings for DHCP, NTP, and TFTP
Chapter 3	Configure DHCP, NTP, and TFTP
Chapter 4	Describe the differences between key system and PBX mode
Chapter 5	Describe the differences between the different types of ephones and ephone-dns
Chapter 5	Configure Cisco Unified Communications Manager Express endpoints
Chapter 6	Configure call-transfer per design specifications
Chapter 6	Configure voice productivity features, including hunt groups, call park, call pickup, paging groups, and paging/intercom
Chapter 6	Configure Music on Hold
Implement voicemail features using Cisco Unity Express	
Chapter 9	Describe the Cisco Unity Express hardware platforms
Chapter 9	Configure the foundational elements required for Cisco Unified Communications Manager Express to support Cisco Unity Express
Chapter 9	Describe the features available in Cisco Unity Express
Chapter 10	Configure AutoAttendant services using Cisco Unity Express
Chapter 10	Configure basic voicemail features using Cisco Unity Express

How This Book Is Organized

Although this book could be read cover-to-cover, it is designed to be flexible and allow you to easily move between chapters and sections of chapters to cover just the material that you need more work with. If you do intend to read all the chapters, the order in the book is an excellent sequence to use.

The core chapters, Chapters 1 through 12, cover the following topics:

- **Chapter 1, "Perspectives on Voice Before Convergence":** This chapter discusses what would be known as the traditional telephony world. It begins where the telephone system originally started: analog connectivity. It then moves into the realm of digital connections and considerations and concludes with the primary pieces that you need to know from the public switched telephone network (PSTN).

- **Chapter 2, "Perspectives on Voice After Convergence":** This chapter focuses primarily on the components of a Cisco VoIP network. By breaking down the voice infrastructure into four distinct areas, each component can be categorized and described. These components include endpoints, call processing agents, applications, and network infrastructure devices.

- **Chapter 3, "Connecting IP Phones to the LAN Infrastructure":** This chapter discusses the preparation and base configuration of the LAN infrastructure to support VoIP devices. This preparation includes support for Power over Ethernet (PoE), voice VLANs, a properly configured DHCP scope for VoIP devices, and the Network Time Protocol (NTP).

- **Chapter 4, "Installing Cisco Unified Communications Manager Express":** This chapter covers everything you need to know to get Cisco Unified Communication Manager Express (CME) ready to support IP phones. It initially walks through the Cisco Unified CME overview and licensing information, then unpacks the installation and base configuration process.

- **Chapter 5, "Basic Cisco Unified CME IP Phone Configuration":** This chapter focuses on the process to create and assign directory numbers to Cisco IP phones. In addition, the chapter walks through the configuration of IP phone auto-registration, which makes your initial network setup much easier, and the configuration of additional phone parameters such as phone locale and system messages.

- **Chapter 6, "Configuring Cisco Unified CME Voice Productivity Features":** This chapter examines feature after feature supported by the CME router. By the time you're done with this chapter, you'll understand how to configure features such as intercom, paging, call park and pickup, and many others.

- **Chapter 7, "Gateway and Trunk Concepts":** Now that the internal VoIP network is operational through the CME configuration, this chapter examines connections to the outside world through the PSTN or over an IP network. Concepts covered in this chapter include the process of converting voice to packetized format, codec considerations, and trunking methods.

- **Chapter 8, "Configuring and Verifying Gateways and Trunks":** This chapter takes the concepts from Chapter 7 and puts them into configuration action. Topics from this chapter include the configuration of physical voice ports, dial-peer and digit manipulation configuration, and quality of service (QoS).

- **Chapter 9, "Cisco Unity Express Concepts":** This chapter introduces the Cisco Unity Express (CUE), describing the differences between hardware platforms, the software components, and licensing options. The features, functions, and management of the voicemail and auto-attendant applications provided by CUE are explored.

- **Chapter 10, "Cisco Unity Express Configuration":** This chapter discusses the configuration of the Cisco Unity Express platform. It begins with the Cisco Unity Express installation process and walks through configuring Cisco Unity Express global options, mailbox settings, and auto-attendant scripts. The chapter concludes with Cisco Unity Express troubleshooting methods.

- **Chapter 11, "Introducing the Smart Business Communications System":** This chapter introduces the concept of Unified Communications (UC) and explains how the Smart Business Communications System (SBCS) is positioned to deliver UC to the small-medium business (SMB) market. Individual components of the SBCS suite and the most common ways they are deployed are discussed to lay a foundation for implementing the UC500 Series for Small Business.

- **Chapter 12, "Configuring and Maintaining the UC500 Series for Voice":** This chapter discusses the process of provisioning the UC500 Series for Small Business. The chapter begins with a discussion of the UC500's function in the SBCS family, moves into a discussion about the Cisco Configuration Assistant (CCA), and then concludes with step-by-step instructions for deploying and maintaining telephony and voice-mail services on the UC500.

In addition to the 12 main chapters, this book includes tools to help you verify that you are prepared to take the exam. Chapter 13, "Final Preparation," includes guidelines that you can follow in the final days before the exam. Also, the CD-ROM includes quiz questions and memory tables that you can work through to verify your knowledge of the subject matter.

Exam topics covered in Part I:

- Describe the function of the infrastructure in a UC environment

- Describe the function of endpoints in a UC environment

- Describe the function of the call processing agent in a UC environment

- Describe the function of messaging in a UC environment

- Describe the function of auto attendants and IVRs in a UC environment

- Describe the function of contact center in a UC environment

- Describe the applications available in the UC environment, including Mobility, Presence, and Telepresence

- Describe how the Unified Communications components work together to create the Cisco Unified Communications Architecture

- Describe the services provided by the PSTN

- Describe time division and statistical multiplexing

- Describe supervisory, informational, and address signaling

- Describe numbering plans

- Describe analog circuits

- Describe digital voice circuits

- Describe PBX, trunk lines, key-systems, and tie lines

Part I: Voice Perspectives

Where It All Began: Analog Connections: This section discusses the simplest type of modern voice communication, analog connections.

The Evolution: Digital Connections: Modern businesses quickly outgrow analog circuits. This section discusses the process of converting analog voice into digital signals and using digital circuits to send multiple calls over a single line.

Understanding the PSTN: Just about all voice circuits currently terminate at the world's largest voice network, the PSTN. This section discusses the components of the PSTN, focusing specifically on PBX and Key Systems, and methods used to connect to the PSTN.

CHAPTER 1

Perspectives on Voice Before Convergence

Welcome to the world of voice. No, not Voice over IP (VoIP); you're not there yet. Before you can enter that world, there is a foundation to be laid. The traditional telephony network has been in place since the early 1900s and it is not going to disappear overnight. Thus, until then, the new VoIP networks must integrate with traditional telephony networks. In order to perform this integration, you must have a basic understanding of the world of traditional voice telephony. This chapter walks you through the foundations of the public switched telephone network (PSTN), private branch exchange (PBX) systems, and analog and digital circuitry.

"Do I Know This Already?" Quiz

The "Do I Know This Already?" quiz allows you to assess whether you should read this entire chapter or simply jump to the "Exam Preparation Tasks" section for review. If you are in doubt, read the entire chapter. Table 1.1 outlines the major headings in this chapter and the corresponding "Do I Know This Already?" quiz questions. You can find the answers in Appendix A, "Answers to the 'Do I Know This Already?' Quizzes."

Table 1.1   *"Do I Know This Already?" Foundation Topics Section-to-Question Mapping*

Foundation Topics Section	Questions Covered in This Section
Where It All Began: Analog Connections	1–3
The Evolution: Digital Connections	4–9
Understanding the PSTN	10

1. Analog phones connected to the PSTN typically use which of the following signal types?

   a. Loop start

   b. Ground start

   c. CAS

   d. CCS

2. Which of the following issues is prevented by using ground start signaling?

   a. Echo

   b. Glare

   c. Reflexive transmissions

   d. Mirrored communication

3. Which of the following signaling types represents supervisory signaling?

   a. Off-hook signal

   b. Dial tone

   c. DTMF

   d. Congestion

4. What are two disadvantages of using analog connectivity?

   a. Conversion complexity

   b. Signal quality

   c. Limited calls per line

   d. Lack of common voice services

5. Which of the following processes samples an analog waveform at timed intervals to obtain a digital measurement of the electrical signal?

   a. Quantization

   b. PAM

   c. PCM

   d. Codec

6. Which of the following systems allows you to send multiple voice calls over a single digital circuit by dividing the calls into specific time slots?

   a. MUX

   b. DE-MUX

   c. TDM

   d. TCP

7. When using T1 CAS signaling, which bits are used to transmit signaling information within each voice channel?

   a. The first bit of each frame

   b. The last bit of each frame

   c. The second and third bits of every third frame

   d. The eighth bit of every sixth frame

8. How large is each T1 frame sent over a digital CAS connection?

   a. 8 bits

   b. 24 bits

   c. 80 bits

   d. 193 bits

9. Which of the following time slots are used for T1 and E1 signaling when using CCS connections? (Choose two.)

   a. Time slot 1

   b. Time slot 16

   c. Time slot 17

   d. Time slot 23

   e. Time slot 24

10. Which of the following standards created by the ITU designates international numbering plans for devices connected to the PSTN?

   a. ITU-T

   b. E.164

   c. ITU-161

   d. T-161

Foundation Topics

Where It All Began: Analog Connections

In 1877, Thomas Edison created a brilliant device known as a phonograph, shown in Figure 1.1.

Sound-Collecting Horn

Cylinder Coated with Tinfoil

(Photo Courtesy of Jason Klobassa)

Figure 1.1   *Replica of Edison's Phonograph*

This device was able to record sounds by pressing a needle into a cylinder covered with tinfoil on a rhythmic basis as a person spoke into a sound collecting horn. The phonograph could then play back this sound by moving the needle at a steady speed back over the indentions made in the tinfoil. This "archaic" form of recording is one representation of an analog signal.

An analog signal uses some property of the device that is capturing the audio signal to convey audio information. In the case of Edison's phonograph, the property was the various indentions in tinfoil. In today's world, where everything is connected through some form of cabling, electric currents are used to send analog signals. When you speak into an analog phone, the sounds that come out of your mouth are converted into electricity. The volume and pitch that you use when speaking result in different variations of electrical current. Electrical voltage, frequency, current, and charge are all used in some combination to convey the properties of your voice. Figure 1.2 illustrates perhaps a more familiar view of using electrical signals to capture the properties of voice.

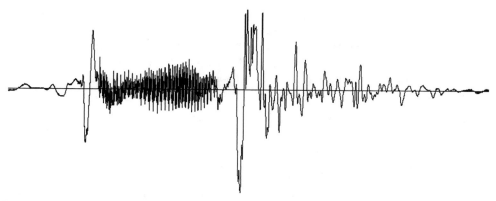

Figure 1.2   *Electrical Analog Waveform of Human Speech*

Note   The analog waveform shown in Figure 1.2 is from me (Jeremy) saying the word "Hello."

Analog phone lines use the properties of electricity to convey changes in voice over cabling. Of course, there is far more than just voice to send over the phone lines. The analog phones you use at home must convey many different types of signaling as well. Signaling includes messages such as dial tone, dialed digits, busy signals, and so on. These signaling types will be discussed in just a moment. For now, let's look at the cabling used to make analog connections function.

Loop Start and Ground Start Signaling

Each analog circuit is composed of a pair of wires. One wire is the ground, or positive side of the connection (this is often called the *tip*). The other wire is the battery, or negative side of the connection (often called the *ring*). You'll commonly hear phone technicians talk about these wires as the "tip and ring." These two wires are what power the analog phone and allow it to function, just like the wires that connect your car battery to the car. Figure 1.3 illustrates the connections of the tip and ring wire to your analog phone.

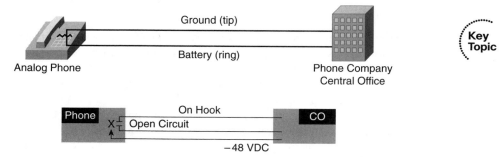

Key Topic

Figure 1.3   *Connections of the Ground and Battery Wires to an Analog Phone*

The jagged line over the wires in the analog phone in Figure 1.3 represents a broken circuit. Anytime the phone is on-hook, the phone separates the two wires, preventing electric signal from flowing through the phone. When the phone is lifted off-hook, the phone connects the two wires, causing an electrical signal (48V DC voltage) to flow from the phone company central office (CO) into the phone. This is known as *loop start signaling*.

Loop start signaling is the typical signaling type used in home environments. Loop start signaling is susceptible to a problem known as *glare*. Glare occurs when you pick up the phone to make an outgoing call at the same time as a call comes in on the phone line before the phone has a chance to ring. This gives you the awkward moment of, "Uhhh...Oh! Hello Bob! I'm sorry; I didn't know you were on the phone." In home environments, this is not usually a problem for a couple reasons. First, the chances of having a simultaneous outgoing and incoming call are very slim. Second, if you do happen to have an incoming call, it's always meant for your house (unless the caller dialed the wrong number).

In business environments, glare can become a significant problem because of the large number of employees and high call volume. For example, a corporation may have a key system (which allows it to run its own, internal phone system) with five analog trunks to the PSTN, as shown in Figure 1.4.

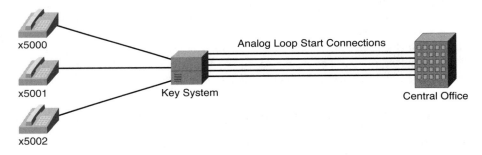

Figure 1.4   *Illustration of Glare*

If a call comes in for x5002 at the same time as x5000 picks up the phone, the key system will connect the two signals, causing x5000 to receive the call for x5002. This happens because the loop start signal from x5000 seizes the outgoing PSTN line at the same time as the key system receives the incoming call on the same PSTN line. This is an instance of glare.

Because of glare, most modern PBX systems designed for larger, corporate environments use *ground start signaling*. Ground start signaling originated from its original implementation in pay phone systems. Many years ago, when a person lifted the handset of a pay phone, they would not receive a dial tone until they dropped in a coin. The coin would brush past the tip and ring wires and temporarily ground them. The grounding of the wires would signal the phone company to send a dial tone on the line. Using this type of signaling in PBX systems allows the PBX to separate an answering phone from an incoming phone line, reducing the problem of glare. In order to receive a dial tone from the CO, the PBX must send a ground signal on the wires. This intentionally signals to the telephone CO that an outgoing call is going to happen, whereas using the loop start method of signaling just connects the wires to receive an incoming call or place an outgoing call.

Supervisory Signaling

In addition to using the of properties of electric signals to generate voice traffic, analog phones are responsible for accepting and sending multiple types of signaling. The first type of signaling the phone handles is considered *supervisory signaling*. Supervisory signaling handles the following:

- **On-hook signal:** When the phone is on-hook, the connection between the tip and ring wires is broken and no electrical signal passes between them.

- **Off-hook signal:** When the phone is off-hook, the phone connects the tip and ring wires, completing the circuit and allowing electrical signal to pass.

Key Topic

- **Ringing:** To cause an analog phone to ring, the phone company sends an alternating current (AC) signal down one of the wires, which the phone detects and generates a ring signal.

Informational Signaling

Once the analog phone generates an off-hook signal, the phone company responds by using informational signaling to generate a dial tone. Informational signaling uses specific electrical frequencies to send a plethora of information to the caller. The following events are results of informational signaling:

- **Dial tone:** Indicates the phone company is ready to receive digits

- **Busy:** Indicates the remote phone is already in use

Key Topic

- **Ringback:** Indicates the remote phone is currently ringing

- **Congestion:** Indicates the long-distance telephone network is not able to complete the call

- **Reorder:** Indicates the local telephone company is not able to complete the call

- **Receiver off-hook:** Indicates the local receiver has been off-hook for an extended period of time

- **No such number:** Indicates the dialed number is invalid

- **Confirmation:** Indicates the telephone company is attempting to complete the call

The phone company generates each of these informational signals using well-known electrical frequencies for the local region (country). All analog phones operating within the same country should have identical informational signals.

Address Signaling

Once the phone company has used informational signaling to generate a dial tone signal, the user can dial digits. There are two types of address signaling in use worldwide:

■ **Dual-tone multifrequency (DTMF):** The buttons on a telephone keypad use a pair of high and low electrical frequencies (thus "dual-tone") to generate a signal each time a caller presses a digit. This type of analog phone is shown in part A of Figure 1.5. DTMF is the predominant signal type used in the United States.

■ **Pulse:** The rotary-dial wheel of a phone connects and disconnects the local loop circuit as it rotates around to signal specific digits. This type of analog phone is shown in part B of Figure 1.5.

A   B

Figure 1.5   *DTMF and Pulse Dialing Analog Phones*

The Evolution: Digital Connections

Analog signaling was a massive improvement over tin cans and string, but still posed plenty of problems of its own. First, an analog electrical signal experiences degradation (signal fading) over long distances. To increase the distance the analog signal could travel, the phone company had to install repeaters (shown in Figure 1.6) to regenerate the signal as it became weak.

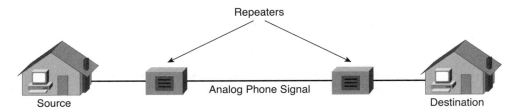

Figure 1.6   *Analog Signal Repeaters*

Unfortunately, as the analog signal was regenerated, the repeater device was unable to differentiate between the voice traveling over the wire and line noise. Each time the repeater regenerated the voice, it amplified the line noise as well. Thus, the more times a phone company regenerated a signal, the more distorted and difficult to understand the signal became.

The second difficulty encountered with analog connections was the sheer number of wires the phone company had to run to support a large geographical area or a business with a large number of phones. Because each phone required two wires, the bundles of wire became massive and difficult to maintain (imagine the hassle of a single pair of wires in the bundle breaking). A solution to send multiple calls over a single wire was needed. A digital connection is that solution.

Converting Analog to Digital Signals

Simply put, digital signals use numbers to represent levels of voice instead of using a combination of electrical signals. When someone talks about "digitizing voice," they are speaking about the process of changing analog voice signals into a series of numbers (shown in Figure 1.7), which you can use to put the voice back together at the other end of the line.

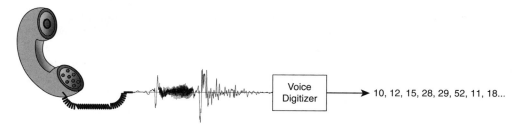

Figure 1.7   *Converting Analog to Digital Signals*

To convert an analog signal into digital format, the converting device goes through a four-step process:

1. Sample the signal.

2. Quantize the signal.

3. Encode the quantized value into binary format.

4. Optionally compress the sample to save bandwidth.

The following sections describe each part of the process in turn.

Sample the Signal

To convert an analog waveform into a numeric value, the digitizing device must sample it many times as the analog signal changes, as shown in Figure 1.8. This sampling process is known as *pulse-amplitude modulation (PAM)*.

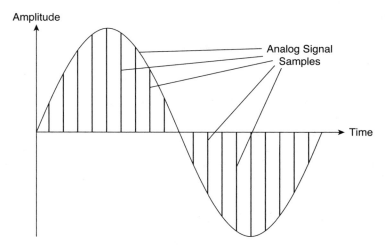

Figure 1.8   *Sampling Analog Voice*

In 1927, Dr. Harry Nyquist, an engineer at Bell Laboratories at the time, found that by sampling a signal at twice the number as the highest electrical frequency of the signal per second, he could regenerate the voice with acceptable audio quality levels. Human speech typically uses frequencies up to 9000 Hz, which would result in 18,000 samples each second. Sending this many samples per second would result in a large bandwidth requirement for each voice call, so Nyquist cut the sampling frequency range for human voice to 4000 Hz (resulting in 8000 digital samples per second). Although limiting the frequency range like this did cut down on the quality of voice, this frequency range is sufficient to allow you to identify the remote caller and sense their mood.

Quantize the Signal

After the digitizing device has taken thousands of samples of the analog audio, it then matches each sample to a voltage scale, as shown in Figure 1.9. This process is known as *quantization*.

Quantization assigns a value from the voltage range based on the amplitude of each audio sample. The quantization process divides the voltage range into 16 total segments (0 to 7 positive, and 0 to 7 negative). Notice in Figure 1.9 that the voltage values are not evenly spaced; the values in the lower segments are much closer together, whereas the voltage values in the higher segments move further and further apart. This allows the digitizing device to obtain accurate readings in the voltage ranges that are common for human voice. As samples move outside the range of normal human voice, the quantization process does not measure them as accurately. This is technically known as *quantization error*, which introduces noise on the line.

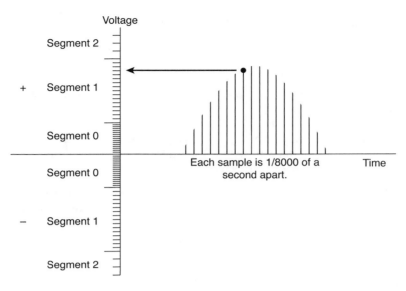

Figure 1.9   *Quantizing the Voice Sample*

Encode the Quantized Value into Binary Format

In the first step of the digitization process, the analog voice is sampled using PAM. The second step of the process then matches the PAM sample to a specific voltage value. In this step, the digitizing equipment converts the sample value into an 8-bit, binary number. This final conversion is known as *pulse-code modulation (PCM)*. By reducing the number of 8-bit samples taken each second to 8000, the amount of bandwidth required for a single voice telephone conversation is 64 kbps (8000 samples × 8 bits per sample = 64,000 bits, or 64 kbps).

The analog-to-digital (and VoIP) conversion process is discussed in more detail in Chapter 7, "Gateway and Trunk Concepts."

Optionally Compress the Sample to Save Bandwidth

Some voice systems allow you to save bandwidth by compressing the audio before sending it to the remote device. The compression methods vary in overhead and audio quality, but many of them can save a significant amount of bandwidth with little quality degradation. These compression methods are commonly used in VoIP communication and are discussed further in Chapter 7.

Sending Multiple Calls over a Single Line

Now, let's come back to the original problems of analog connections:

■ The signal degrades over long distances.

■ You can't send multiple calls over a single line (resulting in massive cabling requirements).

Digitizing voice solves the first problem because you can easily transmit a numeric value any distance a cable can run without any degradation or line noise. *Time-division multiplexing (TDM)* solves the second problem.

TDM allows voice networks to carry multiple conversations at the same time over a single, four-wire path. Because the multiple conversations have been digitized, the numeric values are transmitted in specific time slots (thus the "time-division") that differentiate the separate conversations. Figure 1.10 illustrates three separate voice conversations sent over a digital connection.

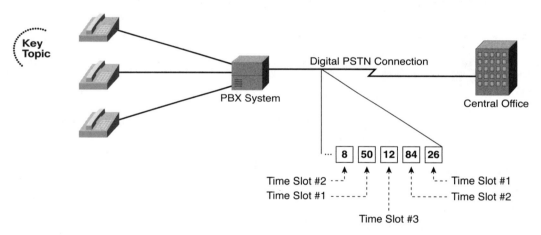

Figure 1.10 *Time-Division Multiplexing Voice Channels*

Notice each of the voice conversations in Figure 1.10 has been digitized and assigned a numeric value and transmitted over the digital PSTN connection. Based on the time the voice data was sent, the PSTN carrier is able to distinguish and reassemble the voice conversations.

Note   While the values in each time slot are shown in decimal in Figure 1.10, they are actually transmitted and interpreted in binary.

Corporations use digital voice connections to the PSTN as T1 circuits in the United States, Canada, and Japan. A T1 circuit is built from 24 separate 64-kbps channels known as a digital signal 0 (DS0). Each one of these channels is able to support a single voice call. Corporations in areas outside the United States, Canada, and Japan use E1 circuits, which allow you to use up to 30 DS0s for voice calls.

Although digital technology solves the problems of signal degradation and the inability to send multiple calls over a single line that occur in analog technology, it creates a new issue: signaling. With analog circuits, supervisory signals were passed by connecting the tip and ring wires together. The phone company generated informational and address signals through specific frequencies of electricity. By solving the problems associated with analog signaling, digital signaling also removed the typical signaling capabilities. To solve this, two primary styles of signaling were created for digital circuits:

- **Channel associated signaling (CAS):** Signaling information is transmitted using the same bandwidth as the voice.

- **Common channel signaling (CCS):** Signaling information is transmitted using a separate, dedicated signaling channel.

Key Topic

The following sections discuss these two styles of signaling.

Channel Associated Signaling

T1 digital connections using CAS actually "steal" binary bits that would typically have been used to communicate voice information and use them for signaling. Initially, this may seem crazy; if you take the binary bits that are used to resynthesize the voice, won't the voice quality drop significantly? Although the voice quality does drop some, the number of binary bits stolen for signaling information is small enough that the change in voice quality is not noticeable.

Note   Because T1 CAS steals bits from the voice channel to transfer signaling information, it is often called *robbed bit signaling (RBS)*.

The voice device running the T1 line uses the eighth bit on every sixth sample in each T1 channel (DS0). Figure 1.11 helps illustrate this concept.

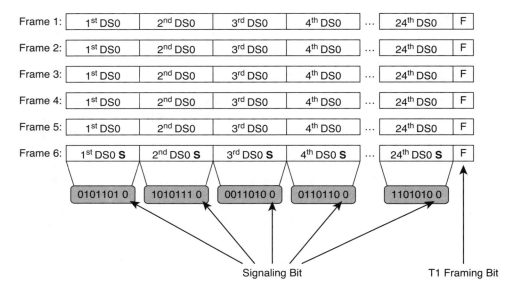

Figure 1.11   *CAS T1 Signaling Bits*

As you can see from Figure 1.11, the 24 channels of the digital T1 circuit carry only voice data for the first five frames that they send. On the sixth frame (marked with an S in Figure 1.11), the eighth bit (also called the *least significant bit*) is stolen for the voice devices to transmit signaling information. This process occurs for every sixth frame after this (12th, 18th, 24th, and so on). This stolen bit relays the signaling information for each respective DS0 channel. For example, the bits stolen from the third DS0 channel relay the signaling information only for that channel.

Notice that at the end of each frame sent for the 24 DS0 channels is an F, signifying the T1 framing bit. When a T1 digital line sends voice data, it does so by sending all 24 of the smaller DS0 frames in one big T1 frame. For example, looking at Figure 1.11, Frame 1 is one big T1 frame composed of the first frame of all the smaller DS0 frames. So, each T1 frame is 193 bits in length. Here's the math:

Each DS0 frame = 8 bits

T1 sends 24 DS0 frames at once (8 bits × 24 frames) = 192 bits

Each T1 frame has a framing bit (1 bit + 192 bits) = 193 bits

How this T1 framing bit is used is dependent on the framing standard used. Digital T1 lines send 8000 of these 193-bit frames every second (because Dr. Nyquist's voice model requires 8000 samples to be sent each second to accurately reconstruct voice). This is why T1 lines run at 1.544 Mbps: (193 bits per frame * 8000 frames per second) = 1,544,000 bps or 1.544 Mbps.

Super Frame (SF) sends groups of 12 T1 frames at a time. When using SF, all 12 of the T1 framing bits are used to keep the T1 equipment synchronized with the other side. This means that all 8000 T1 framing bits sent every second are dedicated to synchronization.

The newer standard, Extended Super Frame (ESF), sends groups of 24 T1 frames at a time. The newer ESF standard uses the framing bits more intelligently than the older SF standard. Of the 8000 bits sent every second, ESF is able to use 2000 bits for synchronization, 2000 bits for error checking, and 4000 bits as a supervisor channel, which is able to send control functions and perform error reporting.

Note   All modern T1 service providers use ESF.

Because one T1 ESF contains 24 frames for each DS0 channel, each DS0 channel is able to send four signaling bits at a time, as shown in Figure 1.12.

Frame 1:	1st DS0	2nd DS0	3rd DS0	4th DS0	...
Frame 2:	1st DS0	2nd DS0	3rd DS0	4th DS0	...
Frame 3:	1st DS0	2nd DS0	3rd DS0	4th DS0	...
Frame 4:	1st DS0	2nd DS0	3rd DS0	4th DS0	...
Frame 5:	1st DS0	2nd DS0	3rd DS0	4th DS0	...
Frame 6:	1st DS0 **A**	2nd DS0 **A**	3rd DS0 **A**	4th DS0 **A**	...
Frame 7:	1st DS0	2nd DS0	3rd DS0	4th DS0	...
Frame 8:	1st DS0	2nd DS0	3rd DS0	4th DS0	...
Frame 9:	1st DS0	2nd DS0	3rd DS0	4th DS0	...
Frame 10:	1st DS0	2nd DS0	3rd DS0	4th DS0	...
Frame 11:	1st DS0	2nd DS0	3rd DS0	4th DS0	...
Frame 12:	1st DS0 **B**	2nd DS0 **B**	3rd DS0 **B**	4th DS0 **B**	...
Frame 13:	1st DS0	2nd DS0	3rd DS0	4th DS0	...
Frame 14:	1st DS0	2nd DS0	3rd DS0	4th DS0	...
Frame 15:	1st DS0	2nd DS0	3rd DS0	4th DS0	...
Frame 16:	1st DS0	2nd DS0	3rd DS0	4th DS0	...
Frame 17:	1st DS0	2nd DS0	3rd DS0	4th DS0	...
Frame 18:	1st DS0 **C**	2nd DS0 **C**	3rd DS0 **C**	4th DS0 **C**	...
Frame 19:	1st DS0	2nd DS0	3rd DS0	4th DS0	...
Frame 20:	1st DS0	2nd DS0	3rd DS0	4th DS0	...
Frame 21:	1stDS0	2nd DS0	3rd DS0	4th DS0	...
Frame 22:	1st DS0	2nd DS0	3rd DS0	4th DS0	...
Frame 23:	1st DS0	2nd DS0	3rd DS0	4th DS0	...
Frame 24:	1st DS0 **D**	2nd DS0 **D**	3rd DS0 **D**	4th DS0 **D**	...

Figure 1.12   *DS0 Signaling Bits in a Single T1 Extended Super Frame*

These four signaling bits (shown as A, B, C, and D in Figure 1.12) are put together to comprise a single signaling pattern that communicates some line state (such as on-hook, off-hook, and so on). For example, if your voice equipment is using foreign exchange office (FXO) loop-start signaling for the T1 line (the signaling will be discussed in just a moment) and the PSTN central office sends a T1 ESF where the ABCD bits are set to 1111, this signals the "ringing" state for the DS0. If the ABCD bits were set to 0101, this signals the "off-hook" state for the DS0.

Note   Although using T1 CAS to steal bits for signaling does not noticeably impact the quality of digital voice transmissions, it does impact the quality of data (modem and fax) transmissions.

Looking at the mechanics of CAS E1 is a little counterintuitive if you are used to T1 deployments. E1 lines have 32 channels, which break down as follows:

- **E1 DS0 1:** Used for E1 framing information

- **E1 DS0 2–16:** Dedicated use for voice (no signaling)

- **E1 DS0 17:** Used for voice signaling information for channels 2–16 and 18–32

- **E1 DS0 18–32:** Dedicated use for voice (no signaling)

It might seem odd to have channel *associated* signaling that is sent in a separate channel (channel 17) in E1 deployments, but that is how E1 CAS operates. It is still considered CAS because the signaling sent in time slot 17 uses the same system of ABCD bits as T1 CAS.

Note   E1 CAS signals using exactly the same method as T1 CAS (ABCD bits), making the two standards interoperable.

There are three types of signaling standards used on T1/E1 CAS connections:

- Loop start

- Ground start

- E&M

Each one of these signaling types has different meanings for the ABCD signaling bits found in the ESF. When configuring your local voice equipment, you must ensure that your signaling type matches the signaling type used by the carrier.

Note   There are five different types of E&M signaling (E&M types 1–5). When using a Cisco router to interface with the legacy voice world, you can support all E&M signaling types *except* type 4.

Common Channel Signaling

Common channel signaling dedicates one of the DS0 channels from a T1 or E1 link for signaling information. This is often called "out of band" signaling because the signaling traffic is sent completely separate from the voice traffic. As a result, a T1 connection using CCS has only 23 usable DS0s for voice. Because CCS dedicates a full channel of the circuit for signaling, the "stolen bit" method of signaling using ABCD bits is no longer necessary. Rather, a full signaling protocol sends the necessary information for all voice channels. The most popular signaling protocol used is Q.931, which is the signaling protocol used for ISDN circuits.

CCS is the most popular connection used between voice systems worldwide because it offers more flexibility with signaling messages, more bandwidth for the voice bearer channels, and higher security (because the signaling is not embedded in the voice channel). CCS also allows PBX vendors to communicate proprietary messages (and features) between their PBX systems using ISDN signaling, whereas CAS does not offer any of these capabilities.

Tip   When using CCS configurations with T1 lines, the 24th time slot is always the signaling channel. When using CCS configurations with E1 lines, the 17th time slot is always the signaling channel.

Key Topic

Note   While ISDN is the most popular protocol used with CCS configurations, CCS can use other protocols. For example, telephone companies use the Signaling System 7 (SS7) protocol (described later in the chapter) with CCS configurations to communicate between COs.

Understanding the PSTN

All the signaling standards and communication methods discussed in the previous section typically focus around the connection to one, massive voice network known as the public switched telephone network (PSTN). If you have ever made a call from a home telephone, you have experienced the results of the traditional telephony network. This network is not unlike many of the data networks of today. Its primary purpose is to establish worldwide pathways allowing people to easily connect, converse, and disconnect.

The Pieces of the PSTN

When the phone system was originally created, individual phones were wired together to allow people to communicate. If you wanted to connect with more than one person, you would need multiple phones. As you can imagine, this solution was short lived as a more scalable system was found. The modern PSTN is now a worldwide network (much like the Internet) built from the following pieces, as shown in Figure 1.13:

Key
Topic

■ **Analog telephone:** Able to connect directly to the PSTN and is the most common device on the PSTN. Converts audio into electrical signals.

■ **Local loop:** The link between the customer premises (such as a home or business) and the telecommunications service provider.

■ **Central office (CO) switch:** Provides services to the devices on the local loop. These services include signaling, digit collection, call routing, setup, and teardown.

■ **Trunk:** Provides a connection between switches. These switches could be CO or private.

■ **Private switch:** Allows a business to operate a "miniature PSTN" inside its company. This provides efficiency and cost savings because each phone in the company does not require a direct connection to the CO switch.

■ **Digital telephone:** Typically connects to a PBX system. Converts audio into binary 1s and 0s, which allows more efficient communication than analog.

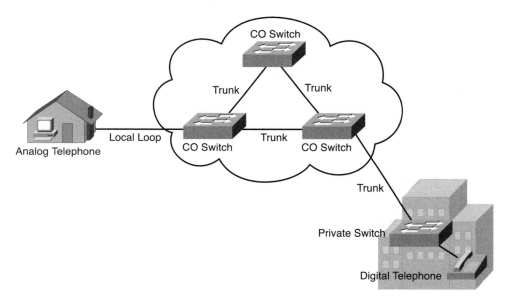

Figure 1.13   *PSTN Components*

Many believe the PSTN will eventually be absorbed into the Internet. While this may be true, advances must be made on the Internet to ensure proper quality of service (QoS) guarantees for voice calls.

Understanding PBX and Key Systems

Many businesses have hundreds or even thousands of phones they support in the organization. If the company purchased a direct PSTN connection for each one of these phones, the cost would be astronomical. Instead, most organizations choose to use a private branch exchange (PBX) or key system internally to manage in-house phones. These systems allow internal users to make phone calls inside the office without using any PSTN resources. Calls to the PSTN will forward out the company's PSTN trunk link (refer to Figure 1.13).

When you first look at a PBX system, it looks like a large box full of cards. Each one of these cards has a specific function:

- **Line cards:** Provide the connection between telephone handsets and the PBX system.

- **Trunk cards:** Provide connections from the PBX system to the PSTN or other PBX systems.

- **Control complex:** Provides the intelligence behind the PBX system; all call setup, routing, and management functions are contained in the control complex.

If you look at a PBX from a network equipment mindset, "single point of failure" might be one of the first thoughts that jump into your mind. While this may be true, most PBX systems offer 99.999 percent uptime with a lifespan of 7 to 10 years. That's a hard statistic to beat in just about any industry.

Key systems are geared around small business environments (typically less than 50 users). As technology has advanced, the line between key systems and PBXs has begun to blur; however, key systems typically support fewer features and have a "shared line" feel. For example, you might see a key system installed in a small insurance office where users all have four lines assigned to their phone. If Joe were to use line 1, the line would appear busy for all users at the insurance office.

Note   Although key systems often have a shared-line feature set, many key systems have numerous features that allow them to operate just like a PBX system, but with fewer ports.

Connections to and Between the PSTN

When you want to connect to the PSTN, you have a variety of options. Home users and small offices can connect using analog ports. Each two-wire analog connection has the ability to support a single call. For home users, a single, analog connection to the PSTN may be sufficient. For small offices, the number of incoming analog connections directly relates to the office size and average call volume. As businesses grow, you can consolidate the multiple analog connections into one or more digital T1 or E1 connections, as shown in Figure 1.14.

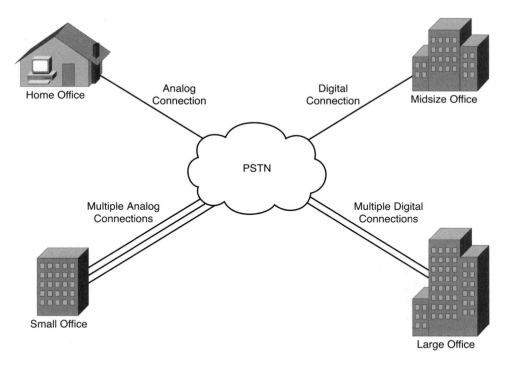

Figure 1.14   *Connections to the PSTN*

Within the PSTN itself lies a network of networks, similar to the Internet, connecting offices from multiple telephony providers together into a massive, worldwide network. In order for all the telephony providers of the world to communicate together, a common signaling protocol must be used, similar to the way TCP/IP operates in the data realm. The voice signaling protocol used around the world is *Signaling System 7 (SS7)*.

SS7 is an out-of-band (CCS-style) signaling method used to communicate call setup, routing, billing, and informational messages between telephone company COs around the world. When a user makes a call, the first CO to receive the call performs an SS7 lookup to locate the number. Once the destination is found, SS7 is responsible for routing the call through the voice network to the destination and providing all informational signaling (such as ring back) to the calling device.

Note   SS7 is primarily a telephony service provider technology. You will not typically interface directly with the SS7 protocol from a telephony customer perspective.

PSTN Numbering Plans

Just as data networks use IP addressing to organize and locate resources, voice networks use a numbering plan to organize and locate telephones all around the world. Organizations managing their own, internal telephony systems can develop any internal number scheme that best fits the company needs (similar to private IP addressing). However, when connecting to the PSTN, you must use a valid, E.164 standard address for your telephone system. E.164 is an international numbering plan created by the International Telecommunication Union (ITU). Each number in the E.164 numbering plan contains the following components:

- Country code

- National destination code

- Subscriber number

Note   E.164 numbers are limited to a maximum length of 15 digits.

As an example, the North American Numbering Plan (NANP) uses the E.164 standard to break numbers down into the following components:

- Country code

- Area code

- Central office or exchange code

- Station code

For example, the NANP number 1-602-555-1212 breaks down as shown in Figure 1.15.

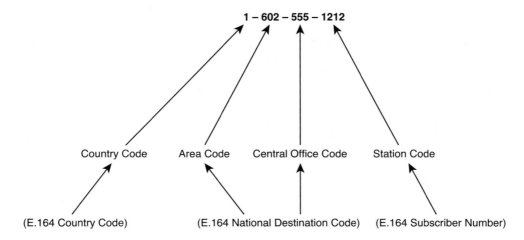

Figure 1.15 *NANP Phone Number Example*

Even though the NANP defines specific categories of numbers that the E.164 standard does not include, the number still falls under the three broad categories, also shown in Figure 1.15.

Exam Preparation Tasks

Review All the Key Topics

Review the most important topics in the chapter, noted with the key topics icon in the outer margin of the page. Table 1.2 lists and describes these key topics and identifies the page numbers on which each is found.

Key
Topic

Table 1.2   *Key Topics for Chapter 1*

Key Topic Element	Description	Page Number
Figure 1.3	Illustrates the wired connections to an analog phone	9
List	List of supervisory signaling types	11
List	List of informational signaling types	11
List	List of address signaling types	12
Figure 1.10	Illustration of TDM	16
List	Two methods used to deliver signaling with digital circuits	17
Tip	Specific signaling time slot for T1 and E1 circuits using CCS	21
List	The components of the PSTN	22

Definitions of Key Terms

Define the following key terms from this chapter, and check your answers in the glossary.

analog signal

loop start signaling

ground start signaling

glare

dual-tone multifrequency (DTMF)

pulse dialing

pulse-amplitude modulation (PAM)

pulse-code modulation (PCM)

time-division multiplexing (TDM)

channel associated signaling (CAS)

common channel signaling (CCS)

robbed bit signaling (RBS)

Super Frame (SF)

Extended Super Frame (ESF)

Q.931

local loop

private branch exchange (PBX)

key system

Signaling System 7 (SS7)

E.164

quantization

VoIP: Why It Is a Big Deal for Businesses: Before you migrate to VoIP, there must be a business objective. This could be cost savings, beneficial new applications, or even ease of use. This section discusses these business benefits of VoIP.

The Cisco VoIP Structure: Cisco has designed a four-layer structure describing the core components of the Cisco VoIP network. This section discusses this structure, and then breaks down each area of the voice network, addressing the individual components in each.

CHAPTER 2

Perspectives on Voice After Convergence

The previous chapter explored the foundation and history of voice communications; it is now time to look into the future by exploring perspectives on voice after convergence. This is our view into the corporate network of the future, where all business communications occur over a single Ethernet cable and applications communicate seamlessly between voice, video, and data networks. This chapter prepares you to discuss the business benefits of VoIP with key individuals at your organization. Likewise, once you are ready to move forward with a VoIP deployment, this chapter will help you identify key applications and services that will exist on the voice network.

"Do I Know This Already?" Quiz

The "Do I Know This Already?" quiz allows you to assess whether you should read this entire chapter or simply jump to the "Exam Preparation Tasks" section for review. If you are in doubt, read the entire chapter. Table 2.1 outlines the major headings in this chapter and the corresponding "Do I Know This Already?" quiz questions. You can find the answers in Appendix A, "Answers to the 'Do I Know This Already?' Quizzes."

Table 2.1 *"Do I Know This Already?" Foundation Topics Section-to-Question Mapping*

Foundation Topics Section	Questions Covered in This Section
VoIP: Why It Is a Big Deal for Businesses	1
Cisco VoIP Structure	2–10

1. Which of the following are advantages of using VoIP over a traditional PBX system? (Choose three.)

    a. Open, compatible standards

    b. Digital and IP phone signaling support

    c. Reduced cabling costs for new buildings

    d. Native support for IP SoftPhones

2. Which of the following is *not* a valid layer in the Cisco Unified Communications model? (Choose two.)

    a. Network

    b. Endpoints

    c. Infrastructure

    d. Carrier

    e. Call processing

3. Which of the following call processing components would be ideal for a 20-person company that intended to double in size over the next 5 years?

    a. Cisco Unified Communications Manager

    b. Cisco Unified Communications Manager Express

    c. Unified Communications 500

    d. Cisco Unified Communications Manager Business Edition

4. Which of the following platforms would you use to run Cisco Unified CME?

    a. Cisco Media Convergence Server (MCS)

    b. Cisco 1861 Router

    c. Cisco 3550 Switch

    d. Cisco 3750 Switch

    e. Cisco UC500

5. What benefit does Unified Communications Manager Business Edition give over Unified Communications Manager?

    a. Support of non-Cisco IP phones

    b. SIP-based signaling support

    c. Support of larger-scale deployments

    d. Integrated voice mail support

6. Which of the following advantages would you gain by using a full Cisco Unity solution over Cisco Unity Connection?

   a. Integration with legacy voice-mail systems

   b. Text-to-speech support

   c. The ability to receive voice mails through an e-mail client

   d. The ability to manage voice mails using a web interface

7. Which of the following applications provides an ACD service for a Cisco VoIP network?

   a. Cisco IVR

   b. Cisco Unified Contact Center

   c. Cisco Auto Attendant

   d. Cisco Communications Manager

8. What is the function of the Cisco Unified Mobility application?

   a. To allow users to log in and log out of IP phones on the network

   b. To auto-forward VoIP devices to different locations based on time of day

   c. To link a single phone number to multiple devices

   d. To track a user's location in the network

9. A manager for a marketing group needs a phone that supports three lines and a custom XML application that he uses to track projects. Which of the following Cisco IP phone models will meet this need? (Choose two.)

   a. Cisco 7911G

   b. Cisco 7941G

   c. Cisco 7945G

   d. Cisco 7960G

   e. Cisco 7971G

10. Which of the following devices allows you to convert signals from an analog fax machine into VoIP packets?

   a. Cisco 3911

   b. Cisco 7985G

   c. Cisco ATA

   d. Cisco Expansion Module

Foundation Topics

VoIP: Why It Is a Big Deal for Businesses

When many people first learn about VoIP, they commonly say, "So we are sending voice over data cables instead of voice cables...what is so big about that?" It seemed that the biggest benefit would be saving cabling costs, nothing more. Once you dig deeper into the ramifications of running voice over data networks, you begin to uncover many business benefits that were previously untapped.

The business benefits of VoIP include the following:

- **Reduced cost of communicating:** Rather than rely on expensive tie lines or toll charges to communicate between offices, VoIP allows you to forward calls over WAN connections.

- **Reduced cost of cabling:** VoIP deployments typically cut cabling costs in half by running a single Ethernet connection rather than both voice and data cables. This cost savings is most realized in newly constructed offices.

- **Seamless voice networks:** Because data networks connect offices, mobile workers, and telecommuters together, VoIP naturally inherits this property. The voice traffic is crossing "your network" (relatively speaking) rather than exiting to the PSTN. This also provides centralized control of all voice devices attached to the network and a consistent dial plan. For example, all users could dial each other using four-digit extensions even though many of them may be scattered around the world.

- **Take your phone with you:** Cost estimates for moves, adds, and changes (MACs) to a traditional PBX system range from $55 to $295 per MAC[1]. With VoIP phone systems, this cost is virtually eliminated. In addition, IP phones are becoming increasingly "plug-and-play," within the local offices, allowing moves with little to no reconfiguration of the voice network. In addition, when combined with a VPN configuration, users can take IP phones home with them and retain their work extension.

- **IP SoftPhones:** SoftPhones represent an ideal example of the possibilities when combining voice and data networks. Users can now plug a headset into their laptop or desktop and allow it to act as their phone. SoftPhones are becoming increasingly more integrated with other applications such as e-mail contact lists, instant messenger, and video telephony.

- **Unified e-mail, voice mail, fax:** All messaging can be sent to a user's e-mail inbox. This allows users to get all messages in one place and easily reply, forward, or archive messages.

- **Increased productivity:** VoIP extensions can forward to ring multiple devices before forwarding to voice mail. This eliminates the "phone tag" games.

- **Feature-rich communications:** Because voice, data, and video networks have combined, users are able to initiate phone calls that communicate with or invoke other applications from the voice or data network to add additional benefits to a VoIP call. For example, calls flowing into a call center can automatically pull up customer records based on caller ID information or trigger a video stream for one or more of the callers.

■ **Open, compatible standards:** In the same way that you can network Apple, Dell, and IBM PCs together, you can now connect devices from different telephony vendors together. While this benefit has yet to be fully realized, this will allow businesses to choose the best equipment for their network, regardless of the manufacturer.

Many believe the PSTN will eventually be absorbed into the Internet. While this may be true, advances must be made on the Internet to ensure proper quality of service (QoS) guarantees for voice calls.

The Cisco VoIP Structure

The OSI reference model was designed to create standard methods of connecting and communicating across data networks. In the realm of voice, similar connection models exist to describe voice communications. Cisco has developed a type of model to describe the Unified Communications system, shown in Figure 2.1.

Key
Topic

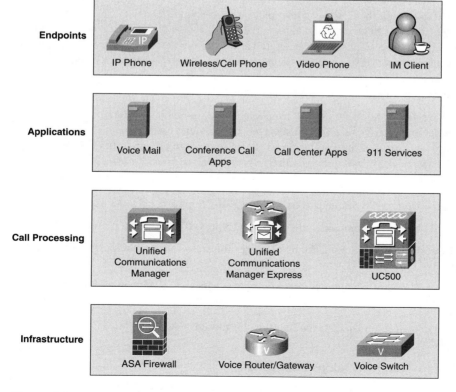

Figure 2.1   *Cisco Voice Unified Communications Layers*

Each of these layers represents an integral piece of the voice network. While the layers work together to create a functional voice network, each layer performs unique functions to the voice network. Let's work through them, layer by layer.

Infrastructure Layer

The infrastructure layer represents the devices that build the infrastructure of the data network. These are devices such as routers, switches, and voice gateways. The infrastructure layer is logically located at the bottom of the model because it represents the foundation that supports the voice network.

When it comes to the infrastructure layer, redundancy and QoS are key. The uptime of traditional PBX systems is 99.999 percent (approximately 5 minutes of downtime per year). In order to achieve this same level of performance in a converged network, your network infrastructure should be tuned for lightning-fast failover should any device or physical link fail. In the same sense, QoS should carry the voice traffic from source to destination using priority bandwidth that is untouched by data traffic. Voice phone calls should never compete for bandwidth from any data application.

Call Processing Layer

The call processing layer is responsible for just that: processing calls and all the functionality that goes with them. When a user picks up their phone handset, the call processing layer gets involved to generate a dial tone. Each digit that is dialed is then analyzed and processed. The ring signal is then generated at the remote device and the call is connected. As the users converse, if one of them presses the Transfer button, for example, the call processing layer steps in to process this request. Just about any time someone touches a phone, the call processing layer gets involved.

When Cisco first moved into the IP telephony space, the initial product offering for the call processing layer was Cisco CallManager. This product could handle a voice network of nearly any size. The only problem was the price point to get into a full Cisco CallManager solution was not attractive to many small to midsize business customers. Cisco has since expanded its call processing portfolio to four different offerings:

■ **Cisco Unified Communications 500 (UC500):** Supports up to 48 users

■ **Cisco Unified Communications Manager Express (CME):** Supports up to 250 users

■ **Cisco Unified Communications Manager Business Edition:** Supports up to 500 users

■ **Cisco Unified Communications Manager (formerly CallManager):** Supports 30,000+ users

Let's dig deeper to understand the functions of these product lines.

Cisco Unified Communications 500 Series

When you think of the UC500 series (shown in Figure 2.2), think "key system replacement."

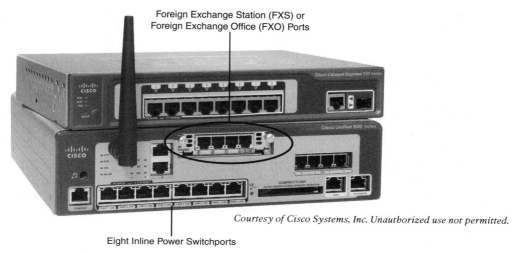

Figure 2.2   *Cisco Unified Communications 500 Series with Eight-Port Expansion Switch*

This small box is designed to fit right into the small business market as an all-in-one product. I (Jeremy) have to admit: when I first saw this product, my mouth dropped open. It is the perfect data and voice product combination.

Note   While the UC500 can replace a traditional key system, it also has many PBX capabilities.

Here is just a partial list of some key UC500 features:

- Phone support for 8 to 48 phones

- Integrated voice mail

- Integrated automated attendant answering system

- Built-in eight-port inline power switch

- External Music on Hold (MoH) jack to attach external audio sources (or play MoH from WAV files stored in UC500 flash memory)

- Support for every common phone feature

- Built-in Foreign Exchange Office (FXO) ports (for analog PSTN connections)

- Built-in Foreign Exchange Station (FXS) ports (for analog phone/modem/fax connections)

- Built-in Network Address Translation (NAT) and firewall support for Internet connectivity

- Built-in Virtual Private Network (VPN) support for up to ten users

- Optional integrated 802.11 wireless network connectivity

This is just a partial list! This is truly an all-in-one data, security, and voice network solution for a small business, all in a pint-size box. Furthermore, the UC500 series is designed for offices that may not have a full-time IT staff in mind. Because of this, nearly all setup, configuration, and maintenance can be performed with an easy-to-manage, web-based interface.

Cisco Unified Communications Manager Express

When businesses outgrow the 48-phone limitation of the UC500 system, the next step is to move into a Cisco Unified CME system, which is scalable to 250 IP phones, depending on the router platform on which you choose to run CME. Table 2.2 breaks down current CME platform limitations.

Table 2.2   *Unified Communications Manager Express Platform Limitations*

Platform	Maximum Number of Phones
Cisco 1861 Integrated Services Router	8
Cisco IAD2430 Integrated Access Device	24
Cisco 2801 Integrated Services Router	25
Cisco 3250 Ruggedize Services Router	10
Cisco 3270 Ruggedize Services Router	50
Cisco 2811 Integrated Services Router	35
Cisco 2821 Integrated Services Router	50
Cisco 2851 Integrated Services Router	100
Cisco 3725 Multiservice Access Router	144
Cisco 3745 Multiservice Access Router	192
Cisco 3825 Integrated Services Router	175
Cisco 3845 Integrated Services Router	250

Keep in mind that these limitations will always shift around, increasing or decreasing slightly as new models of routers and Cisco IOS versions are released.

In addition to the scalability benefits, users upgrading to Cisco Unified CME also receive additional features from the UC500 series. For example, CME supports Cisco Unified CallConnector for Microsoft Office, which allows users to integrate their IP phone with Microsoft Office components such as Outlook and Internet Explorer. Using this feature, a user can click a contact in Outlook and quickly dial them from an IP phone, or even highlight a phone number in a PowerPoint presentation and have their phone auto-dial the number.

Voice mail for the Cisco Unified CME system is typically handled by Cisco Unity Express, which runs using a Linux-based platform installed on a flash card or hard drive inside the router. Because both Cisco Unified CME and Cisco Unity Express run on a fully functional Integrated Services Router (ISR), the business can support a fully functional (WAN, VPN, wireless, and so on) data network and voice network from one device.

Cisco Unified Communications Manager Business Edition

As a business continues to grow beyond the capacity of Cisco Unified CME, the next step in the journey to a full Cisco Unified Communications Manager (CCM) solution is Cisco Unified Communications Manager Business Edition. Moving to this platform means you have now moved away from a router-integrated solution into a dedicated server platform. One example of these dedicated servers is the Cisco Media Convergence Server (MCS) 7835, shown in Figure 2.3.

Courtesy of Cisco Systems, Inc. Unauthorized use not permitted.

Figure 2.3   *Cisco Media Convergence Server 7835*

Cisco Unified Communications Manager Business Edition runs as a Linux-based appliance to provide scalability up to 500 IP phones. The key strength of CCM Business Edition is the ability to provide an all-in-one voice solution from a single server platform. It accomplishes this by including three key applications in one server:

- **Cisco Unified Communications Manager:** The call processing component that provides all features and functionality to the IP phones

- **Cisco Unity Connection:** An integrated voice-mail solution

- **Cisco Unified Mobility:** Allows users to be reached from a single phone number by redirecting incoming calls to multiple devices (configured by the user)

Cisco Unified Communications Manager Business Edition has the same look and feel as the full CCM solution, allowing an organization to upgrade with very little additional training. CCM Business Edition can also integrate with a plethora of additional applications, such as Cisco Unified Contact Center Express and Cisco Unified Presence, that can add functionality to your voice network. You learn about the exact function of these additional applications in the "Cisco Unified Contact Center" and "Additional Applications" sections later in this chapter.

> **Note**   Although Cisco Unified Communications Manager Business Edition is designed as a stand-alone solution, you can achieve a basic level of redundancy by implementing Survivable Remote Site Telephony (SRST) functionality on a Cisco router. This allows the router to support the Cisco IP phones should the Cisco Unified Communications Manager Business Edition server become unavailable.

Cisco Unified Communications Manager

When moving from Cisco Unified Communications Manager Business Edition to a full CCM solution, you are primarily gaining two key benefits: redundancy and scalability. The full Cisco Unified Communications Manager network solution can scale to virtually any size and allows you to implement multiple redundant servers that can support IP phones and applications should any of your primary call processing servers fail.

Table 2.3 compares each of these call processing products.

Table 2.3   *Cisco Call Processing Platforms*

Product	Number of Users	Redundancy Support	Server or Router Based
Cisco UC500	8 to 48	No	Router
Cisco Unified Communications Manager Express	Up to 250 (depending on router)	No	Router
Cisco Unified Communications Manager Business Edition	Up to 500	No	Server
Cisco Unified Communications Manager	30,000 per cluster (many clusters can be supported)	Yes	Server

Applications Layer

As you move up to the next layer of the Cisco VoIP structure, you encounter the applications that expand the functionality of the voice network in some way. Many applications have already been developed for the Cisco VoIP solution, each of them adding its own special features to the voice network. Three of these application servers stand out as "essential applications" for many VoIP networks: Cisco Unity (voice mail), Interactive Voice Response (IVR)/Auto Attendant, and Unified Contact Center.

Cisco Unity Products

Cisco has designed the Cisco Unity product line to encompass everything dealing with messaging. Whereas traditional phone systems are geared to deliver messages to telephone handsets, Cisco Unity allows you to deliver messages to a variety of clients. This allows VoIP network users to unify (thus the name) all messaging into a single point of access. For example, fax messages, voice mail, and e-mail can all be delivered to a single inbox.

The Cisco Unity product line comes in three different flavors, as discussed in the following sections:

- Cisco Unity Express
- Cisco Unity Connection
- Cisco Unity

Cisco Unity Express

The Unity Express option represents the smallest Unity solution you can add to your network. Unity Express runs from either a flash module or hard drive that can be added to a variety of Cisco router platforms. The flash module version of Unity Express is added as an Advanced Integration Module (AIM) card, which plugs in to the motherboard of the router. The hard drive version of Unity Express installs as a network module. Although the flash Unity Express version does not consume a network slot on the router, you are very limited on storage space for voice mails and automated-attendant recordings or scripts. The network module version offers considerably more storage space.

Rather than integrating directly with Cisco IOS, Unity Express boots and runs as a Linux-based appliance on the router, keeping voice-mail functions completely separated from router functions. In addition, Cisco Unity Express provides limited IVR capabilities to provide an automated attendant (for example, press 1 to transfer to sales, press 2 to transfer to customer service, and so on), and message retrieval via phone, web interface, or e-mail. As an integrated solution, Unity Express is geared around networks up to 100 users.

Cisco Unity Connection

Companies that have more than 100 users but less than 7500 users may choose to use Cisco Unity Connection. Unity Connection supports all the basic voice-mail and e-mail integration features of Unity Express, but also adds advanced call routing rules (allowing you to route based on time of day, caller ID, and so on) and speech recognition. A company may choose to deploy Cisco Unity Connection in one of two ways:

- If the organization has fewer than 500 users, they can use Unity Connection in a single-server solution with Cisco Unified Communications Manager, Business Edition. This provides all VoIP call processing and messaging capabilities in a single box.
- As the organization grows beyond 500 users, it can add dedicated Unity Connection servers to scale up to 7500 users.

Cisco Unity

Cisco Unity is a dedicated messaging server solution for VoIP networks. Cisco Unity brings all the capabilities of the Unity Express and Unity Connection platforms and adds scalability and integration with legacy voice-mail systems along with Microsoft Exchange, Lotus Notes, or Novell GroupWise e-mail systems. Cisco Unity is able to support up to 7500 users per server and can be networked with additional servers to support more than 250,000 users.

In addition, Cisco Unity supports fully unified messaging. This feature blends the networks of fax, e-mail, and voice mail into a single, integrated system. The following examples are characteristic of a unified messaging environment:

■ A user is able to forward voice messages as e-mail attachments to any e-mail user, enabling users of different voice-mail systems to share voice-mail messages.

■ Users are able to leave messages for multiple recipients with a single call.

■ Users are able to listen to e-mail messages from a telephone using the text to speech (TTS) feature.

■ A user can respond to an e-mail message over the phone with an audio attachment.

■ A user can view faxes as TIF files from an e-mail client and save them in separate folders.

While Unity Express and Unity Connection support sending voice-mail messages as e-mail attachments, adding true unified messaging offers many more advantages.

Note   Although a rare and strange occurrence, Unity can be integrated with legacy PBX solutions and is not limited to VoIP deployments.

Table 2.4 compares each of these unified messaging products.

Table 2.4   *Cisco Unified Messaging Platforms*

Product	Number of Users	Redundancy Support	E-Mail Support	Server or Router Based
Cisco Unity Express	Up to 250	No	Able to relay voice mail to outside e-mail server	Router
Cisco Unity Connection	Up to 7500	No	Able to relay voice mail to outside e-mail server	Server

Product	Number of Users	Redundancy Support	E-Mail Support	Server or Router Based
Cisco Unity	Up to 7500 per server, network to 250,000	Yes	Integrates directly with MS Exchange, Lotus Notes, or Novell GroupWise	Server

Interactive Voice Response/Auto Attendant

IVR provides prompt and collect features, meaning it can play a recorded message to a user and request that the user press a key in response. These types of systems can be used to provide a variety of information to callers. For example, a bank could use an IVR system to provide balances or transfer options for callers through an automated system. The most popular use of IVR is an auto-attendant application.

An auto attendant can allow callers to direct themselves to the correct person or department in your company without requiring a dedicated receptionist. This could mean building a menu as simple as "Press 1 for Sales, 2 for Engineering, 0 for the operator" or you could allow callers to dial direct extensions in the company. All of the Cisco Unity product lines support an auto-attendant application through IVR. The IVR application gains more functionality as you upgrade from Unity Express to Unity Connection to a full-blown Unity system.

Although the full Cisco Unity software provides a very robust IVR system, it is still a subset of the full features of the standalone Cisco IP IVR software. The full IVR software offers features such as database integration, the ability to send e-mail or SMS messages as a response to a user's input, and integration with HTTP websites.

Cisco Unified Contact Center

Many companies have a corporate call center that fields calls for a variety of purposes. For example, Cisco receives numerous technical support calls every single day. They require a system that distributes calls to the correct specialty groups (such as switching, routing, security, and so on) in the company and then distributes calls accurately to the agents receiving them in the group. For this call center requirement, Cisco has developed the Unified Contact Center product line.

The Contact Center software runs on a dedicated server and provides an automatic call distributor (ACD) service, which distributes calls to different groups in your organization, in addition to IVR capabilities. In addition, the Contact Center uses computer telephony integration (CTI) that can automatically pop up a window on the agent's screen with information about a caller (based on the caller ID), which could include contact information and previous case numbers. In staying true to the VoIP network integration vision, the Contact Center software also supports chat and web collaboration and e-mail integration. This allows what used to be solely a voice call center to become a call center of many communications types.

The Unified Contact Center product line is often called a "call center in a box" because it provides robust call center features in a single-server platform. Cisco distributes the Contact Center software in two flavors: Express and Enterprise. Unified Contact Center Express is designed as a management solution for up to 300 agents. The full Unified Contact Center Enterprise software solution is designed for the larger call center environments.

Additional Applications

Many applications exist in addition to the three "core applications" just mentioned. The following are brief descriptions of the most common additional applications that corporations install in their VoIP environments:

- **Cisco Unified MeetingPlace:** Provides a multimedia conference solution that gives you the capability to conference voice, video, and data into a single conference call. For example, multiple offices could participate in a conference call using IP phones, live video feeds, and instant messenger clients. The conference call could include PowerPoint presentations, shared whiteboards, or live demonstrations. The organization could also choose to record the conference call for playback at a later time.

- **Cisco Unified Presence:** Provides status and reachability information for the users of the voice network. For example, Joe might check the status for Samantha and find that she is available on an instant messenger client but is currently engaged in a video call.

- **Cisco Unified Mobility:** Allows users to have a single contact phone number that they can link to multiple devices. For example, Mike could have the phone number (480) 555-1212 that he links to his desk phone, cell phone, and instant messenger client.

- **Cisco Emergency Responder:** Because VoIP clients have the ability to "roam around" the network using wireless phones, SoftPhones, or extension mobility functionality, emergency calls (911 calls in North America) could pose a location problem. Cisco Emergency Responder (ER) dynamically updates location information for a user based on the current position in the network and feeds that information to the emergency service provider if an emergency call is placed. The Cisco ER product also helps manage emergency calls in a centralized IP telephony deployment, ensuring that branch office emergency calls do not route over any WAN links to the wrong exit point.

Because of the open-standards nature of VoIP, you can expect this application list to grow over time. In addition to applications written by Cisco, many other software publishing companies have and will jump on this VoIP application bandwagon.

Endpoints Layer

The final layer of the Cisco VoIP structure contains the endpoints of the system. This is, most likely, the only layer that your end users will interact with directly. Now, keep this in mind: VoIP allows you to take audio and convert it into IP-based packets. This means that *any* device connecting to a network could potentially be a VoIP endpoint. For example, an instant messenger client or even a website could be considered a VoIP endpoint. So, rather than digress into the many different potential endpoints, let's talk about the most common endpoints you will use in a Cisco-based call processing infrastructure: Cisco IP phones.

You can divide Cisco IP phones into the following categories:

- Entry-level IP phones

- Business-class IP phones

- Touchscreen IP phones

- Specialty devices

Let's break down each of these categories and explore some of the endpoints you will encounter in each.

Note   Due to the rapidly changing VoIP landscape, the devices discussed in the following sections will be continually changing and progressing. For an updated list of Cisco endpoints, visit http://www.cisco.com/go/voice and click the **Cisco Unified IP Phones 7900 Series** hyperlink.

Entry-Level Cisco IP Phones

The entry-level Cisco IP phones are typically single-line, minimal-feature phones that allow you to make and receive calls and perform other basic phone functions such as hold, conference, and transfer. Even in larger businesses, these devices may be ideal for public areas such as a break room, lobby, or copy room. The following IP phones fall under this category:

- Cisco Unified SIP Phone 3911

- Cisco 7906G and 7911G

- Cisco 7931G

Cisco 3911

The Cisco 3911 (shown in Figure 2.4) is about as basic as you can get. This single-line phone provides the following key features:

- **Inline power support:** Can receive power using the Ethernet cable as a source

- **Half-duplex speakerphone:** Built-in microphone and speaker

- **Fixed feature buttons:** Feature buttons built in on the phone versus onscreen display softkeys

Basic Display
(Caller ID, Talk Time)

Feature Buttons

Courtesy of Cisco Systems, Inc. Unauthorized use not permitted.

Figure 2.4   *Cisco 3911 IP Phone*

The display of the Cisco 3911 allows features such as caller ID and call history.

Cisco 7906G and 7911G

Whereas the Cisco 3911 might typically be used in a break room or lobby, the Cisco 7906G and 7911G (shown in Figure 2.5) add enough features that they could be considered for a typical network end user. These single-line phones provide the following key features:

- **Inline power support:** Can receive power using the Ethernet cable as a source

- **Onscreen softkey support:** Four onscreen softkeys for features such as hold, transfer, and redial

- **Basic XML service support:** Provides a scrollable, three-line display for text-based XML applications

Display with Basic XML Support
Softkeys
Menu Rocker

Courtesy of Cisco Systems, Inc. Unauthorized use not permitted.

Figure 2.5   *Cisco 7906G and 7911G IP Phones*

Unlike the 7906G, the 7911G has a built-in 10/100 switch allowing you to co-locate another network device (such as a PC) without requiring additional Ethernet cable drops. These two phones provide a "listen-only" speakerphone capability because they do not have a built-in microphone.

Cisco 7931G

The Cisco 7931G (shown in Figure 2.6) is a 24-line, basic-feature IP phone that is typically used in retail and small commercial environments. It falls under the "entry-level" category because retail and small commercial environments usually have a key-system deployment in which the phones at each location share common lines. The Cisco 7931G provides the following key features:

- **Built-in switch:** Built-in 10/100 Ethernet switch for co-locating other network devices

- **Inline power support:** Can receive power using the Ethernet cable as a source

- **Onscreen softkey support:** Four onscreen softkeys for features such as hold, transfer, and redial

- **Basic XML service support:** Provides a scrollable, three-line display for text-based XML applications and supports audio-based XML applications

Courtesy of Cisco Systems, Inc. Unauthorized use not permitted.

Figure 2.6   *Cisco 7931G IP Phones*

Business-Class Cisco IP Phones

When working with midsize to enterprise-class network environments, you can expect to commonly encounter the following Cisco IP phones: Cisco 7940G, 7941G, 7941G-GE, 7942G, and 7945G. These phones all support two or more lines, larger displays, full-duplex speakerphones, and inline power capabilities. The following sections describe the primary differences between these Cisco IP phone models.

The Cisco 7940G, 7941G, 7941G-GE, 7942G, and 7945G (shown in Figure 2.7) are two-line, fully featured IP phones used in many businesses today. Each of these devices provides the following features:

- **Built-in switch:** Built-in Ethernet switch for co-locating other network devices (such as a laptop or PC)

- **Inline power support:** Can receive power using the Ethernet cable as a source

- **Onscreen softkey support:** Four onscreen softkeys for features such as hold, transfer, and redial

- **XML service support:** Much larger display provides more functionality for a variety of XML-based applications

- **Full-duplex speakerphone and headset support:** High-quality speakerphone and dedicated headset port (which eliminates the need for a separate headset amplifier)

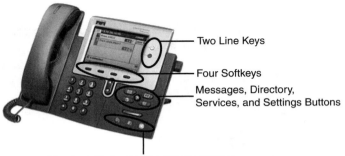

Two Line Keys

Four Softkeys

Messages, Directory, Services, and Settings Buttons

Headset, Mute, Speaker Phone Buttons

Courtesy of Cisco Systems, Inc. Unauthorized use not permitted

Figure 2.7   *Cisco 7940G, 7941G, 7941G-GE, 7942G, and 7945G*

Each Cisco 794x model increment adds its own, unique feature to the base set of 7940 features:

- **Cisco 7941G:** Provides better resolution and backlit display

- **Cisco 7941G-GE:** Provides an integrated 10/100/1000 Gigabit Ethernet switch rather than a 10/100 Fast Ethernet switch

- **Cisco 7942G:** Supports the features of the 7941G and adds high-fidelity audio and the emerging Internet Low Bitrate Codec (iLBC)

- **Cisco 7945G:** Supports the combined features of the 7941G-GE and 7942G, and adds a full 16-bit color display with 320 × 240 resolution

The Cisco 796X series of IP phones mirrors the 794X series, but supports six lines rather than two lines. Every other feature is identical. The Cisco 796X series includes Cisco 7960G, 7961G, 7961G-GE, 7962G, and 7965G.

Touchscreen Cisco IP Phones

While touchscreen Cisco IP phones could easily be categorized under the "business class" category, the touchscreen capabilities add enough flair to move these phones into a class of their own. The touchscreen phones focus solely on the Cisco 797X series eight-line phones, which breaks down into the following models:

- **Cisco 7970G:** The original, full-color, touchscreen display IP phone; mirrors features of 7940G and 7960G

- **Cisco 7971G-GE:** Full-color, touchscreen display IP phone; mirrors Gigabit Ethernet switch features of 7941G-GE and 7961G-GE

- **Cisco 7975G:** Full-color, touchscreen display IP phone that mirrors the features of the 7945G and 7965G, but expands the display to a massive 5.6-inch screen (the 7945G and 7965G support a 5-inch display)

Specialty Devices

In this section, specialty devices include any phones that do not fall under the "day-to-day phone" category that you would find sitting in 90 percent of business areas. There are many devices out there other than what you read about here, but this section should give you a good idea of the types of devices that are available.

Cisco 7985G

The Cisco 7985G model represents the first integrated video and VoIP phone solution from Cisco. Although video could have been integrated into the 797X series, the natural sitting posture of most people would give an unflattering "up the nose" view when using VoIP capabilities. To remedy this, the Cisco 7985G places the camera and video screen at eye level, as shown in Figure 2.8.

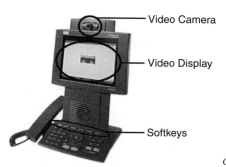

Courtesy of Cisco Systems, Inc. Unauthorized use not permitted.

Figure 2.8   *Cisco 7985G*

Cisco 7921G

The Cisco 7921G phone brings 802.11 wireless and VoIP together. The 7921G wireless IP phone (shown in Figure 2.9) supports 802.11a, b, and g standards to give network users the freedom to roam. This wireless phone has a fairly large (2 inch) display capable of supporting XML-based applications, has a built-in speakerphone, and supports a standby battery life of 200 hours (15.5 hours of talk time).

Courtesy of Cisco Systems, Inc. Unauthorized use not permitted.

Figure 2.9   *Cisco 7921G*

Cisco 7937G Conference Station

The Cisco 7937G (shown in Figure 2.10) is a conference station that resembles a high-tech UFO device landing on a conference room table. The 7937G supports external microphone attachments (which can provide 30 to 40 feet of room coverage) and a backlit display.

Courtesy of Cisco Systems, Inc. Unauthorized use not permitted.

Figure 2.10   *Cisco 7937G*

Cisco ATA 186/188

The Cisco ATA boxes are small devices that can convert up to two analog phones (per ATA) into VoIP devices. This can be the ideal solution to bring legacy fax machines and all-in-one devices into the VoIP network. The ATA 186 provides a single Ethernet interface, while the ATA 188 provides a built-in switch (allowing you to extend service to another co-located network device).

Cisco IP Communicator

Cisco IP Communicator is Cisco's most popular IP SoftPhone solution. IP Communicator emulates a Cisco 7970 IP Phone on the screen of a PC. It provides all the same functionality and features as an actual Cisco 7970 IP Phone. Users can talk and listen using a USB headset or some other speaker/microphone combination.

Cisco VT Advantage

Cisco VT Advantage provides a video integration solution for Cisco IP phone users. VT Advantage represents a webcam and software solution that integrates onscreen video on your PC with the co-located Cisco IP phone. When you make or receive a call, VT Advantage automatically detects and provides video capabilities with the other end. If the other end supports video, the software can automatically establish the video link for the call.

Cisco 7914/7915/7916 Expansion Modules

You can use the Cisco 791X expansion modules to provide additional lines to the 796X and 797X IP Phone series. The modules add up to 15 expansion lines (7914) or 24 expansion lines (7915/7916) with each module. You can add up to two expansion modules per IP phone. Figure 2.11 shows a 7916 expansion module attached to a 7970G Cisco IP Phone.

Courtesy of Cisco Systems, Inc. Unauthorized use not permitted.

Figure 2.11   *Cisco 7970G with 7916 Expansion Module*

Exam Preparation Tasks

Review All the Key Topics

Key Topic

Review the most important topics in the chapter, noted with the key topics icon in the outer margin of the page. Table 2.5 lists and describes these key topics and identifies the page number on which each is found.

Table 2.5 *Key Topics for Chapter 2*

Key Topic Element	Description	Page Number
Figure 2.1	Cisco Voice Unified Communications layers	35
Table 2.3	Cisco call processing platforms	40
Table 2.4	Cisco unified messaging platforms	42

Definitions of Key Terms

Define the following key terms from this chapter, and check your answers in the glossary.

Cisco Unified Communications 500 (UC500)

Cisco Unified Communications Manager Express (CME)

Cisco Media Convergence Server (MCS)

Cisco Unified Communications Manager Business Edition

Cisco Unified Communications Manager

Cisco Unity Express

Cisco Unity Connection

Cisco Unity

Interactive Voice Response (IVR)

Auto Attendant

Cisco Unified Contact Center Express

Cisco Unified MeetingPlace

Cisco Unified Presence

Cisco Unified Mobility

Cisco Emergency Responder

References Used in This Chapter

1. Robin Gareiss, "VoIP by the Numbers," *Network World*, November 3, 2003, http://www.networkworld.com/research/2003/1103voip.html.

Exam topics covered in Part II:

- Describe the purpose of VLANs in a VoIP environment

- Describe the environmental considerations to support VoIP

- Configure switched infrastructure to support voice and data VLANs

- Describe the purpose and operation of PoE

- Describe the appropriate software components needed to support endpoints

- Describe the requirements and correct settings for DHCP, NTP, and TFTP

- Configure DHCP, NTP, and TFTP

- Describe the differences between key system and PBX mode

- Describe the differences between the different types of ephones and ephone-dns

- Configure Cisco Unified Communications Manager Express endpoints

- Configure call-transfer per design specifications

- Configure voice productivity features, including hunt groups, call park, call pickup, paging groups, and paging/intercom

- Configure Music on Hold

Part II: Unified Voice Using Call Manager Express

Connecting and Powering Cisco IP Phones: To provide a centralized power system, the Cisco IP phones must receive their power from a centralized source using Power over Ethernet (PoE). This section discusses the different options for PoE and the selection criterion of each.

VLAN Concepts and Configuration: VLANs allow you to break the switched network into logical pieces to provide management and security boundaries between the voice and data network. This section discusses the concepts and configuration behind VLAN.

Understanding Cisco IP Phone Boot Process: This section discusses the foundations of the Cisco IP phone boot process. Understanding this process is critical to setup troubleshooting issues.

Configuring a Router-Based DHCP Server: This section discusses configuring a Cisco router as a DHCP server for your network.

Setting the Clock of a Cisco Device with NTP: Because a VoIP network is so heavily dependent on accurate time, the sole focus of this section is keeping the clocks accurate on Cisco devices by using NTP.

CHAPTER 3

Connecting IP Phones to the LAN Infrastructure

You walk into the new corporate headquarters for Fizzmo, Corp. On the top of each desk is a Cisco 7945G IP Phone, glowing with a full-color display and two line instances. Smiling, courteous agents are busy taking phone calls from callers excited to purchase the latest Fizzmo wares. Samantha (located in the north corner) is checking her visual voice mail while Emilio (located in the south hall) is getting the latest weather report through an XML IP phone service.

How did we get here? How do you take a newly constructed building and transform it into a bustling call center? That is what this chapter is all about. We will walk through the key concepts and technologies used to build a Cisco VoIP network. By the time you are done with this chapter, you should have all the conceptual knowledge you need to have in place before you can move into the installation and configuration of the Cisco VoIP system.

"Do I Know This Already?" Quiz

The "Do I Know This Already?" quiz allows you to assess whether you should read this entire chapter or simply jump to the "Exam Preparation Tasks" section for review. If you are in doubt, read the entire chapter. Table 3.1 outlines the major headings in this chapter and the corresponding "Do I Know This Already?" quiz questions. You can find the answers in Appendix A, "Answers to the 'Do I Know This Already?' Quizzes."

Table 3.1   *"Do I Know This Already?" Foundation Topics Section-to-Question Mapping*

Foundation Topics Section	Questions Covered in This Section
Connecting and Powering Cisco IP Phones	1–2
VLAN Concepts and Configuration	3–8
Understanding Cisco IP Phone Boot Process	9
Configuring a Router-Based DHCP Server	10
Setting the Clock of a Cisco Device with NTP	11

1. Which of the following methods can you use to power a Cisco 7941G IP Phone? (Choose all that apply.)

    a. Cisco Inline Power

    b. 802.1Q

    c. 802.3af

    d. Local power brick

2. What type of signal is sent by Cisco Inline Power to detect an unpowered Cisco device?

    a. +8 DC voltage

    b. Fast Link Pulse

    c. Cisco Discovery Protocol

    d. Polarity reversal

3. Which of the following terms are synonymous with a VLAN? (Choose two.)

    a. IP subnet

    b. Port security

    c. Broadcast domain

    d. Collision domain

4. Which of the following trunking protocols would be used to connect a Cisco switch to a non-Cisco switch device?

    a. VTP

    b. 802.3af

    c. 802.1Q

    d. ISL

5. Which of the following protocols replicates VLANs over a trunk link?

   a. VTP

   b. 802.1Q

   c. ISL

   d. VRRP

6. Which of the following VTP modes is used by a Cisco switch, by default?

   a. Client

   b. Server

   c. Transparent

   d. VTP is disabled by default.

7. If one switch interface is set to **switchport mode dynamic auto** and is connected to another switch interface set to the same mode, what will be the result?

   a. The interface becomes a trunk port.

   b. The interface becomes an access port.

   c. The interface maintains the default mode.

   d. The interface enters an err-disable state.

8. Which of the following commands would you use to forward DHCP requests from an interface connected to the 172.16.1.0/24 subnet to a DHCP server with the IP address 172.16.100.100?

   a. forward-protocol 172.16.1.0 255.255.255.0 172.16.100.100

   b. forward-protocol dhcp 172.16.1.0 255.255.255.0 172.16.100.100

   c. ip helper-address 172.16.1.0 172.16.100.100

   d. ip helper-address 172.16.100.100

9. How does the Cisco switch communicate voice VLAN information after a Cisco IP phone has received PoE and started the boot process?

   a. Through CDP

   b. Using 802.1Q

   c. Using the proprietary ISL protocol

   d. Voice VLAN information must be statically entered on the Cisco IP phone.

10. Which DHCP option provides the IP address of a TFTP server to a Cisco IP phone?

    a.   Option 10

    b.   Option 15

    c.   Option 150

    d.   Option 290

11. Which of the following NTP stratum numbers would be considered the best?

    a.   Stratum 0

    b.   Stratum 1

    c.   Stratum 2

    d.   Stratum 3

Foundation Topics

Connecting and Powering Cisco IP Phones

Before we can get to the point of plugging in phones and having happy users placing and receiving calls, we must first lay the foundational infrastructure of the network. This includes technologies such as Power over Ethernet, voice VLANs, and DHCP. The network diagram shown in Figure 3.1 represents the placement of these technologies. As you read through this chapter, each section will act as a building block to reach this goal. The first item that must be in place is power for the Cisco IP phones.

Cisco IP phones connect to switches just like any other network device (such as PCs, IP-based printers, and so on). Depending on the model of IP phone you are using, it may also have a built-in switch. Figure 3.2 illustrates the connections on the back of a Cisco 7960 IP Phone.

- **RS232:** Connects to a 7914, 7915, or 7916 expansion module

- **10/100 SW:** Used to connect the IP phone to the network

- **10/100 PC:** Used to connect a co-located PC (or other network device) to the IP phone

After you have physically connected the IP phone to the network, it will need to receive power in some way. There are three potential sources of power in a Cisco VoIP network:

- Cisco Catalyst Switch Power over Ethernet (PoE) (Cisco prestandard or 802.3af power)

- Power Patch Panel PoE (Cisco prestandard or 802.3af power)

- Cisco IP Phone Power Brick (wall power)

Let's dig deeper into each one of these power sources.

Cisco Catalyst Switch PoE

If you were to create an Ethernet cable (Category 5 or 6), you would find that there are eight wires (four pairs of wires) to crimp into an RJ-45 connector on each end of the connection. Further study reveals that only four of the wires are used to transmit data. The other four remain unused and idle...until now.

The terms *inline power* and *Power over Ethernet (PoE)* describe two methods you can use to send electricity over the unused Ethernet wires to power a connected device. There is now a variety of devices that can attach solely to an Ethernet cable and receive all the power they need to operate. In addition to Cisco IP phones, other common PoE devices include wireless access points and video surveillance equipment.

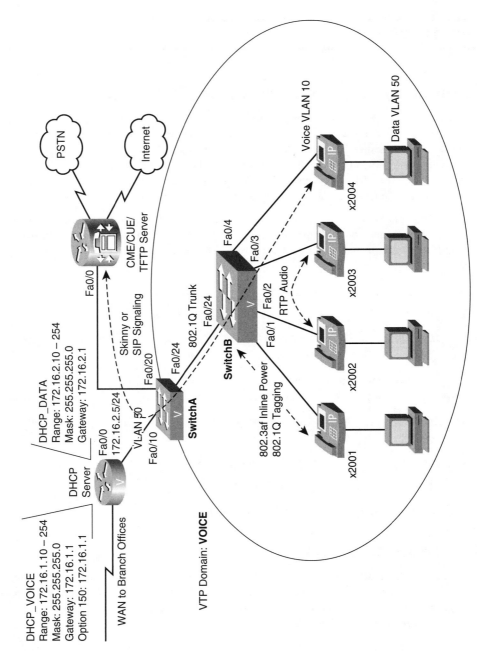

Figure 3.1 *VoIP Network*

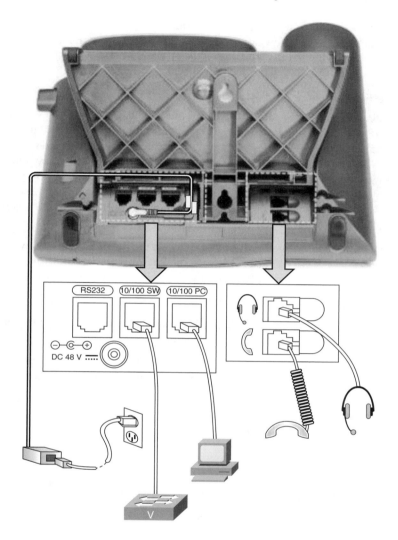

Figure 3.2   *Cisco IP Phone Ethernet Connections*

Powering devices through an Ethernet cable offers many advantages over using a local power supply. First, you have a centralized point of power distribution. Many users expect the phone system to continue to work even if the power is out in the company offices. By using PoE, you can connect the switch powering the IP phones to an uninterruptible power supply (UPS) instead of placing a UPS at the location of each IP phone. PoE also enables you to power devices that are not conveniently located next to a power outlet. For example, it is a common practice to mount wireless access points in the ceiling, where power is not easily accessible. Finally, PoE eliminates much of the "cord clutter" at employees' desks.

PoE became an official standard (802.3af) in 2003. However, the IP telephony industry was quickly developing long before this. In order to power the IP phones without an official PoE standard, some proprietary methods were created, one such method being Cisco Inline Power. The following sections describe these two PoE methods and the methods supported by current Cisco IP phones.

Cisco Inline Power

Cisco Inline Power is often called Cisco prestandard PoE. Because Cisco was one of the early VoIP vendors (Cisco prestandard PoE was created in 2000), many IP phones were purchased before the 802.3af PoE standard was created and implemented in Cisco devices. Whereas an organization typically swaps and upgrades PCs every 3 to 5 years, IP phones can survive the "technology curve" much longer. Because of this, you will run into many Cisco prestandard PoE devices for years to come. To support these devices, most modern Cisco switches support both Cisco prestandard PoE and the industry-standard 802.3af PoE.

To supply power only to an unpowered PoE device, the switch must uniquely detect these devices. The major difference between the PoE methods lies primarily in this detection process. Cisco prestandard PoE uses the following method, as shown in Figure 3.3:

1. The Cisco prestandard PoE device physically connects to the switch.

2. The switch sends an Fast Link Pulse (FLP) tone signal to the device. Only an unpowered, Cisco prestandard PoE device will loop this tone back.

3. When the switch receives the tone back, it realizes the device is an unpowered Cisco prestandard PoE device and applies a minimal amount of power (6.3W) to the line.

4. The unpowered device boots and communicates its actual power requirements to the switch using the Cisco Discovery Protocol (CDP), which Cisco devices traditionally use to detect directly attached neighbors.

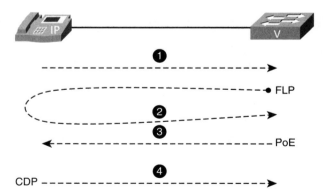

Figure 3.3   *Cisco Prestandard PoE*

Both PoE standards are currently able to deliver power from 0 to 15.4W. If CDP is disabled on the switch (or the connecting device does not support CDP), the switch automatically allocates the maximum amount of power (15.4W) to each port. The device will use only the power it needs; the rest of the power is wasted. Oftentimes, a Cisco switch will only have enough wattage available in its power supply to power all the ports by using a negotiated amount of power. If all the ports attempt to use the full 15.4W of power, the switch will run out of power before all ports can receive it. In this case, the lower port numbers will receive power and the upper port numbers will remain unpowered. This phenomenon is typically referred to as "oversubscription" and is a common design consideration you must take into account when purchasing power supplies for network switches.

802.3af Power over Ethernet

802.3af PoE is similar to Cisco Inline Power but uses a slightly different detection mechanism. Rather than using a FLP tone to detect an unpowered PoE device, 802.3af uses a small DC current that is constantly applied to the line. Non-PoE devices are not harmed by this DC current. An 802.3af-capable device will be equipped with a resistor that returns a specific level of resistance to the line. When the switch detects this resistance level, it will know how much power to send to the attached device. This power can be sent at four different levels, shown in Table 3.2.

Key
Topic

Table 3.2   *802.3af Power Classes*

802.3af Power Class	Power Allocated	Actual Power Used
Class 0	15.4W	0.44 to 12.95W
Class 1	4.0W	0.44 to 3.84W
Class 2	7.0W	3.84 to 6.49W
Class 3	15.4W	6.49 to 12.95W

In Table 3.2, Class 0 and Class 3 seem like duplicates. This design was intentional by the Institute of Electrical and Electronics Engineers (IEEE) standards body. It allows vendors to design PoE-capable devices with very low-cost PoE detection mechanisms that would fall into the Class 0 group. Essentially, the Class 0 PoE device just says, "I need power, please send it!" The switch then allocates the full 15.4W for this device and responds with, "Here's some power, use what you can." The Class 1–3 devices have more sophisticated resistors that allow the PoE device to dictate exactly which class it falls into. Keep in mind that using too many Class 0 devices can prematurely exhaust your switch power supply because each port will get the maximum power allocation regardless of the actual needs of the PoE device.

Note   Also notice that the maximum power used in the "Actual Power Used" column of Table 3.2 is slightly less than the maximum power allocated for each class. This is due to a power loss received through the cabling and in the device power supplies (device power supplies cause a loss of 10 to 20 percent of power).

802.3af PoE is able to send power over all four pairs of wire in an Ethernet cable, thus sharing the same wires as the data. This allows 802.3af to function even over Gigabit Ethernet (1000BASE-T), which uses all four pairs for data transmission. This is also paving the way for future PoE standards that are able to supply significantly more power than 802.3af. In the future, PoE will be able to power more sophisticated devices (perhaps even thin clients).

Note   The IEEE standards body is currently working on an 802.3at PoE standard (also called PoE Plus), the goal of which is to increase the current maximum PoE wattage from 15.4W to 30W or more.

Cisco IP Phone PoE Support

Table 3.3 summarizes the majority of Cisco IP phones and the type of power supported.

Table 3.3   *802.3af Power Classes*

Cisco IP Phone Model	PoE Type
7906G	Cisco prestandard or 802.3af
7911G	Cisco prestandard or 802.3af
7914/7915/7916 Expansion Modules	Local power only
7931G	802.3af only
7937G Conference Station	802.3af only
7940G	Cisco prestandard only
7941G	Cisco prestandard or 802.3af
7941G-GE	802.3af only
7942G	Cisco prestandard or 802.3af
7945G	802.3af only
7960G	Cisco prestandard only
7961G	Cisco prestandard or 802.3af
7961G-GE	802.3af only
7962G	Cisco prestandard or 802.3af
7965G	802.3af only
7970G	Cisco prestandard or 802.3af
7971G-GE	802.3af only
7975G	802.3af only
7985G	802.3af only

Note   For any of the devices that support both power standards, the switch support will determine which power standard is used. If both the switch and IP phone support both power standards, 802.3af is preferred and will be used (Cisco prestandard PoE cannot be forced).

Powering the IP Phone Using a Power Patch Panel or Coupler

Many companies already have a significant investment in their switched network. To upgrade all switches to support PoE would be a significant expense. These organizations may choose to install intermediary devices, such as a patch panel, that are able to inject PoE on the line. The physical layout for this design is demonstrated in Figure 3.4.

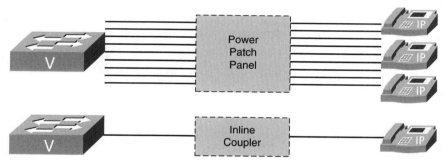

Figure 3.4   *Design for Power Patch Panels or Inline Couplers*

By using the power patch panel, you still gain the advantage of centralized power and backup without requiring switch upgrades.

Note   Keep in mind that Cisco switches must also provide quality of service (QoS) and voice VLAN support capabilities, which may require switch hardware upgrades. Be sure your switch supports these features before you consider a power patch panel solution.

Inline PoE injectors provide a low-cost PoE solution for single devices (one device per coupler). These are typically used to support wireless access points or other "single spot" PoE solutions. Using inline PoE couplers for a large IP phone network would make a mess of your wiring infrastructure and exhaust your supply of electrical outlets (because each inline PoE coupler requires a dedicated plug).

Powering the IP Phone with a Power Brick

Using a power brick to power a device is so simple that it warrants only brief mention. Thus, the reason for this section is primarily to mention that most Cisco IP phones do not ship with power supplies. Cisco assumes most VoIP network deployments will be using PoE. If you are choosing between purchasing power bricks and upgrading your switch infrastructure, it would be wise to check the prices of the power bricks. The average Cisco IP phone power brick price is between $30.00–$40.00 USD. When pricing out a 48-switchport deployment, purchasing power bricks for all the IP phones may very well be in the same price range as upgrading the switch infrastructure.

VLAN Concepts and Configuration

After the IP phone has received power, it must determine its virtual LAN (VLAN) assignment. This section introduces fundamental VLAN concepts such as VLAN trunking and voice VLANs before describing several aspects of VLAN configuration.

VLAN Concepts

When VLANs were introduced a number of years ago, the concept was so radical and beneficial that it was immediately adopted into the industry. Nowadays, it is rare to find any reasonably sized network that is not using VLANs in some way.

VLANs allow you to break up switched environments into multiple broadcast domains. Here is the basic summary of a VLAN:

A VLAN = A Broadcast Domain = An IP Subnet

There are many benefits to using VLANs in an organization, some of which include the following:

- **Increased performance:** By reducing the size of the broadcast domain, network devices run more efficiently.

- **Improved manageability:** The division of the network into logical groups of users, applications, or servers allows you to understand and manage the network better.

- **Physical topology independence:** VLANs allow you to group users regardless of their physical location in the campus network. If departments grow or relocate to a new area of the network, you can simply change the VLAN on their new ports without making any physical network changes.

- **Increased security:** A VLAN boundary marks the end of a logical subnet. To reach other subnets (VLANs), you must pass through a routed (Layer 3) device. Any time you send traffic through a router, you have the opportunity to add filtering options (such as access lists) and other security measures.

Imagine you have an eight-port switch, as shown in Figure 3.5.

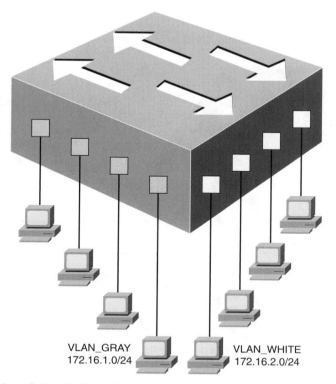

Key
Topic

Figure 3.5   *Switch Divided into Two VLANs*

The four ports on the left side of the switch are in VLAN_GRAY and the four ports on the right side of the switch are in VLAN_WHITE. A switch in this configuration can be seen as two logical switches. Imagine taking this eight-port switch and snapping it in half over your knee (and somehow the two switch halves continued to operate). This is how VLANs are able to separate the devices on the switch. If a device in VLAN_GRAY sends a broadcast, it only reaches the devices in VLAN_GRAY (this is what is meant by separate broadcast domains). Likewise, the devices in the separate VLANs are assigned to different IP subnet addresses because they are seen as separate logical networks. Without a routing solution in place, the devices in VLAN_GRAY are not able to communicate at all with the devices in VLAN_WHITE.

Note   This example uses VLAN_GRAY and VLAN_WHITE for ease of illustration. However, VLANs are actually identified on switches by numbers rather than words.

VLAN Trunking

VLANs are able to transcend individual switches, as shown in Figure 3.6.

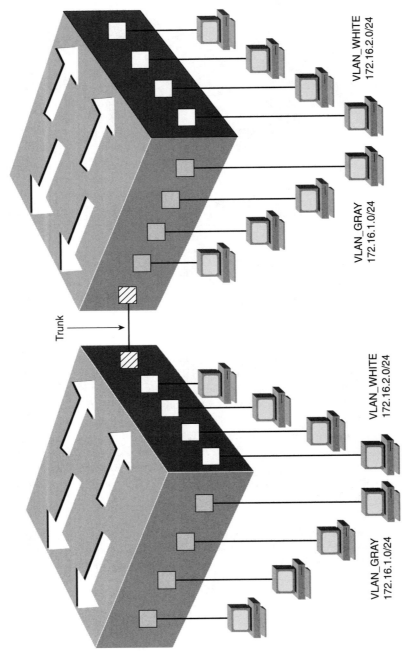

Figure 3.6   *VLANs Move Between Switches*

If a member of VLAN_GRAY sends a broadcast message, it goes to all VLAN_GRAY ports on both switches. The same holds true for VLAN_WHITE. To accommodate this, the connection between the switches must carry traffic for multiple VLANs. This type of port is known as a *trunk port*.

Trunk ports are often called *tagged ports* because the switches send frames between each other with a VLAN "tag" in place. Figure 3.7 illustrates the following process:

1. HostA (in VLAN_GRAY) would like to send data to HostD (also in VLAN_GRAY). HostA transmits the data to SwitchA.

2. SwitchA receives the data and realizes that HostD is available through the FastEthernet 0/24 port (because HostD's MAC address has been learned on this port). Because FastEthernet 0/24 is configured as a trunk port, SwitchA puts the VLAN_GRAY tag in the IP header and sends the frame to SwitchB.

3. SwitchB processes the VLAN_GRAY tag because the FastEthernet 0/24 port is configured as a trunk. Before sending the frame to HostD, the VLAN_GRAY tag is removed from the header.

4. The tagless frame is sent to HostD.

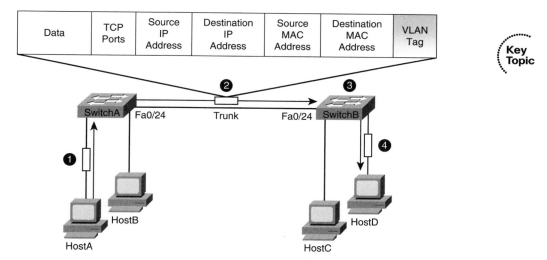

Figure 3.7 *VLAN Tags*

Using this process, the PC never knows what VLAN it belongs to. The VLAN tag is applied when the incoming frame crosses a trunk port. The VLAN tag is removed when exiting the port to the destination PC. Always keep in mind that VLANs are a switching concept; the PCs never participate in the VLAN tagging process.

VLANs are not a Cisco-only technology. Just about all managed switch vendors support VLANs. In order for VLANs to operate in a mixed-vendor environment, a common trunking or "tagging" language must exist between them. This language is known as 802.1Q. All vendors design their switches to recognize and understand the 802.1Q tag, which is what allows us to trunk between switches in any environment.

VLAN Trunking Protocol

Without a doubt, the VLAN Trunking Protocol (VTP) is poorly named. You have already learned about the trunking protocol used today: 802.1Q. A better name for VTP might be "VLAN Replication Protocol," because that is exactly what it does. As you begin to configure your network to support VLANs, it can become quite tedious to create the same VLANs on every switch in your organization. For example, if you wanted to create VLAN 20, you would have to telnet or SSH to every switch that could have a port using VLAN 20 and create the VLAN. By using VTP, you can create VLAN 20 on one switch in your organization and have that information replicate to all the other switches, saving you one step in the VLAN configuration process. Perhaps it received the name "VLAN Trunking Protocol" because it only replicates VLANs over trunk links.

The way VTP works is relatively simple. When you pull a Cisco switch out of the box, it is already configured as a VTP server, which is a switch that is able to add or remove VLANs and replicate those changes to other switches. Every VTP server maintains a VLAN database, which holds all the VLANs that exist in the organization. This database has a revision number that begins incrementing by one for each change that is made. For example:

1. New Cisco switch installed (*VTP Database Rev. 0*)

2. VLAN 10 created (*VTP Database Rev. 1*)

3. VLAN 20 created (*VTP Database Rev. 2*)

4. VLAN 10 deleted (*VTP Database Rev. 3*)

The VTP server sends out updates to the other VTP-capable switches, which replace their VLAN database with the higher revision number as it becomes available. This is illustrated in Figure 3.8.

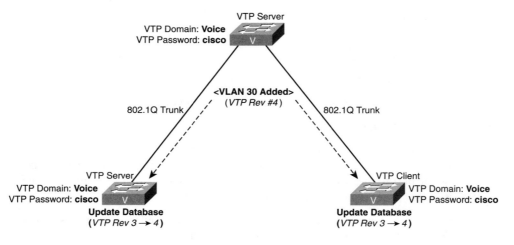

Figure 3.8   *VTP Updates*

You might notice a few new concepts in Figure 3.8 as well. The first is the concept of a VTP domain name and password. In order for the switches to synchronize their databases, they must be configured with the same information for both the VTP domain name and password.

Note   Both the VTP domain name and password are case sensitive.

The second concept shown in Figure 3.8 is the idea of VTP device modes. The following is a list of the supported VTP modes:

- **VTP server:** A VTP server can create, modify, and delete VLANs and replicate those changes to the other switches in your network. This is the default mode of a Cisco switch.

- **VTP client:** A VTP client cannot make any changes to the VLAN database; it can only receive changes from a VTP server and apply them. If you attempt to create, modify, or delete VLANs from a VTP client, the IOS will return an error message.

- **VTP transparent:** A VTP transparent mode switch can create, modify, and delete VLANs, but those VLANs are not replicated to other switches. Likewise, a VTP transparent mode switch ignores any incoming VTP updates. This mode effectively disables VTP.

If you leave all Cisco switches at the default mode (VTP server), you will be able to modify the VLAN database from any switch in your network. The switches will use the VTP database revision number to determine the most recent copy of the database. Some organizations prefer this flexibility, whereas others consider this an unnecessary risk (because unauthorized changes could be made to the VLAN database). For a more secure environment, configure one switch as a VTP server and all the rest as VTP clients or disable VTP completely by configuring all switches in VTP transparent mode.

Caution   Although VTP is a convenient feature, there are many networks that have been completely decimated by a rogue switch with incorrect VLAN information and a high VTP database revision number being introduced into a network. For high-security environments, disable VTP completely.

Understanding Voice VLANs

It is a common and recommended practice to separate voice and data traffic by using VLANs. There are already easy-to-use applications available, such as Wireshark and Voice Over Misconfigured Internet Telephones (VOMIT), that allow intruders to capture voice conversations on the network and convert them into WAV data files. Separating voice and data traffic using VLANs provides a solid security boundary, keeping data applications from reaching the voice traffic. It also gives you a simpler method to deploy QoS, prioritizing the voice traffic over the data.

One initial difficulty you will encounter when separating voice and data traffic is the fact that PCs are often connected to the network using the Ethernet port on the back of a Cisco IP phone. Because you can assign a switchport to only a single VLAN, it initially seems impossible to separate voice and data traffic. That is, until you see that Cisco IP phones support 802.1Q tagging.

The switch built into Cisco IP phones has much of the same hardware that exists inside of a full Cisco switch. The incoming switchport is able to receive and send 802.1Q tagged packets. This gives you the capability to establish a trunk connection between the Cisco switch and IP phone, as shown in Figure 3.9.

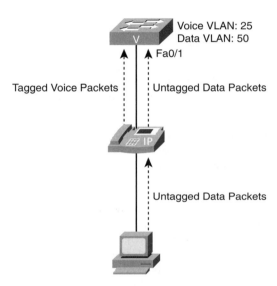

Figure 3.9   *Separating Voice and Data Traffic Using VLANs*

You might call the connection between the switch and IP phone a "mini-trunk" because a typical trunk passes a large number of VLANs (if not all VLANs). In this case, the IP phone tags its own packets with the correct voice VLAN (VLAN 25, in the case of Figure 3.9). Because the switch receives the tagged packets on a port configured as a trunk (or a minitrunk in our case), the switch can read the tag and place the data in the correct VLAN. The data packets pass through the IP phone and into the switch untagged. The switch assigns these untagged packets to whatever VLAN you have configured on the switchport for data traffic.

Note   Technically, any time a switch receives an untagged packet on a trunk port, it is placed into the native VLAN. The native VLAN is configured on a port-by-port basis. In the example shown in Figure 3.9, VLAN 25 would be considered the voice VLAN and VLAN 50 would be considered the native VLAN. The term "native VLAN" describes more of a technical "how it works" rather than how people refer to this VLAN. It would be more common to simply describe VLAN 50 as the data VLAN for the port.

VLAN Configuration

You can break VLAN and trunking configuration down into five major steps:

Step 1. Configure and verify VTP.

Step 2. Configure and verify 802.1Q trunks.

Step 3. Create VLANs.

Step 4. Assign ports to VLANs.

Step 5. (Optional) Configure routing between VLANs.

The last step is optional because configuring inter-VLAN routing is not technically a part of configuring VLANs; however, in any production network, you will need to have some sort of routing in order for the network to function.

To keep this configuration practical, this section slowly works through the configuration of the network diagram shown in Figure 3.1 that opened this chapter, reproduced here for your convenience in Figure 3.10. Let's break these configuration areas down one by one.

Configure and Verify VTP

Rather than start with VTP configuration, you first need to understand the command to verify VTP. This is necessary because you never want to introduce into the network a switch that has an existing VTP configuration (otherwise, the existing VLAN database of your organization could be overwritten, causing a massive network outage).

The command to verify VTP operation is **show vtp status**, which is shown in Example 3.1 on SwitchA.

Example 3.1   *The* **show vtp status** *Output*

```
SwitchA# show vtp status
VTP Version                   : 2
Configuration Revision        : 0
Maximum VLANs supported locally : 1005
Number of existing VLANs      : 5
VTP Operating Mode            : Server
VTP Domain Name               :
VTP Pruning Mode              : Disabled
VTP V2 Mode                   : Disabled
VTP Traps Generation          : Disabled
MD5 digest                    : 0xC4 0xAF 0xA4 0x19 0x0A 0x5F 0x50 0xF0
Configuration last modified by 0.0.0.0 at 0-0-00 00:00:00
```

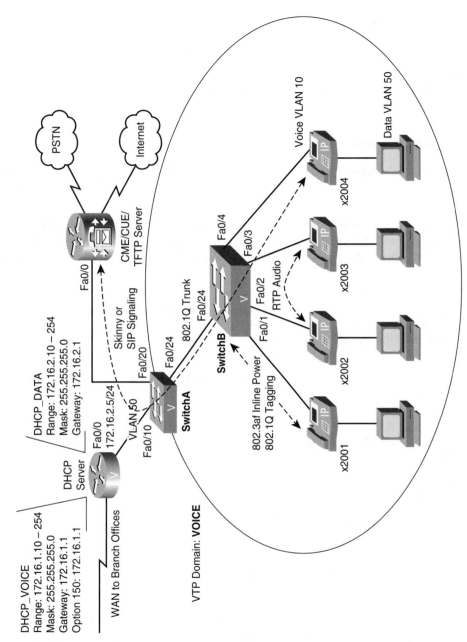

Figure 3.10   *Network Diagram*

It looks like SwitchA is in the default (unmodified) VTP configuration. The key (highlighted) configuration items follow:

- **VTP Version/VTP V2 Mode:** By default, Cisco switches run VTP version 1. Based on the output in Example 3.1, this may seem like a mistype because the switch clearly states "VTP Version 2." However, if you look down in the output, you will see "VTP V2 Mode Disabled," which means the switch is not using the version 2 features. The primary difference between VTP version 1 and 2 is the support for Token Ring VLANs in version 2. Because Token Ring VLAN support is not of the utmost importance in today's networks, you can safely run either version; however, all switches must run the same version.

- **Configuration Revision:** The configuration revision number is the current VTP database revision number that the switches use to determine who has the most current copy of the VLAN database. For a new switch, you would expect to see this set to zero, because no VLAN configuration changes have been made. If this number is anything greater than zero, it means modifications have been made to the VLAN database.

- **VTP Operating Mode:** This switch is currently set as a VTP server, which is the default mode of an unconfigured Cisco switch.

- **VTP Domain Name:** The VTP domain name is currently blank on this switch, which is also indicative of a switch that has not been configured. If the VTP domain name is blank, the switch will join the first VTP domain it hears about. For example, if you connected this switch to another Cisco switch that is already configured for the VTP domain BUBBLES, this switch would automatically set its VTP domain name to BUBBLES and receive the VLAN database for that domain. This behavior only occurs if the VTP domain name is blank. Once the VTP domain name is set, you must manually change it if you would like the switch to join a different VTP domain.

Example 3.2 shows SwitchA and SwitchB in our VoIP network configured with the following settings:

- SwitchA

  VTP Mode: Server

  VTP Domain: VOICE

  VTP Password: cisco

- SwitchB

  VTP Mode: Client

  VTP Domain: VOICE

  VTP Password: cisco

Example 3.2   *Configuring a VTP Server and Clients*

```
SwitchA# configure terminal
Enter configuration commands, one per line.  End with CNTL/Z.
SwitchA(config)# vtp mode ?
  client      Set the device to client mode.
  server      Set the device to server mode.
  transparent  Set the device to transparent mode.
SwitchA(config)# vtp mode server
Device mode already VTP SERVER.
SwitchA(config)# vtp domain VOICE
Changing VTP domain name from NULL to VOICE
05:44:09: %SW_VLAN-6-VTP_DOMAIN_NAME_CHG: VTP domain name changed to VOICE.
SwitchA(config)# vtp password cisco
Setting device VLAN database password to cisco


SwitchB# configure terminal
Enter configuration commands, one per line.  End with CNTL/Z.
SwitchB(config)# vtp mode client
Setting device to VTP CLIENT mode.
SwitchB(config)# vtp domain VOICE
Changing VTP domain name from NULL to VOICE
05:48:49: %SW_VLAN-6-VTP_DOMAIN_NAME_CHG: VTP domain name changed to VOICE.
SwitchB(config)# vtp password cisco
Setting device VLAN database password to cisco
```

Now that the VTP configuration has been put in place, you can verify the settings by using the **show vtp status** command, as shown in Example 3.3.

Example 3.3   *The* **show vtp status** *Output*

```
SwitchA# show vtp status
VTP Version                   : 2
Configuration Revision        : 0
Maximum VLANs supported locally : 1005
Number of existing VLANs      : 5
VTP Operating Mode            : Server
VTP Domain Name               : VOICE
VTP Pruning Mode              : Disabled
VTP V2 Mode                   : Disabled
VTP Traps Generation          : Disabled
MD5 digest                    : 0x1B 0xFD 0x06 0x70 0xA1 0x18 0x56 0x89
Configuration last modified by 0.0.0.0 at 0-0-00 00:00:00
```

Configure and Verify 802.1Q Trunks

Now that VTP is set, you need to configure the 802.1Q trunks between the switches. Looking back at Figure 3.10, you can see that SwitchA and SwitchB connect on FastEthernet 0/24. To configure trunking on the port, you can use the **switchport mode** command. This command has a number of parameters, as shown in Example 3.4.

Example 3.4   *Options Available for the* **switchport mode** *Command*

```
SwitchA(config)# interface fastEthernet 0/24
SwitchA(config-if)# switchport mode ?
  access        Set trunking mode to ACCESS unconditionally
  dot1q-tunnel  set trunking mode to TUNNEL unconditionally
  dynamic       Set trunking mode to dynamically negotiate access or trunk mode
  trunk         Set trunking mode to TRUNK unconditionally

SwitchA(config-if)# switchport mode dynamic ?
  auto       Set trunking mode dynamic negotiation parameter to AUTO
  desirable  Set trunking mode dynamic negotiation parameter to DESIRABLE
```

The two most basic commands in this syntax are **switchport mode access** and **switchport mode trunk**.

The **switchport mode access** command configures the port as a nontrunking port. This is the ideal command to enter on ports connecting to user PCs, servers, printers, or anything else that does not require a trunking connection. By entering this command on all nontrunking ports, you eliminate quite a few known security vulnerabilities of Cisco switches. A common network attack is for a hacker to attempt to negotiate a trunked interface with a switch. If they are successful, they can then gain access to any VLAN in the organization. This is known as a VLAN-hopping attack. The **switchport mode access** command completely disables this type of attack.

The **switchport mode trunk** command configures the port as a trunked connection. Whatever device attaches to the other side must be able to support and understand tagged packets from the switch interface. On some switches, you may receive the following error message when entering the **switchport mode trunk** command:

```
SwitchA(config-if)# switchport mode trunk
Command rejected: An interface whose trunk encapsulation is "Auto" can not be
  configured to "trunk" mode.
```

The reason for this error is that the switch supports multiple trunking protocols. Earlier in the chapter, in the section "VLAN Trunking," you learned about the 802.1Q trunking protocol, but another trunking protocol does exist (for a little while longer, at least): Cisco Inter-Switch Link (ISL). This is a Cisco-proprietary trunking protocol that was released before 802.1Q was fully developed as an industry standard. The ISL protocol is not as efficient as 802.1Q, and is slowly being phased out from future Cisco IOS versions. Until ISL is completely phased out, you may have to enter the command shown in Example 3.5 on switches supporting both trunking protocols.

Example 3.5   *Configuring a Switch Trunk Port*

```
SwitchA(config-if)# switchport trunk encapsulation ?
  dot1q      Interface uses only 802.1q trunking encapsulation when trunking
  isl        Interface uses only ISL trunking encapsulation when trunking
  negotiate  Device will negotiate trunking encapsulation with peer on interface
SwitchA(config-if)# switchport trunk encapsulation dot1q
SwitchA(config-if)# switchport mode trunk
```

Once you have entered these commands on both ends of the connection, a trunk will form between the two switches.

Cisco switches also support a dynamic negotiation of trunk ports. As a matter of fact, the default mode of all switchports on most Cisco switches is **switchport mode dynamic desirable**. This means that the switchport can *dynamically* become an access port or a trunk, depending on the type of device you attach. This can be a convenient setting, because attaching a PC causes the port to automatically become an access port whereas attaching another switch causes the port to automatically become a trunk port. However, convenient settings also have their dark side. In this case, the "dynamic desirable" mode can be exploited by hackers to negotiate a trunk port with the switch and execute a VLAN-hopping attack.

The dynamic trunk negotiation modes function through a protocol known as Dynamic Trunking Protocol (DTP). A switch interface configured to use DTP will send out negotiation packets to attempt to negotiate a trunk link. If the other side accepts, the interface becomes a trunk; otherwise, it remains an access port. Cisco switches support many DTP modes, as follows:

■ **switchport mode dynamic desirable:** This default mode on most Cisco switches dynamically changes the interface between access and trunk modes, depending on the device attached. The *desirable* feature causes the interface to send DTP packets, aggressively trying to negotiate a trunk port configuration with the other side.

■ **switchport mode dynamic auto:** The dynamic auto mode is also able to dynamically change between access and trunk port configurations. However, if you use the dynamic auto mode, the interface does not attempt to aggressively negotiate a trunk port connection with the other side.

■ **switchport mode trunk:** Once you have hard-coded the interface as a trunk port, it can no longer become an access port. However, the interface will still continue to send DTP negotiation packets, attempting to change the other side of the connection to a trunk port, unless you have also entered the **switchport nonegotiate** command.

■ **switchport mode access:** Once you have entered this command, the interface is hard-coded as an access port and cannot become a trunk port, regardless of the settings on the other side of the connection.

■ **switchport nonegotiate:** Entering this command disables DTP messages on the interface.

Table 3.4 provides a summary of the various DTP modes and the resulting negotiated mode. The left column represents one side of the connection and the top row represents the other side of the connection.

Table 3.4   *802.3af Power Classes*

	switchport mode access	switchport mode trunk	switchport mode dynamic desirable	switchport mode dynamic auto
switchport mode	access	invalid connection type	access	access
switchport mode trunk	invalid connection type	trunk	trunk	trunk
switchport mode dynamic desirable	access	trunk	trunk	trunk
switchport mode dynamic auto	access	trunk	trunk	access

Note   My (Jeremy) personal rule on anything "auto" in the Cisco realm is that you auto-not-use-it. In my opinion, it is always better to hard-code each side of the connection as a trunk or access port rather than use the dynamic negotiation modes.

In the network being built throughout this chapter, you could issue the commands shown in Example 3.6 to configure a trunk port between SwitchA and SwitchB. The syntax assumes both SwitchA and SwitchB support both ISL and 802.1Q trunking encapsulations.

Example 3.6   *Configuring SwitchA and SwitchB with Trunk Ports*

```
SwitchA# configure terminal
SwitchA(config)# interface fa0/24
SwitchA(config-if)# switchport trunk encapsulation dot1q
SwitchA(config-if)# switchport mode trunk

SwitchB# configure terminal
SwitchB(config)# interface fa0/24
SwitchB(config-if)# switchport trunk encapsulation dot1q
SwitchB(config-if)# switchport mode trunk
```

Once you have configured the trunk, you can verify the configuration by entering the **show interface** *<interface name/number>* **switchport** command, as shown in Example 3.7 from SwitchA.

Example 3.7   *Verifying Trunk Configuration*

```
SwitchA# show interfaces FastEthernet 0/24 switchport
Name: Fa0/24
Switchport: Enabled
Administrative Mode: trunk
Operational Mode: trunk
Administrative Trunking Encapsulation: dot1q
Operational Trunking Encapsulation: dot1q
Negotiation of Trunking: On
Access Mode VLAN: 1 (default)
Trunking Native Mode VLAN: 1 (default)
Administrative Native VLAN tagging: enabled
Voice VLAN: none
Administrative private-vlan host-association: none
Administrative private-vlan mapping: none
Administrative private-vlan trunk native VLAN: none
Administrative private-vlan trunk Native VLAN tagging: enabled
Administrative private-vlan trunk encapsulation: dot1q
Administrative private-vlan trunk normal VLANs: none
Administrative private-vlan trunk associations: none
Administrative private-vlan trunk mappings: none
Operational private-vlan: none
Trunking VLANs Enabled: ALL
Pruning VLANs Enabled: 2-1001
Capture Mode Disabled
Capture VLANs Allowed: ALL


Protected: false
Unknown unicast blocked: disabled
Unknown multicast blocked: disabled
Appliance trust: none
```

Notice the highlighted administrative and operational modes for the interface in Example 3.7. The administrative mode shows what the port has been configured to do. The operational mode shows what the port is actually doing. In this configuration, I have hard-coded the trunk configuration, so the output indicates the port to be administratively configured to be a trunk, and it is operating as a trunk. In another example, the administrative mode could have been dynamic desirable and the operational mode could have negotiated as an access port.

Create VLANs

After you have configured the trunks, you can move on to creating VLANs. At this point, VTP should be operational between SwitchA and SwitchB (VTP will move into operation once it has a valid trunk connection between switches). As you configure VLANs on SwitchA, they should automatically replicate to SwitchB.

The syntax to create VLANs is simple: move into global configuration mode and enter **vlan** *<vlan number>*. You will then be taken into VLAN configuration mode, where you can assign a logical name to the VLAN. Using the syntax shown in Example 3.8, you can create VLANs on SwitchA.

Example 3.8   *Creating VLANs*

```
SwitchA# configure terminal
SwitchA(config)# vlan 10
SwitchA(config-vlan)# name VOICE
SwitchA(config-vlan)# exit
SwitchA(config)# vlan 50
SwitchA(config-vlan)# name DATA
```

That's it! Now you can drop back to privileged EXEC mode and verify the VLAN configuration, as shown in Example 3.9.

Example 3.9   *Verifying VLAN Database with the* **show vlan brief** *Command*

```
SwitchA# show vlan brief

VLAN Name                             Status    Ports
---- -------------------------------- --------- -------------------------------
1    default                          active    Fa0/2, Fa0/3, Fa0/4, Fa0/5
                                                Fa0/6, Fa0/7, Fa0/8, Fa0/9
                                                Fa0/10, Fa0/11, Fa0/12, Fa0/13
                                                Fa0/14, Fa0/15, Fa0/16, Fa0/17
                                                Fa0/18, Fa0/19, Fa0/20, Fa0/21
                                                Fa0/22, Fa0/23, Fa0/24, Gi0/1
                                                Gi0/2
10   VOICE                            active
50   DATA                             active
1002 fddi-default                     act/unsup
1003 token-ring-default               act/unsup
1004 fddinet-default                  act/unsup
1005 trnet-default                    act/unsup
```

As you can see, VLANs 10 and 50 now exist in the VLAN database. All ports on SwitchA are still assigned to the default VLAN 1. Before moving on to assign the ports to the VLAN, let's verify in Example 3.10 that SwitchA has replicated the VLANs to SwitchB.

Example 3.10 *Verifying VTP Replication with the* **show vtp status** *Command*

```
SwitchB# show vtp status
VTP Version                      : running VTP1 (VTP2 capable)
Configuration Revision           : 2
Maximum VLANs supported locally  : 1005
Number of existing VLANs         : 7
VTP Operating Mode               : Client
VTP Domain Name                  : VOICE
VTP Pruning Mode                 : Disabled
VTP V2 Mode                      : Disabled
VTP Traps Generation             : Disabled
MD5 digest                       : 0xE9 0x09 0x0F 0x55 0x2E 0x92 0xA0 0xB5
Configuration last modified by 172.16.50.10 at 3-13-93 19:41:14
```

The configuration revision number on SwitchB has moved to 2, reflecting the two changes that were made to the VLAN database on SwitchA. Just to be sure, enter the **show vlan** command on SwitchB as shown in Example 3.11.

Example 3.11 *Verifying the VLAN Database on SwitchB*

```
SwitchB# show vlan brief
VLAN Name                             Status     Ports
---- -------------------------------- ---------- -------------------------------
1    default                          active     Fa0/2, Fa0/3, Fa0/4, Fa0/5
                                                 Fa0/6, Fa0/7, Fa0/8, Fa0/9
                                                 Fa0/10, Fa0/11, Fa0/12, Fa0/13
                                                 Fa0/14, Fa0/15, Fa0/16, Fa0/17
                                                 Fa0/18, Fa0/19, Fa0/20, Fa0/21
                                                 Fa0/22, Fa0/23, Fa0/24, Gi0/1
                                                 Gi0/2
10   VOICE                            active
50   DATA                             active
1002 fddi-default                     act/unsup
1003 token-ring-default               act/unsup
1004 fddinet-default                  act/unsup
1005 trnet-default                    act/unsup
```

Sure enough, VLANs 10 and 50 are now appearing as valid VLANs on SwitchB. VTP has done its job!

Assign Ports to VLANs

Now that the VLANs exist, you can assign the necessary ports to each VLAN. Based on the diagram shown earlier in Figure 3.10, the DHCP server will need to join the data VLAN. You will configure FastEthernet 0/20 (connecting to the router/Cisco Unified

Communications Manager Express [CME] device) in the next section when you set up routing between VLANs. Example 3.12 assigns FastEthernet 0/10 on SwitchA to VLAN 50.

Example 3.12   *Assigning Switchport to a VLAN*

```
SwitchA# configure terminal
SwitchA(config)# interface fa0/10
SwitchA(config-if)# switchport mode access
SwitchA(config-if)# switchport access vlan 50
```

FastEthernet 0/10 has now been moved into VLAN 50. To verify this configuration, you can once again use the **show vlan** command, as shown in Example 3.13.

Example 3.13   *Verifying VLAN Assignment*

```
SwitchA# show vlan brief
VLAN Name                             Status    Ports
---- -------------------------------- --------- -------------------------------
1    default                          active    Fa0/2, Fa0/3, Fa0/4, Fa0/5
                                                 Fa0/6, Fa0/7, Fa0/8, Fa0/9
                                                 Fa0/11, Fa0/12, Fa0/13, Fa0/14
                                                 Fa0/15, Fa0/16, Fa0/17, Fa0/18
                                                 Fa0/19, Fa0/20, Fa0/21, Fa0/22
                                                 Fa0/23, Fa0/24, Gi0/1, Gi0/2
10   VOICE                            active
50   DATA                             active    Fa0/10
1002 fddi-default                     act/unsup
1003 token-ring-default               act/unsup
1004 fddinet-default                  act/unsup
1005 trnet-default                    act/unsup
```

FastEthernet 0/10 has now moved into VLAN 50. Because the DHCP server is currently the only device in VLAN 50, it will not have any connectivity with other devices.

Now you can move on to the VLAN assignment on SwitchB. Assigning VLANs here takes one more command because you have both voice and data VLANs on each port. The syntax shown in Example 3.14 will make the assignments on SwitchB.

Example 3.14   *Assigning Voice and Data VLANs*

```
SwitchB# configure terminal
SwitchB(config)# interface range fa0/1 - 4
SwitchA(config-if-range)# switchport mode access
SwitchA(config-if-range)# switchport access vlan 50
SwitchA(config-if-range)# switchport voice vlan 10
```

The ports are now configured to support a voice VLAN of 10 and a data VLAN of 50. This syntax is a newer form of configuration for IP phone connections. In the "old days," you would configure the interface as a trunk port because the switch was really establishing a trunking relationship between it and the IP phone. This was less secure because a hacker could remove the IP phone from the switchport and attach their own device (another managed switch or PC) and perform a VLAN-hopping attack. The more modern syntax configures the port as a "quasi-access port," because an attached PC will only be able to access VLAN 50. Only an attached Cisco IP phone will be able to access the voice VLAN 10.

Key Topic

Note Keep in mind that Cisco IP phones will be able to receive this voice VLAN configuration from the switch via CDP. Once it has received the voice VLAN number, the IP phone will begin tagging its own packets. Non-Cisco IP phones will not be able to understand CDP packets. This typically requires you to manually configure each of the non-Cisco IP phones with its voice VLAN number from a local phone configuration window (on the IP phone).

Configure Routing Between VLANs

All the pieces of the puzzle are in place, with the exception of inter-VLAN routing. With the current setup, all the data devices on VLAN 50 will be able to reach each other, but cannot reach other networks. Likewise, the IP phones will be able to communicate directly, but they cannot reach any other networks or the CME router. As a result, the IP phones will continue to boot cycle endlessly.

To set up inter-VLAN routing, there are three possible designs:

- Separate router ports configured per VLAN

- Router connected to a trunk port (also known as router-on-a-stick)

- Layer 3/multilayer switching

Separate Ports per VLAN

Using the strategy of separate ports per VLAN, you can plug a router interface into each VLAN. The PCs on that VLAN will use the router port as their default gateway, as shown in Figure 3.11.

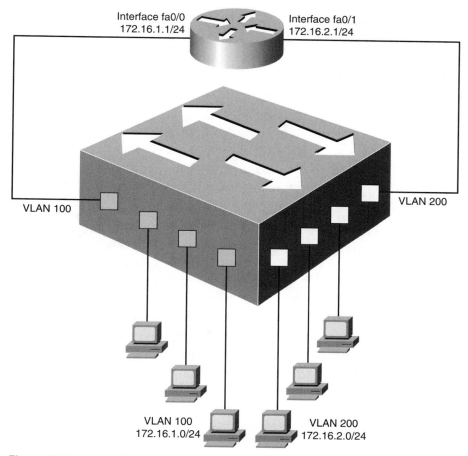

Interface fa0/0
172.16.1.1/24

Interface fa0/1
172.16.2.1/24

VLAN 100

VLAN 200

VLAN 100
172.16.1.0/24

VLAN 200
172.16.2.0/24

Figure 3.11   *Inter-VLAN Routing Using Separate Router Ports per VLAN*

This type of design was one of the first methods to route between VLANs. While effective at accomplishing this goal, you end up with an extremely high cost because each VLAN requires a unique router port. It does not take long for you to run out of router interfaces, requiring an upgrade to a larger router or more routers. To alleviate this load, you might move to a router-on-a-stick design.

Router Connected to a Trunk Port (Router-on-a-Stick)

A router-on-a-stick enables you to route between VLANs using a single router interface connected to a switch trunk port, as shown in Figure 3.12.

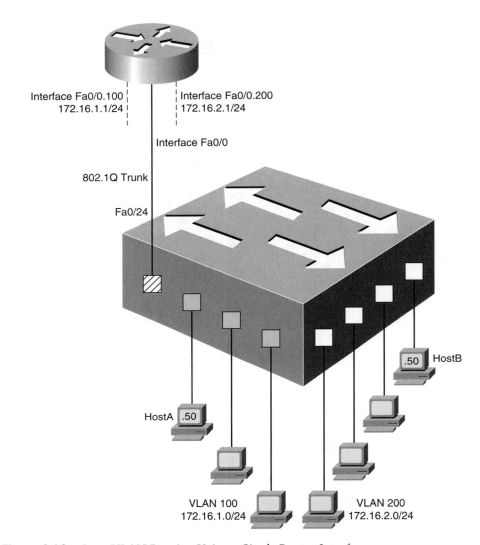

Figure 3.12   *Inter-VLAN Routing Using a Single Router Interface*

As you can see in Figure 3.12, the single, physical router interface that is connected to the switch is now configured with subinterfaces (in this case, FastEthernet 0/0.100 and FastEthernet 0/0.200). This "tricks" the router into believing it has more physical connections than it really does. Let's follow a packet flow as a host from VLAN 100 tries to send a packet to a host in VLAN 200:

   1.   HostA (172.16.1.50) in VLAN 100 attempts to ping HostB (172.16.2.50) in VLAN 200. HostA realizes that HostB is not on its network (due to the subnet mask configured) and sends the data to its default gateway.

2. The switch receives the packet and realizes (due to its MAC address table) that it is destined for port FastEthernet 0/24. Because the port is configured as a trunk, the switch adds an 802.1Q tag to the packet, indicating that the packet belongs to VLAN 100. Once the tag is added to the packet, it is sent to the router.

3. The router receives the packet and sees the tag for VLAN 100. Subinterface FastEthernet 0/0.100 is configured to respond to packets tagged with VLAN 100. The router processes the packet and realizes it is attempting to access an IP address in the 172.16.2.0/24 subnet. Based on the routing table, the router realizes the packet must exit the FastEthernet 0/0.200 subinterface. As the router sends the packet back to the switch, it removes the original tag for VLAN 100 and replaces it with a tag for VLAN 200.

4. Once the switch receives the packet, it removes the VLAN 200 tag and sends it out the switchport connecting to HostB in VLAN 200.

Now you can see why this configuration gets the name "router-on-a-stick." Typically, the router will also be connected to some type of WAN link, such as Internet connectivity, in addition to performing the inter-VLAN routing function.

Layer 3/Multilayer Switching

This final form of inter-VLAN routing uses a router integrated into a switch. This is most often called a Layer 3 or multilayer switch. The concepts are the same as the previous router-on-a-stick design; however, the router is now internal to the switch. To facilitate routing within the switch, you must configure switched virtual interfaces (SVIs), as shown in Figure 3.13. SVIs are virtual interfaces supported on Layer 3 switches that route traffic for their assigned VLAN number.

As soon as the SVI is created, all the users in the SVI VLAN will be able to reach the interface. For example, if you were to create interface VLAN 100, all the ports assigned to VLAN 100 would be able to reach this interface.

The Layer 3 switch design is superior to the previous inter-VLAN routing designs because there is virtually no bandwidth constraints for the hosts assigned to the VLAN to reach the router. In the other inter-VLAN routing designs, the traffic from the hosts needed to leave the switch to reach the router. Therefore, whatever was the speed of the interface connecting to the router was the maximum speed the host could reach. If more than one host was attempting to pass through the router at a time, the bandwidth would then divide between those hosts. Because the SVIs are internal to the switch in the Layer 3 switch design, the only speed constraint becomes the backplane speed of the switch.

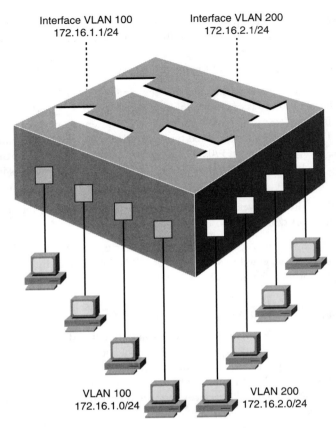
Interface VLAN 100
172.16.1.1/24

Interface VLAN 200
172.16.2.1/24

VLAN 100
172.16.1.0/24

VLAN 200
172.16.2.0/24

Figure 3.13   *Inter-VLAN Routing Using a Layer 3 Switch*

Note   The CCNA Voice exam focuses on inter-VLAN routing using separate router ports and a router-on-a-stick configuration. Layer 3 switching is covered in the CCNP certification track.

In the voice and data network design shown back in Figure 3.10, the CME router will also act as a router-on-a-stick that is able to route between the voice and data VLANs. First, start with the switch side of the configuration. Because SwitchA is connected to the CME router, you need to configure its FastEthernet 0/20 port as a trunk interface, as shown in Example 3.15.

Example 3.15   *Configuring a Trunk to the CME Router*

```
SwitchA# configure terminal
SwitchA(config)# interface fa0/20
SwitchA(config-if)# description CONNECTION TO ROUTER-ON-A-STICK CME ROUTER
SwitchA(config-if)# switchport trunk encapsulation dot1q
SwitchA(config-if)# switchport mode trunk
```

That was easy. Now you need to configure the CME router to perform inter-VLAN routing, as shown in Example 3.16.

Example 3.16   *Configuring Inter-VLAN Routing*

> **Key
> Topic**

```
CME_Router# configure terminal
CME_Router(config)# interface fa0/0
CME_Router(config-if)# no ip address
CME_Router(config-if)# exit
CME_Router(config)# interface fa0/0.10
CME_Router(config-subif)# description ROUTER INTERFACE FOR VOICE VLAN
CME_Router(config-subif)# encapsulation dot1q 10
CME_Router(config-subif)# ip address 172.16.1.1 255.255.255.0
CME_Router(config-subif)# ip helper-address 172.16.2.5
CME_Router(config-subif)# exit
CME_Router(config)# interface fa0/0.50
CME_Router(config-subif)# description ROUTER INTERFACE FOR DATA VLAN
CME_Router(config-subif)# encapsulation dot1q 50
CME_Router(config-subif)# ip address 172.16.2.1 255.255.255.0
```

The CME router is now configured as a router-on-a-stick. In the syntax, there is one command that we have not talked about as of yet: **ip helper-address**. This command instructs the router to forward specific broadcast types to a configured IP address. The primary broadcast type you need to be concerned with in this network design is DHCP requests. Because the DHCP server is assigned to VLAN 50, DHCP requests from the PCs will be able to reach the DHCP server without a problem (because they are in the same VLAN). However, the CME router will block DHCP requests from the Cisco IP phones (on VLAN 10) from reaching the DHCP server. By placing the **ip helper-address 172.16.2.5** command under the subinterface connecting to the voice VLAN, the router will take the DHCP broadcast requests from the IP phones and send them as a unicast message to 172.16.2.5 (the DHCP server). The DHCP server will reply with an IP address offer, which the CME router will pass through to the IP phone.

Note   Nearly all networks that use multiple VLANs also use the **ip helper-address** command. Otherwise, you would need a separate DHCP server for each VLAN.

> **Tip**   Routing DHCP requests to a centralized DHCP server using a helper address is often
> called *DHCP relay*.

Understanding Cisco IP Phone Boot Process

Now that you have learned about VLANs, we can turn our attention back to the Cisco IP phones. With the concepts now in place, you can more fully understand how the Cisco IP phone operates. Here is the Cisco IP phone boot process, start to finish:

Key Topic

1. The Cisco IP phone connects to an Ethernet switchport. If the IP phone and switch support PoE, the IP phone receives power through either Cisco-proprietary PoE or 802.3af PoE.

2. As the Cisco IP phone powers on, the Cisco switch delivers voice VLAN information to the IP phone using CDP as a delivery mechanism. The Cisco IP phone now knows what VLAN it should use.

3. The Cisco IP phone sends a DHCP request asking for an IP address on its voice VLAN. The router connecting to the voice VLAN receives this DHCP request and, through the **ip helper-address** command, forwards the request directly to the DHCP server.

4. The DHCP server responds with an IP address offer. When the Cisco IP phone accepts the offer, it receives all the DHCP options that go along with the DHCP request. DHCP options include items such as default gateway, DNS server information, domain name information, and so on. In the case of Cisco IP phones, a unique DHCP option is included, known as Option 150. This option directs the IP phone to a TFTP server (you learn more about this in the upcoming section, "Configuring a Router-Based DHCP Server").

5. Once the Cisco IP phone has the IP address of the TFTP server, it contacts the TFTP server and downloads its configuration file. Included in the configuration file is a list of valid call processing agents (such as Cisco Unified Communications Manager or CME agents).

6. The Cisco IP phone attempts to contact the first call processing server (the primary server) listed in its configuration file to register. If this fails, the IP phone moves to the next server in the configuration file. This process continues until the IP phone registers successfully or the list of call processing agents is exhausted.

Configuring a Router-Based DHCP Server

We have currently made it up to Step 4 in the preceding IP phone boot process. The phones in our network now need to receive IP address and TFTP server information. In the network design scenario used in this chapter, we are using the WAN branch router as the DHCP server. Using a router as a DHCP server is a somewhat common practice in some small and midsized networks. Once you move into larger organizations, DHCP services are typically centralized onto server platforms. Either DHCP option is capable of sending TFTP server information to the IP phones.

Example 3.17 shows the syntax used to configure the WAN branch router as a DHCP server.

Example 3.17 *Configuring Router-Based DHCP Services*

```
WAN_RTR# configure terminal
WAN_RTR(config)# ip dhcp excluded-address 172.16.1.1 172.16.1.9
WAN_RTR(config)# ip dhcp excluded-address 172.16.2.1 172.16.2.9
WAN_RTR(config)# ip dhcp pool DATA_SCOPE
WAN_RTR(dhcp-config)# network 172.16.2.0 255.255.255.0
WAN_RTR(dhcp-config)# default-router 172.16.2.1
WAN_RTR(dhcp-config)# dns-server 4.2.2.2
WAN_RTR(dhcp-config)# exit
WAN_RTR(config)# ip dhcp pool VOICE_SCOPE
WAN_RTR(dhcp-config)# network 172.16.1.0 255.255.255.0
WAN_RTR(dhcp-config)# default-router 172.16.1.1
WAN_RTR(dhcp-config)# option 150 ip 172.16.1.1
WAN_RTR(dhcp-config)# dns-server 4.2.2.2
```

Key
Topic

The way in which Cisco routers approach DHCP configurations is slightly different from how many other DHCP servers do so. Most DHCP servers allow you to specify a range of IP addresses that you would like to hand out to clients. Cisco routers take the opposite approach: you first specify a range of addresses that you do *not* want to hand out to clients (using the **ip dhcp excluded-address** syntax from global configuration mode). Configuring the excluded addresses before you configure the DHCP pools ensures that the Cisco router does not accidentally hand out IP addresses before you have a chance to exclude them from the range. The DHCP service on the router will begin handing out IP addresses from the first nonexcluded IP address in the network range. In Example 3.17, this will be 172.16.1.10 for the voice scope and 172.16.2.10 for the data scope.

Also notice that the VOICE_SCOPE DHCP pool includes the **option 150** syntax. This creates the custom TFTP server option to be handed out to the Cisco IP phones along with their IP address information. In this case, the TFTP server of the IP phones is the same as the default gateway because we are using the CME router as a call processing agent.

Tip   Notice as well that I assigned a DNS server of 4.2.2.2 to both the data and voice devices. This is a well-known, open DNS server on the Internet. This IP address works fantastically to test connectivity and DNS services in new network deployments because it is such a simple IP address to remember.

The WAN_RTR router is now configured as a DHCP server for the network.

Multiple DHCP Scopes and Helper Addresses

A common question that comes up on DHCP services is, "How does the DHCP server know from which IP address range to pull for a given group of devices?" More specifically in our scenario, how does the DHCP server know to give addresses from the 172.16.1.0/24 network to the Cisco IP phones and addresses from the 172.16.2.0/24 network to the data devices? The answer to this question lies in how the DHCP server receives the DHCP request. In the case of the data devices, the DHCP server receives the request directly on its FastEthernet 0/0 interface because the server is on the same VLAN as the data devices. The DHCP request has no IP address information, as you would expect from a normal DHCP request. Because of this, the router will hand out IP addresses from the subnet to which its FastEthernet 0/0 interface belongs. In this case, the FastEthernet 0/0 interface of the DHCP server belongs to the 172.16.2.0/24 subnet, causing the data devices to receive IP addresses from this range.

In the case of the VoIP devices, the DHCP request is received by the FastEthernet 0/0.10 subinterface of the CME router. Because of the **ip helper-address** command, the CME router forwards the DHCP request to the DHCP server. Technically, the CME router would be referred to as a DHCP relay agent. Whenever a DHCP request is relayed, the DHCP relay agent adds to the packet the IP address of the interface that received the DHCP request. This tells the DHCP server, "This packet has been relayed to you from the 172.16.1.0/24 subnet" because the FastEthernet 0/0.10 subinterface has the IP address 172.16.1.1. When the DHCP server receives the DHCP request, it looks at the relay information and knows to offer an address from the correct subnet.

Key Topic

Note   If you wanted to deliver specific IP address information to an individual phone, you could configure a unique DHCP scope on the router for the phone and use the **hardware address** *<mac-address>* syntax to reserve the scope for a specific device.

Setting the Clock of a Cisco Device with NTP

The final task to prepare the network infrastructure to support a Cisco VoIP network is to set the time. Having an accurate time on Cisco devices is important for many reasons. Here is a quick list of just some of the reasons why you want an accurate clock on your network devices:

■   Allows Cisco IP phones to display the correct date and time to your users

■   Assigns correct date and time to voice-mail tags

- Gives accurate times on Call Detail Records (CDRs), which are used to track calls on the network

- Plays an integral part in multiple security features on all Cisco devices

- Tags logged messages on routers and switches with accurate time information

When Cisco devices boot, many of them default their date and time to noon on March 1, 1993. You have two options in setting the clock: manually, using the **clock set** command from the privileged EXEC mode, or automatically, using the Network Time Protocol (NTP).

Devices setting the clock using NTP always have a more accurate time clock than a manually set clock. Likewise, all the NTP devices on your network will have the exact same time. These advantages make NTP the preferred clock-setting method. The accuracy of the clock on your device depends on the stratum number of the NTP server. A stratum 1 time server is one that has a radio or atomic clock directly attached. The device that receives its time from this server via NTP is considered a stratum 2 device. The device that receives its time from this stratum 2 device via NTP is considered a stratum 3 device, and so on. There are many publicly accessible stratum 2 and 3 (and even some stratum 1) devices on the Internet.

Note	You can obtain a list of publicly accessible NTP servers at http://www.ntp.org.

After you have obtained one or more NTP servers to use, you can configure NTP support on your Cisco devices by using the following syntax:

```
WAN_RTR# configure terminal
WAN_RTR(config)# ntp server 64.209.210.20
WAN_RTR(config)# clock timezone ARIZONA -7
```

The first command, **ntp server** *<ip address>*, configures your Cisco device to use the specified NTP server; 64.209.210.20 is one of many publicly accessible NTP servers. If this is the only command you enter, your clock on your device will set itself to the Universal Time Coordinated (UTC) time zone. To accurately adjust the time zone for your device, use the **clock timezone** *<name> <hours>* command. The previous syntax example set the time zone for Arizona to −7 hours from UTC.

Some areas of the world support daylight saving time (DST), which shifts the clock forward or back an hour throughout the year. To configure DST support on your router, you can use the command shown in Example 3.18.

Example 3.18   *Configuring DST Support on a Cisco Device*

```
WAN_RTR(config)# clock summer-time ?
  WORD  name of time zone in summer
WAN_RTR(config)# clock summer-time CA1_DST ?
  date       Configure absolute summer time
  recurring  Configure recurring summer time
WAN_RTR(config)# clock summer-time CA1_DST recurring ?
  <1-4>  Week number to start
  first  First week of the month
  last   Last week of the month
  <cr>
WAN_RTR(config)# clock summer-time CA1_DST recurring 2 ?
  DAY  Weekday to start
WAN_RTR(config)# clock summer-time CA1_DST recurring 2 sunday ?
  MONTH  Month to start
WAN_RTR(config)# clock summer-time CA1_DST recurring 2 sunday March ?
  hh:mm  Time to start (hh:mm)
WAN_RTR(config)# clock summer-time CA1_DST recurring 2 sunday March 02:00 ?
  <1-4>  Week number to end
  first  First week of the month
  last   Last week of the month
WAN_RTR(config)# clock summer-time CA1_DST recurring 2 sunday March 02:00 1 ?
  DAY  Weekday to end
WAN_RTR(config)# clock summer-time CA1_DST recurring 2 sunday March 02:00 1
  sunday ?
  MONTH  Month to end
WAN_RTR(config)# clock summer-time CA1_DST recurring 2 sunday March 02:00 1 sunday
  November ?
  hh:mm  Time to end (hh:mm)
WAN_RTR(config)# clock summer-time CA1_DST recurring 2 sunday March 02:00 1 sunday
  November 02:00
```

Note   I worked the command through the context-sensitive help to show all the options available when configuring DST.

To verify NTP is working properly, you can use the **show ntp associations** and **show clock** commands, as shown in Example 3.19.

Example 3.19 *Verifying NTP Synchronization Status*

```
WAN_RTR# show ntp associations
      address          ref clock       st  when  poll reach  delay  offset    disp
*~64.209.210.20    138.23.180.126    3    14   64  377    65.5    2.84     7.6
 * master (synced), # master (unsynced), + selected, - candidate, ~ configured
WAN_RTR# show clock
11:25:48.542 CA1_DST Mon Jun 9 2008
```

The key information from the **show ntp associations** command is just to the left of the configured NTP server address. The asterisk indicates that your Cisco device has synchronized with this server. You can configure multiple NTP sources for redundancy, but the Cisco device will only choose one master NTP server to use at a time. Example 3.20 shows an additional (more accurate) NTP server to the WAN_RTR.

Example 3.20 *Verifying Multiple NTP Associations*

```
AdTEC_Voice# show ntp associations
      address          ref clock       st  when  poll reach  delay  offset    disp
*~64.183.56.58     .GPS.             1    55   64  377   253.4   31.53    25.6
 ~64.209.210.20    138.23.180.126    3    54  256  377   212.7   75.64    17.8
 * master (synced), # master (unsynced), + selected, - candidate, ~ configured
```

Notice that the router moved the master asterisk up to the new stratum (st) 1 server, but still keeps the stratum 3 server configured as a backup.

Exam Preparation Tasks

Review All the Key Topics

Review the most important topics in the chapter, noted with the key topics icon in the outer margin of the page. Table 3.5 lists and describes these key topics and identifies the page number on which each is found.

Key Topic

Table 3.5   *Key Topics for Chapter 3*

Key Topic Element	Description	Page Number
List	Protocol used by Cisco IP phones to negotiate PoE requirements with a Cisco switch	64
Paragraph	Understanding the 802.3af Power over Ethernet standard	65
List	VLAN benefits	68
Figure 3.5	VLAN concept	69
Figure 3.7	Trunking concept	71
List	VTP modes	73
Figure 3.9	Understanding voice VLANs	74
Note	Method used to deliver voice VLAN to Cisco IP phones	86
Figure 3.12	Router-on-a-stick design	88
Example 3.16	Router-on-a-stick configuration	91
List	Cisco IP phone boot process	92
Example 3.17	Router-based DHCP server configuration	93
Note	Highlights method to assign IP address information to individual Cisco IP phones via DHCP	94

Definitions of Key Terms

Define the following key terms from this chapter, and check your answers in the glossary.

802.3af Power over Ethernet (PoE)

Cisco Inline Power

Cisco Discovery Protocol (CDP)

virtual LAN (VLAN)

trunking

Inter-Switch Link (ISL)

802.1Q

VLAN Trunking Protocol (VTP)

Dynamic Trunking Protocol (DTP)

router-on-a-stick

switched virtual interface (SVI)

Network Time Protocol (NTP)

Cisco Unified Communications Manager Express Overview: This section gives an overview of the Cisco Unified Communications Manager Express (CME) system, the Cisco hardware it can run on, and features it supports.

Licensing and Models for Cisco Unified CME: As you design your IP telephony network, you can choose a key system, PBX, or hybrid model. This section discusses these models and the licenses required by Cisco to operate a Cisco Unified CME environment.

Installing Unified CME on a Cisco Router: Many routers ship with Cisco Unified CME software preinstalled; on others, it must be installed manually. This section discusses the installation and upgrade process for Cisco Unified CME.

Configuring the Cisco Unified CME Router as a TFTP Server: The Cisco Unified CME router is responsible for serving the correct files to the IP phones during the boot process. This section discusses the configuration of the CME router as a TFTP server.

Configuring the Cisco Unified CME System-Level Functions: In this section, you will see four steps you must take to prepare the Cisco Unified CME router to handle Cisco IP phones.

CHAPTER 4

Installing Cisco Unified Communications Manager Express

At this point, you now understand the difference between TDM and IP-based voice systems. You have seen the foundation network requirements for Power over Ethernet (PoE), Dynamic Host Configuration Protocol (DHCP), virtual LANs (VLANs), and Network Translation Protocol (NTP) and understand the configuration required to build the infrastructure. Now it is time to turn the attention to the Cisco Unified Communications Manager Express (CME) installation process.

"Do I Know This Already?" Quiz

The "Do I Know This Already?" quiz allows you to assess whether you should read this entire chapter or simply jump to the "Exam Preparation Tasks" section for review. If you are in doubt, read the entire chapter. Table 4.1 outlines the major headings in this chapter and the corresponding "Do I Know This Already?" quiz questions. You can find the answers in Appendix A, "Answers to the 'Do I Know This Already?' Quizzes."

Table 4.1   *"Do I Know This Already?" Foundation Topics Section-to-Question Mapping*

Foundation Topics Section	Questions Covered in This Section
Cisco Unified Communications Manager Express Overview	1
Licensing and Models for Cisco Unified CME	2–3
Installing Unified CME on a Cisco Router	4
Configuring the Cisco Unified CME Router as a TFTP Server	5–7
Configuring the Cisco Unified CME System-Level Functions	8–10

1. How many Cisco IP phones can a Cisco 2801 CME Router support?

    a. 8

    b. 24

    c. 50

    d. 144

2. Which of the following are required licenses to operate a Cisco Unified CME router? (Choose three.)

    a. IOS license

    b. User license

    c. Phone license

    d. Phone user license

    e. Feature license

3. Which design model would you use if you wanted the number of lines on each IP phone to match the number of phone lines coming in from the PSTN?

    a. Shared line model

    b. Limited model

    c. Keyswitch model

    d. Hybrid model

    e. PBX model

4. What command can you use to extract a bundle of CME files into the flash of the router?

   a. copy

   b. extract

   c. xtract

   d. archive

5. Which files does the Cisco IP phone download from the TFTP server during the boot process? (Choose two.)

   a. Firmware

   b. Music on Hold

   c. XML templates

   d. Configuration files

6. What is the primary function of the **alias** syntax in the **tftp-server** command?

   a. To make files in subdirectories accessible without entering the full path

   b. To rename files

   c. To hide the original filename to increase network security

   d. To allow multiple files to be accessed through one filename

7. Once phone firmware files are downloaded and copied to the flash memory of a router, how are they made accessible to the IP phones?

   a. The CME telephony service automatically recognizes these files and makes them available via TFTP.

   b. The firmware files must be manually made available by using the **tftp-server** command.

   c. The firmware files are made available through TFTP when entered in the telephony service using the **load** command.

   d. The firmware files are copied to an external TFTP server by the router and downloaded directly to the IP phones.

8. Which three commands must be entered to allow the CME router to begin accepting IP phone registrations?

   a. **max-ephones**

   b. **max-dn**

   c. **no shutdown**

   d. **ip source-address**

   e. **telephony-service enable**

   f. **no telephony-service disable**

9. How does the Cisco Unified CME router create configuration files for the Cisco IP phones? (Choose two.)

   a. Configuration files are automatically created as configuration information is entered.

   b. Configuration files must be downloaded from Cisco and copied to the flash of the router.

   c. Configuration files can be generated by entering the **create cnf-file** syntax.

   d. Configuration files are generated by the IP phones and uploaded to the router's flash during the boot process.

10. The Cisco Unified CME router generates a generic configuration file for IP phones that do not have any configuration information. What is the name of this file?

   a. Config.default

   b. Default.xml

   c. Default.cnf

   d. XMLDefault.cnf.xml

   e. Holiday prompt

   f. Emergency prompt

Foundation Topics

Cisco Unified Communications Manager Express Overview

When Cisco first entered the IP telephony space, it did so with its flagship CallManager product line. CallManager was a dedicated server or servers that was a custom fit for medium to large businesses deploying thousands of phones at a single site or multiple locations. Although CallManager (now known as Cisco Unified Communications Manager) provided a cost-effective solution for these larger businesses, the startup price was far beyond the range that was affordable by small businesses.

As the CallManager product line developed, Cisco released a product known as Survivable Remote Site Telephony (SRST), which allowed a router to act as a failover device for Cisco IP phones if their CallManager server was unreachable. SRST was so fantastic, Cisco eventually turned it into a standalone solution (rather than just a failover solution) that could support a small office environment. The product was initially named IOS Telephony Service (ITS), which then became CallManager Express, which then became the Unified Communications Manager Express (CME) product used today.

Depending on the platform used, Cisco Unified CME can scale to support an environment of up to 240 IP phones. Table 4.2 gives the Cisco Unified CME IOS platforms available and the current maximum number of IP phones supported.

Table 4.2   *Current Cisco Unified Communications Manager Express Platform Limitations*

Platform	Maximum Number of Phones
Cisco 1861 Integrated Services Router	8
Cisco IAD2430 Integrated Access Device	24
Cisco 2801 Integrated Services Router	24
Cisco 3250 Ruggedize Services Router	10
Cisco 3270 Ruggedize Services Router	50
Cisco 2811 Integrated Services Router	35
Cisco 2821 Integrated Services Router	50
Cisco 2851 Integrated Services Router	100
Cisco 3725 Multiservice Access Router	144
Cisco 3745 Multiservice Access Router	192
Cisco 3825 Integrated Services Router	175
Cisco 3845 Integrated Services Router	250

Key Topic

The Cisco Unified CME system supports features you would come to expect from a time-division multiplexing (TDM) PBX or key system. These features can be divided into four categories: system, phone, trunk, and voice mail features. The major features in each category are included in the following list (current as of CME Version 4.3):

- System Features

  - Account codes and Call Detail Record (CDR) field entry

  - Callback busy subscriber and camp-on

  - Per-phone call coverage rules

  - Call hold and retrieve

  - Call park: personal and directed

  - Call transfer and park recall

  - Call park assign to extension

  - Call pickup directed

  - Call pickup local group

  - Call pickup explicit group

  - Call transfer: consultative and blind

  - Call waiting

  - Computer telephony integration (CTI) with Microsoft CRM and Outlook using Cisco IOS Software Telephony Services Provider (TSP)

  - E911 with two emergency location numbers per zone, unlimited zones per site

  - Eight-party impromptu conferencing

  - Directory services using XML

  - Hunt groups: sequential, circular, parallel (blast), and longest idle

  - Hunt-group dynamic login and logout

  - Hunt-groups statistics: daily and hourly

  - Intercom

  - Meet-me conferencing (32 party)

  - Music on Hold (MOH): internal or external source

  - Night service bell or call forwarding

  - Overlay extensions for enhanced call coverage

  - Called-name display for overlay extensions

  - Paging: internal through IP phones or to external system

- Per-call caller ID blocking

- Secondary dial tone

- Standards-based network call transfer and call forwarding using H.450

- Additional system speed-dial option through XML service

- Time-of-day and day-of-week call blocking

- Customizable called-name display

- Support of SRST fallback service phone auto-registration

- Basic automatic call distributor (B-ACD) (three queues) with auto-attendant and call statistics

- Display of number of calls in queue on IP phone

- Agent login and logout of B-ACD hunt group

- Integration with Cisco Unified Contact Center Express 5.0 for advanced call center features with support for up to 50 agents, agent supervisors, call recording, silent monitoring, and reporting features

- Secure Real-Time Protocol (SRTP), providing media encryption for calls on the IP network

- Secure voice IP phone certificate authentication and provisioning plus secure device signaling using Transport Layer Security (TLS)

- Phone Features

  - Maximum 250 phones per system

  - Up to 34 line appearances per phone

  - Attendant console functions using Cisco Unified IP Phone Expansion Module 7914

  - Fast transfer: blind or consult

  - Busy lamp

  - Silent ringing options

  - Automatic line selection for outbound calls

  - Call forward on busy, no answer, and all (internal or external)

  - Call-forward-all restriction control

  - Do not disturb (DND)

  - Feature ring with DND set

  - IP phone display of DND state

  - Dial-plan pattern load on SIP phones

- Diversion of calls directly to voice mail

- Customization of softkeys

- Enable and disable call-waiting notification per line

- Call waiting with overlay directory number

- Call-waiting ring

- Dual or 8 call line appearances per button

- After-hours toll-bar override

- Auto-answer with headset

- European date formats

- Hook flash passthrough across analog PSTN trunks

- Idle URL: periodically push messages or graphics on IP phones

- Last-number redial

- Live record to Cisco Unity Express mailbox

- Local name directory lookup

- On-hook dialing

- Station speed dial with configuration changes from IP phone

- System speed dial for 10,000 numbers

- Silent and feature ring options

- SIP-based line-side subscribe, providing basic presence of phone status

- Transfer to voice mail softkey

- Call barge with privacy on shared lines

- Access features using softkeys or feature access codes

- Remote teleworker IP phone support

- Dynamic hunt-group join or leave

- Support for analog phones using Cisco ATA 186 Analog Telephone Adapter or Cisco VG224 Analog Phone Gateway in SCCP mode

- Support for fax machines on Foreign Exchange Station (FXS) ports or ATA using H.323, SCCP, or SIP

- XML application services on Cisco Unified IP display phones

- Station-to-station video with voice using Cisco Unified Video Advantage or Cisco Unified IP Phone 7985G endpoints

- Extension mobility within the single site

- Wideband audio (G.722) and iLBC codec

- Trunk Features

    - Analog Foreign Exchange Office (FXO) loop and ground start

    - Ear and mouth (E&M)

    - Basic Rate Interface (BRI) and Primary Rate Interface (PRI) support (NI2, 4ESS, 5ESS, EuroISDN, DMS100, and DMS250) and several other switch types currently supported in Cisco IOS Software

    - Caller ID name and number

    - Automatic number identification (ANI)

    - Digital trunk support (T1/E1)

    - Direct inward dialing (DID)

    - Direct outward dialing

    - E1 R2 support

    - Dedicated trunk mapping to phone button

    - H.323 trunks with H.450 support

    - H450.12 automatic detection of H.450 support for remote H.323 endpoints

    - H.323-to-H.323 hairpin call routing for non-H.450-compliant H.323 endpoints

    - SIP trunks and RFC 2833 support

    - Transcoding with G.711, G.729a, and iLBC

    - ISDN Q.SIG supplementary services of basic calls, including call forwarding busy, no answer, all; calling name and line identification (CLIP and CNIP); connected line and name identification (COLP and CONP); message waiting indicator (MWI) and message center support; MWI passthrough QSIG-to-TDM voice mail

- Voice Mail Features

    - Integrated voice mail and auto-attendant solution with Cisco Unity Express

    - Integration with Cisco Unity Voice Mail and Cisco Unity Unified Messaging, or third-party voice mail integration (H.323, SIP, or dual-tone multifrequency [DTMF])

This and other upcoming chapters will discuss many of these features in depth.

Figure 4.1 displays the network diagram built in the previous chapter.

The Cisco Unified CME router in the upper right of Figure 4.1 provides connectivity to the PSTN (allowing for incoming and outgoing PSTN calls) and to the Internet. Cisco designed CME with capabilities to be an all-in-one device. With this one router, you could operate both your data and voice networks.

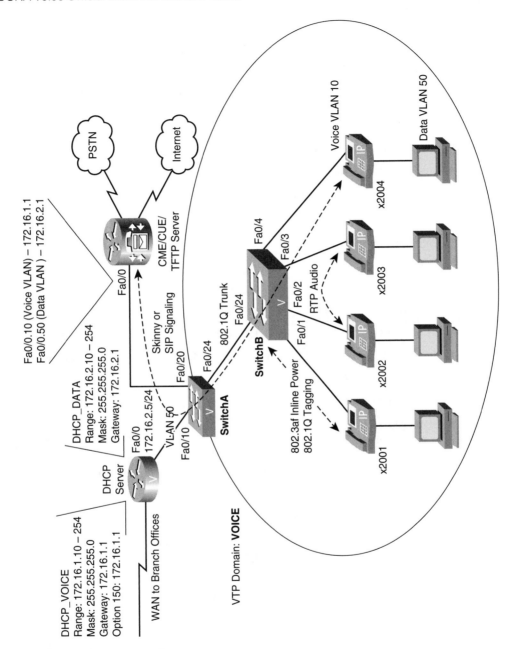

Figure 4.1   *VoIP Network Diagram*

The network diagram pictured in Figure 4.1 shows a separate router connecting to the corporate branch offices. From a design standpoint, this functionality could be integrated into the Cisco Unified CME router as well. CME is able to integrate into other VoIP or TDM network environments. Figure 4.2 illustrates potential integration scenarios.

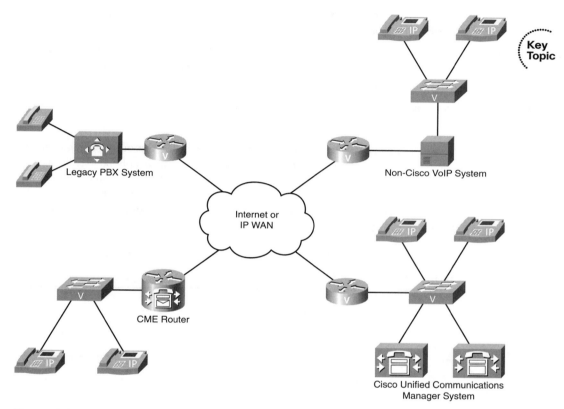

Figure 4.2   *CME Integration Scenarios*

A network using the design shown in Figure 4.2 would be able to place calls between any of the network systems shown using the IP WAN as a transport. The PSTN would still exist at each of these locations but would be used as a backup connection should a WAN failure at any or all of the locations occur.

Note   Chapter 7, "Gateway and Trunk Concepts," and Chapter 8, "Configuring and Verifying Gateways and Trunks," discuss the specifics of integrating the Cisco Unified CME system with other VoIP and TDM systems.

Licensing and Models for Cisco Unified CME

Alas, all is not free in the world of IP telephony. To legally operate a Cisco Unified CME system, you must purchase three types of licenses:

Key Topic

- **IOS license:** The CME router must be licensed to run a version of Cisco IOS that is capable of supporting the CME software.

- **Feature license:** The feature license (also known as seat license) grants the CME router the ability to support a specific number of IP phones. These licenses are sold in incremental blocks

- **Phone user licenses:** You must purchase one phone user license for each Cisco IP phone supported by the CME system.

Often, vendors bundle the licenses with the Cisco Unified CME products being sold. For example, when you purchase a Cisco IP phone, it will come with a phone user license, allowing it to connect to a Cisco Unified CME or Cisco Unified Communications Manager system. The vendor may also bundle the CME router with the IOS license and a 24-seat feature license. Table 4.3 shows the current feature licenses available for the CME system.

Table 4.3   *Cisco Unified Communications Manager Express Feature Licenses*

Number of Phones	License
24	FL-CCME-SMALL
36	FL-CCME-36
48	FL-CCME-MEDIUM
96	FL-CCME-96
144	FL-CCME-144
168	FL-CCME-168
250	FL-CCME-250

You can add feature licenses incrementally to your system. For example, you might start with a network of 80 IP phones and purchase an FL-CCME-96 license, allowing the network to grow up to 96 IP phones. Once you grow beyond that, you could add on a FL-CCME-SMALL license incrementally to add an additional 24 phones per license purchase.

Once all your licensing is in place, you can begin to plan the model you would like to use for Cisco Unified CME. CME supports three different models of configuration:

- PBX

- Keyswitch

- Hybrid

Choosing a model does not "lock you in" to one configuration or another; rather, the model represents more of a design that you can use for your company. This section describes each of the three models.

PBX Model

Using a PBX model of configuration gives most of the IP phones in your system a unique extension number, as shown in Figure 4.3.

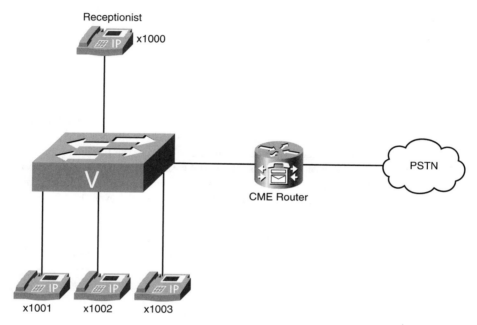

Figure 4.3   *Cisco Unified CME PBX Model*

In this model, users can dial each other using their own, unique extension numbers. To get an outside line to the PSTN, the user would first dial a 9 (or some other access code) and receive a second dial tone. A local receptionist or auto-attendant system running on the Cisco Unified CME router is responsible for distributing incoming calls from the PSTN to the users. If the company is large enough to warrant a Direct Inward Dial (DID) block of phone numbers, the CME can route incoming PSTN calls directly to the users.

Keyswitch Model

Using a keyswitch model of configuration mirrors the TDM keyswitch environment, which provided shared numbers to the phones supported by the system. Figure 4.4 illustrates a keyswitch model design.

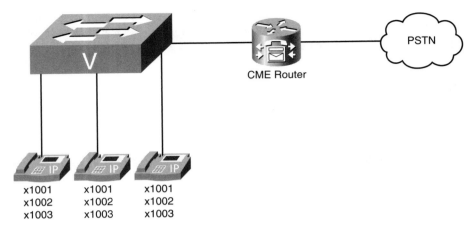

Figure 4.4   *Cisco Unified CME Keyswitch Model*

The receptionist is not included in the design in Figure 4.4 because keyswitch environments typically provide a 1:1 ratio between directory numbers on phones and PSTN circuits. For example, if an office has three incoming PSTN lines, the three lines on each phone map directly to one of these lines. When the Cisco Unified CME router receives an incoming call on the first PSTN line, it rings the first line of all the IP phones connected to the system. A receptionist may be present in the office; however, the office would be small enough that any employee could answer any line.

In a keyswitch environment, intra-office calls are rare because the office environment is small enough for a user to walk to another cubical or yell, "Hey Beth, pick up line 1!" over a cubical wall.

Hybrid Model

The hybrid model is useful for environments that want a keyswitch feel, where each line maps directly to a PSTN line, but also want to allow simple intra-office calling. In a pure keyswitch environment with three lines on each phone, an intra-office call between two employees would use up two of the lines, leaving only one line remaining for incoming or outgoing PSTN calls. In the hybrid model, each user would receive a unique extension in addition to the shared "keyswitch" lines, as shown in Figure 4.5.

Depending on your configuration, the extension unique to each user may or may not be able to reach the PSTN. If you have a limited number of PSTN lines available at the office, you may want to restrict PSTN access from the unique extension on each phone. You can also have this unique extension be the default active line when the user picks up the phone so that a user does not temporarily tie up one of the shared, PSTN lines each time the receiver is lifted.

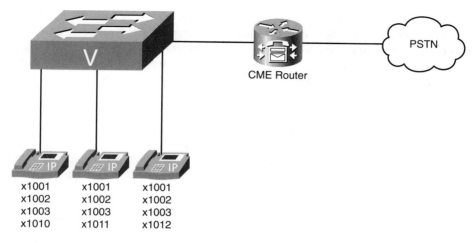

Figure 4.5   *Cisco Unified CME Hybrid Model*

Installing Unified CME on a Cisco Router

One advantage of Cisco IOS is the ease of installation and upgradability. To perform an IOS installation or upgrade, you can set up a TFTP server on your PC, download IOS from Cisco.com, and then enter a command similar to the following:

```
Router# copy tftp://172.16.2.5/c2801-adventerprisek9-mz.124-19.bin flash:
```

Assuming your TFTP server is working correctly and assigned the IP address 172.16.2.5, the single BIN IOS file would copy over. Once you reboot the router, you would be running the new IOS version.

Installing Cisco Unified CME is not quite as simple. Rather than being an all-in-one BIN file, the CME software is a series of files, which breaks down into the following categories:

- **Basic files:** The core files needed to run CME. This file set includes the firmware files that the Cisco IP phones need to operate.

- **GUI files:** The files required to power the CME web-based management utility.

- **XML template file:** The file that dictates the structure of the CME web-based management utility. Editing this file allows you to create different levels of administrators (such as a CME administrator who can only modify IP phone configurations through the web-based utility).

- **MOH files:** Audio files used for Music on Hold (MOH).

- **Script files:** Various Tool Command Language (Tcl) script files to provide more advanced functionality to CME (such as auto-attendant and automatic call distributor [ACD] functions).

- **Miscellaneous files:** Additional files that allow you to have custom ringtones or different backgrounds on select models of Cisco IP phones.

Performing a full installation of the Cisco Unified CME software adds around 150 files to the flash memory of your router. If you were to download each of these files manually and copy them one by one, it could be an all-day process just to get the CME files in place. To save you some pain, Cisco has introduced the **archive** command in the IOS syntax, which allows you to extract a group of files to flash all at once.

Note Many routers ship with the Cisco Unified CME software conveniently preinstalled. However, with the speed of change in the VoIP world, it won't be long before you find yourself upgrading the CME version or firmware files for your Cisco IP phones. You can use the following processes for clean installs or upgrades of the CME software.

To perform an installation of the CME files on your router, you must first download the appropriate files from the Cisco website. Figure 4.6 gives you an idea of what the CME file download area looks like.

Select a File to Download			
Sort by: Filename ▼ Go			
Filename	**Release**	**Date**	**Size (Bytes)**
cme-full-4.3.0.0.tar CME 4.3 Full System Files for IOS 12.4(15)XZ releases, includes MOH and GUI files, BACD prompts, Ringtones, 7970 Backgrounds, and all phone loads (except 7985)	4.3.0.0	02-MAY-2008	68423168
cme-basic-4.3.0.0.tar CME 4.3 basic system files for IOS 12.4(15)XZ releases, includes GUI files and Basic Phone Loads (7906/11, 7921, 7937, 7941/61)	4.3.0.0	02-MAY-2008	32422912
cme-gui-4.2.0.4.tar CME 4.2 GUI files for IOS 12.4(11)XW6 and later releases with updated GUI. Includes additional support for 7942/7945/7965/7975 phones and extension mobility.	4.2.0.4	25-APR-2008	815104
directxfer.aef Direct Transfer system script that allows system to transfer outside caller into users voice mail box on CUE - also used in UCC Mobility installations.	1.0	25-APR-2008	18032
Cisco-CUCME-TSP-2.1.2.exe Cisco Unified Communications Manager Express Telephony Service Provider (TSP) 2.1.2 - Compatible CME Version:4.1 using 12.4(15)T1 or later IOS. Provides support for Windows Vista.	2.1.2	13-MAR-2008	4931954
cme-gui-4.1.0.2.tar CME 4.1 GUI files 4.1.0.2 for IOS 12.4(11)XJ and 12.4(15)T releases, with additional support for 7942/7945/7965/7975 phones	4.1.0.2	11-MAR-2008	827392
moh.zip CME MOH files recorded at different volumes	1.0	10-MAR-2008	1264530

Figure 4.6   *CME Software Download Page*

As you can see, Cisco offers many different "packs" of files, such as the basic files, GUI files, or MOH files. In addition, there is also a full CME pack of files, which includes all the files in the previous bulleted list in a single TAR archive.

Note TAR archives (files with a .tar extension) are the only files that you can extract into the router flash memory by using the **archive** command.

Cisco offers these different file packs as options for you to download and install. These CME file packs give you flexibility to install only the files you want. For example, you may only have enough flash memory on your router for the CME basic and GUI files. In this case, you can install just those components. Likewise, some may prefer to manage the CME system solely from the command line. In this case, there is no reason to use up valuable router flash space with the CME GUI files.

To install the full CME software package onto a router, obtain the full TAR file from Cisco and place the file on your TFTP server (which should be accessible from your Cisco router). Then issue the command shown in Example 4.1.

Example 4.1   *Installing CME Files into Flash Memory*

Key Topic

```
CME_Voice# archive tar /xtract tftp://172.16.2.5/cme-full-4.3.0.0.tar flash:
Loading cme-full-4.3.0.0.tar from 172.16.2.5 (via FastEthernet0/0): !
bacdprompts/ (directory) 0 (bytes)
extracting bacdprompts/app-b-acd-2.1.2.2-ReadMe.txt (18836 bytes)
extracting bacdprompts/app-b-acd-2.1.2.2.tcl (24985 bytes)
extracting bacdprompts/app-b-acd-aa-2.1.2.2.tcl (35485 bytes)
extracting bacdprompts/en_bacd_allagentsbusy.au (75650 bytes)
extracting bacdprompts/en_bacd_disconnect.au (83291 bytes)
extracting bacdprompts/en_bacd_enter_dest.au (63055 bytes)!
extracting bacdprompts/en_bacd_invalidoption.au (37952 bytes)
extracting bacdprompts/en_bacd_music_on_hold.au (496521 bytes)!!
extracting bacdprompts/en_bacd_options_menu.au (123446 bytes)
extracting bacdprompts/en_bacd_welcome.au (42978 bytes)
extracting bacdprompts/en_bacd_xferto_operator.au (34794 bytes)!
extracting CME43-full-readme-v.2.0.txt (22224 bytes)
Desktops/ (directory)
Desktops/320x212x12/ (directory)
extracting Desktops/320x212x12/CampusNight.png (131470 bytes)
extracting Desktops/320x212x12/CiscoFountain.png (80565 bytes)!
extracting Desktops/320x212x12/List.xml (628 bytes)
extracting Desktops/320x212x12/MorroRock.png (109076 bytes)
extracting Desktops/320x212x12/NantucketFlowers.png (108087 bytes)
extracting Desktops/320x212x12/TN-CampusNight.png (10820 bytes)
extracting Desktops/320x212x12/TN-CiscoFountain.png (9657 bytes)
extracting Desktops/320x212x12/TN-Fountain.png (7953 bytes)
extracting Desktops/320x212x12/TN-MorroRock.png (7274 bytes)!
extracting Desktops/320x212x12/TN-NantucketFlowers.png (9933 bytes)
extracting Desktops/320x212x12/Fountain.png (138278 bytes)
gui/ (directory)
extracting gui/Delete.gif (953 bytes)
extracting gui/admin_user.html (3845 bytes)
extracting gui/admin_user.js (647358 bytes)!!!
!output omitted
```

As you can see, the cme-full-4.3.0.0.tar file is expanded into the flash of the router. The output shown in Example 4.1 is only one page out of five pages of files that would copy into the router's flash. Now imagine copying each one of those files one by one using the **copy** command. No thanks!

Note Example 4.1 demonstrates how to install the full CME package onto a router. You can follow a similar process if you only want to install individual components.

Configuring the Cisco Unified CME Router as a TFTP Server

Now that you have the Cisco Unified CME files installed into the router flash, you can configure the CME router as a TFTP server. Before diving right into the syntax, let's review *why* we are making the CME router a TFTP server. The following is the boot process of a Cisco IP phone:

1. The Cisco IP phone connects to an Ethernet switchport. If the IP phone and switch support PoE, the IP phone receives power through either Cisco Proprietary PoE or 802.3af PoE.

2. As the Cisco IP phone powers on, the Cisco switch delivers voice VLAN information to the IP phone using CDP as a delivery mechanism. The Cisco IP phone now knows what VLAN it should use.

3. The Cisco IP phone sends a DHCP request asking for an IP address on its voice VLAN. The router connecting to the voice VLAN receives this DHCP request and, through the **ip helper-address** command, forwards the request directly to the DHCP server.

4. The DHCP server responds with an IP address offer. When the Cisco IP phone accepts the offer, it receives all the DHCP options that go along with the DHCP request. DHCP options include items such as default gateway, DNS server information, domain name information, and so on. In the case of Cisco IP phones, a unique DHCP option is included known as Option 150. This option directs the IP phone to a TFTP server.

5. When the Cisco IP phone has the IP address of the TFTP server, it contacts the TFTP server and downloads its firmware and configuration files. Included in the configuration file is a list of valid call processing agents (such as Cisco Unified Communications Manager or CME agents).

6. The Cisco IP phone attempts to contact the first call processing server (the primary server) listed in its configuration file to register. If this fails, the IP phone moves to the next server in the configuration file. This process continues until the IP phone registers successfully or the list of call processing agents is exhausted.

Chapter 3 completed up through Step 4 of the boot process. The Cisco IP phone received its IP address information from the DHCP server and now has the IP address of the TFTP server (from DHCP Option 150), which is going to be the Cisco Unified CME router. But, as of yet, the CME router is not acting as a TFTP server. The CME router needs to hand out both the phone firmware (for whichever applicable Cisco IP phone models you are using) and the necessary phone configuration files. Otherwise, the Cisco IP phones will reach Step 5 of the boot process and stop.

Cisco routers will allow you to turn them into TFTP servers to serve files from the router's flash memory. Now, you do not want to serve up the *entire* flash memory of your router to the TFTP service. Otherwise, unauthorized users could download copies of your router's IOS or other sensitive files stored in flash. Instead, you must specify exactly what files are served from the flash memory.

In the "old days" of the CME software, this used to be a major challenge, because CME would dump all its software files into a flat directory in your router flash. That's right; you would enter **dir flash:** and see 100+ CME files without any subdirectories to organize them. You would then have to weed through the files and use extensive documentation to figure out which firmware files belonged to each phone (the firmware files have names such as P00308000500.bin, so it was not obvious just based on the filename). Thankfully, in the newer versions of CME software, that has all changed. The phone firmware files are all organized in subdirectories that make it clear which files belong to each. Example 4.2 shows the directory listings of the router's flash after installing the CME full TAR package.

Example 4.2   *Verifying Installed CME Files*

```
CME_Voice# dir flash:
Directory of flash:/


    1  -rw-     32999900   May 12 2008 21:28:00 -07:00  c2801-adventerprisek9-mz.124-
19.bin
    2  drw-            0   Jun 10 2008 14:57:20 -07:00  bacdprompts
   14  -rw-        22224   Jun 10 2008 14:57:30 -07:00  CME43-full-readme-v.2.0.txt
   15  drw-            0   Jun 10 2008 14:57:30 -07:00  Desktops
   28  drw-            0   Jun 10 2008 14:57:36 -07:00  gui
   46  -rw-       496521   May 12 2008 21:30:00 -07:00  music-on-hold.au
   47  drw-            0   May 12 2008 21:30:00 -07:00  phone
  128  drw-            0   May 12 2008 21:35:46 -07:00  ringtones
129996800 bytes total (28583936 bytes free)


CME_Voice# dir flash:/phone
Directory of flash:/phone/
   48  drw-            0   May 12 2008 21:30:00 -07:00  7945-7965
   57  drw-            0   May 12 2008 21:30:34 -07:00  7937
   59  drw-            0   May 12 2008 21:31:12 -07:00  7914
   61  drw-            0   May 12 2008 21:31:12 -07:00  7906-7911
   70  drw-            0   May 12 2008 21:31:46 -07:00  7920
   72  drw-            0   May 12 2008 21:31:52 -07:00  7931
   80  drw-            0   May 12 2008 21:32:24 -07:00  7942-7962
   89  drw-            0   May 12 2008 21:32:58 -07:00  7921
   97  drw-            0   May 12 2008 21:33:54 -07:00  7940-7960
  102  drw-            0   May 12 2008 21:34:02 -07:00  7970-7971
  111  drw-            0   May 12 2008 21:34:36 -07:00  7975
  119  drw-            0   May 12 2008 21:35:12 -07:00  7941-7961
```

continues

Example 4.2   *Verifying Installed CME Files   continued*

```
129996800 bytes total (28583936 bytes free)


CME_Voice# dir flash:/phone/7940-7960
Directory of flash:/phone/7940-7960/
    98   -rw-        129824   May 12 2008 21:33:56 -07:00   P00308000500.bin
    99   -rw-           458   May 12 2008 21:33:56 -07:00   P00308000500.loads
   100   -rw-        705536   May 12 2008 21:34:00 -07:00   P00308000500.sb2
   101   -rw-        130228   May 12 2008 21:34:00 -07:00   P00308000500.sbn
129996800 bytes total (28583936 bytes free)
```

As you dig deeper in the router flash directory listing, you can find the actual firmware files that are used for the IP phones. Example 4.3 shows output for the Cisco 7940 and 7960 IP Phone models. Now that you know the names of the firmware files, you can make them available through TFTP.

Example 4.3   *Configuring Router-Based TFTP Services for IP Phone Firmware Files*

Key
Topic

```
CME_Voice# configure terminal
Enter configuration commands, one per line.  End with CNTL/Z.
CME_Voice(config)# tftp-server flash:/phone/7940-7960/P00308000500.bin alias
  P00308000500.bin
CME_Voice(config)# tftp-server flash:/phone/7940-7960/P00308000500.loads alias
  P00308000500.loads
CME_Voice(config)# tftp-server flash:/phone/7940-7960/P00308000500.sb2 alias
  P00308000500.sb2
CME_Voice(config)# tftp-server flash:/phone/7940-7960/P00308000500.sbn alias
  P00308000500.sbn
```

The **alias** syntax that follows the **tftp-server** command allows the firmware file to be requested simply by asking for the aliased filename. This is necessary in the newer CME versions, which organize the firmware files into subdirectories. The Cisco IP phones do not know the full path to the firmware file; they only ask for the firmware filename.

Note Be sure to make all the firmware files in each subdirectory available through TFTP. The Cisco IP phones will use most, if not all, of these files during the boot process.

The firmware files for the Cisco 7940 and 7960 IP Phones are now available via TFTP from the Cisco Unified CME router. You can repeat this process as many times as necessary to make the firmware files available for the additional models of IP phones you have on your network.

Note There may be models of Cisco IP phones that are supported by Cisco Unified CME whose firmware files are not contained in the CME full TAR package. The firmware files for these IP phone models can be individually downloaded from the Cisco website and placed into the router's flash memory. This same principle also applies for IP phone firmware that has been upgraded since the CME software release you are using.

Configuring the Cisco Unified CME System-Level Functions

Now that the Cisco Unified CME router is serving up the correct firmware files, you can get into the configuration of the CME system itself. You can configure just about all of the CME settings from the telephony-service configuration mode, which you access simply by entering **telephony-service** from global configuration mode.

Four key system-level functions need to be specified in order for the CME router to begin supporting IP phones:

- Maximum phones and directory numbers

- Firmware load files

- Source IP address information

- Generated configuration files

The following sections describe each system-level function.

Maximum Phones and Directory Numbers

Before the Cisco Unified CME router can begin registering and supporting IP phones, it needs to know the number of phones and directory numbers it will be supporting. By default, both values are set to zero, so the router will not support any VoIP devices. To configure this value, you can use the syntax shown in Example 4.4.

Example 4.4 *Provisioning CME Phone and Directory Number Support*

Key
Topic

```
CME_Voice(config)# telephony-service
CME_Voice(config-telephony)# max-ephones ?
  <1-30>  Maximum phones to support
CME_Voice(config-telephony)# max-ephones 24
CME_Voice(config-telephony)# max-dn ?
  <1-150>  Maximum directory numbers supported
  <cr>
CME_Voice(config-telephony)# max-dn 48
```

The **max-ephones** parameter configures the maximum number of IP phones the router will support, whereas the **max-dn** parameter specifies the maximum number of directory numbers.

> **Note** These parameters directly affect how much memory the router reserves to support the CME service. Setting the value much higher than you actually need may reserve excessive resources on your router and impact other network services.
>
> In addition, the **max-ephones** parameter should not be any higher than the number of feature licenses you have purchased for your CME system.

Firmware Load Files

In the section "Configuring the Cisco Unified CME Router as a TFTP Server," you saw how to configure the CME router to serve the phone firmware files via TFTP. You must now tell the telephony service which firmware files it should use for the various models of Cisco IP phones it will be supporting. This can be done under the telephony-service configuration mode by using the **load** command, as shown in Example 4.5.

Example 4.5 *Specifying Firmware Loads for Cisco IP Phones*

```
CME_Voice(config-telephony)# load ?
  12SP      Select the firmware load file for 12SP+ and 30VIP phones
  7902      Select the firmware load file for 7902
  7905      Select the firmware load file for 7905
  7910      Select the firmware load file for Telecaster 7910 phones
  7912      Select the firmware load file for 7912
  7914      Select the firmware load file for sidecar 7914
  7920      Select the firmware load file for 7920
  7935      Select the firmware load file for 7935 Conference Station
  7936      Select the firmware load file for 7936
  7960-7940 Select the firmware load file for Telecaster 7960 & 7940 phones
  7970      Select the firmware load file for 7970
  7971      Select the firmware load file for 7971
  ATA       Select the firmware load file for ATA
CME_Voice(config-telephony)# load 7960 ?
  WORD   firmware filename for Telecaster 7960 & 7940 [without .bin]
CME_Voice(config-telephony)# load 7960 P00308000500
Updating CNF files
CNF files updating complete
CME_Voice(config-telephony)#
```

Notice that after you enter the **load ?** command, the CME router displays all supported Cisco IP phone models. You need to enter a unique **load** command for each IP phone model you are using in your Cisco Unified CME system. Only enter the firmware filename; do not enter the .bin extension.

> **Note** Because the newer Cisco Unified CME software creates a directory structure in the flash memory, be sure you have aliased each of the firmware files using the **tftp-server** syntax discussed earlier in this chapter. The Cisco IP phones simply ask for a firmware filename during the boot process; they do not specify subdirectory information.

To put all the pieces into place, the syntax in Example 4.6 walks through the complete TFTP server and load configuration for the Cisco 7970 and 7971 IP Phones.

Example 4.6   *Configuring CME for 7970 and 7971 Firmware Loads*

```
CME_Voice# dir flash:/phone
Directory of flash:/phone/
    48  drw-           0  May 12 2008 21:30:00 -07:00   7945-7965
    57  drw-           0  May 12 2008 21:30:34 -07:00   7937
    59  drw-           0  May 12 2008 21:31:12 -07:00   7914
    61  drw-           0  May 12 2008 21:31:12 -07:00   7906-7911
    70  drw-           0  May 12 2008 21:31:46 -07:00   7920
    72  drw-           0  May 12 2008 21:31:52 -07:00   7931
    80  drw-           0  May 12 2008 21:32:24 -07:00   7942-7962
    89  drw-           0  May 12 2008 21:32:58 -07:00   7921
    97  drw-           0  May 12 2008 21:33:54 -07:00   7940-7960
   102  drw-           0  May 12 2008 21:34:02 -07:00   7970-7971
   111  drw-           0  May 12 2008 21:34:36 -07:00   7975
   119  drw-           0  May 12 2008 21:35:12 -07:00   7941-7961
129996800 bytes total (28583936 bytes free)
CME_Voice# dir flash:/phone/7970-7971
Directory of flash:/phone/7970-7971/
   103  -rw-     2494499  May 12 2008 21:34:14 -07:00   apps70.8-3-2-27.sbn
   104  -rw-      547706  May 12 2008 21:34:16 -07:00   cnu70.8-3-2-27.sbn
   105  -rw-     2456051  May 12 2008 21:34:28 -07:00   cvm70sccp.8-3-2-27.sbn
   106  -rw-      530601  May 12 2008 21:34:32 -07:00   dsp70.8-3-2-27.sbn
   107  -rw-      538527  May 12 2008 21:34:34 -07:00   jar70sccp.8-3-2-27.sbn
   108  -rw-         638  May 12 2008 21:34:36 -07:00   SCCP70.8-3-3S.loads
   109  -rw-         642  May 12 2008 21:34:36 -07:00   term70.default.loads
   110  -rw-         642  May 12 2008 21:34:36 -07:00   term71.default.loads
129996800 bytes total (28583936 bytes free)
CME_Voice# configure terminal
Enter configuration commands, one per line.  End with CNTL/Z.
CME_Voice(config)# tftp-server flash:/phone/7970-7971/apps70.8-3-2-27.sbn alias
  apps70.8-3-2-27.sbn
```

continues

Example 4.6   *Configuring CME for 7970 and 7971 Firmware Loads*   *continued*

```
CME_Voice(config)# tftp-server flash:/phone/7970-7971/cnu70.8-3-2-27.sbn alias
  cnu70.8-3-2-27.sbn
CME_Voice(config)# tftp-server flash:/phone/7970-7971/cvm70sccp.8-3-2-27.sbn alias
  cvm70sccp.8-3-2-27.sbn
CME_Voice(config)# tftp-server flash:/phone/7970-7971/dsp70.8-3-2-27.sbn alias
  dsp70.8-3-2-27.sbn
CME_Voice(config)# tftp-server flash:/phone/7970-7971/jar70sccp.8-3-2-27.sbn alias
  jar70sccp.8-3-2-27.sbn
CME_Voice(config)# tftp-server flash:/phone/7970-7971/SCCP70.8-3-3S.loads alias
  SCCP70.8-3-3S.loads
CME_Voice(config)# tftp-server flash:/phone/7970-7971/term70.default.loads alias
  term70.default.loads
CME_Voice(config)# tftp-server flash:/phone/7970-7971/term71.default.loads alias
  term71.default.loads
CME_Voice(config)# telephony-service
CME_Voice(config-telephony)# load ?
  12SP      Select the firmware load file for 12SP+ and 30VIP phones
  7902      Select the firmware load file for 7902
  7905      Select the firmware load file for 7905
  7910      Select the firmware load file for Telecaster 7910 phones
  7912      Select the firmware load file for 7912
  7914      Select the firmware load file for sidecar 7914
  7920      Select the firmware load file for 7920
  7935      Select the firmware load file for 7935 Conference Station
  7936      Select the firmware load file for 7936
  7960-7940 Select the firmware load file for Telecaster 7960 & 7940 phones
  7970      Select the firmware load file for 7970
  7971      Select the firmware load file for 7971
  ATA       Select the firmware load file for ATA
CME_Voice(config-telephony)# load 7970 SCCP70.8-3-3S.loads
Updating CNF files
CNF files update complete
CME_Voice(config-telephony)# load 7971 SCCP70.8-3-3S.loads
Updating CNF files
CNF files update complete
```

Note You might be wondering how to determine which of the firmware files should be specified in the **load** command. This information is available at Cisco.com by searching for **Cisco Unified CME Supported Firmware, Platforms, Memory, and Voice Products.** From the search results, pick the version of Cisco Unified CME you are using. The resulting page will show all the firmware files supported for each Cisco IP phone model. One of those files will have an asterisk next to it; this represents the file you should use with the **load** command.

Source IP Address Information

Before the Cisco Unified CME router can respond to the Cisco IP phones it is support-ing, it must know what source IP address to use when communicating. This is specified using the command **ip source-address** from the telephony service configuration mode. Based on the network diagram shown earlier in Figure 4.1, the CME router should use the source IP address 172.16.1.1, which also acts as the default gateway for the Cisco IP phones in the network, as follows:

```
CME_Voice(config-telephony)# ip source-address 172.16.1.1
```

If the Cisco Unified CME router supports IP phones on multiple VLANs or has multiple interfaces the IP phones could use to reach the CME router, it is common to use a loop-back interface as the source IP address. A loopback interface is a virtual interface on the router that is reachable as long as the router is online. The previous syntax set the CME source IP address to 172.16.1.1, which will work as long as the FastEthernet 0/0.10 inter-face is online. However, if that interface were to go offline, the CME router would not be able to provide service to IP phones through any other interface. Example 4.7 shows how to create a loopback interface on a Cisco router.

Example 4.7 *Configuring the CME Source IP Address*

```
CME_Voice# configure terminal
Enter configuration commands, one per line.  End with CNTL/Z.
CME_Voice(config)# interface loopback ?
  <0-2147483647>  Loopback interface number
CME_Voice(config)# interface loopback 0
CME_Voice(config-if)# ip address 172.16.254.254 255.255.255.255
CME_Voice(config-if)# exit
CME_Voice(config)# telephony-service
CME_Voice(config-telephony)# ip source-address 172.16.254.254
```

A few items to note about this configuration: first, notice the range of loopback interface numbers. Cisco enables you to create more than two billion loopback interfaces. Your router would most likely run out of memory if you tried this; however, this enables you to create as many loopback interfaces as you could practically use on the router.

Second, take a look at the subnet mask on the loopback interface IP address. This is known as a *host mask*. The router now knows that the loopback interface connects to only a single IP address instead of using up an entire subnet, as it would if you were to use a less-specific subnet mask. For example, if you used a Class C subnet mask (255.255.255.0 or /24) on the loopback interface, the router would now believe that the loopback interface connects to an entire Class C subnet of addresses. You would not be able to use the 172.16.254.0/24 addresses on any other interfaces of your router.

Finally, loopback interfaces come up automatically as long as the router is running. There is no need to enter the **no shutdown** command unless the loopback interface was manual-ly shut down.

Once you create the loopback interface, you can then change the **ip source-address** command on the router to use the new loopback interface as a means of communicating with the IP phones.

> **Note** In the VoIP network diagram shown in Figure 4.1 (and also Figure 3.1), there would be no real advantage to using a loopback interface because all the IP phones are located on VLAN 10 and can get to the router only through the single FastEthernet 0/0 interface. The loopback configuration would be advantageous when the IP phones have more than one path to reach the CME router.

Generated Configuration Files

The last area of configuration focuses on generating configuration files for the Cisco IP phones. Think back to the IP phone boot process: once the IP phone gets an IP address and TFTP server information from the DHCP server, it then attempts to contact the TFTP server to download its configuration file and firmware. Up to this point, there has been no discussion about that configuration file. So what is it?

The IP phone uses its configuration file to determine which IP address to use when contacting the CME router (specified via the **ip source-address** command in the previous section), the firmware file it should download, the IP phone's extension number (if it has one), and many other configuration items. You may have noticed the following output when looking through the previous syntax examples:

```
Updating CNF files
CNF files update complete
```

That output represents the Cisco Unified CME router updating the configuration files that are sent to the IP phones. This process occurs any time a change is made to the CME router that would affect the IP phone boot process (such as specifying new firmware files or source-address information). If you ever want to manually instruct the router to create the configuration files, use the command shown in Example 4.8 from telephony service configuration mode.

Example 4.8   *Generating IP Phone Configuration Files*

```
CME_Voice(config-telephony)# create cnf-files
CNF file creation is already On
Updating CNF files
CNF files update complete
```

At this point, the CME router does not have any configured IP phones, so it generates only generic configuration files. These generic configuration files allow IP phones to reach the CME router and download the necessary firmware files, but not much else. Once you configure the router to support IP phones, the CME router generates a unique configuration file for each phone with the information specific to the IP phone. Let's take a look at the generic configuration files generated so far, shown in Example 4.9.

Example 4.9 *Verifying Files Served by the CME TFTP Service*

```
CME_Voice# show telephony-service tftp-bindings
tftp-server system:/its/SEPDEFAULT.cnf
tftp-server system:/its/SEPDEFAULT.cnf alias SEPDefault.cnf
tftp-server system:/its/XMLDefault.cnf.xml alias XMLDefault.cnf.xml
tftp-server system:/its/ATADefault.cnf.xml
tftp-server system:/its/united_states/7960-tones.xml alias United_States/7960-
   tones.xml
tftp-server system:/its/united_states/7960-font.xml alias English_United_States/
   7960-font.xml
tftp-server system:/its/united_states/7960-dictionary.xml alias English_United_
   States/7960-dictionary.xml
tftp-server system:/its/united_states/7960-kate.xml alias English_United_States/
   7960-kate.xml
tftp-server system:/its/united_states/SCCP-dictionary.xml alias English_United_
   States/SCCP-dictionary.xml
```

The **show telephony-service tftp-bindings** command shows all the files the CME service itself is serving to the IP phones via TFTP. This is in addition to the files manually specified using the **tftp-server** command in global configuration mode. There is one file specifically that is of interest right now: XMLDefault.cnf.xml. This is the default configuration file handed out to any IP phone that does not have an existing configuration in the CME router (which is all IP phones at this point). Notice that all these files are located on the system: drive of your router. This drive represents the router's RAM. Each time the router is rebooted, these configuration files are rebuilt by the CME process using the configuration you have saved in NVRAM and placed back into the router's memory.

Using the **more** command, you can dig deeper into the contents of the XMLDefault.cnf.xml file, as shown in Example 4.10.

Example 4.10 *Inspecting the IP Phone Generic Configuration File*

```
CME_Voice# more system:/its/XMLDefault.cnf.xml
<Default>
<callManagerGroup>
<members>
<member  priority="0">
<callManager>
<ports>
```

Key
Topic

Example 4.10   *Inspecting the IP Phone Generic Configuration File*   *continued*

```
<ethernetPhonePort>2000</ethernetPhonePort>
</ports>
<processNodeName>172.16.1.1</processNodeName>
</callManager>
</member>
</members>
</callManagerGroup>
<loadInformation6  model="IP Phone 7910"></loadInformation6>
<loadInformation124  model="Addon 7914"></loadInformation124>
<loadInformation9  model="IP Phone 7935"></loadInformation9>
<loadInformation8  model="IP Phone 7940">P00308000500</loadInformation8>
<loadInformation7  model="IP Phone 7960">P00308000500</loadInformation7>
<loadInformation20000  model="IP Phone 7905"></loadInformation20000>
<loadInformation30008  model="IP Phone 7902"></loadInformation30008>
<loadInformation30002  model="IP Phone 7920"></loadInformation30002>
<loadInformation30019  model="IP Phone 7936"></loadInformation30019>
<loadInformation30006  model="IP Phone 7970">SCCP70.8-3-3S.loads
  </loadInformation30006>
<loadInformation119  model="IP Phone 7971">SCCP70.8-3-3S.loads
  </loadInformation119>
<loadInformation30018  model="IP Phone 7961"></loadInformation30018>
<loadInformation30007  model="IP Phone 7912"></loadInformation30007>
</Default>
```

As you can see, XML files are formatted into various tags (if you have had experience with HTML, this is very similar). Each configuration item will have an open and close tag. For example, consider the following line:

```
<processNodeName>172.16.1.1</processNodeName>
```

This line tells the Cisco IP phone the IP address of the Cisco Unified CME router. The <processNodeName> tag opens the line and the </processNodeName> tag closes the line. The IP address information of the CME router is in between the tags. Looking through this default configuration file, you can see that three pieces of information are provided to the IP phone:

■ The correct Ethernet port to use (which is always 2000, by default)

■ The CME router IP address

■ Phone firmware information

The Cisco Unified CME router has been configured with the correct firmware information only for the Cisco 7940, 7960, 7970, and 7971 IP Phone models, so the XMLDefault.cnf.xml file displays only these firmware images.

If you were to connect a Cisco IP phone to the network at this point, it would boot, retrieve the correct VLAN information, get its IP address, contact the TFTP server, and download the generic configuration and firmware files. If you were to look at one of these devices, the display screen would look like the image shown in Figure 4.7.

Figure 4.7   *Cisco IP Phone Using the CME Router Generic Configuration File*

You can see that the phone has registered, is receiving the correct date and time information, and has active softkeys on the bottom of the display window. However, there is no line information shown next to the line buttons. When the handset of the phone is lifted, no dial tone is played. You learn more about this topic in Chapter 5, "Basic CME IP Phone Configuration," where you will configure the IP phones in the CME router.

Exam Preparation Tasks

Review All the Key Topics

Key Topic

Review the most important topics in the chapter, noted with the key topics icon in the outer margin of the page. Table 4.4 lists and describes these key topics and identifies the page number on which each is found.

Table 4.4   *Key Topics for Chapter 4*

Key Topic Element	Description	Page Number
Table 4.2	Lists hardware platforms supporting CME	105
Figure 4.2	Shows possible CME integration scenarios	111
List	Discusses three types of CME licenses	112
Example 4.1	Configuration to install CME	117
List	Cisco IP phone boot process	118
Example 4.3	Configuration allowing CME router to act as TFTP server	120
Example 4.4	Key **max-ephones** and **max-dn** commands to enable CME services	121
Syntax	Key **ip source-address** command to enable CME services	125
Example 4.8	Command to generate IP phone configuration files	126
Example 4.10	Inside view of the XML Default.cnf.xml configuration file	127

Complete the Tables and Lists from Memory

Print a copy of Appendix C, "Memory Tables" (found on the CD), or at least the section for this chapter, and complete the tables and lists from memory. Appendix D, "Memory Tables Answer Key," also on the CD, includes completed tables and lists to check your work.

Definitions of Key Terms

Define the following key terms from this chapter, and check your answers in the glossary.

Survivable Remote Site Telephony (SRST)

IOS license

feature license

phone user license

Ensuring the Foundation: This section provides a quick review of the foundation that must be in place to allow for a working IP telephony environment.

Ephone and Ephone-DN—The Keys to Ringing Phones: This section is the primary focus of the chapter as it covers the process to create and assign directory numbers to Cisco IP phones.

Supporting Auto-Registration and Auto-Assignment of IP Phones: To make the process of configuring IP phones simpler, Cisco allows you to auto-register the phones and auto-assign directory numbers. These concepts are covered in this section.

Additional IP Phone Configuration Parameters: Once the IP phones have been assigned phone numbers, you can tune a few settings to customize their look and feel. This section discusses changing the date and time format, phone locale, and system messages.

*

CHAPTER 5

Basic CME IP Phone Configuration

The anticipation must be killing you! You've gone through four chapters on VoIP technology and a phone has yet to ring. That is about to change in this chapter. The foundation system is in place and now the configuration of the Cisco IP phones can begin. Ninety percent of this configuration focuses on two configuration concepts: ephone and ephone-dn. These two configurations represent the logical representation of IP phones and directory numbers, respectively.

This chapter explains the configuration of ephone and ephone-dn on your CME router. Using these skills, you will be able to configure a local working phone system.

"Do I Know This Already?" Quiz

The "Do I Know This Already?" quiz allows you to assess whether you should read this entire chapter or simply jump to the "Exam Preparation Tasks" section for review. If you are in doubt, read the entire chapter. Table 5.1 outlines the major headings in this chapter and the corresponding "Do I Know This Already?" quiz questions. You can find the answers in Appendix A, "Answers to the 'Do I Know This Already?' Quizzes."

Table 5.1   *"Do I Know This Already?" Foundation Topics Section-to-Question Mapping*

Foundations Topics Section	Questions Covered in This Section
Ensuring the Foundation	1
Ephone and Ephone-DN— The Keys to Ringing Phones	2–7
Supporting Auto-Registration and Auto-Assignment of IP Phones	8
Additional IP Phone Configuration Parameters	9–10

1. Which of the following commands specifies the firmware file that a Cisco 7960 Phone should use when contacting the CME router?

   a.   tftp-server

   b.   load

   c.   firmware-load 7960

   d.   firmware-load

2. When you enter the command **ephone-dn 20** from global configuration mode, what mode does the CME router use for the ephone-dn?

   a.   Distinct

   b.   Single-line

   c.   Dual-line

   d.   Limited

3. Which of the following features would not be allowed with an ephone-dn configured in single-line mode?

   a.   Hold

   b.   Speaker

   c.   Redial

   d.   Conference

4. What criteria does the CME router use to link an ephone to a physical Cisco IP phone?

   a.   MAC address

   b.   IP address

   c.   MAC address and IP address

   d.   Serial number

5. You would like to assign ephone-dn 11 (DN 2703) to ephone 8, line 4. You would like the line to ring with three pulses. Which of the following commands will make this assignment?

   a.   button 4:2703 feature

   b.   button 4:11 feature

   c.   button 4f11

   d.   button 4f2703

6. You have entered the following configuration on the CME router:

```
CME_Voice(config)# ephone-dn 10 dual-line
CME_Voice(config-ephone-dn)# number 1010
CME_Voice(config-ephone-dn)# preference 0
CME_Voice(config-ephone-dn)# huntstop channel
CME_Voice(config)# ephone-dn 11 dual-line
CME_Voice(config-ephone-dn)# number 1010
CME_Voice(config-ephone-dn)# huntstop
CME_Voice(config-ephone-dn)# preference 1
```

You assign ephone-dn 10 to ephone 1 and ephone-dn 11 to ephone 2. What will be the results of this configuration?

   a.   Both ephone 1 and 2 will ring on an incoming call to 1010.

   b.   Only ephone 1 will ring on an incoming call to 1010; ephone 2 will never ring, even if ephone 1 is on a call.

   c.   Only ephone 1 will ring on an incoming call to 1010; ephone 2 will only ring if ephone 1 is currently on a call.

   d.   The configuration is invalid; multiple ephone-dns cannot be assigned the same number.

7. How does CME support shared-line environments that allow multiple phones to receive calls on the same DN simultaneously?

   a. Using feature-ring configurations

   b. Using shared-dn configurations

   c. Using overlay configurations

   d. Using dual-line configurations

8. A Cisco IP phone attempts to register with the CME router. Currently, the IP phone has no explicit ephone configuration in CME. What will the CME router do by default?

   a. Reject the registration

   b. Register the phone and create an ephone entry in the running-config

   c. Register the phone but not create an ephone entry in the running-config

   d. Register the phone, create an ephone entry, and auto-assign a DN

9. You have just updated ephone 9 to use DN 1010 on line 5. Which of the following represents the minimum configuration necessary to apply the changes?

   a. No additional configuration is necessary; the CME router updates the phone via SCCP.

   b. The phone must be restarted using the **restart** command.

   c. The phone must be restarted using the **reset** command.

   d. The phone must be hard booted by performing a **shutdown** followed by a **no shutdown** on the connecting switch interface.

10. Which of the following commands will change the default "Cisco Unified CME" title displayed on the bottom of all Cisco IP phones?

   a. banner

   b. phone banner

   c. prompt

   d. system message

Foundation Topics

Ensuring the Foundation

Chapter 3, "Connecting IP Phones to the LAN Infrastructure," and Chapter 4, "Installing Cisco Unified Communications Manager Express," put configurations in place that are key to a working CME system. It would be wise to take a high-level review of those concepts before jumping straight into the configuration of the IP phones.

Just about all the concepts discussed so far focus on the boot process of the Cisco IP phone. The following list outlines the Cisco IP phone boot process, which is illustrated in Figure 5.1:

1. The 802.3af PoE switch sends a small DC voltage on the Ethernet cable, detects an unpowered 802.3af device, and supplies power to the line.

2. The switch delivers voice VLAN information to the Cisco IP phone using Cisco Discovery Protocol (CDP).

3. The IP phone sends a DHCP request on its voice VLAN. The DHCP server replies with IP addressing information, including DHCP Option 150, which directs the IP phone to the TFTP server.

4. The IP phone contacts the TFTP server and downloads its configuration file and firmware.

5. Based on the IP address listed in the configuration file, the IP phone contacts the call processing server (the CME router in this case), which supports VoIP functions.

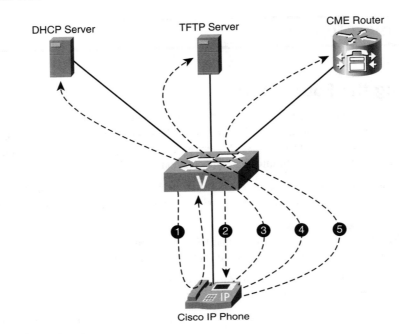

Figure 5.1   *Cisco IP Phone Boot Process*

Note   Figure 5.1 shows the DHCP server, TFTP server, and CME router as three separate devices. To save resources, smaller networks typically combine all three of these functions into one device. In this case, the CME router would also act as the DHCP and TFTP server for the network.

To meet the demands of this boot process, we have put the following configuration in place over the last two chapters:

- Voice VLAN

- DHCP services

- TFTP services

Voice VLAN

To separate the voice and data traffic, you must configure each port connecting to a Cisco IP phone for a voice VLAN. In Example 5.1, the voice VLAN is 100 and the data VLAN (for the PC device attaching to the IP phone) is 200.

Example 5.1   *Configuring Voice VLANs*

```
Switch# configure terminal
Switch(config)# interface fa0/1
Switch(config-if)# switchport mode access
Switch(config-if)# switchport voice vlan 100
Switch(config-if)# switchport access vlan 200
Switch(config-if)# spanning-tree portfast
```

This configuration also includes the command **spanning-tree portfast**, which disables the Spanning Tree Protocol (STP) on interfaces connecting to Cisco IP phones. STP is a protocol designed to detect loops in a switched network. For example, if you connected two switches with two crossover cables as shown in Figure 5.2, it would cause a loop in the network.

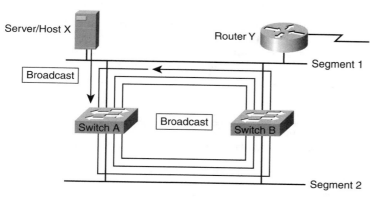

Figure 5.2   *Broadcast Storm Caused by Redundant Switch Connections*

As shown in Figure 5.2, a broadcast packet will loop around the network, because the very nature of a switch is to send a broadcast packet out all ports. STP stops these types of loops and is a critical component in managing redundant switch connections.

Unfortunately, STP adds a 30-second delay any time a new device is connected to a switch. This delay allows the port to detect other switches connected to the port (and try to determine if there is a loop in the network) and learn the Media Access Control (MAC) address of the attached device. With the speed of our network devices today, this 30-second delay can prolong the boot process of a Cisco IP phone considerably because the initial DHCP requests from the phone will fail. The **spanning-tree portfast** command eliminates this 30-second delay, allowing the port to become active immediately.

DHCP Services

Once the IP phone receives its voice VLAN information, it begins sending DHCP requests. The configuration in Example 5.2 allows a Cisco router to become a DHCP server for the voice VLAN and deliver the needed IP address information to the IP phones.

Example 5.2   *Configuring a DHCP Scope on a Router*

```
ROUTER(config)# ip dhcp pool VOICE_SCOPE
ROUTER(dhcp-config)# network 172.16.1.0 255.255.255.0
ROUTER(dhcp-config)# default-router 172.16.1.1
ROUTER(dhcp-config)# option 150 172.16.1.1
ROUTER(dhcp-config)# dns-server 4.2.2.2
```

In addition to delivering the standard DHCP information (IP address, subnet mask, default gateway, DNS), the DHCP server delivers phone Option 150, which gives the IP phone the IP address of the TFTP server.

TFTP Services

The TFTP server plays the role of "file server" in the IP telephony network. The IP phones download their configuration and firmware files from this server. The CME router generates these configuration files as you work through the initial configuration. For example, you must specify the correct firmware loads for the CME router to use with the IP phones. As you do this, it generates or modifies existing configuration files to reflect these changes, as shown in Example 5.3.

Example 5.3   *Configuring Firmware Loads in CME*

```
CME_Voice(config)# telephony-service
CME_Voice(config-telephony)# load 7970 SCCP70.8-3-3S.loads
Updating CNF files
CNF files update complete
```

Because there has been no individual phone configurations entered up to this point, the only configuration file sent to the Cisco IP phones is the XMLDefault.cnf.xml file. This file contains the IP address and port number used to connect to the call processing server (the CME router, in our case) and the names of the firmware file the IP phone should use. Once the IP phone has this configuration file, it downloads the necessary firmware and contacts the CME router.

Note   In CME 4.0 and later, configuration and firmware files can be stored on an external TFTP server using the command **cnf-file location tftp://**<*ip address of TFTP server*> from telephony service configuration mode. This can save some valuable flash space on your router.

And that's where the last two chapters have led you. The Cisco IP phone has come to the CME router and said, "I would like to use *you* as my call processing device." The CME router receives this request and says, "Great! But who are you?" The CME router delivers no additional configuration to the IP phone because you have yet to enter it. So let's enter away! Welcome to the world of ephones and ephone-dn.

Ephone and Ephone-DN—The Keys to Ringing Phones

In the movie *The Matrix*, Thomas Anderson (also known as Neo) finds out that the world around him is not real, but rather a computer-generated environment. He soon becomes a part of the Resistance, who fights against the forces behind this computer-generated world. He soon meets up with Morpheus, who teaches him more about this new world. Let's pick up with their dialog here:

> **Morpheus:** This is the construct. It's our loading program. We can load anything from clothing, to equipment, weapons, training simulations, anything we need.
>
> **Neo:** Right now we're inside a computer program?
>
> **Morpheus:** Is it really so hard to believe? Your clothes are different. The plugs in your arms and head are gone. Your hair is changed. Your appearance now is what we call residual self image. It is the mental projection of your digital self.

The concepts of ephone and ephone-dn are not too far beyond this. You must now configure the CME router to support IP phones. Think about this as your construct, "the mental projection of your digital phones." Each ephone you configure is a representation of the settings of a physical Cisco IP phone sitting in your office somewhere. Each ephone-dn represents a directory number that you can assign to one or more ephones. Because ephone-dns are assigned to ephones, you should configure them first.

> **Note**   While viewing of *The Matrix* is not yet required for Cisco certification, I (Jeremy) believe about 90 percent of the concepts in Cisco can somehow be linked back to this movie, which I highly recommend.

Understanding and Configuring Ephone-DNs

An ephone-dn in its simplest form is just a directory number that can be assigned to one or more buttons on one or more Cisco IP phones. You can configure each ephone-dn you create as either a single- or dual-line mode ephone-dn. Here's the difference:

- **Single-line ephone-dn:** In single-line mode, the ephone-dn is only able to make or receive one call at a time. If a call arrives on an ephone-dn where there is already an active call, the caller will receive a busy signal.

- **Dual-line ephone-dn:** In dual-line mode, the ephone-dn is able to handle two simultaneous calls. This is useful for supporting features like call waiting, conference calling, and consultative transfers.

In most network environments, dual-line configurations are useful for user IP phones, whereas single-line configurations are useful for network functions (such as intercom or paging). The syntax in Example 5.4 configures two ephone-dns, the first as a single-line and the second as a dual-line.

Example 5.4 *Configuring Ephone-DNs*

```
CME_Voice# config t
Enter configuration commands, one per line.  End with CNTL/Z.
CME_Voice(config)# ephone-dn ?
  <1-150>  ephone-dn tag
CME_Voice(config)# ephone-dn 1
CME_Voice(config-ephone-dn)# number ?
  WORD  A sequence of digits - representing telephone number
CME_Voice(config-ephone-dn)# number 1000
CME_Voice(config-ephone-dn)# exit
CME_Voice(config)# ephone-dn 2 ?
  dual-line  dual-line DN (2 calls per line/button)
  <cr>
CME_Voice(config)# ephone-dn 2 dual-line
CME_Voice(config-ephone-dn)# number 1001
```

That's all there is to it! Notice the range of ephone-dn tags from the context-sensitive help is 1–150. This tag is a logical number, which will be useful when assigning the ephone-dn to an ephone. You can choose any ephone-dn tag from the range when creating the ephone-dn as long as the total number of ephone-dns does not exceed the number specified using the **max-dn** command.

Note Creating more ephone-dns than you have specified using the **max-dn** command will result in the following error message:

```
CME_Voice(config)# ephone-dn 49
dn tag 49 exceeds legal range 1 to max-dn 48
```

To correct this error, increase the max-dn value from telephony service configuration mode.

The **number** syntax (which is used to assign a directory number to an ephone-dn) also supports a secondary number value. For example, you could enter

```
CME_Voice(config)#ephone-dn 2 dual-line
CME_Voice(config-ephone-dn)#number 1001 secondary 4805551001
```

This allows the ephone-dn to answer for multiple phone numbers. This could be useful if you wanted an internal extension to be reachable if someone on the internal network dialed a four-digit extension or the full PSTN Direct Inward Dial (DID) number.

Note Direct Inward Dial (DID) is a feature supported by PSTN carriers that allows internal extensions to be reached by PSTN callers directly without the need to route calls through a receptionist.

Understanding and Configuring Ephones

When you configure an ephone in CME, it represents the configuration applied directly to a single Cisco IP phone or SoftPhone managed by the CME router. Just as with the ephone-dns, the **max-ephone** parameter directly impacts the number of ephones you are able to create and manage on a CME router. The syntax in Example 5.5 adds an ephone to the CME router.

Example 5.5   *Creating an Ephone*

```
CME_Voice(config)# ephone ?
  <1-24>  Ethernet phone tag
CME_Voice(config)# ephone 1
CME_Voice(config-ephone)#
```

Once you enter the command **ephone** *<tag>*, the CME router moves you into ephone configuration mode. Every command you enter after this directly affects the Cisco IP phone matched to this ephone.

After initially creating the ephone, you need to logically link it to the physical IP phone it represents. The CME router uses the MAC address of a Cisco IP phone for this purpose. There are three ways to find the MAC address of a Cisco IP phone:

- **On the box of the Cisco IP phone:** The box the Cisco IP phone ships in has the MAC address of the phone on it next to a UPC code.

- **On the back of the Cisco IP phone:** A sticker on the back side of the phone lists the MAC address of the device. The address appears next to a UPC code.

- **From the Settings menu of the Cisco IP phone:** All Cisco IP phones have a Settings button that allows you to manually configure various settings for the device. On most models of Cisco IP phones, choosing **Settings** and then **Network Configuration** will display the MAC address of the phone on the LCD display.

Note   Having a UPC code containing the MAC address information of the IP phone is beneficial if you have a handheld UPC scanner (barcode scanner). You can set up the scanner to allow you to scan the MAC address of each device and then input the extension number into an Excel spreadsheet. You can then export this information for bulk entry of devices.

When you have the MAC address of the IP phone, you can enter it from ephone configuration mode, as shown in Example 5.6.

Example 5.6　*Assigning a MAC Address to an Ephone*

Key Topic

```
CME_Voice(config)# ephone 1
CME_Voice(config-ephone)# mac-address ?
  H.H.H  Mac address
  <cr>
CME_Voice(config-ephone)# mac-address 0014.1c48.e71a
```

After you have entered the ephone MAC address information, you can verify the IP phone registration status by using the **show ephone** command, shown in Example 5.7.

Example 5.7　*Verifying Ephone Registration Status*

```
CME_Voice# show ephone
ephone-1 Mac:0014.1C48.E6D1 TCP socket:[2] activeLine:0 REGISTERED in SCCP ver 11
  and Server in ver 8
mediaActive:0 offhook:0 ringing:0 reset:0 reset_sent:0 paging 0 debug:0 caps:8
IP:172.30.60.31 52777 Telecaster 7960  keepalive 0 max_line 6

ephone-2 Mac:000C.2957.ACF5 TCP socket:[-1] activeLine:0 UNREGISTERED
mediaActive:0 offhook:0 ringing:0 reset:0 reset_sent:0 paging 0 debug:0 caps:0
IP:0.0.0.0 0 Unknown 0  keepalive 0 max_line 0
```

This **show ephone** output shows two configured ephones: one currently registered (ephone 1) with the IP address 172.30.60.31 and the other currently unregistered (ephone 2).

Tip　If you ever see a phone's status shown as DECEASED in the **show ephone** output, the CME router has lost connectivity with the IP phone through a TCP keepalive failure. The UNREGISTERED status indicates the CME router closed the connection to the IP phone in a normal manner.

With the ephone linked to a physical Cisco IP phone, you can now begin assigning the buttons to the ephone-dns.

Associating Ephones and Ephone-DNs

Linking ephones and ephone-dns is probably the most confusing section of the CME configuration because there are so many options. You can assign ephone-dns by using the **button** command from ephone configuration mode. The basic syntax of this command is as follows:

```
button <physical button> <separator> <ephone-dn>
```

Example 5.8 demonstrates the basic use of the **button** command.

Example 5.8   *Assigning Ephone-DN 2 to Button 1 on Ephone 1*

```
CME_Voice(config)# ephone 1
CME_Voice(config-ephone)# button 1:2
CME_Voice(config-ephone)# restart
```

The **button 1:2** syntax assigns ephone-dn 2 (configured in the prior section) to button 1 of ephone 1. The colon (:) separator designates that this is a "normal ring" button assignment. That is, calls to 1001 (the number of ephone-dn 2) will cause the IP phone to audibly ring and the light on the handset to blink. The **restart** syntax causes the phone to perform a warm reboot and redownload its configuration file from the TFTP server. Figure 5.3 illustrates what the physical IP phone looks like after making this assignment.

Figure 5.3   *Ephone 1 Following Ephone-DN Assignment*

You can assign multiple lines to a phone by either entering multiple **button** commands, as shown in Example 5.9, or putting multiple entries on the same line, as shown in Example 5.10.

Example 5.9   *Assigning Buttons Using Multiple Commands*

```
CME_Voice(config)# ephone 1
CME_Voice(config-ephone)# button 1:2
CME_Voice(config-ephone)# button 2:1
```

Example 5.10   *Assigning Buttons Using One Command*

```
CME_Voice(config)# ephone 1
CME_Voice(config-ephone)# button 1:2 2:1
```

The **show ephone** command is also useful for verifying button assignments, as shown in Example 5.11.

Example 5.11   *Verifying Button Assignments Using the* **show ephone** *Command*

```
CME_Voice# show ephone
ephone-1 Mac:0014.6A16.C2DA TCP socket:[5] activeLine:0 REGISTERED in SCCP ver 8
  and Server in ver 8
mediaActive:0 offhook:0 ringing:0 reset:0 reset_sent:0 paging 0 debug:0 caps:7
IP:172.30.60.32 14719 7912   keepalive 2701 max_line 2 dual-line
button 1: dn 2 number 1001 CH1   IDLE          CH2   IDLE
button 2: dn 1 number 1000 CH1   IDLE
```

Notice the last two lines of this **show** output. You are now able to verify the ephone-dns assigned to the ephone. As an added benefit, the output displays the actual extension as well. Notice the first button shows CH1 and CH2 as IDLE while the second button just shows CH1 as IDLE. This is because ephone-dn 2 was configured with the dual-line syntax, which allows two active channels.

As mentioned previously, using the colon separator with the **button** command makes a normal ephone-dn assignment to a device. There are a host of different characters you can use for a separator, as shown in Table 5.2.

Table 5.2   *Separators for Use with the* **button** *Command*

Separator Character	Function
:	**Normal ring:** Line rings normally on incoming call and handset light flashes as phone rings.
b	**Call waiting beep, no ring:** The line ringer is suppressed on incoming call, but the handset light still flashes. Call waiting beeps are allowed during active calls.
f	**Feature ring:** The line performs a triple ring on incoming calls. This can be useful as a distinctive ring feature.
m	**Monitor mode:** The line does not ring for incoming calls and is unable to place outgoing calls. This mode simply monitors the status of a shared line. For example, if DN 1001 was assigned to ephone 1, you might also assign DN 1001 to the receptionist ephone 2 in monitor mode. This allows the receptionist to see if DN 1001 is currently in use, but not make or receive calls using the line.
o	**Overlay line (no call waiting):** Overlay lines are used to create a shared-line experience between multiple ephones. Overlay lines will be discussed later in this chapter.
c	**Overlay line (with call waiting):** Same idea as the prior separator, but adds call waiting functionality. Overlay lines will be discussed later in this chapter.

Key Topic

Separator Character	Function
x	**Overlay expansion/rollover:** Allows calls to roll over to additional lines of the IP phone when a call is received on an overlay line on which there is already an active call established.
s	**Silent ring:** Disables ring and call waiting beep for incoming calls. The visual lights and onscreen indicators remain active.
w	**Watch mode:** Performs the same function as monitor mode (**m**), but watches *all* the lines on the phone for which the watched line is the primary. For example, if you configured a receptionist to watch DN 1001, which was the primary extension for ephone 1, the receptionist would see that ephone 1 was busy if DN 1001 was in use or if *any of the other lines* on the ephone using DN 1001 as its primary extension were in use. Again, this is primarily for receptionist use; a line in watch mode cannot receive or make phone calls.

For example, a company might want to create four DNs for their three IP phones to meet these requirements:

- IP phone 1 (normal employee)
  - Line 1: directory number 1010 (normal ring)
  - Line 2: directory number 1015 (feature ring)
- IP phone 2 (normal employee)
  - Line 1: directory number 1011 (normal ring)
  - Line 2: directory number 1015 (feature ring)
- IP phone 3 (receptionist)
  - Line 1: directory number 1012 (normal ring)
  - Line 2: directory number 1010 (monitor phone 1 status)
  - Line 3: directory number 1011 (monitor phone 2 status)
  - Line 4: directory number 1015 (feature ring)

The configuration in Example 5.12 will accomplish this scenario.

Example 5.12   *Multiple Ephone-DN and Ephone Configuration*

```
CME_Voice(config)# ephone-dn 10 dual-line
CME_Voice(config-ephone-dn)# number 1010
CME_Voice(config)# ephone-dn 11 dual-line
CME_Voice(config-ephone-dn)# number 1011
CME_Voice(config)# ephone-dn 12 dual-line
CME_Voice(config-ephone-dn)# number 1012
CME_Voice(config)# ephone-dn 13 dual-line
CME_Voice(config-ephone-dn)# number 1015
CME_Voice(config)# ephone 5
CME_Voice(config-ephone)# mac-address 00a0.932a.b34c
CME_Voice(config-ephone)# button 1:10 2f13
CME_Voice(config-ephone)# exit
CME_Voice(config)# ephone 6
CME_Voice(config-ephone)# mac-address 00a0.aa25.431b
CME_Voice(config-ephone)# button 1:11 2f13
CME_Voice(config-ephone)# exit
CME_Voice(config)# ephone 7
CME_Voice(config-ephone)# mac-address 00a0.a819.90a1
CME_Voice(config-ephone)# button 1:12
CME_Voice(config-ephone)# button 2m10
CME_Voice(config-ephone)# button 3m11
CME_Voice(config-ephone)# button 4f13
CME_Voice(config-ephone)# exit
```

Note   The buttons for the receptionist phone also could have been entered using the command **button 1:12 2m10 3m11 4f13**. Example 5.12 shows them entered on separate lines to make it a little easier to understand.

Working with Shared-Line and Overlay Options

At this point, you know have the knowledge to assign individual extensions to IP phones using the **button** command. This gives you the ability to configure a PBX model environment in which each phone has a unique extension number. However, because Cisco designed the CME product line for small-to-midsized business environments, you will eventually encounter the need to configure a keyswitch or hybrid model system that uses shared lines.

Configuring a basic shared line in CME is easy. Simply assign the same ephone-dn to multiple ephones, as shown in Example 5.13.

Example 5.13   *Configuring a Basic Shared-Line System*

```
CME_Voice(config)# ephone-dn 10 dual-line
CME_Voice(config-ephone-dn)# number 1010
CME_Voice(config)# ephone 8
CME_Voice(config-ephone)# button 1:10
CME_Voice(config-ephone)# restart
CME_Voice(config-ephone)# exit
CME_Voice(config)# ephone 9
CME_Voice(config-ephone)# button 1:10
CME_Voice(config-ephone)# restart
CME_Voice(config-ephone)# exit
```

Once the phones restart, the same DN (1010) appears on both. Incoming calls to DN 1010 will ring on both phones, and whoever answers the call first gets the call. The main problem with this configuration is that only one person can use the shared line at a time. If the line is in use, it appears on other phones using the same line, as shown in Figure 5.4.

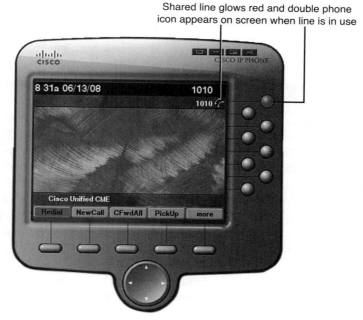

Figure 5.4   *Shared Line in Use*

On Cisco IP phones that support LED-lit line keys, the line indicator will change to red, preventing additional calls from being made. In some shared-line environments, this is a desirable outcome because each shared line directly maps to an incoming PSTN connection. If one person is using the line, the PSTN line is truly "in use" and should restrict others from using it.

Other environments may desire the shared line be made available to others (to place and receive calls) even if the shared line is in use. For example, take a technical support group of five employees who all receive support calls from the organization on the shared DN 1010. Just because one person from the support group is on a call should not mean that the others cannot make or receive calls. This situation calls for multiple ephone-dns with the same extension number. Example 5.14 shows the configuration.

Example 5.14   *Configuring a Shared-Line System with Multiple Ephone-DNs*

```
CME_Voice(config)# ephone-dn 10 dual-line
CME_Voice(config-ephone-dn)# number 1010
CME_Voice(config)# ephone-dn 11 dual-line
CME_Voice(config-ephone-dn)# number 1010
CME_Voice(config)# ephone 8
CME_Voice(config-ephone)# button 1:10
CME_Voice(config-ephone)# restart
CME_Voice(config-ephone)# exit
CME_Voice(config)# ephone 9
CME_Voice(config-ephone)# button 1:11
CME_Voice(config-ephone)# restart
CME_Voice(config-ephone)# exit
```

The configuration in Example 5.14 takes care of the outgoing call issue because the two ephones are using truly unique, dual-line ephone-dns. If ephone 8 picks up the line, the CME system only sees ephone-dn 10 in use and does not show the line-in-use indicator on ephone 9.

Incoming calls do pose a problem. When the CME router receives a call for 1010, it now sees two equal cost paths to get there (ephone-dn 10 and ephone-dn 11). So how is it going to handle this dilemma? Just pick one completely at random. So, sometimes ephone 8 will get the call and sometimes ephone 9 will get the call. If this is your desired behavior, great! You are done with the configuration. However, most people would like more control over how the call flows than a random line selection.

You can achieve control over which ephone receives the call by using the **preference** and **huntstop** commands. The **preference** command dictates which ephone-dn is more preferred than the other by assigning a value from 0–10, where the *lower* preference numbers are better (that doesn't make much sense, does it?). For example, if you were to modify the ephone-dn configuration from Example 5.14 to look like Example 5.15, ephone-dn 10 would *always* receive incoming calls for the DN 1010. Only if the ephone-dn 10 was busy or unavailable would ephone-dn 11 begin receiving incoming calls.

Example 5.15   *Using the* preference *Command with Multiple Ephone-DNs*

```
CME_Voice(config)# ephone-dn 10 dual-line
CME_Voice(config-ephone-dn)# number 1010
CME_Voice(config-ephone-dn)# preference 0
CME_Voice(config)# ephone-dn 11 dual-line
CME_Voice(config-ephone-dn)# number 1010
CME_Voice(config-ephone-dn)# preference 1
```

> **Note**   Preference 0 is the default preference for all ephone-dn configurations. Most default configurations are not visible in the running configuration of the router. Don't be alarmed if you do a **show run** command and see the **preference 0** syntax you entered disappear from the ephone-dn configuration.

That brings up another potential problem. Each of the ephone-dns are configured with the **dual-line** syntax. This enables them to place calls on hold and make an additional call, transfer a call, start a conference call, or receive calls via call waiting. Whoa, put the brakes on right there. Because ephone-dn 10 was configured as a lower preference than ephone-dn 11, the first call to DN 1010 would go to ephone-dn 10. If a second call came in to DN 1010 while ephone-dn 10 was still on the active call, the call would be received via call waiting on ephone-dn 10 rather than rolling over to ephone-dn 11. So, you would have one employee (on ephone-dn 10) taking on two calls while the other employee (on ephone-dn 11) sits idle. That doesn't seem efficient, does it? This is where the **huntstop** command comes in handy.

The **huntstop** command has two forms: **huntstop** and **huntstop channel**. The name of this command describes its function. It *stops* the CME router from *hunting* for other matches to the destination pattern. Simply entering **huntstop** tells the CME router, "stop hunting for other matches with *this* ephone-dn." Entering **huntstop channel** says to the router, "stop hunting for other matches with *one channel* of this ephone-dn." Example 5.16 shows how to stop the problems with the configuration in Example 5.15.

Example 5.16   *Using the* **preference** *Command with* **huntstop**

```
CME_Voice(config)# ephone-dn 10 dual-line
CME_Voice(config-ephone-dn)# number 1010
CME_Voice(config-ephone-dn)# preference 0
CME_Voice(config-ephone-dn)# huntstop channel
CME_Voice(config-ephone-dn)# no huntstop
CME_Voice(config)# ephone-dn 11 dual-line
CME_Voice(config-ephone-dn)# number 1010
CME_Voice(config-ephone-dn)# huntstop channel
CME_Voice(config-ephone-dn)# preference 1
```

> **Key Topic**

Notice the configuration of ephone-dn 10 uses the **huntstop channel** command followed by the **no huntstop** command. This may seem counterintuitive at first, but follow the logic: if you use *only* the **huntstop channel** command, the router will simply stop hunting if the first channel of ephone-dn 10 is in use. Additional calls to DN 1010 will result in a busy signal. By combining the **huntstop channel** command with the **no huntstop** command, you are telling the CME router, "Stop hunting for other channels on ephone-dn 10, but don't stop hunting completely! Look for other ephone-dns with this DN." This results in ephone-dn 11 receiving a call to DN 1010 if ephone-dn 10 is currently active on a call. If both ephone-dns 10 and 11 are on an active call, an incoming call to DN 1010 will receive a busy signal.

Now back to the original scenario: There are five employees in an organization's technical support group who receive calls on DN 1010. The configuration in Example 5.16 will accomplish this objective (if there were an additional three ephone-dns added with DN 1010 for the other employees), but the tech support employees who have the preference 0 and 1 ephone-dns assigned to their IP phone will get lots of calls while the tech support employees with the preference 2, 3, and 4 ephone-dns will only get calls if the first two are busy. A better system might have *all* the IP phones ring when on a call to DN 1010, and whichever tech support employee answers the call first will take the call.

This design is a custom fit for ephone-dn button overlays. Overlaying ephone-dns allows you to assign multiple DNs to a single extension. Back in Table 5.2, there were three "overlay separators" listed that you can use with the **button** command. To save page flipping, here they are:

- **o separator:** Overlay line with no call waiting

- **c separator:** Overlay line with call waiting

- **x separator:** Overlay line with line rollover to other lines on Cisco IP phone

So, to change the previous configuration into a shared-line configuration where all IP phones would ring on an incoming call to DN 1010, you could use the syntax shown in Example 5.17.

Example 5.17   *Using Button Overlays*

```
CME_Voice(config)# ephone-dn 10
CME_Voice(config-ephone-dn)# number 1010
CME_Voice(config-ephone-dn)# preference 0
CME_Voice(config-ephone-dn)# no huntstop
CME_Voice(config)# ephone-dn 11
CME_Voice(config-ephone-dn)# number 1010
CME_Voice(config-ephone-dn)# preference 1
CME_Voice(config-ephone-dn)# exit
CME_Voice(config)# ephone 8
CME_Voice(config-ephone)# button 1o10,11
CME_Voice(config-ephone)# exit
CME_Voice(config)# ephone 9
CME_Voice(config-ephone)# button 1o10,11
CME_Voice(config-ephone)# exit
CME_Voice(config)# telephony-service
CME_Voice(config-telephony)# restart all
```

> **Tip**   Rather than restart each IP phone individually, you can use the **restart all** command from telephony service configuration mode to restart all IP phones managed by the CME router.
>
> Also, you can assign up to ten overlay lines per line instance of an IP phone.

An incoming call to DN 1010 would now ring both ephones 8 and 9 because ephone-dns 10 and 11 are overlayed on button 1. Notice that Example 5.17 uses the **o** separator, which means overlay with no call waiting. The first call that comes in to DN 1010 will cause both ephones 8 and 9 to ring. Whichever phone answers the call will take responsibility for it and the CME router will flag the ephone as "busy" (in a call). If a second call comes in while the first call is still active, the ephone that did not answer the first call will ring. The ephone that is still active on the first call will not hear a call waiting beep while the line is ringing. If you wanted to have call waiting active for the overlay lines, you could change the **button** command syntax to **button 1c10,11** for both phones. If you have changed to a **c** button separator, the phone currently on an active call would hear a call waiting beep. This is not the call waiting beep of ephone-dn 10 (which received the first call) but the call waiting beep of ephone-dn 11 (which is receiving the second call).

Combining Overlay and Dual-Line Functions

You may or may not have noticed that the configuration in Example 5.17 was modified so that ephone-dn 10 and ephone-dn 11 were *not* configured with the **dual-line** syntax. This allows the **o** and **c** overlay separators to act as advertised. If the **dual-line** syntax was added to the ephone-dn configuration shown in Example 5.17, the results would depend on the separator used for the overlay configuration.

If the **ephone-dn dual-line** syntax was used with the **o** separator for the **button** command, the first phone call to DN 1010 would ring both phones. Whichever phone answers first gets the call. When a second call comes in, the phone that did not answer the first call rings and the phone that is currently on a call hears a call waiting beep. Even though the **o** separator states "overlay with no call waiting," the nature of the **dual-line** syntax allows the DN to receive calls while on call waiting. If the phone that took the first call placed the first caller on hold and took the second call, the third call to DN 1010 would only ring the second phone.

If the **ephone-dn dual-line** syntax was used with the **c** separator for the **button** command, the first phone call to DN 1010 would ring both phones. Whichever phone answers first gets the call. When a second call comes in, the phone that did not answer the first call rings and the phone that is currently on a call hears a call waiting beep. This call waiting beep is due to the **dual-line** syntax rather than the **c** separator. The CME router still sees the second channel of ephone-dn 10 available, so it uses that. If the phone user who took the first call placed the first caller on hold and took the second call, the third call to DN 1010 would cause a call waiting beep on the first phone and ring the second phone. This second call waiting beep is due to the c separator because all channels on the first ephone-dn are now used up.

You are recommended to either use only ephone-dns *not* configured with the dual-line configuration or add the **huntstop channel** and **no huntstop** commands under each line in the overlay group, to prevent confusion.

Tip   After you configure an ephone-dn as single-line or dual-line, you cannot change the mode without deleting the ephone-dn (**no ephone-dn** <*number*>) and re-creating it. Attempting to change the configuration results in this error message:

```
CME_Voice(config)#ephone-dn 10 dual-line
Line mode can't be changed, need to remove the dn and reconfig again.
```

The last separator you can use with line overlay is **x**. This allows you to assign other lines on a Cisco IP phone to the overlay group, giving users a little more ease in answering multiple calls. Example 5.18 shows the syntax.

Example 5.18   *Using x Separator to Assign More Overlay Lines*

```
CME_Voice(config)# ephone 9
CME_Voice(config-ephone)# button 1c10,11
CME_Voice(config-ephone)# button 2x1
CME_Voice(config-ephone)# restart
```

The **x** separator does not link button 2 of the IP phone to ephone-dn 1; rather, *it allows button 2 to be an overflow of button 1*. Once you have put this configuration in place, Figure 5.5 shows what the interface of the IP phone will look like.

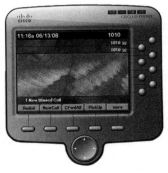

Figure 5.5   *IP Phone Using x Expansion Separator for Line 2*

Two lines now appear as 1010, giving the user the ease of use to use a second line from the overlay set for incoming or outgoing calls.

Finally, just to put all the pieces in place, Example 5.19 shows a full configuration of all five IP phones of the technical support employees using dual-line ephone-dns with the **huntstop channel** command (to prevent wild call waiting scenarios). Each technical support employee has one additional instance of the overlay line group on their phone for ease of managing the incoming and outgoing calls.

Example 5.19 *Full Configuration of the Technical Support Employees*

```
CME_Voice(config)# ephone-dn 10
CME_Voice(config-ephone-dn)# number 1010
CME_Voice(config-ephone-dn)# preference 0
CME_Voice(config-ephone-dn)# huntstop channel
CME_Voice(config-ephone-dn)# no huntstop
CME_Voice(config-ephone-dn)# exit
CME_Voice(config)# ephone-dn 11
CME_Voice(config-ephone-dn)# number 1010
CME_Voice(config-ephone-dn)# preference 1
CME_Voice(config-ephone-dn)# huntstop channel
CME_Voice(config-ephone-dn)# no huntstop
CME_Voice(config-ephone-dn)# exit
CME_Voice(config)# ephone-dn 12
CME_Voice(config-ephone-dn)# number 1010
CME_Voice(config-ephone-dn)# preference 2
CME_Voice(config-ephone-dn)# huntstop channel
CME_Voice(config-ephone-dn)# no huntstop
CME_Voice(config-ephone-dn)# exit
CME_Voice(config)# ephone-dn 13
CME_Voice(config-ephone-dn)# number 1010
CME_Voice(config-ephone-dn)# preference 3
CME_Voice(config-ephone-dn)# huntstop channel
CME_Voice(config-ephone-dn)# no huntstop
CME_Voice(config-ephone-dn)# exit
CME_Voice(config)# ephone-dn 14
CME_Voice(config-ephone-dn)# number 1010
CME_Voice(config-ephone-dn)# preference 4
CME_Voice(config-ephone-dn)# huntstop channel
CME_Voice(config)# ephone 8
CME_Voice(config-ephone)# button 1o10,11,12,13,14
CME_Voice(config-ephone)# button 2x1
CME_Voice(config-ephone)# exit
CME_Voice(config)# ephone 9
CME_Voice(config-ephone)# button 1o10,11,12,13,14
CME_Voice(config-ephone)# button 2x1
CME_Voice(config-ephone)# exit
```

continues

Example 5.19 *Full Configuration of the Technical Support Employees*   *continued*

```
CME_Voice(config)# ephone 10
CME_Voice(config-ephone)# button 1o10,11,12,13,14
CME_Voice(config-ephone)# button 2x1
CME_Voice(config-ephone)# exit
CME_Voice(config)# ephone 11
CME_Voice(config-ephone)# button 1o10,11,12,13,14
CME_Voice(config-ephone)# button 2x1
CME_Voice(config-ephone)# exit
CME_Voice(config)# ephone 12
CME_Voice(config-ephone)# button 1o10,11,12,13,14
CME_Voice(config-ephone)# button 2x1
CME_Voice(config-ephone)# exit
CME_Voice(config)# telephony-service
CME_Voice(config-telephony)# restart all
```

Troubleshooting IP Phone Registration

One of the most common troubleshooting areas in a CME deployment is the registration of IP phones. This is why understanding the boot process of the Cisco IP phones is so critical. Messages from the onscreen display of the phone can also point you in the right direction for troubleshooting if you understand the boot process.

Right after the Cisco IP phone receives voice VLAN information from the switch, it begins sending DHCP requests. During this time, the onscreen display will display the words "Configuring IP." If the phone seems to stay there for an extended period of time (1 to 2 minutes) and then reboots itself, there may be an issue with DHCP services (or the voice VLAN configuration). One of the fastest ways to diagnose this problem is to check if the IP phone is receiving an IP address from the phone itself. On most Cisco IP phones, pressing the **Settings** button, selecting the **Network Configuration** area, and scrolling down to the IP address section (which is usually item 6, as shown in Figure 5.6) allows you to verify the IP address of the phone.

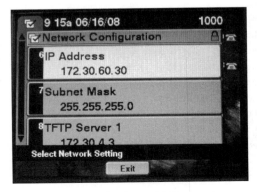

Figure 5.6 *Verifying the IP Address of a Cisco IP Phone*

If the phone consistently does not display an IP address, the problem you are encountering is most likely related to a voice VLAN or DHCP configuration issue. Verify the voice VLAN settings on the interface, verify the DHCP pool configuration, and ensure that you have properly configured the **ip helper-address** command (if necessary).

> **Tip**   If the Cisco IP phone is not "new out of the box," there may be an existing configuration in place on the Cisco IP phone that prevents the phone from registering. To ensure that the IP phone configuration has been cleared, use the **Settings** button to access the Network Configuration section of the configuration. By default, all settings on the IP phone are locked from user changes. Enter the * * # key sequence (commonly spoken star-star-pound) on the telephone keypad to unlock the settings. On some IP phone models, an Erase softkey will appear after you have entered this key sequence. Press this softkey to clear any hard-coded IP phone settings from memory. On other IP phone models, you need to scroll down to the **Erase Configuration** line item from the Network Configuration section (usually line 33 of this section).

When the IP phone does have an IP address assignment, you can move on to the next step of the boot process: the TFTP server.

After the phone passes the "Configuring IP" message on the LCD display, it will change to "Configuring CM List." During this time, the IP phone is attempting to download the configuration file from the TFTP server. If the phone stays on this message for an extended time (more than 30 seconds), there might be a communication issue with the TFTP server.

The first step you can take to troubleshoot this area of communication is to ping the IP address of the phone from the TFTP server. This ensures that the path of communication from the TFTP server to the IP phone is good. Second, verify that the TFTP server is serving up the right files. If you are using your CME router as the TFTP server, a great way to verify this is to use the **debug tftp events** command, as shown in Example 5.20.

Example 5.20   *Troubleshooting TFTP Communication Using* **debug tftp events**

```
CME_Voice# debug tftp events
*Jun 16 16:43:40.285: TFTP: Looking for CTLSEP00141C48E71A.tlv
*Jun 16 16:43:40.345: TFTP: Looking for SEP00141C48E71A.cnf.xml
*Jun 16 16:43:42.713: TFTP: Opened system:/its/XMLDefault7960.cnf.xml, fd 0, size
  931 for process 194
*Jun 16 16:43:42.765: TFTP: Finished system:/its/XMLDefault7960.cnf.xml, time
  00:00:00 for process 194
*Jun 16 16:43:42.953: TFTP: Looking for English_United_States/7960-font.xml
*Jun 16 16:43:42.953: TFTP: Opened system:/its/united_states/7960-font.xml, fd 0,
  size 8777 for process 194
*Jun 16 16:43:43.017: TFTP: Finished system:/its/united_states/7960-font.xml, time
  00:00:00 for process 194
*Jun 16 16:43:43.721: TFTP: Looking for English_United_States/SCCP-dictionary
  ext.xml
```

continues

Example 5.20   *Troubleshooting TFTP Communication Using* **debug tftp events**
continued

```
*Jun 16 16:43:43.813: TFTP: Looking for English_United_States/SCCP-dictionary.xml
*Jun 16 16:43:43.817: TFTP: Opened system:/its/united_states/SCCP-dictionary.xml,
  fd 0, size 2711 for process 194
*Jun 16 16:43:43.837: TFTP: Finished system:/its/united_states/SCCP-dictionary.xml,
  time 00:00:00 for process 194
*Jun 16 16:43:44.145: TFTP: Looking for English_United_States/7960-dictionary
  ext.xml
*Jun 16 16:43:44.237: TFTP: Looking for English_United_States/7960-dictionary.xml
*Jun 16 16:43:44.241: TFTP: Opened system:/its/united_states/7960-dictionary.xml,
  fd 0, size 19750 for process 194
*Jun 16 16:43:44.377: TFTP: Finished system:/its/united_states/7960-dictionary.xml,
  time 00:00:00 for process 194
*Jun 16 16:43:45.657: TFTP: Looking for English_United_States/7960-kate.xml
*Jun 16 16:43:45.661: TFTP: Opened system:/its/united_states/7960-kate.xml, fd 0,
  size 1313 for process 194
*Jun 16 16:43:45.669: TFTP: Finished system:/its/united_states/7960-kate.xml, time
  00:00:00 for process 194
*Jun 16 16:43:45.789: TFTP: Looking for United_States/7960-tones.xml
*Jun 16 16:43:45.789: TFTP: Opened system:/its/united_states/7960-tones.xml, fd 0,
  size 903 for process 194
*Jun 16 16:43:45.797: TFTP: Finished system:/its/united_states/7960-tones.xml, time
  00:00:00 for process 194
*Jun 16 16:43:50.301: %IPPHONE-6-REG_ALARM: 21: Name=SEP00141C48E71A Load=8.0(5.0)
  Last=Phone-Re-IP
*Jun 16 16:43:50.301: %IPPHONE-6-REGISTER: ephone-1:SEP00141C48E71A IP:172.30.60.26
  Socket:1 DeviceType:Phone has registered.
*Jun 16 16:44:54.689: TFTP: Looking for RINGLIST.XML
*Jun 16 16:44:54.709: TFTP: Opened flash:/ringtones/RingList.xml, fd 1, size 495
  for process 196
*Jun 16 16:44:54.713: TFTP: Finished flash:/ringtones/RingList.xml, time 00:00:00
  for process 196
*Jun 16 16:44:54.717: TFTP: Finished system:/its/XMLDefault7960.cnf.xml, time
  00:00:00 for process 194
*Jun 16 16:44:54.833: TFTP: Looking for DISTINCTIVERINGLIST.XML
*Jun 16 16:44:54.849: TFTP: Opened flash:/ringtones/DistinctiveRingList.xml, fd 0,
  size 2823 for process 194
*Jun 16 16:44:54.869: TFTP: Finished flash:/ringtones/DistinctiveRingList.xml, time
  00:00:00 for process 194
```

Each one of the lines from the Example 5.20 output represents either an IP phone sending a TFTP request for a file or the CME router sending a file via TFTP to the IP phone. If you see a "TFTP: Looking" request in the debug output that is not followed by "TFTP: Opened" and "TFTP: Finished" messages, the TFTP server might not be making the correct files available. To verify the files provided by the CME telephony service, you can use the command **show telephony-service tftp-bindings**, as shown in Example 5.21.

Example 5.21   *Verifying TFTP Files Served by the CME Telephony Service*

```
CME_Voice# show telephony-service tftp-bindings
tftp-server system:/its/XMLDefaultCIPC.cnf.xml alias SEP0019D122DCF3.cnf.xml
tftp-server system:/its/XMLDefault7912.cnf.xml alias SEP00146A16C2DA.cnf.xml
tftp-server system:/its/XMLDefault7960.cnf.xml alias SEP00141C48E6D1.cnf.xml
tftp-server system:/its/XMLDefaultCIPC.cnf.xml alias SEP000C2957ACF5.cnf.xml
tftp-server system:/its/SEPDEFAULT.cnf
tftp-server system:/its/SEPDEFAULT.cnf alias SEPDefault.cnf
tftp-server system:/its/XMLDefault.cnf.xml alias XMLDefault.cnf.xml
tftp-server system:/its/ATADefault.cnf.xml
tftp-server system:/its/XMLDefault7960.cnf.xml alias SEP00141C48E71A.cnf.xml
tftp-server system:/its/united_states/7960-font.xml alias English_United_States/
   7960-font.xml
tftp-server system:/its/united_states/7960-font.xml alias English_United_States/
   7920-font.xml
tftp-server system:/its/united_states/7960-dictionary.xml alias
   English_United_States/7960-dictionary.xml
tftp-server system:/its/united_states/7960-kate.xml alias English_United_States/
   7960-kate.xml
tftp-server system:/its/united_states/7960-kate.xml alias English_United_States/
   7920-kate.xml
tftp-server system:/its/united_states/SCCP-dictionary.xml alias
English_United_States/
   SCCP-dictionary.xml
```

Notice that all these files exist on the system drive (which is the RAM of the CME router). These files are created in the RAM of the CME router as the router processes ephone configurations. There are also numerous firmware and locale files that you should make available from the router's flash memory by using the **tftp-server** command. You can quickly verify the files that the CME router is serving by using a filtered version of the **show run** command, as shown in Example 5.22.

Example 5.22   *Verifying TFTP Files Served by the* **tftp-server** *Command*

```
CME_Voice# show run | include tftp-server
tftp-server flash:/phone/7940-7960/P00308000500.bin alias P00308000500.bin
tftp-server flash:/phone/7940-7960/P00308000500.loads alias P00308000500.loads
tftp-server flash:/phone/7940-7960/P00308000500.sb2 alias P00308000500.sb2
tftp-server flash:/phone/7940-7960/P00308000500.sbn alias P00308000500.sbn
tftp-server flash:/phone/7970-7971/apps70.8-3-2-27.sbn alias apps70.8-3-2-27.sbn
tftp-server flash:/phone/7970-7971/cnu70.8-3-2-27.sbn alias cnu70.8-3-2-27.sbn
tftp-server flash:/phone/7970-7971/cvm70sccp.8-3-2-27.sbn alias cvm70sccp.8-3-2
   27.sbn
tftp-server flash:/phone/7970-7971/dsp70.8-3-2-27.sbn alias dsp70.8-3-2-27.sbn
tftp-server flash:/phone/7970-7971/jar70sccp.8-3-2-27.sbn alias jar70sccp.8-3-2
   27.sbn
```

continues

Example 5.22   *Verifying TFTP Files Served by the* **tftp-server** *Command   continued*

```
tftp-server flash:/phone/7970-7971/SCCP70.8-3-3S.loads alias SCCP70.8-3-3S.loads
tftp-server flash:/phone/7970-7971/term70.default.loads alias term70.default.loads
tftp-server flash:/phone/7970-7971/term71.default.loads alias term71.default.loads
tftp-server flash:/ringtones/DistinctiveRingList.xml alias DistinctiveRingList.xml
tftp-server flash:/ringtones/RingList.xml alias RingList.xml
```

If you see any files requested by the IP phone in the **debug tftp events** output that the CME router does not return, you may need to add **tftp-server** commands to make these files available from the router's flash memory.

After the IP phone downloads its necessary support files, it then contacts the CME router to receive line assignments and feature support. All communication between the IP phone and CME router occurs using the Skinny Client Control Protocol (SCCP). Watching this communication can be very helpful in the troubleshooting process (and really interesting too). To observe CME-to-IP phone communication, use the **debug ephone** command. To focus *just* on the registration process, you can filter the output by using the **debug ephone register** command instead, as shown in Example 5.23.

Example 5.23   *Verifying the Ephone Registration Process Using* **debug ephone register**

Key
Topic

```
CME_Voice# debug ephone register
*Jun 16 17:03:10.520: ephone-(1)[1] StationRegisterMessage (3/5/24) from
172.30.60.26
*Jun 16 17:03:10.520: ephone-(1)[1] Register StationIdentifier DeviceName
SEP00141C48E71A
*Jun 16 17:03:10.520: ephone-(1)[1] StationIdentifier Instance 1    deviceType 7
*Jun 16 17:03:10.520: ephone-1[-1]:stationIpAddr 172.16.1.16
*Jun 16 17:03:10.520: ephone-(1) Allow any Skinny Server IP address 172.30.4.3
*Jun 16 17:03:10.520: ephone-1[-1][SEP00141C48E71A]:Found entry 0 for 00141C48E71A
*Jun 16 17:03:10.520: ephone-1[1][SEP00141C48E71A]:phone SEP00141C48E71A
  re-associate OK on socket [1]
*Jun 16 17:03:10.520: %IPPHONE-6-REGISTER: ephone-1:SEP00141C48E71A
  IP:172.30.60.26 Socket:1 DeviceType:Phone has registered.
*Jun 16 17:03:10.520: Phone 0 socket 1
*Jun 16 17:03:10.520: Skinny Local IP address = 172.30.4.3 on port 2000
*Jun 16 17:03:10.760: ephone-1[1][SEP00141C48E71A]:StationLineStatReqMessage from
  ephone line 6
*Jun 16 17:03:10.760: ephone-1[1][SEP00141C48E71A]:StationLineStatReqMessage from
  ephone line 6 Invalid DN -1
*Jun 16 17:03:10.760: ephone-1[1][SEP00141C48E71A]:StationLineStatResMessage sent
  to ephone (1 of 6)
*Jun 16 17:03:10.768: ephone-1[1][SEP00141C48E71A]:StationLineStatReqMessage from
  ephone line 5
*Jun 16 17:03:10.768: ephone-1[1][SEP00141C48E71A]:StationLineStatReqMessage from
  ephone line 5 Invalid DN -1
*Jun 16 17:03:10.768: ephone-1[1][SEP00141C48E71A]:StationLineStatResMessage sent
  to ephone (2 of 6)
```

```
*Jun 16 17:03:10.800: ephone-1[1][SEP00141C48E71A]:StationLineStatReqMessage from
  ephone line 4
*Jun 16 17:03:10.800: ephone-1[1][SEP00141C48E71A]:StationLineStatReqMessage from
  ephone line 4 Invalid DN -1
*Jun 16 17:03:10.800: ephone-1[1][SEP00141C48E71A]:StationLineStatResMessage sent
  to ephone (3 of 6)
*Jun 16 17:03:10.808: ephone-1[1][SEP00141C48E71A]:StationLineStatReqMessage from
  ephone line 3
*Jun 16 17:03:10.808: ephone-1[1][SEP00141C48E71A]:Expansion line on button 3 for
  line 1
*Jun 16 17:03:10.808: ephone-1[1]:StationLineStatReqMessage ephone line
  3 DN 10 = 1010 desc = 1010 label =
*Jun 16 17:03:10.808: ephone-1[1][SEP00141C48E71A]:StationLineStatResMessage sent
  to ephone (4 of 6)
*Jun 16 17:03:10.816: ephone-1[1][SEP00141C48E71A]:StationLineStatReqMessage from
ephone line 2
*Jun 16 17:03:10.820: ephone-1[1][SEP00141C48E71A]:Expansion line on button 2 for
  line 1
*Jun 16 17:03:10.820: ephone-1[1]:StationLineStatReqMessage ephone line 2 DN 10 =
  1010 desc = 1010 label =
*Jun 16 17:03:10.820: ephone-1[1][SEP00141C48E71A]:StationLineStatResMessage sent
  to ephone (5 of 6)
*Jun 16 17:03:10.828: ephone-1[1][SEP00141C48E71A]:StationLineStatReqMessage
  from ephone line 1
*Jun 16 17:03:10.828: ephone-1[1]:StationLineStatReqMessage ephone line 1 DN 10 =
  1010 desc = 1010 label =
*Jun 16 17:03:10.828: ephone-1[1][SEP00141C48E71A]:StationLineStatResMessage sent
  to ephone (6 of 6)
*Jun 16 17:03:10.828: ephone-1[1]:SkinnyCompleteRegistration
```

Note   The prior debug output has been trimmed down considerably to allow you to see the key information provided by the **debug ephone register** command.

The areas of the previous debug output highlighted in gray represent key configuration changes. Initially, you can see the SCCP request from the IP phone (172.16.1.16). The CME router searches and finds the configuration file for the IP phone. The CME router then begins sending SCCP messages to configure each line of the IP phone. Notice that lines 6, 5, and 4 receive "Invalid DN" messages. This indicates that these lines have no DN assignment. Lines 3, 2, and 1 receive messages showing they are Expansion (overlay) lines with the DN 1010.

Supporting Auto-Registration and Auto-Assignment of IP Phones

Since its 4.0 version, CME has supported auto-registration of Cisco IP phones by default. This allows IP phones with no ephone configuration in the CME running configuration to automatically register with the CME router. The CME router does not automatically create an ephone entry in the running configuration; however, the registered phones can be verified by using the **show ephone** command, as shown in Example 5.24.

Example 5.24   *Auto-Registered Ephone Verification*

```
CME_Voice# show ephone
ephone-1 Mac:0014.1C48.E71A TCP socket:[3] activeLine:0 REGISTERED in SCCP ver 11
  and Server in ver 8
mediaActive:0 offhook:0 ringing:0 reset:0 reset_sent:0 paging 0 debug:0 caps:8
IP:172.30.60.29 52850 Telecaster 7960   keepalive 277 max_line 6
button 1: dn 10 number 1010 CH1    IDLE           overlay
button 2: expand-line 1   (DN -1 selected)
button 3: expand-line 1   (DN -1 selected)
overlay 1: 10(1010) 11(1010)
phone has expansion line(s)
ephone-2 Mac:0019.D122.DCF3 TCP socket:[5] activeLine:0 REGISTERED in SCCP ver 9
  and Server in ver 8
mediaActive:0 offhook:0 ringing:0 reset:0 reset_sent:0 paging 0 debug:0 caps:7
IP:172.30.2.50 50645 CIPC   keepalive 0 max_line 8
ephone-3 Mac:0014.6A16.C2DA TCP socket:[2] activeLine:0 REGISTERED in SCCP ver 8
  and Server in ver 8
mediaActive:0 offhook:0 ringing:0 reset:0 reset_sent:0 paging 0 debug:0 caps:7
IP:172.30.60.32 14728 7912   keepalive 1 max_line 2
```

Note   In the Example 5.24 output, ephone-2 (a Cisco IP Communicator) and ephone-3 (a 7912) are auto-registered devices with no ephone configuration in the CME router.

The benefit of having the auto-registration turned on is that you now have ephone entries and MAC addresses for the Cisco IP phones that are trying to register with the CME router. You can then copy and paste the MAC address into a real ephone entry and begin your line configuration for the devices.

Because the auto-registration feature is enabled in CME 4.0 and later by default, there is nothing you need to do to turn it on. If you would like to disable auto-registration, you can access telephony service configuration mode and enter **no auto-reg-ephone**. IP phones that attempt to register without an explicit ephone configuration will receive a "Registration Rejected" message, as shown in Figure 5.7.

Figure 5.7 *IP Phone Message with Auto-Registration Disabled*

If you do have auto-registration disabled, you will be able to see the devices that are failing the registration process by entering the **show ephone attempted-registrations** command, as shown in Example 5.25.

Example 5.25 *Verifying Failed Ephone Registrations*

```
CME_Voice# show ephone attempted-registrations
Attempting Mac address:


Num    Mac Address        DateTime                         DeviceType


- - - - - - - - - - - - - - - - - - - - - - - - - - - - - - - - - - - - - - - - -
1      0014.6A16.C2DA     13:38:13 ARIZONA Fri Jun 13 2008    7912
2      0014.1C48.E6D1     13:38:11 ARIZONA Fri Jun 13 2008    Telecaster 7960
3      0019.D122.DCF3     13:38:25 ARIZONA Fri Jun 13 2008    CIPC
- - - - - - - - - - - - - - - - - - - - - - - - - - - - - - - - - - - - - - - - -
```

Auto-registration is handy because it allows you to see the MAC addresses of the IP phones attempting to register (which you can use for manual configuration). However, it would be much handier if the CME router could assign phone extensions for you...Oh wait; it can! That's the idea behind the **auto assign** command performed from telephony service configuration mode. This command allows you to specify a range of ephone-dns to distribute to IP phones that register but have no explicit ephone configuration in the CME router.

The **auto assign** command allows you to distribute specific ephone-dn ranges to specific types of phones or to any phone requesting an extension. For example, you could use the syntax in Example 5.26 to auto-assign ephone-dns 20 through 24 to Cisco 7940 IP Phones, ephone-dns 25 through 30 to Cisco 7960 IP Phones, and ephone-dns 31 through 39 to any other phone model that attempts to register.

Example 5.26   *Assigning Ephone-DNs Using the* **auto assign** *Command*

Key
Topic

```
CME_Voice(config)# telephony-service
CME_Voice(config-telephony)# auto assign 20 to 24 type ?
  WORD  7960, 7940, 7910, 7905, 7906, 7935, 7902, 7911, 7912,
        7961, 7961GE, 7941, 7941GE, 7920, 7921, 7970, 7971, 7936, 7931, CIPC, ata,
        7962, 7942, 7945, 7965, 7975, 7985, anl or bri
CME_Voice(config-telephony)#auto assign 20 to 24 type 7940
CME_Voice(config-telephony)#auto assign 25 to 30 type 7960
CME_Voice(config-telephony)#auto assign 31 to 39
```

As new phones auto-register, the CME router will begin to auto-assign extensions to them. CME distributes the lowest-numbered ephone-dns first and works its way to the high end of the range. If the first IP phone to register was a 7940 model, it would receive ephone-dn 20. If the first IP phone to register was a 7912, it would receive ephone-dn 31. Once the IP phones have auto-registered, the new ephone configuration will appear in the CME router's running configuration. The CME router even adds the optional **type** command under each ephone to identify the model of IP phone that has auto-registered, as shown in Example 5.27.

Example 5.27   *Verifying the Running Configuration After Ephone-DN Auto-Assignment*

```
CME_Voice# show running-config
…output truncated…
ephone  1
 device-security-mode none
 mac-address 0019.D122.DCF3
 type CIPC
 button  1:21
ephone  2
 device-security-mode none
 mac-address 0014.6A16.C2DA
 type 7912
 button  1:20
ephone  3
 device-security-mode none
 mac-address 0014.1C48.E6D1
 type 7960
 button  1:22
```

Key
Topic

Note   The CME router can auto-detect any supported Cisco IP phone model with the exception of the 7914 Expansion Module. You must manually configure this module under ephone configuration mode.

As soon as you enter the **auto-reg-ephone** command (which is entered by default) under telephony service configuration mode, IP phones begin to auto-register with the CME router. After they have auto-registered, they will simply sit with a blank line configuration until you restart them. After issuing the **auto-assign** command, you can then use the **restart all** command from telephony service configuration mode to get all the lazy auto-registered phones rebooted and assigned new extensions.

Note   If you don't plan on using auto ephone-dn assignment to distribute DNs to the IP phones, consider disabling auto-registration for Cisco IP phones in CME, for the following reasons:

- The **show ephone attempted-registrations** command gives much cleaner output than the **show ephone** or **show ephone summary** command. This makes it much easier to get the MAC addresses of all the IP phones for which you do not have ephone entries. Then, you can manually create the ephones as needed.

- Even though auto-registered phones don't have an ephone entry in the running configuration, they deduct against the **max-ephones** value your CME router can support.

- I steer clear of just about anything with the word "auto" in the Cisco world. My mantra is, "I auto-not use that."

Additional IP Phone Configuration Parameters

By this point, you should have a good idea of how to manage ephone and ephone-dns on the CME router. In addition to the base configuration, CME supports settings that allow you to tune and tweak the connection and interface of the Cisco IP phones it manages. The settings fall under these categories:

- Rebooting IP Phones

- Phone Language Settings

- Date and Time Format

- System Message

Rebooting IP Phones

As you make configuration changes to the CME router, you may need to reboot the Cisco IP phones managed by the system. You can do this by using either the **restart** or **reset** command. The **restart** command does a warm boot of the IP phone. The phone reboots, but keeps its existing IP address and TFTP configuration files. Because DHCP and TFTP take the most time during IP phone boot process, the phone is able to restart very quickly. Most Cisco IP phones are able to restart in 1 to 2 seconds (you'll notice the display screen blinks on and off once and you're back up and running). The **reset** command does a hard reboot of the IP phone. Table 5.3 summarizes the usage of the **restart** and **reset** commands.

Table 5.3 restart *Versus* reset *Commands*

Command	Used For
restart	Phone line changes
	Speed dial changes
reset	DHCP scope changes
	Date and time changes
	Firmware changes
	Locale changes
	Changes to button (services, messages, directories) URLs
	Voicemail number changes

You can enter the **restart** and **reset** commands from ephone or telephony service configuration mode. If entered under the ephone, it will affect only the Cisco IP phone controlled by the specific ephone. If entered from telephony service configuration mode, you have a few options, as shown in Example 5.28.

Example 5.28 restart *Command Options*

```
CME_Voice(config-telephony)# reset ?
  H.H.H        mac address
  all          reset all ethernet phones
  cancel       cancel in progress reset
  sequence-all reset all ethernet phones sequentially, wait for each phone to
    re-register before resetting the next phone. This prevents possible conflict
    between phones when accessing IOS TFTP services

CME_Voice(config-telephony)#reset all ?
  <0-60>  time interval in seconds between each phone reset
  <cr>
```

As you can see, the **reset** command gives you the flexibility to restart a specific IP phone via its MAC address or all phones. Restarting all phones in the network can be overwhelming to the CME router because it could potentially be hit with up to 240 TFTP downloads and registrations at the same time. Thankfully, the CME router automatically paces itself. When you issue the **reset all** command, the CME router replies with the following:

```
CME_Voice(config-telephony)# reset all
Reset 4 phones: at 15 second interval        - this could take several minutes
   per phone
Starting with 7960 phones
```

The CME router then resets the phones, one genre of phones at a time, with a 15-second delay between devices. If you are confident in your router's resource utilization level and would prefer to specify a faster reboot time, you can enter the amount of time the CME router should wait between device resets.

Phone Language Settings

Cisco CME has the ability to support other, non-English locale settings for the IP phones. These locale settings come in two different flavors:

- **User locale:** Affects the language settings for the softkeys, help messages, and buttons on the Cisco IP phones

- **Network locale:** Affects the locale of the tones played by the Cisco IP phone

Although Cisco CME supports many locales for the phones by default (these differ by CME version), you might need to download additional locale support packs from Cisco.com. These support packs are TAR files (which you can extract to the router's flash using the **archive** command) that contain all the necessary tones and translations for Cisco IP phones. Once you extract these files to the CME router's flash memory, you then make them available to the IP phones by using the **tftp-server** command.

Once you have copied the necessary locale support files into the CME router flash memory (if necessary), you can change the locale settings for the CME router. To do this, you can use the syntax shown in Example 5.29.

Example 5.29   *Changing CME Locale Settings*

```
CME_Voice(config)# telephony-service
CME_Voice(config-telephony)# user-locale ?
  <0-4>   user locale index 0 to 4 (0 is default)
  DE      Germany
  DK      Denmark
  ES      Spain
  FR      France
  IT      Italy
  JP      Japan
  NL      Netherlands
  NO      Norway
  PT      Portugal
  RU      Russian Federation
  SE      Sweden
  US      United States
```

continues

Example 5.29   *Changing CME Locale Settings   continued*

```
CME_Voice(config-telephony)# user-locale FR
Updating CNF files
CNF files update complete
Please issue 'create cnf' command after the locale change
CME_Voice(config-telephony)# network-locale ?
  <0-4>  network locale index 0 to 4 (0 is default)
  AT      Austria
  CA      Canada
  CH      Switzerland
  DE      Germany
  DK      Denmark
  ES      Spain
  FR      France
  GB      United Kingdom
  IT      Italy
  JP      Japan
  NL      Netherlands
  NO      Norway
  PT      Portugal
  RU      Russian Federation
  SE      Sweden
  US      United States
CME_Voice(config-telephony)# network-locale FR
Updating CNF files
CNF files update complete
Please issue 'create cnf' command after the locale change
```

Tip   The countries listed under the context-sensitive help for the **user-locale** and **network-locale** commands are those for which the CME router has built-in support. You can add support for additional countries by downloading the language support packs from Cisco.com.

Most CME environments will need to support only a single language for all devices because CME typically manages IP phones in a single location. Changing the **user-locale** and **network-locale** settings from telephony service configuration mode changes the locale support on *all* devices supported by the CME system. If you would like to support different locale settings for the IP phones in a single location, you can do so by using the **ephone-template** command. Example 5.30 demonstrates the process to assign one IP phone (ephone 2) the French locale settings and another IP phone (ephone 3) the Norway locale settings.

Example 5.30   *Multiple Locale Support in CME*

```
CME_Voice(config)# telephony-service
CME_Voice(config-telephony)# user-locale ?
  <0-4>  user locale index 0 to 4 (0 is default)
  DE     Germany
  DK     Denmark
  ES     Spain
  FR     France
  IT     Italy
  JP     Japan
  NL     Netherlands
  NO     Norway
  PT     Portugal
  RU     Russian Federation
  SE     Sweden
  US     United States
CME_Voice(config-telephony)# user-locale 1 FR
CME_Voice(config-telephony)# user-locale 2 NO
CME_Voice(config-telephony)# network-locale 1 FR
CME_Voice(config-telephony)# network-locale 2 NO
CME_Voice(config-telephony)# exit
CME_Voice(config)# ephone-template 1
CME_Voice(config-ephone-template)# user-locale ?
  <0-4>  user locale index (0 is default)
CME_Voice(config-ephone-template)# user-locale 1
CME_Voice(config-ephone-template)# network-locale 1
CME_Voice(config-ephone-template)# exit
CME_Voice(config)# ephone-template 2
CME_Voice(config-ephone-template)# user-locale 2
CME_Voice(config-ephone-template)# network-locale 2
CME_Voice(config-ephone-template)# exit
CME_Voice(config)# ephone 2
CME_Voice(config-ephone)# ephone-template 1
The ephone template tag has been changed under this ephone, please restart or reset
  ephone to take effect.
CME_Voice(config-ephone)# ephone 3
CME_Voice(config-ephone)# ephone-template 2
The ephone template tag has been changed under this ephone, please restart or reset
  ephone to take effect.
CME_Voice(config-ephone)#
```

Note   CME currently supports up to five different locale settings for the devices.

Date and Time Format

Just as there are different locale preferences, different regions of the world prefer different date and time formats. You can set these preferences from telephony service configuration mode using the syntax shown in Example 5.31.

Example 5.31 *Multiple Locale Support in CME*

```
CME_Voice(config)# telephony-service
CME_Voice(config-telephony)# date-format ?
  dd-mm-yy  Set date to dd-mm-yy format
  mm-dd-yy  Set date to mm-dd-yy format
  yy-dd-mm  Set date to yy-dd-mm format
  yy-mm-dd  Set date to yy-mm-dd format
CME_Voice(config-telephony)# date-format mm-dd-yy
CME_Voice(config-telephony)# time-format ?
  12  Set time to 12Hrs(AM/PM) format
  24  Set time to 24Hrs format
CME_Voice(config-telephony)# time-format 12
```

Note This is a great point at which to emphasize the importance of using NTP to set the clock of the CME router. In the data realm, having the accurate time is a good practice and helpful for security logs, but definitely is not mandatory. In the IP telephony realm, many more features revolve around the CME router having an accurate clock.

System Message

By default, every IP phone in your network displays the message "Cisco Unified CME" on the phone LCD screen. While this is great marketing for Cisco, you may want to change the message. This can be accomplished from telephony service configuration mode using the following syntax:

```
CME_Voice(config)# telephony-service
CME_Voice(config-telephony)# system message Don't Worry Be Happy
```

Once you enter the system message, it changes on all Cisco IP phones immediately, as shown in Figure 5.8, without requiring a restart.

Figure 5.8   *IP Phone System Message*

Note   The system message can be up to 32 characters in length.

Exam Preparation Tasks

Review All the Key Topics

Review the most important topics in the chapter, noted with the key topics icon in the outer margin of the page. Table 5.4 lists a reference of these key topics and the page numbers on which each is found.

Key
Topic

Table 5.4   *Key Topics for Chapter 5*

Key Topic Element	Description	Page Number
Figure 5.1	Visually describes Cisco IP phone boot process	138
List	Highlights difference between single- and dual-line configurations	141
Example 5.4	Configuration of ephone-dns	142
Example 5.6	Configuration of an ephone	144
Example 5.8	Assigning ephone-dns to an ephone	145
Table 5.2	Description of button separators	146
Example 5.16	Configuration of **preference** and **huntstop** commands	151
List	Description of the three button overlay methods	152
Example 5.17	Configuration of button overlay	152
Tip	Method to change ephone-dn from single- to dual-line and vice versa	154
Example 5.23	Verifying phone registration with the **debug ephone register** command	160
Example 5.26	Auto-assigning ephone-dns using **auto assign** command	164
Note	Mentions support for auto-detection of all Cisco devices except 7914 expansion module	164
Table 5.3	Summarizes the difference between restarting and resetting devices	166
List	Compares user- and network-locale settings	167

Complete the Tables and Lists from Memory

Print a copy of Appendix C, "Memory Tables" (found on the CD), or at least the section for this chapter, and complete the tables and lists from memory. Appendix D, "Memory Tables Answer Key," also on the CD, includes completed tables and lists to check your work.

Definitions of Key Terms

Define the following key terms from this chapter, and check your answers in the glossary.

Spanning Tree Protocol (STP)

ephone-dn

ephone

feature ring

overlay line

monitor mode

watch mode

auto-registration

auto-assignment

Configuring a Voice Network Directory: This section walks through the creation of a local directory of CME devices, which gives your users an easier method to find and dial local DNs.

Configuring Call Forwarding: This section discusses the concepts and configuration of call forwarding features in the CME environment.

Configuring Call Transfer: This section discusses the concepts and configuration of call transfer features in the CME environment.

Configuring Call Park: This section discusses the concepts and configuration of call park features in the CME environment.

Configuring Call Pickup: This section discusses the concepts and configuration of call pickup features in the CME environment.

Configuring Intercom: This section discusses the concepts and configuration of intercom features in the CME environment.

Configuring Paging: This section discusses the concepts and configuration of paging features in the CME environment.

Configuring After-Hours Call Blocking: This section discusses the methods you can use to allow or deny specific dialing patterns in the after-hours time frame for all or specific IP phones.

Configuring CDRs and Call Accounting: This section discusses the configuration of CDRs and call accounting features.

Configuring Music on Hold: This section discusses the configuration of Music on Hold (MoH) with CME.

Enabling the CME GUI: This section walks through the installation and configuration of this utility.

CHAPTER 6

Configuring Cisco Unified CME Voice Productivity Features

After implementing the ephone and ephone-dn concepts, you now have an IP telephony network that is able to make and place internal organizational calls. If only voice networks stayed this simple! Organizations expect modern telephony systems to support a whole host of features, such as call transfer, music on hold, conference calling, and so on. This chapter is dedicated to adding these types of features to the voice network.

"Do I Know This Already?" Quiz

The "Do I Know This Already?" quiz allows you to assess whether you should read this entire chapter or simply jump to the "Exam Preparation Tasks" section for review. If you are in doubt, read the entire chapter. Table 6.1 outlines the major headings in this chapter and the corresponding "Do I Know This Already?" quiz questions. You can find the answers in Appendix A, "Answers to the 'Do I Know This Already?' Quizzes."

Table 6.1   *"Do I Know This Already?" Foundation Topics Section-to-Question Mapping*

Foundation Topics Section	Questions Covered in This Section
Configuring a Voice Network Directory	1
Configuring Call Forwarding	2–3
Configuring Call Transfer	4–5
Configuring Call Park	6–7
Configuring Call Pickup	8
Configuring Intercom	9
Configuring Paging	10
Configuring After-Hours Call Blocking	11
Configuring CDRs and Call Accounting	12

1. What process must you follow to build the local phone **directory** for the CME environment?

    a. Assign directory entries under each ephone-dn using the **directory** command.

    b. CME automatically builds the directory when you assign caller-id information with the **name** command.

    c. Assign directory entries under each ephone using the **directory** command.

    d. Enter the directory configuration mode and begin associating ephone-dn values with directory entry values.

2. You enter the command **call-forward max-length 0** from telephony service configuration mode. How does this affect the voice network?

    a. Users can forward their phone for an unlimited amount of time.

    b. Users can forward their phones to any destination that is reachable from their IP phone.

    c. The CFwdAll softkey on users' IP phones dims and becomes unavailable.

    d. All IP phones that are currently forwarding calls will transfer calls directly to voice mail.

3. Which of the following categories of standards prevents calls from hairpinning on the network when they are forwarded or transferred?

    a. H.450

    b. H.225

    c. H.323

    d. H.240

4. Which of the following transfer modes does a Cisco router support by default?

    a. Blind

    b. Consult

    c. Full-blind

    d. Full-consult

5. When you enter the command **transfer-pattern 95...** from telephony service configuration mode, what is the result?

    a. Call transfers are restricted to only numbers matching the 95... pattern.

    b. Transferred calls have "95" added to the front of the dialed number information.

    c. Transferred calls have "95" added to the end of the dialed number information.

    d. Users are now able to transfer calls to numbers matching the 95... pattern.

6. You have entered the following configuration on the CME router:

```
CME_Voice(config)#ephone-dn 51
CME_Voice(config-ephone-dn)#number 3002
CME_Voice(config-ephone-dn)#park-slot timeout 60 limit 10 recall
```

What effect does this have on the voice environment?

    a. This creates a call park slot reserved for ephone-dn 3002 that can have up to ten parked calls for 60 seconds each.

    b. This creates a call park slot numbered 3002 that can have up to ten parked calls for 60 seconds each.

    c. This creates a call park slot numbered 3002 that can have a call parked for 60 seconds, at which point the original phone is recalled. If this occurs ten times, the parked call is disconnected.

    d. This creates a call park slot numbered 3002 that can have up to ten calls parked for 60 seconds each, at which point the original phone is recalled.

7. By default, what does pressing the PickUp softkey allow you to do in a Cisco Unified CME environment?

    a. Pick up a ringing phone in your group

    b. Pick up a ringing phone in another group

    c. Answer your own ringing phone

    d. Pick up a specific ringing extension (which you must specify)

8. You are watching an administrator configure an intercom line. After creating a new ephone-dn, she enters the command **number A100** and presses the Enter key. What is the purpose of this command?

   a. To designate extension 100 as an intercom line

   b. To prevent the number from being dialed from an IP phone

   c. To match the number with **number B100** on the other side of the intercom connection

   d. To list the line as the first intercom in the configuration

9. What is the maximum number of paging groups to which a Cisco IP phone can belong?

   a. 1

   b. 5

   c. 25

   d. There is no practical limit.

10. What process can a user use to exempt their IP phone from an after-hours call block configured with the 24/7 keyword?

    a. An after-hours 24/7 call block cannot be exempted.

    b. Enter the correct PIN number.

    c. You must configure the user's phone as exempt.

    d. Enter the correct Accounting code.

11. What are two destinations to which the Cisco Unified CME can send CDRs? (Choose two.)

    a. TFTP server

    b. Syslog server

    c. Logging buffer

    d. HTTP server

12. What two areas does Cisco Unified CME *not* allow you to modify from the CME GUI, by default? (Choose two.)

    a. Ephone-dn

    b. Ephone

    c. The time on the router

    d. The system message

Foundation Topics

Configuring a Voice Network Directory

When most people think of a corporate phone directory, visions of Microsoft Excel spreadsheets e-mailed out monthly come to mind. Isn't there a better way? Sure there is! Cisco IP phones support a local directory that you can update from the CME router as you are configuring devices.

You can enter names under ephone-dn configuration mode either as you are configuring new lines for the organization or separately, after you have configured the lines. These names are used both for building the internal corporate phone directory (often called the "local directory") and for caller ID information. Example 6.1 shows names being added to individual ephone-dns currently in use in the organization.

Example 6.1   *Configuring Local Directory and Internal Caller ID Information*

```
CME_Voice(config)# ephone-dn 20
CME_Voice(config-ephone-dn)# name Joshua Bellman
CME_Voice(config-ephone-dn)# exit
CME_Voice(config)# ephone-dn 21
CME_Voice(config-ephone-dn)# name Ruth Hopper
CME_Voice(config-ephone-dn)# exit
CME_Voice(config)# ephone-dn 22
CME_Voice(config-ephone-dn)# name Esther Billford
CME_Voice(config-ephone-dn)# exit
CME_Voice(config)# ephone-dn 23
CME_Voice(config-ephone-dn)# name Job Smith
CME_Voice(config-ephone-dn)# exit
CME_Voice(config)# ephone-dn 24
CME_Voice(config-ephone-dn)# name Samuel Oldham
CME_Voice(config-ephone-dn)# exit
```

Key Topic

After you enter these names in ephone-dn configuration mode, they take effect immediately. If ephone-dn 24 were to call ephone-dn 21, Ruth would see "Samuel Oldham" appear on her caller ID information, as shown in Figure 6.1.

In addition, all modern Cisco IP phone models allow you to browse the corporate directory by pressing the Directory button on the phone itself. Some low-end IP phones may not have a dedicated Directory button, but instead have a menu-driven process to get there. Once you have pressed the Directory button, you will be able to browse categories including Missed Calls, Received Calls, and so on. Move down to the option showing Local Directory, as shown in Figure 6.2.

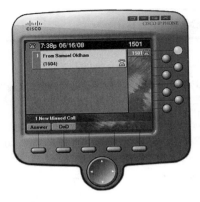

Figure 6.1   *Name Command Affects Directory and Caller ID Information*

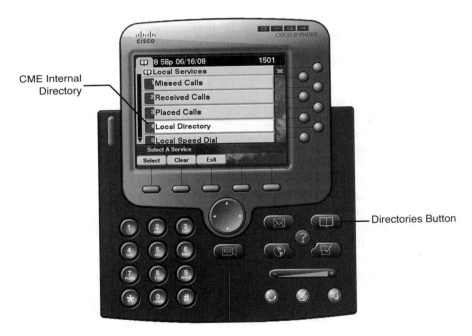

Figure 6.2   *Browsing Phone Directories*

After you select the Local Directory, the IP phone will give you the option to search by first or last name by typing in a user's name as a string on the IP phone. You can enter as many characters as you like to filter down the number of results, or simply press the Select softkey to see the entire corporate directory, as shown in Figure 6.3.

Figure 6.3   *The Local CME Directory*

By default, Cisco Unified CME organizes the local directory alphabetically by first name. You can change this setting by using the **directory** command from telephony service configuration mode. In addition, you can also add manual entries to the directory by using the **directory entry** command. This is useful for devices in the company that do not have an explicit ephone-dn configuration. Example 6.2 demonstrates these two commands in action.

Example 6.2   *Configuring Manual Local Directory Entries*

```
CME_Voice(config-telephony)# directory ?
  entry             Define new directory entry
  first-name-first  first name is first in ephone-dn name field
  last-name-first   last name is first in ephone-dn name field
CME_Voice(config-telephony)# directory last-name-first
CME_Voice(config-telephony)# directory entry ?
  <1-100>  Directory entry tag
  clear    clear all directory entries
CME_Voice(config-telephony)# directory entry 1 ?
  WORD  A sequence of digits representing dir. number
CME_Voice(config-telephony)# directory entry 1 1599 ?
  name  Define directory name
CME_Voice(config-telephony)# directory entry 1 1599 name ?
  LINE  A string - representing directory name (max length: 24 chars)
CME_Voice(config-telephony)# directory entry 1 1599 name Corporate Fax
```

Note   As you can see from the context-sensitive help, you can add up to 100 manual entries to the local CME directory. Also, keep in mind that sorting alphabetically by last name will flip all the information in the directory to list last name first. CME will list the "Corporate Fax" directory entry just added as "Fax Corporate."

Configuring Call Forwarding

There are two methods used to forward calls to a different destination: from the IP phone (the user's method) and from the Cisco IOS CLI (the administrator's method). This section describes both methods and also provides an overview of the **call-forward pattern** command.

Forwarding Calls from the IP Phone

To forward calls from the IP phone, simply press the **CFwdAll** softkey button, shown in Figure 6.4. The IP phone will beep twice and allow you to enter a number. Enter the number to which all calls on the IP phone will forward, and then press the pound key (#) on the phone so that it knows you are done entering the number. To cancel call forwarding, press the **CFwdAll** button a second time.

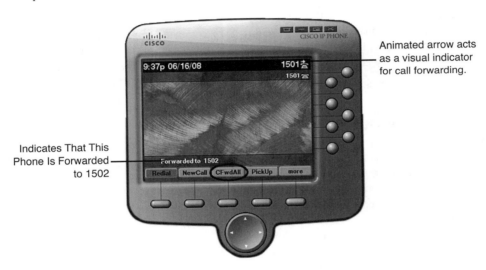

Figure 6.4 *Forwarding Calls from the Cisco IP Phone*

Forwarding Calls from the CLI

Forwarding calls from the command line gives you more options than does forwarding calls from the IP phone, as shown in Example 6.3.

Example 6.3 *Forwarding Calls from the Cisco IOS CLI*

```
CME_Voice(config)# ephone-dn 21
CME_Voice(config-ephone-dn)# call-forward ?
  all            forward all calls
  busy           forward call on busy
  max-length     max number of digits allowed for CFwdAll from IP phone
  night-service  forward call on activated night-service
```

```
  noan            forward call on no-answer
CME_Voice(config-ephone-dn)# call-forward busy 1599
CME_Voice(config-ephone-dn)# call-forward noan 1599 ?
  timeout   Ringing no answer timeout duration
CME_Voice(config-ephone-dn)# call-forward noan 1599 timeout ?
  <3-60000>  Ringing no answer timeout duration in seconds
CME_Voice(config-ephone-dn)# call-forward noan 1599 timeout 25
```

These options allow you to forward calls that are busy or not answering (noan) to a different extension. While this is typically a voice-mail number (which 1599 represents in Example 6.3), this could also be another IP phone if this DN was a member of a hunt group.

Tip   In the United States, the phone rings for 2 seconds followed by 4 seconds of silence. Knowing this can be useful in calculating a good no answer (noan) timeout value.

Also notice that you can specify a **max-length** value after the **call-forward** command. Using this, you can restrict the IP phone from forwarding to external destinations. If you enter the command **call-forward max-length 0**, CME makes the IP phone call forwarding feature unavailable to the Cisco IP phone. The CFwdAll button will dim on the IP phone and become inaccessible.

Tip   At this point, you should have a pretty good idea that there is plenty of configuration under each ephone-dn that is in common with all the others. Make an ephone-dn (and ephone) template in Notepad (or some other text editor) in which you list all the common configuration commands you'll be applying in your environment. That way, if you ever need to add new ephone-dns, you will already have a template listing the common commands you need to enter.

Using the call-forward pattern Command to Support H.450.3

There is one additional command to discuss here, which is available from telephony service configuration mode: **call-forward pattern**. This command allows you to enter a pattern for numbers that will support the H.450.3 call forwarding standard.

To understand the benefits of H.450.3, you must first understand what happens with typical VoIP forwarding. When a call enters the network and hits a forwarded device, that device takes responsibility for the call and becomes a tandem hop in the call flow. That means that the voice traffic now forwards *through* the IP phone that forwarded the call. This can cause quality problems if the device that forwarded the call is a large geographical distance away from the phone receiving the forwarding call. The H.450.3 standard represents a method that allows the CME router to redirect the call directly to the final destination instead of acting as a tandem hop. Figure 6.5 illustrates this concept.

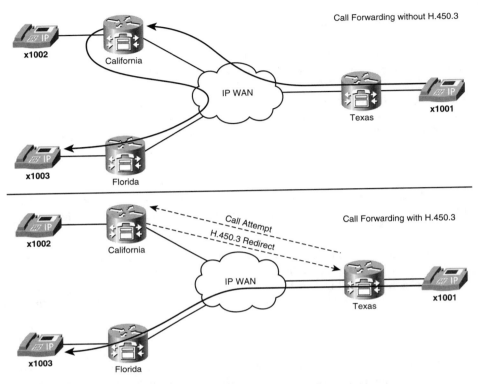

Figure 6.5   *Forwarding Calls With and Without H.450.3 Standards*

Key Topic

In Figure 6.5, the IP phone with x1002 is forwarded to the IP phone with x1003. The top part shows the VoIP call flow without H.450.3 when x1001 places a call to x1002. Notice that the VoIP traffic must pass through the California CME router to reach Florida. This can cause intense quality of service (QoS) problems with the call, such as audio clipping, distortion, and even call drops. This symptom is commonly called "hair-pinning" the call.

The bottom part shows the call with H.450.3 support enabled. When the call reaches California, CME sends an H.450.3-based redirect message, instead of accepting the call and forwarding it on to Florida. The VoIP traffic then travels directly from x1001 in Texas to Florida rather than passing through California to get there.

Entering **call-forward pattern** *<pattern>* from telephony service configuration mode tells CME which numbers should support the H.450.3 standard. Entering the pattern **15..** tells CME, "I want all four-digit numbers that begin with 15 to support H.450.3." Thus, all calls to 15XX extensions would support H.450.3 call forwarding.

> **Note**   There is much more to be said about the H.450.3 standard. There is also more configuration that should be in place to fully support H.450.3. This was intended to be a "sneak peak" of the standard, which the CCVP certification track fully explores.

Configuring Call Transfer

Transferring calls represents another common function in voice networks. To transfer a call, hit the Trnsfer softkey while on an active call. (Note that this is not a typo: "Trnsfer" without the *a* is correct.) When you do, you will hear another dial tone, at which point you can dial the phone number to which you want to transfer your active call. What happens from there depends on the transfer method configured on the CME router. There are two transfer methods available:

- **Consult:** Consult transfer allows you to speak with the other party before transferring the call. After you dial the number to which you would like to transfer the call, you can wait for the other party to answer and speak with them before transferring the call. Pressing the Trnsfer softkey a second time transfers the call, dropping you out of the conversation. Consult transfers require a second line (or dual-line configuration). This is the default transfer mode in CME.

- **Blind:** Blind transfer immediately transfers the call after you have dialed the number (you do not hit the Trnsfer softkey a second time). Blind transfers can work in a single-line configuration.

Key
Topic

To configure the transfer method used, see Example 6.4.

Example 6.4   *Configuring CME Transfer Methods System-Wide*

```
CME_Voice(config)# telephony-service
CME_Voice(config-telephony)# transfer-system ?
  full-blind    Perform call transfers without consultation using H.450.2 or SIP
    REFER standard methods
  full-consult  Perform H.450.2/SIP call transfers with consultation using second
    phone line if available, fallback to full-blind if second line unavailable.
    This is the recommended mode for most systems. See also 'supplementary-service'
    commands under 'voice service voip' and dial-peer.
  local-consult Perform call transfers with local consultation using second phone
    line if available, fallback to blind for non-local consultation/transfer
    target. Uses Cisco  proprietary method.

CME_Voice(config-telephony)# transfer-system full-consult
```

As you can see from the context-sensitive help, there are three transfer methods available: full-blind, full-consult, and local-consult. The full-blind, full-consult, and local-consult describe the transfer methods introduced at the beginning of this section. The full-blind and full-consult methods use the industry-standard H.450.2 method of transferring. Just like call forwarding, you don't want to hairpin the call and cause potential QoS issues each time you transfer. By using the H.450.2 standard when transferring a call, the CME router completely drops the call from the transferring phone and starts a new call at the phone to which the call was transferred.

The local-consult method uses a Cisco proprietary transfer method that will perform a consult transfer if multiple lines or dual-line configurations are available, but will revert to blind transfers if only a single line is available. Cisco proprietary transfers work similar to the H.450 standard. The only problem is this transfer method results in hairpinned calls if you have non-Cisco IP telephony systems on your network.

> **Note**   You can also configure transfer modes individually for each ephone-dn by using the **transfer-mode <blind/consult>** syntax from ephone-dn configuration mode. Configuring the transfer mode this way uses H.450 standards and overrules the system-wide setting.

By default, the Cisco router restricts transfers to devices that are not locally managed. This is usually a good policy, because transferring outside of the company can result in toll fraud. For example, a user could transfer an outside caller to an international number, causing the toll charges to be billed to the organization rather than the outside caller. If you would like to allow transfers outside of the locally managed devices, you can use the **transfer-pattern** *<pattern>* command from telephony service mode, where *pattern* represents numbers to which you would like to allow transfers. Example 6.5 configures the Cisco Unified CME router to allow transfers to 5XXX extensions and local ten-digit PSTN numbers.

Example 6.5   *Configuring CME Transfer Patterns to Allow Outside Transfers*

```
CME_Voice(config)# telephony-service
CME_Voice(config-telephony)# transfer-pattern ?
  WORD  digit string pattern for permitted non-local call transfers

CME_Voice(config-telephony)# transfer-pattern 5...
CME_Voice(config-telephony)# transfer-pattern 9.........
```

> **Note**   Up to this point, you have not learned about the wildcards you are able to use in the **transfer-pattern** command (or any other commands that require a pattern). Chapter 8, "Configuring and Verifying Gateways and Trunks," discusses this topic thoroughly. In the second transfer pattern in Example 6.5, the 9 is used for an outside line followed by the ten-digit number (represented by the ten "." wildcards).

Configuring Call Park

Typically, when you place a call on hold, you can retrieve the call only from the original phone where you placed the call on hold. Shared-line systems bend the rules a little by allowing you to retrieve the call from any phone with the same shared line assignment. The call park feature takes this one step further by allowing you to retrieve the call from any phone in the organization. Call park "parks" the caller on hold at an extension rather than on a specific line. Any IP phone that is able to dial the park extension number can retrieve the call.

The call park system works by finding free ephone-dns in the Cisco Unified CME configuration that you have not assigned to an IP phone and have specifically designated as a call park slot. You can either allow CME to park calls randomly at the first available ephone-dn or allow users to choose the extension where the call is parked. Each of these scenarios fits different environments. Calls being parked at random extensions might work well for a warehouse environment with a voice paging system. When an employee has a call, the receptionist could announce, "Larry, you have a call on 5913" over the loudspeaker, at which point Larry could go to a phone and dial the extension to pick up the call on hold.

Choosing extensions would work well for an electronics superstore in which each department responded to a known extension number. For example, software could be extension 301, cameras could be extension 302, and so on. The receptionist can then park multiple calls on a single call park number (this would require multiple ephone-dns assigned the same extension). As the specific department retrieves the calls, CME would distribute them in the order in which they were parked. The call parked longest would be answered first.

You can configure call park simply by adding an ephone-dn designated for call park purposes. Example 6.6 creates two ephone-dns designated for call park.

Example 6.6   *Configuring Call Park Ephone-DNs*

```
CME_Voice(config)# ephone-dn 50
CME_Voice(config-ephone-dn)# number 3001
CME_Voice(config-ephone-dn)# name Maintenance
CME_Voice(config-ephone-dn)# park-slot
CME_Voice(config-ephone-dn)# exit
CME_Voice(config)# ephone-dn 51
CME_Voice(config-ephone-dn)# number 3002
CME_Voice(config-ephone-dn)# name Sales
CME_Voice(config-ephone-dn)# park-slot ?
  reserved-for  Reserve this park slot for the exclusive use of the phone with the
  extension   indicated by the transfer target extension number
  timeout       Set call park timeout
  <cr>
```

Key Topic

continues

Example 6.6 *Configuring Call Park Ephone-DNs* *continued*

```
CME_Voice(config-ephone-dn)# park-slot timeout ?
  <0-65535>  Specify the park timeout (seconds) before the call is returned to the
    number it was  parked from
CME_Voice(config-ephone-dn)# park-slot timeout 60 ?
  limit  Set call park timeout count limit
CME_Voice(config-ephone-dn)# park-slot timeout 60 limit ?
  <1-65535>  Specify the number of park timeout cycles before the call is
    disconnected
CME_Voice(config-ephone-dn)# park-slot timeout 60 limit 10 ?
  notify    Define additional extension number to notify for park timeout
  recall    recall transfer back to originator phone after timeout
  transfer  Transfer to originator or specified destination after timeout limit
    exceeded
  <cr>
CME_Voice(config-ephone-dn)# park-slot timeout 60 limit 10 recall ?
  alternate  Transfer to alternate target if original target is busy
  retry      Set recall/transfer retry interval if target is in use
  <cr>
CME_Voice(config-ephone-dn)# park-slot timeout 60 limit 10 recall
```

Look at the configuration of ephone-dn 50 in Example 6.6. Designating a call park extension is as simple as entering the **park-slot** command under ephone-dn configuration mode.

> **Note**   When planning to configure call park, keep in mind that each parked call consumes an ephone-dn slot (regardless of single- or dual-line configurations). You may need to increase the number of ephone-dns (**max-dn**) that your CME deployment supports.

Example 6.6 also shows that you have many options when you designate call park–specific ephone-dns. Table 6.2 explains where you can use these options.

Table 6.2   *Options for Use With the* **park slot** *Command*

Command	Function
reserved-for *<dn>*	Allows you to reserve the call park slot for the directory number (DN) you enter. Other phones will not be able to use the call park slot.
timeout *<seconds>*	Specifies the number of seconds CME should wait before notifying the phone that parked the call that the call is still parked. To notify, CME rings that phone for one second and displays a message on the LCD display.

Command	Function
limit <count>	Limits the number of timeout intervals a parked call can reach. After this limit is reached, the parked call is disconnected. As a side note, setting this value quite high is recommended. Customers tend to get bothered when they are on hold for an extended period and then are disconnected.
notify <dn>	Notifies a different DN, in addition to the phone that parked the call, when the parked call reaches timeout period.
only	Used with the prior notify syntax; instructs CME to only ring the DN specified with the notify command rather than ring the original phone.
recall	Causes the call to return (transfer back) to the original phone that parked the call after the parked call reaches the timeout period.
transfer <dn>	Causes the call to transfer to a specified DN after the parked call reaches the timeout period.
alternate <dn>	Allows you to specify an alternate transfer destination should the destination DN specified in the transfer command be on the phone.
retry <seconds>	Sets the amount of time before CME attempts to transfer a parked call again.

There's plenty of flexibility in configuring your call park options. Once you have at least one ephone-dn designated for call park (by using the park-slot command), the Park softkey will appear on the IP phones on an active call.

Note You must restart or reset the IP phones after you have configured the initial ephone-dn designated call park before the Park softkey will appear on active calls. You can accomplish this by using the restart or reset command from telephony service configuration mode.

To park a call, simply press the Park softkey while on an active call. CME will find a parking slot for the call and send a message back to the phone that parked the call, as shown in Figure 6.6.

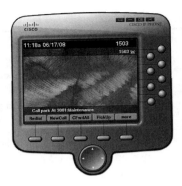

Figure 6.6   *IP Phone After Parking a Call*

When the user parks the call, CME will allocate the first available park slot. Sometimes, you may want to designate which parking slot the call gets, in cases such as those in which each department of the company is assigned a unique call park number. In this case, you can transfer the call (using the Trnsfer softkey) directly into the parking slot you want.

Note   If you want to use a call park system in which each department has its own call park slot, it may be beneficial to configure multiple ephone-dns assigned to each department designated for call park. Otherwise, you will be able to park only one call for each department.

You can answer parked calls in one of three ways:

■ Dial directly into the call park slot. For example, lifting a phone handset and dialing 3001 will answer whatever call you have parked at 3001.

■ Press the PickUp softkey and dial the call park number you wish to answer.

■ From the phone at which the call was parked, press the PickUp softkey followed by an asterisk (*) to recall the most recently parked call back to the phone.

Configuring Call Pickup

Michael works in the sales department at Widget Things, Inc. Being the newest member to the group, he works the late shift, covering calls from 10:30 a.m. to 7:30 p.m. Around 6:00 p.m., the last coworker leaves and Michael handles all the incoming calls alone. Unfortunately, many of Widget Things' customers have the direct contact information for other sales employees, so a typical evening for Michael consists of running around answering phone calls coming in on the IP phones of the five other sales reps. This is where call pickup features can help.

Call pickup allows you to answer another ringing phone in the organization from your local phone. This is accomplished by pushing the PickUp softkey on the IP phone while another phone is ringing. The call automatically transfers to the local phone, where you can answer it. Of course, the organization is large and there could be many ringing phones at the same time, so call pickup gives you the opportunity to divide the phones into groups. You assign each of these groups a number in the CME configuration, as shown in Figure 6.7.

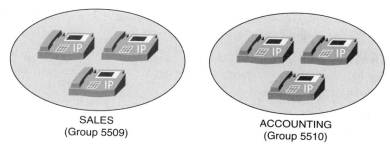

SALES
(Group 5509)

ACCOUNTING
(Group 5510)

Figure 6.7 *Designing Call Pickup Groups*

Based on the softkey used, the users can answer other ringing phones in their own group or enter other group numbers to answer the ringing phones in that group.

The configuration of call pickup is incredibly simple: just design your groups of phones and assign the ephone-dns to the groups. Example 6.7 assigns ephone-dns 1, 2, and 3 to the SALES group and ephone-dns 4, 5, and 6 to the ACCOUNTING group, shown in Figure 6.7.

Example 6.7 *Configuring Call Pickup*

```
CME_Voice(config)# ephone-dn 1
CME_Voice(config-ephone-dn)# pickup-group 5509
CME_Voice(config-ephone-dn)# ephone-dn 2
CME_Voice(config-ephone-dn)# pickup-group 5509
CME_Voice(config-ephone-dn)# ephone-dn 3
CME_Voice(config-ephone-dn)# pickup-group 5509
CME_Voice(config-ephone-dn)# ephone-dn 4
CME_Voice(config-ephone-dn)# pickup-group 5510
CME_Voice(config-ephone-dn)# ephone-dn 5
CME_Voice(config-ephone-dn)# pickup-group 5510
CME_Voice(config-ephone-dn)# ephone-dn 6
CME_Voice(config-ephone-dn)# pickup-group 5510
```

Key
Topic

Note   When you assign the first ephone-dn to a call pickup group number, CME creates the call pickup group. There is no additional command needed for the call pickup group creation.

After you have assigned the ephone-dns to the respective call pickup groups, users can begin answering other ringing phones. CME permits three methods to answer other ringing phones:

Key Topic

- **Directed pickup:** You can pick up another ringing phone directly by pressing the PickUp softkey and dialing the DN of the ringing phone. CME then transfers the call and immediately answers it at your local phone.

- **Local group pickup:** You can pick up another ringing phone in the same call pickup group as your phone by pressing the GPickUp button and entering an asterisk (*) when you hear the second dial tone.

- **Other group pickup:** You can pick up a ringing phone in another group by pressing the GPickUp button and entering the other group number when you hear the second dial tone.

If multiple phones are ringing in the user's call pickup group, CME will answer the oldest ringing phone when the user invokes call pickup.

Note   The GPickUp softkey functions differently depending on the call pickup configuration in CME. If there is only one group configured in CME, pressing the GPickUp button automatically answers the call from your own group number. You will not hear a second dial tone and you do not need to dial an asterisk to signify your own group, because only one group is defined. Once you have configured multiple groups in CME, you will hear a second dial tone after pressing the GPickUp softkey, at which point you can dial either an asterisk for the local group or another group number.

Tip   By default, users can pick up other ringing phones managed by CME by using the directed pickup method, described previously, regardless of the destination device being assigned to a call pickup group. To disable this feature, enter the command **no service directed-pickup** from telephony service configuration mode. Once you enter this command, the PickUp softkey on the IP phones operates as a local group pickup button. Pressing the softkey will then immediately answer ringing calls in your own local pickup group.

Configuring Intercom

Intercom configurations are common in traditional phone systems. This feature allows an administrative assistant and executive to work closely together by having a speakerphone "tether" between them.

Technically, the way intercom deployments work is through a speed-dial and auto-answer speed-dial configuration. If the administrative assistant presses the button configured as an intercom, it speed dials the executive's phone, which auto-answers the call on muted speakerphone. To establish two-way communication, the executive deactivates mute (by pressing the Mute button). Understanding this helps make the intercom configuration much clearer.

To configure intercom functionality, you must configure two new ephone-dns, one for each side of the intercom connection. These intercom lines should be assigned a number, just like any other ephone-dn. However, in order to prevent others from accidentally (or purposely) dialing the intercom and ending up on muted speakerphone for a random IP phone, the number should be something users cannot dial from other IP phones. The configuration in Example 6.8 accomplishes this objective.

Example 6.8   *Configuring Intercom*

```
CME_Voice(config)# ephone-dn 60
CME_Voice(config-ephone-dn)# number A100
CME_Voice(config-ephone-dn)# intercom A101 label "Manager"
CME_Voice(config-ephone-dn)# exit
CME_Voice(config)# ephone-dn 61
CME_Voice(config-ephone-dn)# number A101
CME_Voice(config-ephone-dn)# intercom A100 label "Assistant"
CME_Voice(config-ephone-dn)# exit
CME_Voice(config)# ephone 1
CME_Voice(config-ephone)# button 2:60
CME_Voice(config-ephone)# restart
restarting 0014.1C48.E71A
CME_Voice(config-ephone)# exit
CME_Voice(config)# ephone 2
CME_Voice(config-ephone)# button 2:61
CME_Voice(config-ephone)# restart
restarting 0019.D122.DCF3
```

Key Topic

Notice the number assigned to ephone-dn 60 is A100. You cannot dial this number from a Cisco IP phone keypad, but you can assign it to a speed-dial button. The **intercom** command acts like a speed-dial button on the ephone-dn. In the case of ephone-dn 60, the command **intercom A101** dials the number A101, which is assigned to ephone-dn 61. Because ephone-dn 61 is also configured with the **intercom** command, it auto-answers the incoming call on muted speakerphone. The **label** syntax allows you to assign a logical name to the speed-dial; otherwise, the A101 or A100 label will show up next to the line button on the phone. There are three other arguments you can use with the **intercom** command to tune the functionality:

- **barge-in:** Automatically places an existing call on hold and causes the intercom to immediately answer.

- **no-auto-answer:** Causes the phone to ring rather than auto-answer on speakerphone.

- **no-mute:** Causes the intercom to answer with unmuted speakerphone rather than muted. While this is beneficial to allow immediate two-way conversation, you also run the risk of one side barging into existing conversations or background noise.

Configuring Paging

Paging is similar to the intercom concept; however, it provides only a one-way automatic path for communication. This is useful to allow broadcast messages, such as emergency notifications or to notify employees of holding calls.

The CME paging system works by designating an ephone-dn as a paging number. Calls to the DN of this ephone-dn will broadcast to the IP phones that you have assigned to this paging group. Figure 6.8 illustrates this concept.

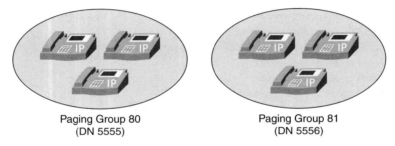

Paging Group 80   Paging Group 81
   (DN 5555)   (DN 5556)

Figure 6.8   *Call Paging Functionality*

As shown in Figure 6.8, calls to DN 5555 will page the three phones assigned to that paging group. Calls to 5556 will do the same for the paging group 81.

Note   You can assign an IP phone to only one paging group. However, CME does allow you to create paging numbers that page multiple paging groups, thus providing directed and company-wide paging functionality.

CME supports paging in unicast and multicast configurations. Paging in unicast configuration causes the CME router to send individual messages to each one of the IP phones in the group. So, if there were six IP phones assigned to paging group 80, a page to the group would cause the CME router to stream six individual audio signals to the devices. Because of the overhead this causes, CME limits unicast paging groups to a maximum of ten IP phones.

Multicast configuration allows the CME router to send one audio stream, which only the IP phones assigned to the paging group will receive. This allows a virtually limitless number of IP phones in each paging group. Sounds like the winning option, right? The catch is this: in order to support multicast paging, you must configure the foundation network environment to support multicast traffic. Some of these configurations can get quite complex and are covered in the CCNP certification track.

The three paging configurations are unicast paging, multicast paging, and multiple-group paging. Example 6.9 shows unicast, single-group paging.

Example 6.9   *Configuring Unicast, Single-Group Paging*

```
CME_Voice(config)# ephone-dn 80
CME_Voice(config-ephone-dn)# number 5555
CME_Voice(config-ephone-dn)# paging
CME_Voice(config-ephone-dn)# exit
CME_Voice(config)# ephone 1
CME_Voice(config-ephone)# paging-dn 80
CME_Voice(config-ephone)# exit
CME_Voice(config)# ephone 2
CME_Voice(config-ephone)# paging-dn 80
```

Key Topic

Calls to the paging number 5555 now page both ephones 1 and 2 using unicast paging. To convert the configuration in Example 6.9 to multicast paging, you could modify the **paging** command with the following syntax:

```
CME_Voice(config)# ephone-dn 80
CME_Voice(config-ephone-dn)# paging ip 239.1.1.100 port 2000
```

The IP address that follows the **paging** command is a multicast address. Think of this as a "radio frequency" that the IP phones tune to each time a page occurs. Just like a car radio tuning to a specific FM frequency to hear a radio station, the IP phones tune into the IP address 239.1.1.100 and hear the audio stream for the paging system. As mentioned before, you must configure your network to properly support multicast traffic. Otherwise your switches will treat this multicast traffic just like it treats broadcasts, flooding your network on all ports each time a page occurs.

The paging configuration in Example 6.10 demonstrates the configuration of a multiple-group paging system. Ephones 1 and 2 will continue to use ephone-dn 80 as their dedicated paging group. Ephones 3 and 4 will use ephone-dn 81. This time, a third paging group enables you to page both paging groups at once. This can give an organization the flexibility to page specific departments or the company as a whole.

Example 6.10   *Configuring Multiple-Group Paging*

```
CME_Voice(config)# ephone-dn 80
CME_Voice(config-ephone-dn)# number 5555
CME_Voice(config-ephone-dn)# paging
CME_Voice(config-ephone-dn)# exit
CME_Voice(config)# ephone-dn 81
CME_Voice(config-ephone-dn)# number 5556
CME_Voice(config-ephone-dn)# paging
CME_Voice(config-ephone-dn)# exit
CME_Voice(config)# ephone-dn 82
CME_Voice(config-ephone-dn)# number 5557
```

continues

Example 6.10   *Configuring Multiple-Group Paging*   *continued*

```
CME_Voice(config-ephone-dn)# paging group 81,82
CME_Voice(config-ephone-dn)# exit
CME_Voice(config)# ephone 1
CME_Voice(config-ephone)# paging-dn 80
CME_Voice(config-ephone)# exit
CME_Voice(config)# ephone 2
CME_Voice(config-ephone)# paging-dn 80
CME_Voice(config-ephone)# exit
CME_Voice(config)# ephone 3
CME_Voice(config-ephone)# paging-dn 81
CME_Voice(config-ephone)# exit
CME_Voice(config)# ephone 4
CME_Voice(config-ephone)# paging-dn 81
```

With the configuration shown in Example 6.10, a call to DN 5555 will page ephones 1 and 2, a call to DN 5556 will page ephones 3 and 4, and a call to DN 5557 will page all ephones. You do not need to assign any ephones to paging-dn 82 because this ephone-dn represents a group of both paging-dns 80 and 81.

Note   CME allows you to list up to ten paging numbers using the **paging group** command.

Configuring After-Hours Call Blocking

In the traditional telephony realm, there have been many recorded incidents of unauthorized phone calls being placed after-hours, when most, if not all, staff has left for the evening. To prevent this, you can implement after-hours call blocking on CME.

After-hours call blocking allows you to define ranges of times specified as after-hours intervals. You can then list number patterns that are disallowed during those intervals. If a user places a call during the after-hours time range that matches one of the defined patterns, CME will play a reorder tone and disconnect the call.

Of course, there are exceptions to every rule. You may want to have some phones completely exempt from the policy, or give users a "back door" around the restrictions if they are working late and need to make business-related calls that CME would typically restrict. The after-hours call blocking configuration on CME provides for both of these scenarios. You have the option to completely exempt certain IP phones from the after-hours restrictions or to provide users with a PIN they can enter into the IP phone. If they enter the PIN correctly, CME exempts the IP phone from the after-hours policy for a configurable amount of time.

Note   There are some patterns that may be beneficial to block all the time. For example, 1-900 numbers in the United States often represent high-cost, less-than-reputable business-es that are typically banned from all corporate environments. CME also allows you to cre-ate a 24/7, nonexemptible pattern that is disallowed at all times, using the after-hours call blocking system.

After-hours call blocking has three major steps of configuration:

Step 1.   Define days and/or hours of the day that your company considers off-hours.

Step 2.   Specify patterns that you would like to block during the times specified in Step 1.

Step 3.   Create exemptions to the policy, if needed.

You will perform most of the configuration for the after-hours call blocking restrictions from telephony service configuration mode. Example 6.11 demonstrates the configura-tion of after-hours time intervals.

Example 6.11   *Configuring After-Hours Time Ranges and Dates*

```
CME_Voice(config)# telephony-service
CME_Voice(config-telephony)# after-hours ?
  block   define after-hours block pattern
  date    define month and day
  day     define day in week
CME_Voice(config-telephony)# after-hours day ?
  DAY  day of week (Mon, Tue, Wed, etc)
CME_Voice(config-telephony)# after-hours day mon ?
  hh:mm  Time to start (hh:mm)
CME_Voice(config-telephony)# after-hours day mon 17:00 ?
  hh:mm  Time to stop (hh:mm)
CME_Voice(config-telephony)# after-hours day mon 17:00 8:00
CME_Voice(config-telephony)# after-hours day tue 17:00 8:00
CME_Voice(config-telephony)# after-hours day wed 17:00 8:00
CME_Voice(config-telephony)# after-hours day thu 17:00 8:00
CME_Voice(config-telephony)# after-hours day fri 17:00 8:00
CME_Voice(config-telephony)# after-hours date ?
  MONTH  Month (Jan, Feb, Mar, etc)
CME_Voice(config-telephony)# after-hours date dec ?
  <1-31>  day of month in date
CME_Voice(config-telephony)# after-hours date dec 25 ?
  hh:mm  Time to start (hh:mm)
CME_Voice(config-telephony)# after-hours date dec 25 00:00 ?
  hh:mm  Time to stop (hh:mm)
CME_Voice(config-telephony)# after-hours date dec 25 00:00 00:00
CME_Voice(config-telephony)# after-hours date jan 1 00:00 00:00
```

Key
Topic

The configuration in Example 6.11 defines weekdays, from 5:00 p.m. to 8:00 a.m. the next day, as after-hours, along with the entire day on December 25 (Christmas) and January 1 (New Year's Day).

In the next step of the after-hours configuration, you define the patterns that CME should block during the after-hours time slots you have configured. See Example 6.12.

> **Note**   Chapters 8 and 9 discuss the patterns you can use for matching fully. For now, examples in this chapter use the "." wildcard, which matches any digit dialed, and the "T" wildcard, which matches any number of digits.

Example 6.12   *Configuring After-Hours Block Patterns*

```
CME_Voice(config)# telephony-service
CME_Voice(config-telephony)# after-hours block ?
  pattern  block pattern
CME_Voice(config-telephony)# after-hours block pattern ?
  <1-32>  index of patterns
CME_Voice(config-telephony)# after-hours block pattern 1 ?
  WORD  digits string for after hour block pattern
CME_Voice(config-telephony)# after-hours block pattern 1 91..........
CME_Voice(config-telephony)# after-hours block pattern 2 9011T
CME_Voice(config-telephony)# after-hours block pattern 3 91900....... ?
  7-24  block pattern works for 7 * 24
  <cr>
CME_Voice(config-telephony)# after-hours block pattern 3 91900....... 7-24
```

You might have noticed based on the context-sensitive help output in Example 6.12 that the CME router allows you to configure up to 32 indexes of block patterns. The initial block pattern 1 matches and blocks long distance numbers; block pattern 2 matches and blocks international numbers; block pattern 3 matches and blocks 1-900 toll calls. Notice that block pattern 3 is followed by the **7-24** keyword. This additional syntax tells the CME router to block calls to this pattern at all times. If you enter block patterns with this keyword, phones exempted from other after-hours blocked numbers will not be exempt from these patterns.

> **Note**   If you need more flexibility than after-hours blocking provides, you can also use Class of Restriction (COR) features with CME. *Cisco Voice over IP (CVOICE) Authorized Self-Study Guide*, Third Edition, by Kevin Wallace (Cisco Press, 2008) has more information on the configuration of COR on Cisco routers.
>
> For more information on the web, use the following URL: http://tinyurl.com/64256f.

The final step in the configuration of after-hours blocking is to allow any necessary exemptions to the policy, as shown in Example 6.13. You can add exemptions on a per–IP phone basis or by using one or more PIN numbers to allow on-demand access to block patterns (with the exception of the patterns defined with the **7-24** keyword) from any IP phone. Example 6.13 configures ephone 1 to be exempt from the after-hours call blocking policy. Ephones 2 and 3 are configured with PIN numbers. In order to become exempt from the after-hours call blocking policy, the user using the phone must enter the necessary PIN number.

Example 6.13   *Configuring After-Hours Exemptions*

```
CME_Voice(config)# ephone 1
CME_Voice(config-ephone)# after-hour exempt
CME_Voice(config-ephone)# exit
CME_Voice(config)# ephone 2
CME_Voice(config-ephone)# pin ?
  WORD  A sequence of digits - representing personal identification number
CME_Voice(config-ephone)# pin 1234
CME_Voice(config-ephone)# exit
CME_Voice(config)# ephone 3
CME_Voice(config-ephone)# pin 4321
CME_Voice(config-ephone)# exit
CME_Voice(config)# telephony-service
CME_Voice(config-telephony)# login timeout 120 clear 23:00
```

Note   The PIN number can be any number between four and eight digits.

The last line in Example 6.13 is a key to allowing the PIN numbers to function properly. By default, all the CME-supported Cisco IP phones have a Login softkey on the LCD display. This softkey is dimmed and unusable until you enter the **login** command from telephony service configuration mode. The **timeout** value that follows this command represents the amount of idle time before the phone automatically revokes the last PIN number entered. The **clear** value is an absolute time at which the last-entered PIN number becomes invalid. In the case of Example 6.13, the PIN will clear at 11:00 p.m. regardless of the last time it was entered. This does not prevent users from logging back in by entering their PIN number a second time after 11:00 p.m.

Note   The default timeout for the **login** command is 60 minutes. Also, you will need to restart or reset all phones before the **login** command will take effect.

Configuring CDRs and Call Accounting

"Who made that call?" That question could arise for many reasons. Perhaps the entire police and fire departments arrive at the front door of your company because of an emergency call originating from your business. Perhaps management is reviewing the recent long distance bill and came across an international call to Aruba that was four hours in length. Whatever the reason, you can find the answer by looking through the archived Call Detail Records (CDRs), as long as you have configured the CME router to support them.

CDRs contain valuable information about the calls coming into, going out of, and between the IP phones on your network. These records contain all the information you need to find who called whom and how long they were talking. The CME router can log CDRs to the buffered memory (RAM) of the router, to a syslog server, or to both. Storing the CDRs in the RAM of the router is better than nothing, but not very effective. If the CME router ever loses power, all the CDRs will be lost. Likewise, the RAM of the router has limited storage and is not an effective solution. Viewing CDRs from the log file on the CME router is very cryptic and tedious to understand. Example 6.14 demonstrates the syntax you can use to enable logging of CDRs to the buffered memory of the router.

Example 6.14   *Configuring CDR Logging to Buffered Memory*

```
CME_Voice(config)# logging buffered 512000
CME_Voice(config)# dial-control-mib ?
  max-size      Specify the maximum size of the dial control history table
  retain-timer  Specify timer for entries in dial control history table
CME_Voice(config)# dial-control-mib retain-timer ?
  <0-35791>  Time (in minutes) for removing an entry
CME_Voice(config)# dial-control-mib retain-timer 10080
CME_Voice(config)# dial-control-mib max-size ?
  <0-1200>  Number of entries in the dial control history table
CME_Voice(config)# dial-control-mib max-size 700
```

Example 6.14 specifies the following parameters for CDR buffered logging:

- 512,000 bytes of memory dedicated to the logging functions of the router.

- CDRs are kept for 10,080 minutes (7 days).

- The CME router keeps a maximum of 700 CDRs in memory.

To view the CDRs recorded by CME, use the **show logging** command, as shown in Example 6.15.

Example 6.15   *The* **show logging** *Command Output*

```
CME_Voice# show logging
Syslog logging: enabled (12 messages dropped, 1 messages rate-limited,
                0 flushes, 0 overruns, xml disabled, filtering disabled)
    Console logging: level debugging, 168 messages logged, xml disabled,
                    filtering disabled
<…output omitted>
Log Buffer (512000 bytes):

*Jun 18 01:57:08.987: %SYS-5-CONFIG_I: Configured from console by Jeremy on vty0
  (172.30.3.28)
*Jun 18 01:57:48.640: %VOIPAAA-5-VOIP_CALL_HISTORY: CallLegType 1, ConnectionId
  B71427FB3C1011DD80EEB6A01B061E9, SetupTime *18:57:17.970 ARIZONA Tue Jun 17
  2008, PeerAddress 1503, PeerSubAddress , DisconnectCause 1    , DisconnectText
  unassigned number (1), ConnectTime *18:57:48.640 ARIZONA Tue Jun 17 2008,
  DisconnectTime *18:57:48.640 ARIZONA Tue Jun 17 2008, CallOrigin 2, ChargedUnits
  0, InfoType 2, TransmitPackets 0, TransmitBytes 0, ReceivePackets 0, ReceiveBytes
  0
*Jun 18 01:57:48.640: %VOIPAAA-5-VOIP_FEAT_HISTORY: FEAT_VSA=fn:CFBY,ft:06/17/2008
  18:57:18.623,frs:0,fid:129,fcid:B77841E83C1011DD80F3B6A01B061E9,legID:0,frson:2,
  fdcnt:1,fwder:1501,fwdee:1503,fwdto:1599,frm:1501,bguid:B71427FB3C1011DD80EEB6A
  001B061E9
*Jun 18 01:57:48.640: %VOIPAAA-5-VOIP_FEAT_HISTORY: FEAT_VSA=fn:TWC,ft:06/17/2008
  18:57:17.967,cgn:1503,cdn:,frs:0,fid:126,fcid:B71427FB3C1011DD80EEB6A01B061E9,
  legID:4B,bguid:B71427FB3C1011DD80EEB6A001B061E9
<…output omitted>
```

What you see here are three CDR entries that record a call from x1503 to x1501. If you are able to decode most of what is displayed in that log, you are definitely ahead of the game.

Sending messages to a syslog server is better than sending them to the RAM of the CME router. A syslog server is a PC or server running a dedicated application that receives and stores logging messages from one or more devices. There are many syslog server platforms available for download on the Internet.

Note   The Kiwi Syslog Daemon (http://www.kiwisyslog.com) is by far my (Jeremy) favorite syslog platform available. The fact that it is free helps quite a bit, but it is also easy to install and manage.

After you have set up a syslog server, you can direct the CME router to send CDR records to it by using the following syntax:

```
CME_Voice(config)# gw-accounting syslog
CME_Voice(config)# logging 172.30.100.101
```

The initial command in this syntax directs the CDR records to the syslog server. The second command tells the CME router where the syslog server is located; in this case 172.30.100.101. Figure 6.9 shows the CDR records being received by the Kiwi Syslog application.

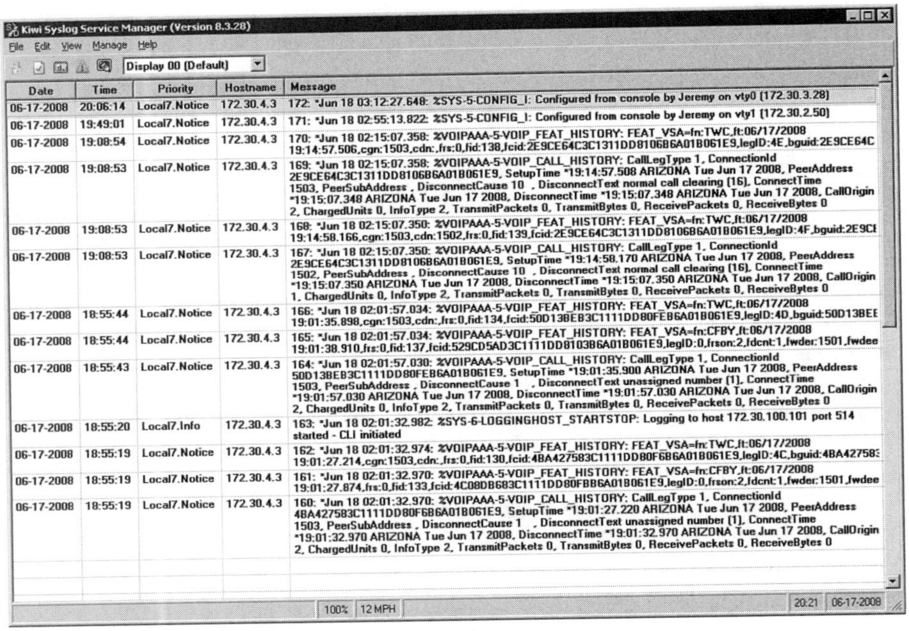

Figure 6.9   *CDR Records Logged to a Kiwi Syslog Server*

The output shown on the syslog server is the same messages received in the buffered logging. Although it is a little easier to read than scrolling through wrapped terminal output, the messages are just as cryptic. For this reason, many third-party vendors have created CDR interpreters that format the syslog data into easy-to-understand spreadsheets and HTML pages.

Tip   Cisco offers a web-based utility that can show many third-party software applications geared around CDR interpretation. You can find the partner search application at this URL: http://tinyurl.com/5okclk.

It is quite common for an organization to use these CDRs for billing purposes. Businesses track the long distance and international calls to the department level to assist in budget accounting. Although it is possible to keep track of the extension numbers that are in each department and the calls they make, the call data is easier to manage if CME can flag the CDR with an account code.

Businesses can distribute account codes to each department in the organization. For example, the East Coast sales group might get account code 1850, the West Coast sales group 1851, management 1852, and so on. You could then train the users in each department to enter this account code each time they make a long distance or international call by pressing the Acct softkey on the phone. This softkey appears when the IP phone is in the ring out or connected state, as shown in Figure 6.10.

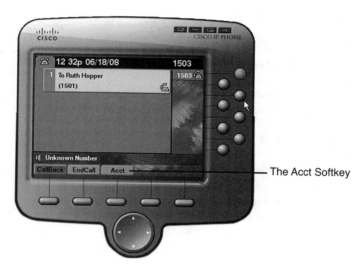

Figure 6.10   *The Acct Softkey in the Ring Out State*

After the user has pressed the Acct softkey, an Acct prompt appears at the bottom of the phone, where the user can enter their department account number followed by the pound key (#). Entering this number during the ring out or connected call state does not interrupt the call in any way. After the user enters the account number, CME flags the CDR records with the account number dialed. This allows for easy filtering and accurate billing to each department.

Configuring Music on Hold

What voice network would be complete without the sound of music coming through handsets on hold everywhere? CME has the ability to stream Music on Hold (MoH) from specified WAV or AU audio files that you copy to the flash memory of the router.

CME can stream this audio either in multiple unicast streams (which is more resource intensive) or in a single multicast stream (which is less resource intensive, but requires a multicast network configuration). In addition, CME can stream the MoH using G.711 or G.729 codecs.

Note Because the G.729 audio codec is designed for human voice, the quality of MoH streamed using G.729 is significantly lower than MoH streamed using G.711. In addition, CME will use transcoding DSP resources to convert the MoH to the G.729 codec. With all these factors, using G.711 for your MoH, if at all possible, is highly recommend.

Example 6.16 configures a CME router to support multicast MoH, streaming music from a file in flash called bonjovi.wav.

Example 6.16 *Configuring MoH Support*

```
CME_Voice(config)# telephony-service
CME_Voice(config-telephony)# moh ?
  WORD  music-on-hold filename containing G.711 A-law or u-law 8KHz encoded audio
    file (.wav or .au format). The file must be loaded into the routers flash
    memory.
CME_Voice(config-telephony)# moh bonjovi.wav
CME_Voice(config-telephony)# multicast moh ?
  A.B.C.D  Define music-on-hold IP multicast address from flash
CME_Voice(config-telephony)# multicast moh 239.1.1.55 ?
  port  Define media port for multicast moh
CME_Voice(config-telephony)# multicast moh 239.1.1.55 port ?
  <2000-65535>  Specify the RTP port: 2000 - 65535
CME_Voice(config-telephony)# multicast moh 239.1.1.55 port 2123
```

Note Because the U.S. government sees MoH as a type of broadcasting, you must purchase a license if you intend to play any songs covered by a copyright (such as music by Bon Jovi) over MoH. With that in mind, there are thousands of royalty-free songs available on the Internet that you could use for MoH.

Enabling the CME GUI

Cisco provides a graphical user interface (GUI) that allows you to manage some of the CME basic functions through a web interface. These basic functions include configuring and managing ephones, ephone-dns, some system and voice-mail functions, and reports.

Note   After being in the Cisco world for some time, you will definitely get the feeling that real Cisco techs use the command-line interface (CLI). Seeing the CME GUI will only reinforce that feeling; although it does enable you to configure some basic settings, you can accomplish far more by using the command line. The GUI would suffice for a phone administrator whose primary job is the configuration of new phones and phone lines.

Before you are able to access the GUI, there are a few preliminary configuration steps you need to have in place. First and foremost, you need to ensure that you have loaded into the flash memory of the CME router the files that power the GUI. If you extracted the TAR file that contains the full CME installation into the flash of the CME router, the GUI files should be included. If you installed the CME files individually, be sure to download and install the CME GUI TAR file pack from Cisco.com. For more information on downloading and installing CME files into the flash of the router, check out Chapter 4, "Installing Cisco Unified Communications Manager Express."

Tip   You can always verify that you have installed the GUI files by performing a directory list of your router's flash. Different CME versions organize the file structure differently, but should have relatively the same files. Here's a directory listing of CME version 4.3:

```
CME_Voice# dir flash:
Directory of flash:/
     1  drw-           0  Jun 10 2008 14:57:20 -07:00  bacdprompts
    13  -rw-       22224  Jun 10 2008 14:57:30 -07:00  CME43-full-readme-
        v.2.0.txt
    14  drw-           0  Jun 10 2008 14:57:30 -07:00  Desktops
    27  drw-           0  Jun 10 2008 14:57:36 -07:00  gui
    45  -rw-      496521  May 12 2008 21:30:00 -07:00  music-on-hold.au
    46  drw-           0  May 12 2008 21:30:00 -07:00  phone
   127  drw-           0  May 12 2008 21:35:46 -07:00  ringtones
   161  -rw-    45460908  Jun 12 2008 15:17:22 -07:00  c2801-adventerprisek9_
        ivs-mz.124-15.T5.bin
129996800 bytes total (16123904 bytes free)
CME_Voice# dir flash:gui
Directory of flash:/gui/

    28  -rw-         953  Jun 10 2008 14:57:36 -07:00  Delete.gif
    29  -rw-        3845  Jun 10 2008 14:57:38 -07:00  admin_user.html
    30  -rw-      647358  Jun 10 2008 14:57:40 -07:00  admin_user.js
    31  -rw-        1029  Jun 10 2008 14:57:40 -07:00  CiscoLogo.gif
    32  -rw-         174  Jun 10 2008 14:57:40 -07:00  Tab.gif
    33  -rw-       16344  Jun 10 2008 14:57:42 -07:00  dom.js
    34  -rw-         864  Jun 10 2008 14:57:42 -07:00  downarrow.gif
    35  -rw-        6328  Jun 10 2008 14:57:42 -07:00  ephone_admin.html
    36  -rw-        4558  Jun 10 2008 14:57:42 -07:00  logohome.gif
```

```
37   -rw-        3724   Jun 10 2008 14:57:42 -07:00  normal_user.html
38   -rw-           0   Jun 10 2008 14:57:42 -07:00  normal_user.js
39   -rw-         843   May 12 2008 21:29:56 -07:00  sxiconad.gif
40   -rw-        1347   May 12 2008 21:29:56 -07:00  Plus.gif
41   -rw-        2399   May 12 2008 21:29:56 -07:00  telephony_service.html
42   -rw-         870   May 12 2008 21:29:56 -07:00  uparrow.gif
43   -rw-        9968   May 12 2008 21:29:56 -07:00  xml-test.html
44   -rw-        3412   May 12 2008 21:29:58 -07:00  xml.template
129996800 bytes total (16123904 bytes free)
```

Because you will be accessing the GUI through a web interface, you need to turn the CME router into a mini-web server to serve up the CME pages. The configuration in Example 6.17 accomplishes this feat.

Example 6.17   *Configuring the CME Router as a Web Server*

```
CME_Voice(config)# ip http server
CME_Voice(config)# ip http secure-server
% Generating 1024 bit RSA keys, keys will be non-exportable...[OK]


CME_Voice(config)# ip http path flash:/gui
CME_Voice(config)# ip http authentication local
```

Example 6.17 enables both the HTTP (**ip http server**) and HTTPS (**ip http secure-server**) services on the router. Of course, HTTPS is the preferred method of accessing the CME GUI because the CME router encrypts all communication. The **ip http path flash:/gui** command sets the HTTP server to use files from the GUI subdirectory of flash memory of the CME router for HTTP requests. Finally, the CME router will use its local user database to authenticate users attempting to access the web interface.

Note   You might need to change the argument of the **ip http path** command based on where the HTML files are located for the CME GUI. Earlier versions of CME placed all CME files directly into flash without any directory structure. In this case, the command should be entered as **ip http path flash:**.

The next step in enabling the CME GUI is to create a user account with permission to access and manage the CME router. Example 6.18 configures this.

Example 6.18   *Creating a CME Web Administrator Account and Adding Permissions*

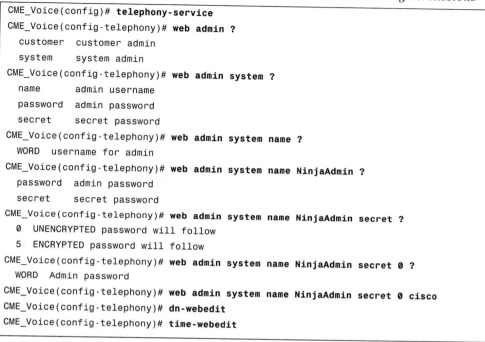

```
CME_Voice(config)# telephony-service
CME_Voice(config-telephony)# web admin ?
  customer   customer admin
  system     system admin
CME_Voice(config-telephony)# web admin system ?
  name      admin username
  password  admin password
  secret    secret password
CME_Voice(config-telephony)# web admin system name ?
  WORD  username for admin
CME_Voice(config-telephony)# web admin system name NinjaAdmin ?
  password  admin password
  secret    secret password
CME_Voice(config-telephony)# web admin system name NinjaAdmin secret ?
  0  UNENCRYPTED password will follow
  5  ENCRYPTED password will follow
CME_Voice(config-telephony)# web admin system name NinjaAdmin secret 0 ?
  WORD  Admin password
CME_Voice(config-telephony)# web admin system name NinjaAdmin secret 0 cisco
CME_Voice(config-telephony)# dn-webedit
CME_Voice(config-telephony)# time-webedit
```

The CME router is now equipped with a user account called NinjaAdmin with the password cisco.

By default, the CME GUI is not able to add ephone-dns to the CME configuration or modify the time on the CME router. The **dn-webedit** and **time-webedit** commands unlock these functions.

Note   If you are synchronizing your router's clock via NTP, do *not* enter the **time-webedit** command, to ensure that the time remains set to the more accurate NTP server.

The CME router's web interface is now ready to go. The final step is to connect to the CME router using a supported web browser platform.

Note   At the time of this writing, the only supported web browser for CME is Internet Explorer version 6 or later. However, with the continued popularity of alternative browsers such as Mozilla Firefox and Safari, this is likely to change in the near future.

Key Topic

From the supported web browser, enter the URL **http://<CME_IP_Address>/ccme.html** to access the CME GUI. After authenticating with your web admin account, the CME management console is displayed, as shown in Figure 6.11.

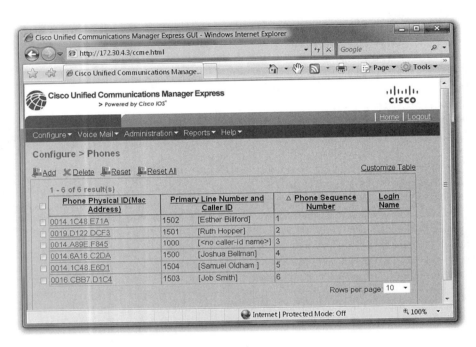

Figure 6.11   *CME Web-Based Management Interface*

Note   The image shown in Figure 6.11 was captured after clicking **Configure > Phones** in the CME GUI. This gives you something a little more exciting to look at than the opening gray screen.

Exam Preparation Tasks

Review All the Key Topics

Review the most important topics in the chapter, noted with the key topics icon in the outer margin of the page. Table 6.3 lists a reference of these key topics and the page numbers on which each is found.

Table 6.3   *Key Topics for Chapter 6*

Key Topic Element	Description	Page Number
Example 6.1	Creating local directory and caller ID information	179
Example 6.3	Configuration of busy and no answer call forwarding	182–193
Figure 6.5	Illustrates the concept of call hairpinning	184
List	The differentiation between blind and consult call transfer methods	185
Example 6.5	Allowing outside call transfers using the **transfer-pattern** command	186
Example 6.6	Configuration of call park	187–188
Example 6.7	Configuration of call pickup	191
List	Three types of call pickup methods	192
Example 6.8	Configuration of intercom	193
Note	Key note regarding the number of paging groups to which a Cisco IP phone can belong	194
Example 6.9	Configuring unicast paging	195
Example 6.11	Configuring after-hours time designations	197
Example 6.12	Configuring after-hours block patterns	198
Example 6.17	Configuring the CME router as a web server	206
Example 6.18	Configuring the CME web administrator account	207

Definitions of Key Terms

Define the following key terms from this chapter, and check your answers in the glossary.

local directory

H.450.3

H.450.2

hairpinning

call park

call pickup

directed pickup

local group pickup

other group pickup

Exam topics covered in Part III:

- Describe the process of voice packetization

- Describe RTP and RTCP

- Describe the function of and differences between codecs

- Describe H.323, MGCP, SIP, and SCCP signaling protocols

- Describe the function and application of a dial plan

- Describe the function and application of voice Gateways

- Describe the function and application of voice ports in a Gateway

- Describe the function and operation of call-legs

- Describe and configure voice dial peers

- Describe the differences between PSTN and Internet Telephony Service Provider circuits

- Identify the factors that impact voice quality

- Describe how QoS addresses voice quality issues

- Identify where QoS is deployed in the UC infrastructure

Part III: Connecting via Gateways and Trunks

The Process of Converting Voice to Packets: This section discusses the Nyquist theorem as it relates to converting the audio coming into a telephone into a digital packet.

Choosing a Voice Codec: One of the key facts you'll need to know before deploying VoIP is how much network bandwidth the audio will use. This section discusses a variety of voice codec considerations along with the necessary bandwidth calculation formulas.

Trunking CME to the PSTN: The PSTN remains the key connection for any voice network. This section discusses multiple analog and digital methods to connect to the PSTN.

Trunking CME to Other VoIP Systems: In the next-generation voice network, communication can occur between offices over the PSTN or IP WAN. Because of the cost savings, the IP WAN is typically the preferred path. This section discusses the protocols used to establish inter-office VoIP communication.

CHAPTER 7

Gateway and Trunk Concepts

At this point, you now have the knowledge to assemble, configure, and operate a VoIP network internal to your organization. At some point, this voice network will have to grow beyond itself and connect to other voice networks, perhaps most importantly the PSTN. This chapter is dedicated to describing the methods you can use to connect your VoIP network to other networks. The chapter begins by discussing the process of converting spoken audio into packets. From there, this chapter discusses the hardware and signaling used to establish a connection. After the public switched telephone network (PSTN) connection is running, you can turn your attention to the connections to other VoIP networks.

"Do I Know This Already?" Quiz

The "Do I Know This Already?" quiz allows you to assess whether you should read this entire chapter or simply jump to the "Exam Preparation Tasks" section for review. If you are in doubt, read the entire chapter. Table 7.1 outlines the major headings in this chapter and the corresponding "Do I Know This Already?" quiz questions. You can find the answers in Appendix A, "Answers to the 'Do I Know This Already?' Quizzes."

Table 7.1   *"Do I Know This Already?" Foundation Topics Section-to-Question Mapping*

Foundation Topics Section	Questions Covered in This Section
The Process of Converting Voice to Packets	1–3
Choosing a Voice Codec	4–7
Trunking CME to the PSTN	8
Trunking CME to Other VoIP Systems	9–10

1. What frequency range is accurately reproduced by the Nyquist theorem?

    a. 200–9000 Hz

    b. 300–3400 Hz

    c. 300–4000 Hz

    d. 20–20,000 Hz

2. Which of the following G.711 forms is used in the United States?

    a. G.711a

    b. G.711ab

    c. G.711 a-law

    d. G.711 μ-law

3. What amount of bandwidth is consumed by the audio payload of G.729a?

    a. 4.3 kbps

    b. 6.3 kbps

    c. 8 kbps

    d. 16 kbps

4. How many bytes per packet are transmitted by G.729 assuming a 20-ms sample size?

    a. 20

    b. 40

    c. 100

    d. 120

5. What amount of data does the IP, UDP, and RTP header information add to each packet transmitted?

    a. 20 bytes

    b. 40 bytes

    c. 56 bytes

    d. 58 bytes

6. What function does VAD have on the voice network?

    a. The creation of redundant voice paths over the PSTN

    b. Significant bandwidth savings due to silence suppression

    c. Improved DSP utilization

    d. Permits additional, compressed calls over the IP WAN

7. Which of the following are high complexity codecs? (Choose two.)

    a. G.711 μ-law

    b. G.729

    c. G.729a

    d. iLBC

8. You would like to trunk your small office environment to the PSTN using analog connections. With which of the following interfaces would you equip your router?

    a. FXS

    b. FXS-DID

    c. FXO

    d. E&M

9. You would like to configure your VoIP environment to allow for centralized control over all voice gateways. Which of the following protocols would you use?

    a. H.323

    b. MGCP

    c. SIP

    d. SCCP

10. SIP signaling is based on what common standard?

    a. HTTP

    b. IETF

    c. TCP

    d. UDP

Foundation Topics

The Process of Converting Voice to Packets

Long ago, Dr. Harry Nyquist (and many others) created a process that allows equipment to convert analog signals (flowing waveforms) into digital format (1s and 0s). It is important to understand this process as it will guide your configuration of sample sizes, Digital Signal Processor (DSP) resources, and codecs.

The origin of the digital conversion process takes us back to the 1920s, a far throw from our VoIP world. The Bell Systems Corporation was trying to find a way to deploy more voice circuits with less wire, because analog voice technology required one pair of wires for each voice line. For organizations requiring many voice circuits, this meant running bundles of cable. After plenty of research, Nyquist found that he could accurately reconstruct audio streams by taking samples that numbered twice the highest audio frequency used in the audio.

Here is how it breaks down. Audio frequencies vary based on the volume, pitch, and so on that comprise the sound. Here are a few key facts:

- The average human ear is able to hear frequencies from 20–20,000 Hz.

- Human speech uses frequencies from 200–9000 Hz.

- Telephone channels typically transmit frequencies from 300–3400 Hz.

- The Nyquist theorem is able to reproduce frequencies from 300–4000 Hz.

Now, you might be thinking, "If human speech uses frequencies between 200–9000 Hz and the normal telephone channel only transmits frequencies from 300–3400 Hz, how can you understand human conversation over the phone?" That's a great question! Studies have found that telephone equipment can accurately transmit understandable human conversation by sending only a limited range of frequencies. The telephone channel frequency range (300–3400 Hz) gives you enough sound quality to identify the remote caller and sense their mood. The telephone channel frequency range does not send the full spectrum of human voice inflection and lowers the actual quality of the audio. For example, if you've ever listened to talk radio, you can always tell the difference in quality between the radio host and the telephone caller.

Key Topic

Nyquist believed that you could accurately reproduce an audio signal by sampling at twice the highest frequency. Because he was after audio frequencies from 300–4000 Hz, it would mean sampling 8000 times (2 * 4000) every second. So what's a sample? A *sample* is a numeric value. More specifically, in the voice realm, a sample is a numeric value that consumes a single byte of information. As Figure 7.1 illustrates, during the process of sampling, the sampling device puts an analog waveform against a Y-axis lined with numeric values.

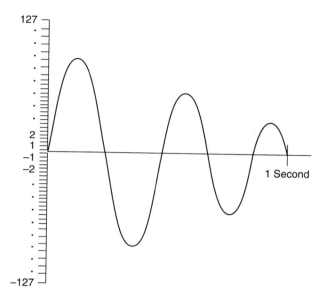

Figure 7.1   *Converting Analog Voice Signals to Digital*

This process of converting the analog wave into digital, numeric values is known as *quantization*. Because 1 byte of information is only able to represent values 0–255, the quantization of the voice scale is limited to values measuring a maximum peak of +127 and a maximum low of –127. Notice in Figure 7.1 that the 127 positive and negative values are not evenly spaced. This is by design. To achieve a more accurate numeric value (and thus, a more accurate reconstructed signal at the other end), the frequencies more common to voice are tightly packed with numeric values, whereas the "fringe frequencies" on the high and low end of the spectrum are more spaced apart.

The sampling device breaks the 8 binary bits in each byte into two components: a positive/negative indicator and the numeric representation. As shown in Figure 7.2, the first bit indicates positive or negative, and the remaining seven bits represent the actual numeric value.

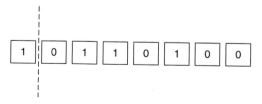

Figure 7.2   *Encoding Voice into Binary Values*

Because the first bit in Figure 7.2 is a 1, you read the number as positive. The remaining seven bits represent the number 52. This would be the digital value used for one voice sample. Now, remember, the Nyquist theorem dictates that you need to take 8000 of those samples every single second. Doing the math, figure 8000 samples a second times the 8 bits in each sample, and you get 64,000 bits per second. It's no coincidence that uncompressed audio (including the G.711 audio codec) consumes 64 kbps. Once the sampling device assigns numeric values to all these analog signals, a router can place them into a packet and send them across a network.

Note   There are two forms of the G.711 codec: μ-law (used primary in the United States and Japan) and a-law (used everywhere else). The quantization method described in the preceding paragraph represents G.711 a-law. G.711 μ-law codes in exactly the opposite way. If you were to take all the 1 bits in Figure 7.2 and make them 0s and take all the 0 bits and make them 1s, you would have the G.711 μ-law equivalent. Yes, it doesn't make sense to code it that way, but who said things we do in the United States should make sense?

The last and optional step in the digitization process is to apply compression measures. Advanced codecs, such as G.729, allow you to compress the number of samples sent and thus use less bandwidth. This is possible because sampling human voice 8000 times a second produces many samples that are very similar or identical. For example, say the word "cow" out loud to yourself (provided you are in a relatively private area). That takes about a second to say, right? If not, say it slower until it does. Now, listen to the sounds you are making. There's the very distinguished "k" sound that starts the word, then you have the "ahhhhhh" sound in the middle, followed by the "wa" sound at the end. If you were to break that into 8000 individual samples, chances are most of them would sound the same.

The process G.729 (and most other compressed codecs) uses to compress this audio is to send a sound sample once and simply tell the remote device to continue playing that sound for a certain time interval. This is often described as "building a codebook" of the human voice traveling between the two endpoints. Using this process, G.729 is able to reduce bandwidth down to 8 kbps for each call; a fairly massive reduction in bandwidth.

Unfortunately, chopping the amount of bandwidth down comes with a price. Quality is usually impacted by the compression process. Early on in the voice digitization years, the powers that be created a measurement system known as a Mean Opinion Score (MOS) to rate the quality of the various voice codecs. The test used to rate the quality of voice is simple: a listener would listen to a caller say the sentence, "Nowadays, a chicken leg is a rare dish," and rate the clarity of this sentence on a scale of 1–5. Table 7.2 shows how each audio codec fared in MOS testing.

Table 7.2   *Audio Codec Bandwidth and MOS Values*

Codec	Bandwidth Consumed	MOS
G.711	64 kbps	4.1
Internet Low Bitrate Codec (iLBC)	15.2 kbps	4.1
G.729	8 kbps	3.92
G.726	32 kbps	3.85
G.729a	8 kbps	3.7
G.728	16 kbps	3.61

Key Topic

Table 7.2 leads into a much needed discussion about audio coder/decoders (codecs). There are quite a few different audio codecs you can use on your network, each geared for different purposes and environments. For example, there are some codecs geared specifically for military environments where audio is sent through satellite link and bandwidth is at a premium. These codecs sacrifice audio quality to achieve very streamlined transmissions. Other codecs are designed to meet the need for quality.

If you stay in the Cisco realm for long, you will hear two codecs continually repeated: G.711 and G.729. This is because Cisco designed all its IP phones with the ability to code in either of these two formats. G.711 is the "common ground" between all VoIP devices. For example, if a Cisco IP phone is attempting to communicate with an Avaya IP phone, they may support different compressed codecs, but can at least agree on G.711 when communicating.

Note   G.729 comes in two different variants: G.729a (annex A) and G.729b (annex B). G.729a sacrifices some audio quality to achieve a much more processor-efficient coding process. G.729b introduces support for Voice Activity Detection (VAD), which makes voice transmissions more efficient. You learn more about these variants in the following section.

Key Topic

Choosing a Voice Codec

When selecting a voice codec for your network, you should ask the following questions regarding the codec:

- Is the codec supported on all VoIP devices in my network?

- How many Digital Signal Processor (DSP) resources does it take to code audio using the codec?

- Does the codec meet satisfactory quality levels for my network for all audio types?

- How much bandwidth does the codec consume?

- How does the codec handle packet loss?

- Does the codec support multiple sample sizes? What are the ramifications of using them?

Some of these questions have been covered up to this point; others will be discussed in the following subsections describing codec selection criteria.

Calculating Codec Bandwidth Requirements

Before you deploy VoIP over your WAN connections, you'll want to know exactly how much bandwidth the codec you are using will consume. Although it is easy to look at a table of codec bandwidth amounts (such as the earlier Table 7.2), these amounts do not take into account other factors such as sample size, header information, and link-efficiency mechanisms. You can use the following process to calculate the impact voice will have on your network bandwidth:

Step 1.   Determine the audio bandwidth required for the audio codec itself.

Step 2.   Determine data link, network, and transport layer overhead.

Step 3.   Add any additional overhead amounts.

Step 4.   Add it all together.

Step 5.   Subtract bandwidth savings measures.

You can use multiple methods to find the amount of bandwidth required for a voice call. The process presented here and described in the following sections is one of the easiest to remember.

Step 1: Determine the Audio Bandwidth Required for the Audio Codec Itself

To find the amount of bandwidth required for the audio codec, you need to determine the size (in bytes) of audio contained in each packet. This size is directly impacted by the audio sample size contained in each packet. The sample size is a specific time interval of audio. For most audio codecs, the sample size is 20 milliseconds (ms), by default. Increasing the sample size gives you a bandwidth savings benefit because the router sends fewer packets overall (and fewer packets mean less header information). The drawback to increasing the sample size is that the overall delay in building the packet is increased. If the two devices communicating already have significant delay between them (due to distance, traffic sharing the link, and so on), the additional coding delay could cause quality of service (QoS) issues.

You can use the following formula to determine the voice payload size:

```
Bytes_Per_Packet = (Sample_Size * Codec_Bandwidth) / 8
```

The Sample_Size variable in the formula uses a unit value of seconds and the Codec_Bandwidth variable uses a unit value of bits per second (bps). So, if you had a G.711 call using a 20-ms sample size, the formula would calculate like this:

```
Bytes_Per_Packet = (.02 * 64000) / 8
Bytes_Per_Packet = 1280 / 8
Bytes_Per_Packet = 160
```

Here's another example of a G.729 call using a 20-ms sample size:

```
Bytes_Per_Packet = (.02 * 8000) / 8
Bytes_Per_Packet = 160 / 8
Bytes_Per_Packet = 20
```

Step 2: Determine Data Link, Network, and Transport Layer Overhead

After you've found the amount of voice contained in each packet, you then need to calculate the amount of data contained in the header in each packet. The following values represent the amount of overhead for common data link layer network technologies:

- **Ethernet:** 20 bytes

- **Frame Relay:** 4–6 bytes

- **Point-to-Point Protocol (PPP):** 6 bytes

At the network and transport layers of the OSI model, the values are fixed amounts:

- **IP:** 20 bytes

- **UDP:** 8 bytes

- **Real-time Transport Protocol (RTP):** 12 bytes

Because every voice packet uses RTP, UDP, and IP, you can save a little brain space by just remembering that the network and transport layers always add 40 bytes of data per packet.

Note   The RTP protocol has not been fully covered yet; for now, just know that it is the protocol responsible for streaming audio. RTP will be covered later in this chapter in the section "Understanding RTP and RTCP."

Step 3: Add Any Additional Overhead Amounts

Additional overhead gets added into the equation primarily if you are using VoIP over a VPN connection. The following are common overhead values based on the type of VPN used:

- **GRE/L2TP:** 24 bytes

- **MPLS:** 4 bytes

- **IPsec:** 50–57 bytes

Step 4: Add It All Together

When you have all the values from the first three steps, you can add them together in a final equation:

```
Total_Bandwidth = Packet_Size * Packets_Per_Second
```

Now remember, you're after the total bandwidth per call. So, first you need to add together the values from Steps 1–3 to form the packet size. For example, if you were using the G.729 codec with a 20-ms sample size over an Ethernet network, the packet size would be as follows:

```
+ 20 bytes (voice payload)
+ 20 bytes (IP header)
+ 8 bytes (UDP header)
+ 12 bytes (RTP header)
+ 20 bytes (Ethernet header)
--------------------
80 bytes per packet
```

That gives you one piece of the equation, the packet size. To find the number of packets per second, some simple reasoning can come into play. Remember, each packet contains a 20-ms sample size, and 1 second is 1000 milliseconds. So, if you take 1000 ms / 20 ms = 50 ms, this helps you find that it will take 50 packets per second to generate the full second of audio. This now give you all the pieces you need to find the final amount of bandwidth per call:

```
Total_Bandwidth = Packet_Size * Packets_Per_Second
Total_Bandwidth = 80 bytes * 50 Packets_Per_Second
Total_Bandwidth = 4000 bytes per second
```

Because network engineers do not usually assess network speed in bytes per second, you might want to multiply the final answer by 8 to find the bits per second (because there are 8 bits in a byte):

```
4000 * 8 = 32,000 bits per second (more commonly written 32 kbps)
```

That is how you can find the amount of bandwidth consumed per VoIP call on the network.

This is a skill that you have to practice a few times, so here are two practice problems for you. See if you arrive at the same answer:

1. Find the bandwidth per call when using the G.711 codec with a 30-ms sample size over an Ethernet network. (Answer: 80 kbps.)

2. Find the bandwidth per call when using the G.729 codec with a 20-ms sample size over a Frame Relay network using 4-byte headers. (Answer: 25.6 kbps.)

Step 5: Subtract Bandwidth Savings Measures

In the realm of VoIP, there are two primary bandwidth savings measures that you can enable to improve the efficiency of your voice network. They are Voice Activity Detection (VAD) and RTP header compression.

VAD allows the router to detect the "sound of silence" in a VoIP conversation. By default, the routers will send RTP data, even if no one is talking. Through many studies, findings show that on average, 35–40 percent of a phone call is silence. By enabling VAD, you are able to recoup this bandwidth back into your budget.

Note   The actual amount of bandwidth savings due to VAD varies from company to company, because it is affected greatly by dialect, mood, excitement levels, background noise, and so on. It is best to calculate only a minimal amount of VAD-based bandwidth savings in your voice calculations.

RTP header compression (often called *compressed RTP*) allows routers to cache network and transport layer header information in voice packets, allowing routers to strip this redundant header information from future packets. Think about it this way: once two devices establish a VoIP call between each other, what type of information appears in the network and transport layer headers? IP addresses, port numbers, QoS markings, and so on. Now, how much of that information changes during the course of a voice conversation? None of it. The IP addresses stay the same, the port numbers don't change, and the QoS markings are consistent. So, rather than send this redundant information in every packet, RTP header compression sends the first packet as a full packet, then strips the redundant information out of future packets. This results in the 40-byte IP/RTP/UDP header information compressing down to approximately 2–5 bytes.

The impact of this bandwidth savings depends on the codec you are using. For example, using G.711 creates bigger packets, so the impact of compressing headers will be less noticeable than if you were using G.729. RTP header compression provides nearly a 40 percent bandwidth savings when used with G.729.

The Role of Digital Signal Processors

Cisco designed its routers with one primary purpose in mind: routing. Moving packets between one location and another is not a very processor-intensive task, thus Cisco routers are not equipped with the kind of memory and processing resources typical PCs are equipped with. For example, from a router's perspective, having 256 MB of RAM is quite a bit. From a PC's perspective, 256 MB will barely help you survive the Microsoft Windows boot process.

Moving into the realm of VoIP, the network now requires the router to convert loads of voice into digitized, packetized transmissions. This task would easily overwhelm the resources you have on the router. This is where Digital Signal Processors (DSP) come into play. DSPs offload the processing responsibility for voice-related tasks from the processor of the router. This is very similar to the idea of purchasing an expensive video card for a PC to offload the video processing responsibility from the PC's processor.

Specifically, a DSP is a chip that performs all the sampling, encoding, and compression functions on audio coming into your router. If you were to equip your router with voice interface cards (VIC), allowing it to connect to the PSTN or analog devices, but did not equip your router with DSPs, the interfaces would be worthless. The interfaces would be able to actively connect to the legacy voice networks, but would not have the power to convert any voice into packetized form.

DSPs typically come in chips to install in your Cisco router that look like old memory SIMMs, as shown in Figure 7.3.

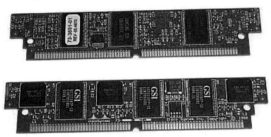

Figure 7.3   *Digital Signal Processor Chip*

Some Cisco routers could also have DSPs embedded on the motherboard or added in riser cards. Above all, it is important for you to add the necessary number of DSPs to your router to support the number of active voice call, conferencing, and transcoding (converting one codec to another) sessions you plan to support.

Tip   Cisco provides a DSP calculator that provides the number of DSP chips you need to purchase based on the voice network you are supporting. This tool can be found at http://www.cisco.com/pcgibin/Support/DSP/dsp-calc.pl (Cisco.com login required). Keep in mind that a growing network will always require more DSP resources. It is usually best to pack the router full with as many DSP resources as you can fit in it; you're going to need them!

You can add DSP chips either directly to a router's motherboard (if the router supports this) or to the network modules you add to the router to support voice cards. Cisco bundles these DSP chips into packet voice DSP modules (PVDM), which resemble the old memory SIMMs (see image in Figure 7.3). Based on the DSP requirements given by the Cisco DSP calculator, you can then purchase one or more of the following PVDMs:

Key
Topic

- **PVDM2-8:** Provides .5 DSP chip

- **PVDM2-16:** Provides 1 DSP chip

- **PVDM2-32:** Provides 2 DSP chips

- **PVDM2-48:** Provides 3 DSP chips

- **PVDM2-64:** Provides 4 DSP chips

Alas, not all codecs are created equal. Some codecs consume more DSP resources to pass through the audio conversion process than other codecs consume. Table 7.3 shows the codecs considered medium and high complexity.

Table 7.3 *Medium and High-Complexity Codecs*

Medium Complexity	High Complexity
G.711 (a-law and μ-law)	G.728
G.726	G.723
G.729a, G.729ab	G.729, G.729b
—	iLBC

Generally speaking, the DSP resources are able to handle roughly double the number of medium-complexity calls per DSP as high-complexity calls.

Note   Newer DSP chips are able to process calls more efficiently and can handle more high-complexity calls per chip than older DSP hardware. To find the exact amount of calls per DSP, use the Cisco DSP calculator tool mentioned in the previous tip.

Understanding RTP and RTCP

When you walk into the VoIP world, you encounter a whole new host of protocol standards. Think of the Real-time Transport Protocol (RTP) and Real-time Transport Control Protocol (RTCP) as the protocols of voice. RTP operates at the transport layer of the OSI model *on top of UDP*. Having two transport layer protocols is a bit odd, but that's exactly what is happening here. UDP provides the services it always does: port numbers (that is, session multiplexing) and header checksums (which ensure that the header information does not become corrupted). RTP adds time stamps and sequence numbers to the header information. This allows the remote device to put the packets back in order when it receives them at the remote end (function of the sequence number) and use a buffer to remove jitter (slight delays) between the packets to give a smooth audio playout (function of the time stamp). Figure 7.4 gives a visual representation of the RTP header information contained in a packet.

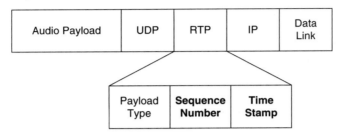

Figure 7.4   *RTP Header Information*

The Payload Type field in the RTP header is used to designate what *type* of RTP is in use. You can use RTP for audio or video purposes.

Once two devices attempt to establish an audio session, RTP engages and chooses a random, even UDP port number from 16,384 to 32,767 for each RTP stream. Keep in mind that RTP streams are one-way. If you are having a two-way conversation, the devices will establish dual RTP streams, one in each direction. The audio stream stays on the initially chosen port for the duration of the audio session (the devices will not dynamically change ports during a phone call).

At the time the devices establish the call, RTCP also engages. While this protocol *sounds* extremely important, its primary job is statistics reporting. It delivers statistics between the two devices participating in the call, which include

- Packet count
- Packet delay
- Packet loss
- Jitter (delay variations)

Although this information is useful, it is not nearly as critical as the actual RTP audio streams. Keep this in mind when you are configuring QoS settings.

As the devices establish the call, the RTP audio streams use an even UDP port from 16,384 to 32,767, as previously discussed in this section. RTCP creates a separate session over UDP between the two devices by using an *odd*-numbered port from the same range. Throughout the call duration, the devices send RTCP packets at least once every 5 seconds. The CME router can log and report this information, which allows you to determine the issues that are causing call problems (such as poor audio, call disconnects, and so on) on the network.

Note   RTCP will use the odd-numbered port following the RTP port. For example, if the RTP audio uses port 17,654, the RTCP port for the session will be 17,655.

Internet Low Bitrate Codec: One Codec to Rule Them All

The VoIP industry has long desired a compressed codec that can be as universally supported as G.711. Unfortunately, most of the existing compressed codecs are either proprietary in nature, do not deliver on quality requirements, or are unable to meet bandwidth demands. All of that is changing with the creation of the Internet Low Bitrate Codec (iLBC).

iLBC was developed in 2000 as a nonproprietary, high-quality, bandwidth-savvy codec that industry-wide vendors could use when communicating between VoIP devices. Arguably, the task force was successful in creating this codec. Here are the statistics on iLBC:

- **Bit rate:** 15.2 kbps (when coded using a 20-ms sample size) or 13.3 kbps (when coded using a 30-ms sample size)

- **Codec complexity:** High

- **Quality:** Comparable to G.711; one of the best quality levels for any compressed codec

Key Topic

In addition, iLBC has one of the best audio loss covering methods around. This means if packets are dropped during a conversation, impact on the conversation is lower with iLBC than with nearly any other codec.

As the time of this writing, only the newest Cisco IP phones support iLBC. These IP phones include

- Cisco 7906G

- Cisco 7911G

- Cisco 7921G

- Cisco 7942G

- Cisco 7945G

- Cisco 7962G

- Cisco 7965G

- Cisco 7975G

Trunking CME to the PSTN

Connecting your CME router to the PSTN typifies what is meant by a voice gateway. The router is now translating the legacy voice world to the VoIP world, and vice versa. In order to make the connection to the PSTN, you must equip the CME router with traditional telephony interfaces. These can be either analog connections or digital connections.

Understanding Analog Connections

As mentioned before, analog connections are single-connection circuits, typically used in a small business. A router typically uses Foreign Exchange Station (FXS) analog interfaces to connect to analog devices such as telephones, fax machines, and modems. Foreign Exchange Office (FXO) analog interfaces are used to connect to the PSTN central office (CO) or to a legacy PBX system. The number of incoming FXO connections from the PSTN directly impacts the number of concurrent PSTN phone calls that can be active from the organization. The last type of analog connection you can use is an Ear and Mouth (E&M) interface. E&M signaling is designed to connect directly to a PBX system that also supports E&M interfaces. Figure 7.5 illustrates a CME voice gateway supporting analog voice connections.

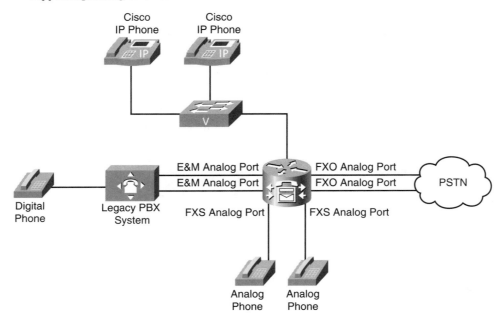

Figure 7.5   *Analog Voice Connectivity*

> **Note**   Whenever you install analog voice interfaces, always be sure the router or supporting voice module has enough DSP resources to support those analog interfaces.

The FXS and FXO ports (and DSP resources) shown in Figure 7.5 now have the job of converting the analog audio coming from the port into VoIP packets, and vice versa.

Understanding Digital Connections

As an office grows, analog connectivity can become cumbersome and expensive. Digital connections allow multiple conversations to share a single circuit. The digital channels are built using DS0 channels as "building blocks." Depending on the interface you are using to connect to the PSTN service provider, you can support a different number of DS0 channels. Each DS0 provides a 64-kbps channel, which supports a single audio call. The following are the available digital ports you can use in your router:

- **Channel associated signaling (CAS) T1/E1:** CAS interfaces attempt to "squeeze" signaling (which provides features such as caller ID, ring, off-hook, and so on) into the same channel as the audio. By doing this, you are able to support 24 DS0 audio channels out of a T1 interface (used primarily in the United States, Japan, and Korea). E1 interfaces (typically used outside of the United States, Japan, and Korea) support 30 channels.

> **Key Topic**

- **Common channel signaling (CCS) or Primary Rate Interface (PRI) T1/E1:** CCS/PRI interfaces separates the audio signaling into a dedicated channel, leaving the full 64 kbps of each DS0 for audio only. Because of this, a T1 using CCS uses only 23 DS0 audio channels (because the 24th is dedicated to signaling). PRI describes the ISDN implementation of CCS, which is more commonly used by PSTN COs and PBX vendors. Because of its architecture, E1 still provides 30 channels with CCS signaling.

- **Basic Rate Interface (BRI):** Each BRI interface provides two DS0 channels and a small signaling channel.

When purchasing a digital circuit from a service provider, the carriers typically allow you to build a circuit using any number of DS0 channels you would like, provided you do not exceed the maximum number of DS0 channels an interface can handle. If you purchase fewer channels than what the full interface can support, this is typically called a "fractional" connection. For example, if you chose to use a T1 interface but only leased 12 DS0s from the PSTN carrier, you would call this a fractional T1 connection.

Trunking CME to Other VoIP Systems

As VoIP becomes more popular, businesses will prefer to use interoffice connectivity over data networks rather than the PSTN, due to long-distance cost savings and bandwidth efficiency (VoIP calls can use less bandwidth than traditional PSTN). The single-office CME deployment will need to connect with other offices or providers over the VoIP network, as illustrated in Figure 7.6.

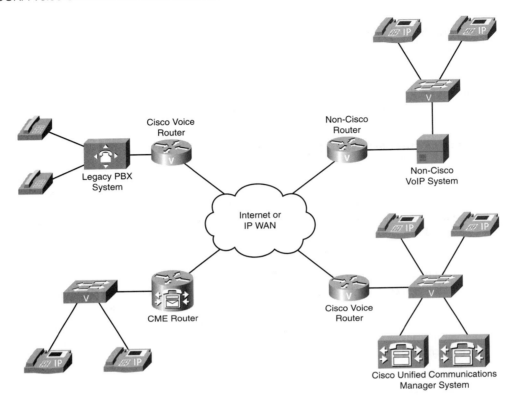

Figure 7.6 *Interoffice VoIP Connectivity*

To communicate with these other VoIP systems, CME needs a common VoIP communications protocol. This is very similar to the world of data communications. Because all devices now support the TCP/IP protocol, they can all communicate over the network regardless of manufacturer. The voice world also needs a protocol, not so much for voice communication (because this is the job of RTP), but rather for voice signaling. Voice signaling includes call setup messages, call maintenance messages, relaying dialed digits, and so on. While the data realm has settled on TCP/IP as the protocol of choice, the voice world still has multiple signaling protocols you can use. The following list provides an overview of each of these protocols:

- **H.323:** H.323 was the first of the four voice signaling protocols and definitely has maturity on its side. The International Telecommunication Union, Telecommunication Standardization Sector (ITU-T) originally created H.323 to allow simultaneous voice, video, and data to transmit across ISDN connections. It has since been adapted to work over LAN environments.

- **Session Initiation Protocol (SIP):** SIP is often called the "next generation" of H.323. Developed by the Internet Engineering Task Force (IETF), SIP is a much more lightweight and scalable protocol than H.323. While support for SIP is widespread, it is an evolving standard that does not currently support many of the advanced features of VoIP networks. As SIP becomes more mature and robust, it is poised to become the primary VoIP signaling standard used worldwide (similar to the way data networks use TCP/IP today).

- **Media Gateway Control Protocol (MGCP):** MGCP is the first true "client/server" VoIP signaling protocol. If you are using MGCP, you will perform the vast majority of your gateway configuration from a centralized system known as a *call agent*. Because this is a newer IETF standard, it is not as widely supported as H.323 or SIP.

- **Skinny Client Control Protocol (SCCP):** SCCP is the only Cisco-proprietary VoIP protocol currently in use. Although SCCP is not specifically designed for gateway signaling and control, a limited number of Cisco gateways do support it. The primary goal of SCCP is to provide a signaling protocol between the Cisco Unified Communications Manager and Cisco IP phones. Similar to MGCP, the SCCP devices report every action to the Communications Manager server, which then responds with the action the device should take.

Now, let's look deeper into each one of these protocols.

H.323

ITU officially approved H.323 as a standard in February 1996. Because the group designed H.323 to provide a multimedia user experience over ISDN connections, ITU modeled much of its architecture from the ISDN signaling protocol Q.931. If you have studied ISDN signaling and communications, moving into the H.323 world is not much different. Many of the same terms, signaling messages, and so on are identical. Unfortunately, because modern-day data networks have moved away from ISDN to cheaper and more bandwidth-savvy connection types, Q.931 protocol signaling is quite cryptic to most. This makes understanding the signaling of H.323 equally cryptic when attempting to troubleshoot or debug communications.

The designers of H.323 created it as a peer-to-peer protocol. This allows every device running H.323 to be completely independent from other devices. This allows you to configure each H.323 device uniquely and prevent reliance on any other device for normal operation. This way, if the H.323 gateway loses communication with other routers, it continues to operate and support voice devices without losing any call processing capabilities. The disadvantage of this peer-to-peer design is the amount of configuration you must put into each device. Because you configure each H.323 gateway independently from others, it needs full knowledge of the network.

For example, consider the network shown in Figure 7.7. In this network, you would need to configure each H.323 gateway to know about all the extensions at the remote offices. For example, you would have to configure H.323 Gateway 1 to point to 10.1.1.2 to reach the 2XXX extensions, to point to 10.1.1.3 to reach the 3XXX extensions, and to point to 10.1.1.4 to reach the 4XXX extensions. You would then need to repeat this process on each of the other H.323 gateways to reach the other offices. You can imagine that, as your network grows from 4 offices to 10, and then from 10 to 20, the amount of configuration on each of these voice gateways would soon become unmanageable.

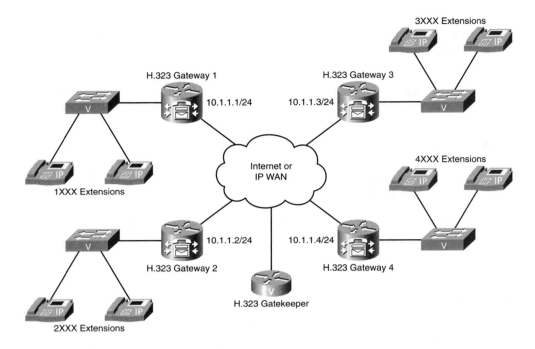

Figure 7.7   *H.323 Gateway Topology Design*

You can ease this configuration by implementing an H.323 gatekeeper (also shown in Figure 7.7). This gatekeeper acts as a centralized reference point in the H.323 network for phone numbers, access control, and bandwidth management. For example, if you were to configure the network shown in Figure 7.7 using a gatekeeper device, only the gatekeeper would require full knowledge of the voice network. You would configure the H.323 gatekeeper to know that 1XXX extensions are reachable through 10.1.1.1, 2XXX extensions are reachable through 10.1.1.2, and so on. You would then configure all the other H.323 gateways to ask the gatekeeper for the location of a dialed number anytime they attempted to reach another device on the network.

In addition to acting as a "centralized phonebook" to the H.323 network, the gatekeeper can also provide call admission control (CAC) and bandwidth management. Not only do the H.323 gateways ask the gatekeeper to locate a given phone extension, but they also ask the questions "Am I allowed to make this call?" (CAC) and "Is there enough bandwidth available to make this call?" (bandwidth management). This enables you to have an independent device watching the bandwidth available on the WAN, ensuring that each link is not saturated with voice traffic.

Of course, once you begin to rely on an H.323 gatekeeper as a central point of contact, you give up some of the benefits of peer-to-peer configurations. If the H.323 gatekeeper fails or becomes unreachable by the H.323 gateways, the gateways no longer have the intelligence they need to make site-to-site calls. Because of this, gatekeepers are usually configured to be redundant. In addition, Figure 7.7 might give the impression that the gatekeeper floats "out there" connected to the WAN, doing nothing more than being a gatekeeper. This is usually not the case. Most often, you will co-locate the H.323 gatekeeper functions with one of the H.323 gateways. For example, if the H.323 Gateway 1 in Figure 7.7 represented the central site of your organization, you might also configure this gateway as the H.323 gatekeeper for the network.

Table 7.4 summarizes the primary advantages and disadvantages of the H.323 protocol.

Table 7.4   *H.323 Advantages and Disadvantages*

Advantages	Disadvantages
Industry standard.	The peer-to-peer architecture can lead to complex configurations on multiple devices.
Widely supported across many VoIP equipment vendors.	Signaling messages are encoded in binary, which makes troubleshooting more difficult than it is for other VoIP signaling protocols.
Mature, stable.	Because H.323 represents a suite of protocols (for data, video, and voice sharing), it consumes more processor and memory resources than the other protocols dedicated only to voice and video signaling.
Supports most modern VoIP features.	—

Note   Cisco IP phones do not support the H.323 protocol due to its excessive resource consumption.

SIP

SIP was designed by the IETF as an alternative to H.323. Comparing the two protocols is like comparing the TCP/IP protocol suite to the File Transfer Protocol (FTP). When you think of H.323, think of it as a package of protocols to allow the sharing of voice, video, and data over a network environment. This is similar to the TCP/IP protocol suite, which creates network communications using a variety of protocols that are in the TCP/IP "package." On the other hand, FTP has one purpose: transferring files from one device to another. Many other protocols help FTP make this happen (such as TCP, IP, and Ethernet), but these are just seen as supporting protocols. In the same way, the purpose of SIP is to set up sessions primarily between voice and video endpoints. Period. SIP is *not* designed to transfer audio, video, and so on. Rather, it just sets up the session. There are many other protocols that are called into play to make this happen (such as TCP, UDP, RTP, and so on), but they are seen as supporting protocols rather than part of the SIP "package." All SIP does is start, manage, and end the session; it passes off the responsibility of the voice or video call to other protocols. This characteristic is one of the primary differentiators between H.323 and SIP.

One of the goals of the IETF when creating SIP was to make the communications between SIP devices easy to understand. The IETF accomplished this by coding all communications between SIP devices, known as user agents (UA), as ASCII text-based messages rather than binary (which H.323 uses). When you are troubleshooting SIP communications, the debug messages actually make sense. For example, a call from one device to another (extension 5001 to 6001, shown in Figure 7.8) produces the messages shown in the figure, which are easily seen in debug output on a router.

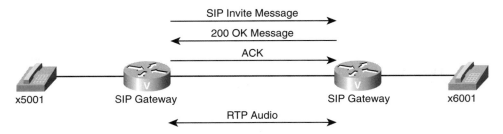

Figure 7.8   *SIP Gateway Communication*

On the contrary, H.323 uses binary encoding based on the ISDN Q.931 standard, which is easier for the routers to process, but much more difficult to understand and troubleshoot.

Tip   SIP signaling is based on HTTP. Many of the same messages you see when browsing the web are seen in SIP signaling. For example, if you incorrectly dial an extension, the SIP signaling device will return a 404: NOT FOUND error message. This is the same error message you would receive if trying to access website content that did not exist.

Because the IETF designed SIP simply to start and end voice and video sessions between devices, many organizations and VoIP vendors have decided to expand SIP signaling to add features or protocols to the session. Think of this like the Mozilla Firefox web browser. You can download Firefox with a base set of features that allows for web browsing, pop-up blocking, and bookmarking capabilities. However, if you would like a feature that Firefox does not include in the base set, you can access a directory of thousands of "add-on" applications to the Firefox web browser. These application add-ons include features such as PDF translation, weather reports, and FTP management. If an add-on becomes extremely popular, Mozilla will often add the functionality to a future version of Firefox.

In the same way, SIP is still evolving. The base SIP 2.0 protocol used today (at the time of this writing) provides most signaling and features you would expect from a VoIP system. However, there are some features that SIP 2.0 does not support at this time; for these features, VoIP vendors create their own, proprietary SIP signaling or protocol "add-ons." Anytime an organization creates one of these additions to SIP, it inevitably becomes a proprietary function. For example, imagine that Cisco created an IP phone that also made a cup of coffee every morning, based on a SIP signal from a remote device (you could call your desk extension in the morning and dial the necessary pass code to start the coffee brew cycle). The "coffee brew" function would be a proprietary add-on to SIP. If you used non-Cisco IP phones on your network, you would not be able to use this SIP signal with them, even if they also came equipped with coffee brewing capabilities.

The consensus in the VoIP industry is that SIP will become the final voice and video signaling protocol in the future. However, at this time it is still seen as an evolving standard because it does not support all features on all VoIP devices without using proprietary additions. One day, once the SIP standard reaches maturity, you will be able to use VoIP equipment from any vendor on the same network, managed by the same system. In addition, SIP signaling is commonly used in instant messenger (IM) applications, online games, and online video conference solution. Using this common protocol across the network will allow calls from any of these software applications to physical VoIP devices. For example, you could place a call from an IM application to a Cisco 7960 IP Phone or vice versa.

Note   Most Internet telephony service providers (ITSP), which allow businesses to use the Internet to make outside telephone calls using VoIP, use SIP as their primary signaling protocol.

Table 7.5 summarizes the primary advantages and disadvantages of the SIP protocol.

Table 7.5   *SIP Advantages and Disadvantages*

Advantages	Disadvantages
Wide support across multiple vendors.	ASCII text-based signaling consumes more bandwidth than binary-based signaling.
ASCII text-based signaling provides easier understanding and troubleshooting.	SIP is still considered an evolving standard; proprietary additions prevent full, cross-vendor feature support from all management systems.
Leverages many familiar standards (such as DNS, HTTP, and RTP) for addressing and signaling functions.	—

MGCP

Cisco played a significant role in the development of MGCP, which is now an IETF standard. MGCP allows you to put your voice gateways under the control of a centralized call agent. Anytime the MGCP gateway interacts with the voice network, it relies on the call agent for its intelligence. The call agent tells the gateway how to process digits, where to send the calls, what codec it should be using, and so on. Using MGCP is like turning your voice gateway into a dumb terminal, where the call agent is now the mainframe. The gateway does not have any intelligence in itself; it receives everything from the centralized call agent system.

Consider an example. An analog phone connected to the FXS port of an MGCP gateway goes off-hook. The MGCP gateway immediately sends a message to the call agent that says, "Call agent, a phone just went off-hook. What should I do?" The call agent responds, "Play a dial tone." After the MGCP gateway sends a dial tone to the phone, the phone user dials the digit 9. Once again, the MGCP gateway sends a message to the call agent that says, "Call agent, the phone just dialed the digit 9. What should I do?" The call agent responds, "Stop the dial tone and play a beep," which the MGCP gateway then does. This process continues for each step of the voice call. The router basically becomes a "dumb terminal" interfacing with the call agent "mainframe."

Note   The commands are sent from the call agent to the MGCP-controlled gateway using UDP port 2427.

The beauty of MGCP is in its centralized configuration. As you manage more VoIP gateways and devices in a growing voice network, you will appreciate having a centralized place of configuration rather than equipping each device with its own configuration. This is also a benefit for managed voice service provider environments. Corporations pay these service providers to manage their entire voice network. If the service provider uses MGCP, it can centralize the configuration in its call agents; the equipment that it installs at the customer premises will have minimal local configuration.

Note   The Cisco Unified Communication Manager Express (CME) platform does not use MGCP because it requires a complete configuration to support the voice network (it does not rely on any call agent servers). Networks using Cisco Unified Communication Manager or Cisco Unified Communication Manager Business Edition are able to use MGCP to manage network devices.

Table 7.6 summarizes the primary advantages and disadvantages of the MGCP protocol.

Table 7.6   *MGCP Advantages and Disadvantages*

Advantages	Disadvantages
Centralized configuration.	Not as widely supported as H.323 or SIP (primarily supported on Cisco devices only).
Requires minimal configuration on voice gateways.	Because the MGCP gateway relies so heavily on the call agent, if the communication between the voice gateway and call agent fails, the voice gateway becomes useless.

SCCP

SCCP (more often called "Skinny"), the only Cisco-proprietary protocol of the four signaling protocols, is used to control Cisco IP phones and other Cisco endpoint devices (such as the ATA 186/188). Skinny functions as a stimulus/response protocol similar to MGCP. Any interaction with a Cisco IP phone (such as lifting the handset, dialing a digit, and so on) causes the IP phone to send Skinny messages to the call processing software, which then responds with a Skinny message instructing the device with the action to take.

The main advantage of the Skinny protocol is also its main weakness: it is proprietary. By using a proprietary protocol to control Cisco IP phones, Cisco can deploy new features and capabilities for the IP phones without requiring major revisions to an industry-standard protocol. Of course, the drawback of using a proprietary protocol is that Cisco IP phones will only work with Cisco call processing software (such as Cisco Unified CME or Cisco Unified Communications Manager) by default. Cisco IP phones can also use SIP (and MGCP in some cases) by downloading a replacement firmware from Cisco.com.

Note   Although you can use SIP on Cisco IP phones, you must currently use SCCP to receive full feature functionality.

Table 7.7 provides a summary look at each of the four voice signaling protocols.

Table 7.7   *Protocol Summary*

	Standards Body	Industry Support	Used on Gateways	Used on Cisco IP Phones	Architecture
H.323	ITU	Excellent	Yes	No	Peer-to-peer
MGCP	IETF	Fair	Yes	Yes, limited	Client/server
SIP	IETF	Very good	Yes	Yes	Peer-to-peer
SCCP	None	Proprietary	Yes, very limited	Yes	Client/server

Understanding Internet Telephony Service Providers

Since a new generation of VoIP communication has arrived, a new generation of telephony service provider has emerged. Internet telephony service providers (ITSP) allow your business to connect to the PSTN using VoIP communication, as shown in Figure 7.9.

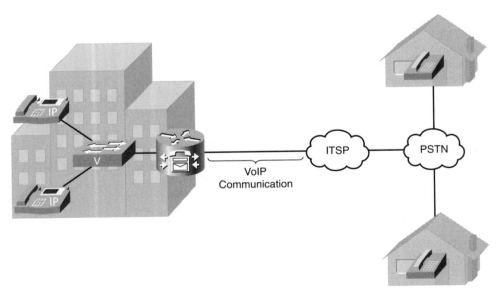

Figure 7.9   *ITSP Architecture*

By allowing you to use VoIP trunks to the PSTN, the ITSP is able to provide cheaper rates (per call and long distance) than traditional TSPs. Using an ISTP also provides the benefit of bundling both your voice and data connection over a single, IP-based circuit. If you have a lower number of voice calls, more bandwidth is available for data communications.

Exam Preparation Tasks

Review All the Key Topics

Review the most important topics in the chapter, noted with the key topics icon in the outer margin of the page. Table 7.8 lists and describes these key topics and identifies the page number on which each is found.

Table 7.8   *Key Topics for Chapter 7*

Key Topic Element	Description	Page Number
Paragraph	Explains the Nyquist theory of digital audio conversion	218
Table 7.2	Compares common codec bandwidth amounts and MOS values	221
Note	Summarizes the step-by-step process of converting spoken voice into digital audio	221
List	Describes the difference between G.729, G.729a, and G.729b	221
Formula	Shows the formula for determining the number of bytes contained in each voice packet	223
List	Lists common Layer 2 overhead for various network types	223
List	Lists Layers 3 and 4 overhead for voice communications	223
Formula	Shows the formula for determining total bandwidth required for a VoIP call	224
List	Lists the five chips you can install to add DSP resources to a router	227
Paragraph	Describes the process of establishing RTP communications	228
List	Lists the key statistics about the iLBC codec	229
Paragraph	Describes the use of analog FXS and FXO ports	230
List	Describes digital PSTN connectivity methods	231
List	Lists the four VoIP signaling protocols	232–233
Table 7.7	Summarizes VoIP signaling protocol characteristics	240

Complete the Tables and Lists from Memory

Print a copy of Appendix C, "Memory Tables" (found on the CD), or at least the section for this chapter, and complete the tables and lists from memory. Appendix D, "Memory Tables Answer Key," also on the CD, includes completed tables and lists to check your work.

Definitions of Key Terms

Define the following key terms from this chapter, and check your answers in the glossary.

Nyquist theorem

Mean Opinion Score (MOS)

G.711

G.726

G.728

G.729

Internet Low Bitrate Codec (iLBC)

Real-time Transport Protocol (RTP)

Real-time Transport Control Protocol (RTCP)

Foreign Exchange Station (FXS)

Foreign Exchange Office (FXO)

Ear and Mouth (E&M)

H.323

Media Gateway Control Protocol (MGCP)

Session Initiation Protocol (SIP)

Skinny Client Control Protocol (SCCP)

Internet telephony service provider (ITSP)

quantization

Configuring Physical Voice Port Characteristics:
Before you can configure your voice reachability information, you must first configure the ports connecting to
the voice network. This section discusses the configuration of FXS, FXO, and digital T1/E1 voice interfaces.

Understanding and Configuring Dial Peers: Dial
peers assemble the "routing table" for dialed digits. This
section discusses the configuration and verification of
POTS and VoIP dial peers.

**Understanding Router Call Processing and Digit
Manipulation:** This section discusses the methods the
router uses to handle incoming and outgoing calls, along
with the various ways you can implement digit manipulation on the network.

Quality of Service: Without quality of service (QoS),
your voice communications will quickly be overrun by
data traffic. This section presents a high-level view of the
purpose of QoS, along with the configuration of
AutoQoS.

CHAPTER 8

Configuring and Verifying Gateways and Trunks

Connecting a voice gateway to another voice network is similar to connecting a router to a data network: plugging in the cable is the smallest part of the configuration. When the physical connections are in place, let the configuring begin. Instead of routing tables, voice gateways build the logical dial plan through a system of dial peers. This chapter explores the configuration and testing of dial peers in a voice environment.

A voice network is only as good as the foundation infrastructure. If the foundation network does not have any method of differentiating the network traffic passing to and fro, there is a good chance that your voice traffic will soon be overrun by data traffic. The latter part of this chapter discusses QoS measures that you can put in place to protect and prioritize the voice traffic.

"Do I Know This Already?" Quiz

The "Do I Know This Already?" quiz allows you to assess whether you should read this entire chapter or simply jump to the "Exam Preparation Tasks" section for review. If you are in doubt, read the entire chapter. Table 8.1 outlines the major headings in this chapter and the corresponding "Do I Know This Already?" quiz questions. You can find the answers in Appendix A, "Answers to the 'Do I Know This Already?' Quizzes."

Table 8.1 *"Do I Know This Already?" Foundation Topics Section-to-Question Mapping*

Foundation Topics Section	Questions Covered in This Section
Configuring Physical Voice Port Characteristics	1–2
Understanding and Configuring Dial Peers	3–6
Understanding Router Call Processing and Digit Manipulation	7–9
Quality of Service	10

1. Which of the following interface types would you use to connect an analog fax machine to the VoIP network?

   a. FXS

   b. FXO

   c. E&M

   d. BRI

2. Which of the following commands would you use to configure a T1 line to use channels 1–6 to connect to the PSTN using FXO loop start signaling?

   a. pri-group 1-6 type fxo-loop-start

   b. pri-group 1 timeslots 1-6 type fxo-loop-start

   c. ds0-group 1-6 type fxo-loop-start

   d. ds0-group 1 timeslots 1-6 type fxo-loop-start

3. You would like to configure a dial peer to connect to a PBX system using a digital T1 CAS configuration. What type of dial peer would you create?

   a. Analog

   b. Digital

   c. POTS

   d. VoIP

4. You have the following configuration entered on your voice router:

   ```
   dial-peer voice 99 pots
    destination-pattern 115.
    port 1/0/0
   ```

   A user dials the number 1159. What digits does the router send out the port 1/0/0?

   a. 1159

   b. 115

   c. 11

    d. 59

    e. 9

5. What is the default codec used by a VoIP dial peer?

    a. G.711 µ-law

    b. G.711 a-law

    c. G.723

    d. G.729

6. Which of the following destination patterns could you use to match any dialed number up to 32 digits in length? (Choose two.)

    a. .+

    b. [0-32]

    c. T

    d. &

7. After you have created a translation rule, how is it applied?

    a. To an interface

    b. To a translation profile

    c. Globally

    d. To a dial peer

8. Which of the following digit manipulation commands will work under a VoIP dial peer?

    a. prefix

    b. forward-digits

    c. translation-profile

    d. digit-strip

9. What is the final method used by a router to match an inbound dial peer for incoming calls?

    a. Using the **answer-address** command

    b. Using dial peer 0

    c. Using the **port** command

    d. Using the **destination-pattern** command

10. Which of the following is *not* an area you can use QoS to manage?

    a.   Packet jitter

    b.   Variable delay

    c.   Fixed delay

    d.   Router queuing

Foundation Topics

Configuring Physical Voice Port Characteristics

Before you can dive fully into the configuration of dial plans using dial peers, you first have to think about the physical characteristics of the voice ports on the router. Obviously, the voice ports plug into a cable, which eventually connects to a far-end device. Beyond that, there are a few additional settings on the router that you can tune to allow the voice ports to operate exactly to your specification. This section divides the discussion of these configurations into analog and digital forms.

Configuring Analog Voice Ports

Similar to Ethernet, when you connect a cable to an analog voice port on a router, it just works (provided there is a signal coming from the other end). The router receives the electrical signals from the line and processes them normally. In addition to normal call processing, there are a few settings you can tune on each interface type to change the way it operates with the other end of the connection. This section describes configuration options for Foreign Exchange Station (FXS) ports and Foreign Exchange Office (FXO) ports.

Foreign Exchange Station Ports

FXS ports connect to *end stations*, that is, typical analog devices such as telephones, fax machines, and modems (shown in Figure 8.1).

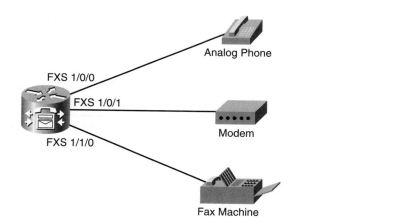

Key
Topic

Figure 8.1   *FXS Port Connections*

When you are getting ready to configure your FXS voice ports, the best place to start is to find out what voice ports your router is equipped with. You can do this quickly by using the **show voice port summary** command, as shown in Example 8.1.

Example 8.1   *Identifying Voice Ports Using* show voice port summary

```
CME_Voice# show voice port summary
                              IN       OUT
PORT           CH  SIG-TYPE  ADMIN OPER STATUS   STATUS   EC
============== == ========== ===== ==== ======== ======== ==
0/0/0          —  fxs-ls     up    dorm on-hook  idle     y
0/0/1          —  fxs-ls     up    dorm on-hook  idle     y
0/2/0          —  fxo-ls     up    dorm idle     on-hook  y
0/2/1          —  fxo-ls     up    dorm idle     on-hook  y
0/2/2          —  fxo-ls     up    dorm idle     on-hook  y
0/2/3          —  fxo-ls     up    dorm idle     on-hook  y
```

Note   If you are using your router for CME, each ephone-dn you configure shows up under the **show voice port summary** output as an EXFS port.

Based on the output from Example 8.1, you can see that this router is equipped with two FXS ports and four FXO ports.

When working with FXS ports, there are three common areas of configuration:

■   Signaling

■   Call progress tones

■   Caller ID information

There are two types of signaling you can use for analog FXS interfaces: ground start and loop start. This signal type dictates the method used by the attached device to signal that a phone is going off-hook. Table 8.2 briefly describes the differences between ground start and loop start signaling.

Table 8.2   *Comparing Ground Start and Loop Start*

Ground Start	Loop Start
Signals a new connection by grounding two of the wires in the cable temporarily	Signals by completing a circuit (by lifting the handset off-hook) and dropping the total DC voltage down on the line
Must be configured	Is the default
Typically used when connecting to PBX equipment	Typically used when connecting to analog devices such as telephones, fax machines, and modems

You can use the syntax shown in Example 8.2 to set the signaling type on the voice port.

Example 8.2   *Configuring FXS Voice Port Signaling*

```
CME_Voice(config)# voice-port 0/0/0
CME_Voice(config-voiceport)# signal ?
  groundStart  Ground Start
  loopStart    Loop Start
CME_Voice(config-voiceport)# signal loopStart
```

If you have traveled the world, you may have noticed that phones sound different in different regions. Based on your geographical location, dial tones may be higher or lower and busy signals may be fast or slow. These are all considered call progress tones: audio signals that inform the caller how the call is progressing. By default, the FXS port of your router uses the call progress tones from the United States. If your router is serving some other part of the world, use the command shown in Example 8.3 to adjust the call progress tones.

Example 8.3   *Adjusting Call Progress Tones*

```
CME_Voice(config)# voice-port 0/0/0
CME_Voice(config-voiceport)# cptone ?
  locale   2 letter ISO-3166 country code
```

AR Argentina	IN India	PE Peru
AU Australia	ID Indonesia	PH Philippines
AT Austria	IE Ireland	PL Poland
BE Belgium	IL Israel	PT Portugal
BR Brazil	IT Italy	RU Russian Federation
CA Canada	JP Japan	SA Saudi Arabia
CN China	JO Jordan	SG Singapore
CO Colombia	KE Kenya	SK Slovakia
C1 Custom1	KR Korea Republic	SI Slovenia
C2 Custom2	KW Kuwait	ZA South Africa
CY Cyprus	LB Lebanon	ES Spain
CZ Czech Republic	LU Luxembourg	SE Sweden
DK Denmark	MY Malaysia	CH Switzerland
EG Egypt	MX Mexico	TW Taiwan
FI Finland	NP Nepal	TH Thailand
FR France	NL Netherlands	TR Turkey
DE Germany	NZ New Zealand	AE United Arab Emirates
GH Ghana	NG Nigeria	GB United Kingdom
GR Greece	NO Norway	US United States
HK Hong Kong	OM Oman	VE Venezuela
HU Hungary	PK Pakistan	ZW Zimbabwe
IS Iceland	PA Panama	

Simply enter the two-digit country code to change the sound of all the progress tones on the device attached to the FXS port.

Finally, you can use the syntax shown in Example 8.4 to configure caller ID information for the device attached to the FXS port.

Example 8.4 *Configuring FXS Port Caller ID Information*

```
CME_Voice(config)# voice-port 0/0/0
CME_Voice(config-voiceport)# station-id name 3rd Floor Fax
CME_Voice(config-voiceport)# station-id number 5551000
```

This configuration allows other devices in your system to receive caller ID name and number information anytime the device attached to the FXS port places a call to them.

Foreign Exchange Office Ports

FXO ports act as a trunk to the PSTN central office (CO) or PBX systems, as shown in Figure 8.2.

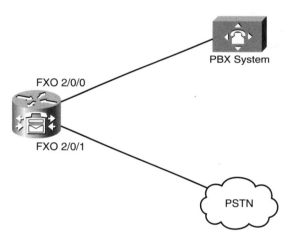

Figure 8.2 *FXO Port Connections*

FXO ports use many of the same commands as FXS cards, such as **signal** to set loop start or ground start signaling, and **station-id** to set caller ID information. There are two additional commands that are of note:

- **dial-type**

- **ring number**

The **dial-type <dtmf/pulse>** command allows you to choose to use dual-tone multifrequency (DTMF) or pulse dialing. Yes, there are still some areas of the world that require the use of pulse dialing (and rotary phones). If you are installing a voice network into one of these areas, this command is for you.

The **ring number** *\<number\>* command allows you to specify the number of rings that should pass before the router answers an incoming call to the FXO port. By default, this is set to one ring, which causes the router to answer an incoming call immediately. There may be instances where the FXO port of the router is attached to a loop of other devices (such as in a home office environment) and the user wants the other devices to have a chance to answer the call before the router picks up the line and processes it. In this case, you can set the ring number to a higher value.

Configuring Digital Voice Ports

Cisco provides digital T1 and E1 ports in the form of Voice and WAN Interface Cards (VWIC) for routers. These cards offer you the flexibility to configure them for a data connection or a voice connection. Unlike analog interfaces, you must configure digital interfaces before they will operate correctly, because the router does not know the type of network you will be using. As discussed in Chapter 7, "Gateway and Trunk Concepts," there are two types of voice network configurations you can use: T1/E1 channel associated signaling (CAS) or T1/E1 common channel signaling (CCS; commonly referred to as ISDN Primary Rate Interface [PRI]). The type of network to which you are connecting dictates the command you will use to configure your VWIC card: **ds0-group** for T1/E1 CAS connections or **pri-group** for T1/E1 CCS connections.

Example 8.5 demonstrates configuring all 24 channels of a T1 CAS interface to connect to a PSTN carrier.

Example 8.5 *Configuring a T1 CAS PSTN Interface*

```
CME_Voice# show controllers t1
T1 1/0 is down.
  Applique type is Channelized T1
  Cablelength is long gain36 0db
  Transmitter is sending remote alarm.
  Receiver has loss of signal.
  alarm-trigger is not set
  Soaking time: 3, Clearance time: 10
  AIS State:Clear  LOS State:Clear  LOF State:Clear
  Version info Firmware: 20050620, FPGA: 20, spm_count = 0
  Framing is SF, Line Code is AMI, Clock Source is Line.
   Current port master clock:local osc on this network module
  Data in current interval (215 seconds elapsed):
     0 Line Code Violations, 0 Path Code Violations
     0 Slip Secs, 0 Fr Loss Secs, 0 Line Err Secs, 0 Degraded Mins
     0 Errored Secs, 0 Bursty Err Secs, 0 Severely Err Secs, 215 Unavail Secs
CME_Voice# configure terminal
Enter configuration commands, one per line.  End with CNTL/Z.
CME_Voice(config)# controller t1 1/0
CME_Voice(config-controller)# framing ?
  esf  Extended Superframe
  sf   Superframe
```

continues

Example 8.5   *Configuring a T1 CAS PSTN Interface   continued*

```
CME_Voice(config-controller)# framing esf
CME_Voice(config-controller)# linecode ?
  ami   AMI encoding
  b8zs  B8ZS encoding
CME_Voice(config-controller)# linecode b8zs
CME_Voice(config-controller)# clock source ?
  free-running  Free Running Clock
  internal      Internal Clock
  line          Recovered Clock

CME_Voice(config-controller)# clock source line
CME_Voice(config-controller)# ds0-group ?
  <0-23>  Group Number
CME_Voice(config-controller)# ds0-group 1 ?
  timeslots  List of timeslots in the ds0-group
CME_Voice(config-controller)# ds0-group 1 timeslots ?
  <1-24>  List of T1 timeslots
CME_Voice(config-controller)# ds0-group 1 timeslots 1-24 ?
  type  Specify the type of signaling
  <cr>
CME_Voice(config-controller)# ds0-group 1 timeslots 1-24 type ?
  e&m-delay-dial      E & M Delay Dial
  e&m-fgd             E & M Type II FGD
  e&m-immediate-start E & M Immediate Start
  e&m-lmr             E & M land mobil radio
  e&m-wink-start      E & M Wink Start
  ext-sig             External Signaling
  fgd-eana            FGD-EANA BOC side
  fxo-ground-start    FXO Ground Start
  fxo-loop-start      FXO Loop Start
  fxs-ground-start    FXS Ground Start
  fxs-loop-start      FXS Loop Start
  none                Null Signalling for External Call Control
  <cr>
CME_Voice(config-controller)# ds0-group 1 timeslots 1-24 type fxo-loop-start ?
CME_Voice(config-controller)#^Z
CME_Voice# show voice port summary
                              IN        OUT
PORT      CH  SIG-TYPE    ADMIN OPER STATUS   STATUS   EC
========= == ============ ===== ==== ======== ======== ==
1/0:1     01  fxo-ls       up   down idle     on-hook  y
```

```
1/0:1    02   fxo-ls    up    down idle    on-hook  y
1/0:1    03   fxo-ls    up    down idle    on-hook  y
1/0:1    04   fxo-ls    up    down idle    on-hook  y
1/0:1    05   fxo-ls    up    down idle    on-hook  y
1/0:1    06   fxo-ls    up    down idle    on-hook  y
1/0:1    07   fxo-ls    up    down idle    on-hook  y
1/0:1    08   fxo-ls    up    down idle    on-hook  y
1/0:1    09   fxo-ls    up    down idle    on-hook  y
1/0:1    10   fxo-ls    up    down idle    on-hook  y
1/0:1    11   fxo-ls    up    down idle    on-hook  y
1/0:1    12   fxo-ls    up    down idle    on-hook  y
1/0:1    13   fxo-ls    up    down idle    on-hook  y
1/0:1    14   fxo-ls    up    down idle    on-hook  y
1/0:1    15   fxo-ls    up    down idle    on-hook  y
1/0:1    16   fxo-ls    up    down idle    on-hook  y
1/0:1    17   fxo-ls    up    down idle    on-hook  y
1/0:1    18   fxo-ls    up    down idle    on-hook  y
1/0:1    19   fxo-ls    up    down idle    on-hook  y
1/0:1    20   fxo-ls    up    down idle    on-hook  y
1/0:1    21   fxo-ls    up    down idle    on-hook  y
1/0:1    22   fxo-ls    up    down idle    on-hook  y
1/0:1    23   fxo-ls    up    down idle    on-hook  y
1/0:1    24   fxo-ls    up    down idle    on-hook  y
```

There are many commands to discuss from Example 8.5, starting with the **show controllers t1** command. This command allows you to identify the T1 interfaces on your router. These interfaces do not appear in the **show ip interface brief** output, because the router does not know if you will configure the interface as a voice or data connection. Once you identify the slot and port of your T1 interface, you can then configure the necessary **framing** and **linecode** commands. These commands let you change how the T1 or E1 interface formats the frames it sends to the service provider. Set these values based on the service provider to which you are connecting.

Note   If you are in the United States, most service providers use ESF framing and B8ZS linecoding.

After you have set the framing and linecoding, you can move into the clocking. The command **clock source line** instructs the router to receive its interface clocking from the service provider. If you are connecting to a PSTN carrier, this is the norm. If your router is connecting to a PBX system inside your company, you may enter the command **clock source internal**, which allows the router to provide clocking information to the PBX system.

Finally, the **ds0-group** command configures the line as a T1 CAS connection and allows you to enter the specific number of time slots you would like to provision. In Example 8.5, all 24 time slots were provisioned under DS0 group 1. The group number you choose can be any value from 0–23. This value acts as an identifier for the time slots you place into it. You could provision a single T1 line for many different purposes. For example, you could create DS0 group 5 with time slots 1–5 that connect to an onsite PBX system. You could then create DS0 group 6 using time slots 6–24 that connect to the PSTN (provided the PBX system and PSTN carrier were provisioned for these same time slot settings). Figure 8.3 illustrates the physical design of this network type.

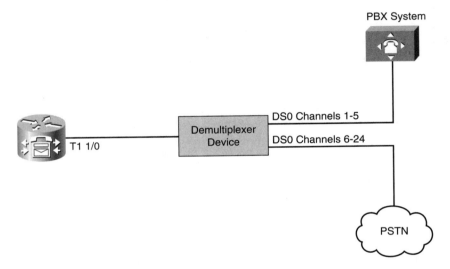

Figure 8.3   *Provisioning Multiple Connections with a Single T1 Interface*

Note   The demultiplexing device shown in Figure 8.3 allows you to break the single T1 interface into multiple interfaces with specific channel assignments.

Notice that the **ds0-group** command also allows you to set the signaling type. This gives you the ability to connect to many different network types. The PSTN carrier typically uses FXO loop start signaling over the T1 CAS connection (this may differ depending on your location and service provider). PBX systems often support one of the various E&M signaling types.

Once you have entered the **ds0-group** command, the router automatically creates a voice port for each time slot you provision, as you can see from the **show voice port summary** output of Example 8.5. The port is listed as 1/0:1 because 1/0 represents the physical interface and the additional 1 represents the DS0 group number. You will want to make a note of this port identifier; you will need it when you configure the dial peers. Each of the ports listed represents a different channel on the T1 interface.

Configuring the digital T1/E1 interface for a CCS (ISDN PRI) PSTN connection uses similar syntax as the CAS. Example 8.6 demonstrates a configuration that provisions all 24 time slots of the VWIC interface as a PRI PSTN connection.

Example 8.6   *Configuring a T1 CCS PSTN Interface*

```
CME_Voice(config)# isdn switch-type ?
  primary-4ess     Lucent 4ESS switch type for the U.S.
  primary-5ess     Lucent 5ESS switch type for the U.S.
  primary-dms100   Northern Telecom DMS-100 switch type for the U.S.
  primary-dpnss    DPNSS switch type for Europe
  primary-net5     NET5 switch type for UK, Europe, Asia and Australia
  primary-ni       National ISDN Switch type for the U.S.
  primary-ntt      NTT switch type for Japan
  primary-qsig     QSIG switch type
  primary-ts014    TS014 switch type for Australia (obsolete)
CME_Voice(config)# isdn switch-type primary-5ess
CME_Voice(config)# controller t1 1/0
CME_Voice(config-controller)# pri-group ?
  nfas_d     Specify the operation of the D-channel timeslot.
  service    Specify the service type
  timeslots  List of timeslots in the pri-group
  <cr>
CME_Voice(config-controller)# pri-group timeslots ?
  <1-24>  List of timeslots which comprise the pri-group

CME_Voice(config-controller)# pri-group timeslots 1-24 ?
  nfas_d   Specify the operation of the D-channel timeslot.
  service  Specify the service type
CME_Voice(config-controller)# pri-group timeslots 1-24
CME_Voice(config-controller)#^Z
CME_Voice# show voice port summary
                                 IN      OUT
PORT     CH  SIG-TYPE     ADMIN OPER STATUS  STATUS   EC
======== == ============ ===== ==== ======== ======== ==
1/0:23   01  isdn-voice   up    dorm none     none     y
1/0:23   02  isdn-voice   up    dorm none     none     y
1/0:23   03  isdn-voice   up    dorm none     none     y
1/0:23   04  isdn-voice   up    dorm none     none     y
1/0:23   05  isdn-voice   up    dorm none     none     y
1/0:23   06  isdn-voice   up    dorm none     none     y
1/0:23   07  isdn-voice   up    dorm none     none     y
1/0:23   08  isdn-voice   up    dorm none     none     y
1/0:23   09  isdn-voice   up    dorm none     none     y
1/0:23   10  isdn-voice   up    dorm none     none     y
1/0:23   11  isdn-voice   up    dorm none     none     y
```

continues

Example 8.6   *Configuring a T1 CCS PSTN Interface   continued*

```
1/0:23    12   isdn-voice   up   dorm none   none   y
1/0:23    13   isdn-voice   up   dorm none   none   y
1/0:23    14   isdn-voice   up   dorm none   none   y
1/0:23    15   isdn-voice   up   dorm none   none   y
1/0:23    16   isdn-voice   up   dorm none   none   y
1/0:23    17   isdn-voice   up   dorm none   none   y
1/0:23    18   isdn-voice   up   dorm none   none   y
1/0:23    19   isdn-voice   up   dorm none   none   y
1/0:23    20   isdn-voice   up   dorm none   none   y
1/0:23    21   isdn-voice   up   dorm none   none   y
1/0:23    22   isdn-voice   up   dorm none   none   y
1/0:23    23   isdn-voice   up   dorm none   none   y
```

When configuring this CCS connection, the first step is to set the ISDN switch type. This needs to match the type of switch your local service provider is using. Example 8.6 sets this to primary-5ess. Once you have configured the switch type, the router will allow you to enter the **pri-group** command. This works identically to the **ds0-group** command in that it allows you to provision a specific number of time slots for use with the PSTN carrier. This command does not allow you to select a signaling type because the router assumes ISDN PRI signaling.

Once you have entered this command, the router creates 24 ISDN voice ports, verified with the **show voice port summary** command, which it will use for incoming and outgoing voice calls. Notice that the voice port is represented by the identifier 1/0:23. This represents channel 23 (time slot 24) of the T1 ISDN PRI connection (channels are listed from 0–23, whereas time slots are listed 1–24). This is the dedicated signaling channel used to bring up the other 23 voice bearer channels.

Note   When using T1 interfaces, channel 23 (time slot 24) is always the signaling channel. When using E1 interfaces, channel 16 (time slot 17) is always the signaling channel.

As before, you will want to make note of this port identifier for the ISDN circuit. The router will require you to identify this interface when configuring your dial peers.

Understanding and Configuring Dial Peers

When you initially entered the Cisco world, you probably learned about the concept of static routing. This method of routing allows you to manually enter destinations the router is able to reach on the data network. Using dial peers is a similar concept to this; think of dial peers as static routes for your voice network. By default, the CME router only knows how to reach the ephone-dns you configure for the Cisco IP phones. You can connect the CME router to any number of FXS, FXO, or digital T1/E1 connections, but until you create dial peers for these connections, the router will not use them.

Dial peers define voice reachability information. Simply put, these are the phone numbers you are able to dial. For example, you might connect an analog phone to the FXS port of the router. As soon as you make the connection, the analog phone receives a dial tone and is able to place calls. However, no one will be able to call the analog phone because it does not yet have a phone number. Using a dial peer, you can assign one or more phone numbers to this analog device. Furthermore, dial peers allow you to use wildcards to define ranges of phone numbers. This is useful when you want to define large groups of numbers available from a destination such as a PBX system or PSTN connection.

There are two primary types of dial peers that you can create:

- **POTS dial peer:** Used to define voice reachability information for any traditional voice connection (that is, any device connected to an FXS, FXO, E&M, or digital voice port)

- **VoIP dial peer:** Used to define voice reachability information for any VoIP connection (that is, any device that is reachable through an IP address)

Figure 8.4 illustrates the placement of plain old telephone service (POTS) and Voice over IP (VoIP) dial peers in a network.

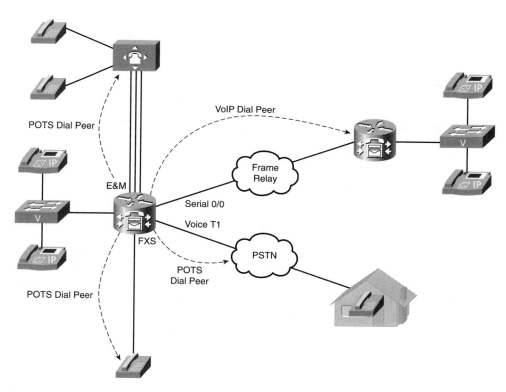

Figure 8.4   *POTS and VoIP Dial Peers*

Because these dial peers define voice reachability information on a hop-by-hop basis, they are commonly referred to as call legs.

Voice Call Legs

To accurately configure dial peers, you must first understand the concept of call legs. A call leg represents a connection to or from a voice gateway from a POTS or VoIP source. For example, Figure 8.5 illustrates a voice connection scenario.

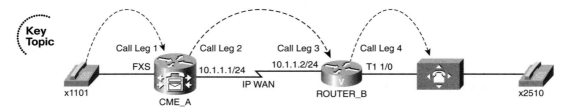

Figure 8.5   *Voice Connection Call Legs*

As illustrated in Figure 8.5, the phone on the left (extension 1101) makes a call to the phone on the right (extension 2510). For this call to pass through successfully, four call legs must exist:

■ **Call leg 1:** The incoming POTS call leg from x1101 on CME_A

■ **Call leg 2:** The outgoing VoIP call leg from CME_A to ROUTER_B

■ **Call leg 3:** The incoming VoIP call leg on ROUTER_B from CME_A

■ **Call leg 4:** The outgoing POTS call leg to x2510 from ROUTER_B

If the call were placed in the opposite direction (from x2510 to x1101), the same number of call legs would be needed, but in reverse. Thus, in order to provide a two-way calling environment in which x1101 can call x2510 and vice versa, you would need a total of eight call legs.

Understanding the concept of call legs is critical to a proper configuration of dial peers on your router. Each one of the call legs identified in Figure 8.5 represents a dial peer that must exist on your router. These dial peers define not only the reachability information (phone numbers) for the devices, but also the path the audio must travel. From CME_A's perspective, it will be receiving audio from x1101 on an FXS port (call leg 1). CME_A must then pass that voice information over the IP network to 10.1.1.2 (call leg 2). From ROUTER_B's perspective, it will receive a call from x1101 on the IP WAN network (call leg 3). It must then take that call and pass it to the PBX system out the digital T1 1/0 interface (call leg 4).

As you can see from Figure 8.5, call legs are matched on the inbound and outbound direction. In the same way, you must configure dial peers to match voice traffic in both directions. In some cases, you can use a single dial peer for bidirectional traffic. For example, creating a single POTS dial peer for x1101 will match incoming and outgoing calls to x1101. At other times, you must create more than one dial peer for inbound and outbound traffic. For example, CME_A required an outbound VoIP dial peer to send the call to ROUTER_B (10.1.1.2). ROUTER_B then needed an inbound VoIP dial peer to receive the call from CME_A. As you see multiple examples of dial peers in the upcoming sections, these concepts will become clearer.

Configuring POTS Dial Peers

As mentioned previously, you can use POTS dial peers to define reachability information for anything connected to your VoIP network from the traditional telephony world. This includes devices connected to FXO, FXS, E&M, and digital BRI/T1/E1 interfaces.

Tip   If you are connecting to something without an IP address (such as an analog phone, fax machine, PBX, or the PSTN), it is a POTS dial peer.

The network in Figure 8.6 demonstrates the configuration of POTS dial peers.

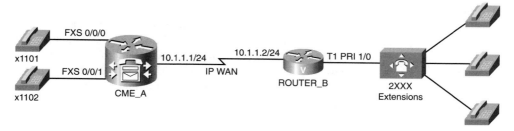

Figure 8.6   *Dial Peer Configuration Scenario*

The configuration will begin with the CME_A router. To create POTS dial peers, you can use the syntax **dial-peer voice** *<tag>* **pots** from global configuration mode. The *tag* value can be any number you want (from 1 to 2,147,483,647), as long as it is unique on the router. Although this tag does not have any impact on the reachability information you assign to the devices, many administrators have a common practice of relating a dial-peer tag value to the phone number of the device. Example 8.7 assigns the extensions shown in Figure 8.6 to the analog phones attached to the CME_A router's FXS ports.

Example 8.7   *Configuring POTS Dial Peers for FXS Ports*

```
CME_A(config)# dial-peer voice ?
  <1-2147483647>  Voice dial-peer tag
CME_A(config)# dial-peer voice 1101 ?
  mmoip  Multi Media Over IP
  pots   Telephony
  vofr   Voice over Frame Relay
  voip   Voice over IP
CME_A(config)# dial-peer voice 1101 pots
CME_A(config-dial-peer)# destination-pattern ?
  WORD  A sequence of digits - representing the prefix or full telephone number
CME_A(config-dial-peer)# destination-pattern 1101
CME_A(config-dial-peer)# port 0/0/0
CME_A(config-dial-peer)# exit
CME_A(config)# dial-peer voice 1102 pots
CME_A(config-dial-peer)# destination-pattern 1102
CME_A(config-dial-peer)# port 0/0/1
```

After you create the dial peer, you can then assign the phone number to the attached device(s) by using the **destination-pattern** and **port** commands. After you have entered this configuration, you can place calls between the phones attached to the CME_A router. Before you place any calls, it is always best to verify the dial-peer configuration.

The **show dial-peer voice** command (without the **summary** keyword) does show you all the dial peers on your router, but uses about a page of output for each dial peer. Although this information may be useful at times, the **summary** view, which is shown in Example 8.8, is usually much easier to digest. Notice at the bottom of the output are the dial-peer tags 1101 and 1102, displayed as POTS dial peers with the proper destination pattern and port assignments. The other dial peers listed (with tags 20005–20014) are dial peers created by the CME routers for the ephone-dns configured in Chapter 5, "Basic CME IP Phone Configuration."

Example 8.8   *Verifying Dial Peers*

```
CME_A# show dial-peer voice summary
dial-peer hunt 0
                    AD                           PRE PASS              OUT
  TAG    TYPE  MIN  OPER PREFIX    DEST-PATTERN   FER THRU SESS-TARGET  STAT PORT
  20005  pots  up   up             1500$          0                         50/0/20
  20006  pots  up   up             1501$          0                         50/0/21
```

20007	pots	up	up	1502$	0		50/0/22
20008	pots	up	up	1503$	0		50/0/23
20009	pots	up	up	1504$	0		50/0/24
20010	pots	up	up	1505$	0		50/0/25
20011	pots	up	up	1506$	0		50/0/26
20012	pots	up	up	1507$	0		50/0/27
20013	pots	up	up	1508$	0		50/0/28
20014	pots	up	up	1509$	0		50/0/29
1101	pots	up	up	1101	0	up	0/0/0
1102	pots	up	up	1102	0	up	0/0/1

You can test the configuration by placing a call between the devices. Because this is a book, you will not actually hear the phones ring, so Example 8.9 shows a useful **debug** command in which you can see the router process the dialed digits from the phone attached to the FXS port.

Example 8.9   *Using the* **debug voip dialpeer** *Command to Analyze Digit Processing*

```
CME_A# debug voip dialpeer
voip dialpeer default debugging is on
.Jul  2 17:16:44.698: //-1/77671F238035/DPM/dpMatchPeersCore:
   Calling Number=, Called Number=1, Peer Info Type=DIALPEER_INFO_SPEECH
.Jul  2 17:16:44.698: //-1/77671F238035/DPM/dpMatchPeersCore:
   Match Rule=DP_MATCH_DEST; Called Number=1
.Jul  2 17:16:44.698: //-1/77671F238035/DPM/dpMatchPeersCore:
   Result=Partial Matches(1) after DP_MATCH_DEST
.Jul  2 17:16:44.702: //-1/77671F238035/DPM/dpMatchPeersMoreArg:
   Result=MORE_DIGITS_NEEDED(1)
.Jul  2 17:16:45.114: //-1/77671F238035/DPM/dpMatchPeersCore:
   Calling Number=, Called Number=11, Peer Info Type=DIALPEER_INFO_SPEECH
.Jul  2 17:16:45.114: //-1/77671F238035/DPM/dpMatchPeersCore:
   Match Rule=DP_MATCH_DEST; Called Number=11
.Jul  2 17:16:45.114: //-1/77671F238035/DPM/dpMatchPeersCore:
   Result=Partial Matches(1) after DP_MATCH_DEST
.Jul  2 17:16:45.114: //-1/77671F238035/DPM/dpMatchPeersMoreArg:
   Result=MORE_DIGITS_NEEDED(1)
.Jul  2 17:16:45.914: //-1/77671F238035/DPM/dpMatchPeersCore:
   Calling Number=, Called Number=110, Peer Info Type=DIALPEER_INFO_SPEECH
.Jul  2 17:16:45.914: //-1/77671F238035/DPM/dpMatchPeersCore:
   Match Rule=DP_MATCH_DEST; Called Number=110
.Jul  2 17:16:45.914: //-1/77671F238035/DPM/dpMatchPeersCore:
   Result=Partial Matches(1) after DP_MATCH_DEST
```

continues

Example 8.9   *Using the* **debug voip dialpeer** *Command to Analyze Digit Processing* *continued*

```
.Jul  2 17:16:45.914: //-1/77671F238035/DPM/dpMatchPeersMoreArg:
   Result=MORE_DIGITS_NEEDED(1)
.Jul  2 17:16:48.426: //-1/77671F238035/DPM/dpMatchPeersCore:
   Calling Number=, Called Number=1101, Peer Info Type=DIALPEER_INFO_SPEECH
.Jul  2 17:16:48.426: //-1/77671F238035/DPM/dpMatchPeersCore:
   Match Rule=DP_MATCH_DEST; Called Number=1101
.Jul  2 17:16:48.426: //-1/77671F238035/DPM/dpMatchPeersCore:
   Result=Success(0) after DP_MATCH_DEST
.Jul  2 17:16:48.426: //-1/77671F238035/DPM/dpMatchPeersMoreArg:
   Result=SUCCESS(0)
   List of Matched Outgoing Dial-peer(s):
     1: Dial-peer Tag=1101
```

Notice the highlighted output from the **debug** command in Example 8.9. This shows the router performing digit-by-digit call processing. As the attached phone dials each digit, the router processes that digit and attempts to find a match from among its dial peer configuration. For the first three dialed digits, the result is clear: more digits needed. Once the caller dials the fourth digit, the router matches dial-peer tag 1101 and processes the call.

Now we can turn our attention to the POTS dial-peer configuration on ROUTER_B, which has a T1 PRI connection to a PBX system hosting 2XXX extensions (four-digit extensions beginning with the number 2). In the earlier "Configuring Digital Voice Ports" section of this chapter, the physical characteristics of the T1 VWIC interface were configured to support T1 PRI connectivity (by using the **pri-group** command). When that command was entered, the router automatically created the voice port 1/0:23, which represented the signaling channel of the T1 PRI connection. Example 8.10 now configures the router to use this T1 PRI port anytime it receives a call for a 2XXX extension.

Example 8.10   *Configuring a POTS Dial Peer for a T1 Interface*

```
ROUTER_B(config)# dial-peer voice 2000 pots
ROUTER_B(config-dial-peer)# destination-pattern 2...
ROUTER_B(config-dial-peer)# no digit-strip
ROUTER_B(config-dial-peer)# port 1/0:23
```

It is that simple. Notice that you can use the "." wildcard to represent any dialed digit. This instructs the router to send all 2XXX extensions out port 1/0:23 (the T1 PRI interface). There is one additional command in this example that brings up a big point of discussion: **no digit-strip**. This command prevents the router from automatically stripping dialed digits from this dial peer. Now, why would the router do that? Because of the POTS dial-peer rule Cisco has programmed into Cisco IOS. Here's the rule:

Digit Stripping Rule of POTS Dial Peers:

The router will automatically strip any explicitly defined digit from a POTS dial peer before forwarding the call.

An explicitly defined digit is any non-wildcard digit. In the case of Example 8.10, 2 is an explicitly defined digit. This rule is in place primarily to assist with stripping outside dialing codes before sending calls to the PSTN. For example, organizations commonly require users to dial 9 to access an outside line (often receiving a second dial tone after they have dialed 9). However, if you keep this access digit prepended to the dialed phone number, the PSTN carrier will reject the call. Thus, you could create a POTS dial peer with the **destination-pattern 9.......** command (for seven-digit dialing), and the router will automatically strip the explicitly defined 9 digit before sending the call to the PSTN.

In the case of Example 8.10, stripping the 2 digit before sending the call to the PBX system would not be a desired behavior. Thus, the **no digit-strip** command prevents this automatic digit stripping process. This concept will be revisited in the upcoming "Understanding Router Call Processing and Digit Manipulation" section.

Note The automatic digit stripping function is specific to POTS dial peers. VoIP dial peers (discussed in the following section) do not automatically strip digits.

Configuring VoIP Dial Peers

Looking at the scenario shown in Figure 8.7, the POTS dial peers now provide connectivity to the legacy voice equipment. However, CME_A and ROUTER_B are divided by an IP WAN connection that the legacy voice equipment must cross to achieve end-to-end communication.

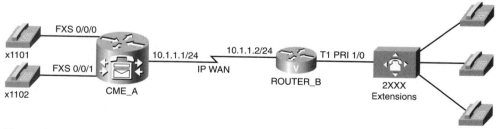

Figure 8.7 *Dial Peer Configuration Scenario*

To accomplish this connectivity, you must use VoIP dial peers, because you are crossing an IP-based network. Example 8.11 configures the necessary VoIP dial peers on the CME_A and ROUTER_B devices.

Example 8.11 *Configuring VoIP Dial Peers*

Key Topic

```
CME_A(config)# dial-peer voice 2000 voip
CME_A(config-dial-peer)# destination-pattern 2...
CME_A(config-dial-peer)# session target ?
  WORD  A string specifying the session target
CME_A(config-dial-peer)# session target ipv4:10.1.1.2
CME_A(config-dial-peer)# codec ?
  clear-channel  Clear Channel 64000 bps (No voice capabilities: data transport
    only)
  g711alaw       G.711 A Law 64000 bps
  g711ulaw       G.711 u Law 64000 bps
  g722-48        G722-48K 64000 bps - Only supported for H.320<->H.323 calls
  g722-56        G722-56K 64000 bps - Only supported for H.320<->H.323 calls
  g722-64        G722-64K 64000 bps - Only supported for H.320<->H.323 calls
  g723ar53       G.723.1 ANNEX-A 5300 bps (contains built-in vad that cannot be
    disabled)
  g723ar63       G.723.1 ANNEX-A 6300 bps (contains built-in vad that cannot be
    disabled)
  g723r53        G.723.1 5300 bps
  g723r63        G.723.1 6300 bps
  g726r16        G.726 16000 bps
  g726r24        G.726 24000 bps
  g726r32        G.726 32000 bps
  g728           G.728 16000 bps
  g729br8        G.729 ANNEX-B 8000 bps (contains built-in vad that cannot be
    disabled)
  g729r8         G.729 8000 bps
  ilbc           iLBC 13330 or 15200 bps
CME_A(config-dial-peer)# codec g711ulaw

ROUTER_B(config)# dial-peer voice 1100 voip
ROUTER_B(config-dial-peer)# destination-pattern 110.
ROUTER_B(config-dial-peer)# session target ipv4:10.1.1.1
ROUTER_B(config-dial-peer)# codec g711ulaw
```

The primary difference between the POTS and VoIP dial peer configuration is the use of the **session target** command rather than the **port** command. When you use the context-sensitive help after the **session target** command, the router simply replies with WORD. This means that whatever you enter after the command is somewhat freeform. Most of the time, you will use the syntax **ipv4:***ip address* to enter a remote IP address, as shown in Example 8.11. This command also allows you to direct calls to DNS names (by using **dns:***name* syntax) or to a variety of call management servers, such as H.323 gatekeepers or SIP proxy servers.

After you have set the session target destination, you can optionally use the **codec** command to select the codec the router should use when placing a call to this destination.

Note   If the codec values do not match between the two routers, the call will fail and return a reorder tone (fast busy signal). This is commonly called a codec mismatch. The default codec value for VoIP dial peers is G.729.

Finally, notice that the dial peer 1100 on ROUTER_B uses the command **destination-pattern 110.** to direct all calls starting with the digits 110 to the CME_A router. Without using this wildcard, you would need to create two VoIP dial peers on ROUTER_B: one for x1101 and one for x1102.

Note   Notice that dial-peer tag 2000 was used on the CME_A router for a VoIP dial peer, and was used on the ROUTER_B router for a POTS dial peer. This combination will work just fine. The only restriction to keep in mind is that you cannot use the same dial-peer tag value for different functions on the *same* router.

Using Dial-Peer Wildcards

As you have seen in the previous few sections, configuring dial peers (and destination patterns) without using wildcards would be extremely time consuming. By far, the most commonly used wildcard is the dot (.), which represents any dialed digit. There are a few other wildcards in addition to this that you will find useful in your configurations. Table 8.3 provides a description for these wildcards.

Table 8.3   *Wildcards You Can Use with the* **destination-pattern** *Command*

Wildcard	Description
Period (.)	Matches any dialed digit from 0–9 or the * key on the telephone keypad. For example, 20.. matches any number from 2000 through 2099.
Plus (+)	Matches one or more instances of the preceding digit. For example, 5+23 matches 5523, 55523, 555523, and so on. This trend continues up to 32 digits, which is the maximum length of a dialable number.
Brackets ([])	Matches a range of digits. For example, [1-3]22 matches 122, 222, and 322. You can include a caret (^) before the entered numbers to designate a "does not match" range. For example, [^1-3]22 matches 022, 422, 522, 622, 722, 822, 922, and *22.
T	Matches any number of dialed digits (from 0–32 digits).
Comma (,)	Inserts a one-second pause between dialed digits.

Key Topic

Note   The pound symbol (#) on a telephone keypad is not a wildcard symbol. This key immediately processes a dialed number when it is entered without waiting for additional digits.

Tip   If you plan to create a dial peer using only the T wildcard as the destination pattern, Cisco recommends that you create the destination as .T. This requires a user to dial at least one digit to match the destination pattern. Otherwise, a phone left off-hook for too long without a dialed digit will match the destination pattern.

Typically, the brackets wildcard is the most difficult to understand, primarily because it is the most flexible. Take the examples shown in Table 8.4.

Table 8.4   *Destination-Pattern Brackets Wildcard Examples*

Pattern	Description
555[1-3]...	Matches dialed numbers beginning with 555, having 1, 2, or 3 as the fourth digit, and ending in any three digits
[14-6]555	Matches dialed numbers where the first digit is 1, 4, 5, or 6 and the last three digits are 555
55[59]12	Matches dialed numbers where the first two digits are 55, the third digit is 5 or 9, and the last two digits are 12
[^1-7]..[135]	Matches dialed numbers where the first digit is *not* 1–7, the second and third digits are any number, and the last digit is 1, 3, or 5

These wildcards are most often used when creating dial plans for PSTN access. Initially, the most logical destination pattern choice for the PSTN may seem to be 9T (9 for an outside line followed by any number of digits). The problem with this is that Cisco designed the T wildcard to match variable-length strings from 0–32 digits. When a user dials an outside number, such as 14805551212, the router configured with the T wildcard will sit silently and wait for the user to dial more digits. By default, the router will wait for additional dialed digits for 10 seconds, which is the interdigit timeout (also called the T302 timer). Although you can force the router to process the call immediately after dialing the number by pressing the pound key (#), this is not something you would want to train all your users to do.

Creating a PSTN dialing plan using wildcards other than T is not extremely difficult as long as you think through the reachable PSTN numbers. Table 8.5 provides a sample PSTN dial plan that you could use in the United States.

Table 8.5   *Sample PSTN Destination Patterns for North America*

Key
Topic

Pattern	Description
[2-9]......	Used for 7-digit dialing areas
[2-9]..[2-9]......	Used for 10-digit dialing areas
1[2-9]..[2-9]......	Used for 11-digit long-distance dialing
[469]11	Used for service numbers such as 411, 611, and 911
011T	Used for international dialing

Note   Although you can manually create an international dial plan without using the T symbol, doing so can become quite tedious.

The configuration in Example 8.12 illustrates the configuration of a North American PSTN dial plan on a router. In this example, the T1 CAS voice port 1/0:1 is connected to the PSTN and internal users must dial 9 for outside PSTN access.

Example 8.12   *Configuring a North American PSTN Dial Plan*

```
VOICE_RTR(config)# dial-peer voice 90 pots
VOICE_RTR(config-dial-peer)# description Service Dialing
VOICE_RTR(config-dial-peer)# destination-pattern 9[469]11
VOICE_RTR(config-dial-peer)# forward-digits 3
VOICE_RTR(config-dial-peer)# port 1/0:1
VOICE_RTR(config-dial-peer)# exit
VOICE_RTR(config)# dial-peer voice 91 pots
VOICE_RTR(config-dial-peer)# description 10-Digit Dialing
VOICE_RTR(config-dial-peer)# destination-pattern 9[2-9]..[2-9]......
VOICE_RTR(config-dial-peer)# port 1/0:1
VOICE_RTR(config-dial-peer)# exit
VOICE_RTR(config)# dial-peer voice 92 pots
VOICE_RTR(config-dial-peer)# description 11-Digit Dialing
VOICE_RTR(config-dial-peer)# destination-pattern 91[2-9]..[2-9]......
VOICE_RTR(config-dial-peer)# forward-digits 11
VOICE_RTR(config-dial-peer)# port 1/0:1
VOICE_RTR(config-dial-peer)# exit
VOICE_RTR(config)# dial-peer voice 93 pots
VOICE_RTR(config-dial-peer)# description International Dialing
VOICE_RTR(config-dial-peer)# destination-pattern 9011T
VOICE_RTR(config-dial-peer)# prefix 011
VOICE_RTR(config-dial-peer)# port 1/0:1
VOICE_RTR(config-dial-peer)# exit
```

Two commands in this syntax deal with the automatic digit stripping feature of POTS dial peers: **forward-digits** *<number>* and **prefix** *<number>*. The **forward-digits** *<number>* command allows you to specify the number of right-justified digits you wish to forward. Notice the first dial peer 90 in Example 8.12. With a destination pattern of 9[469]11, the router would automatically strip the 9 and the two 1s from the pattern before sending the call. By entering the command **forward-digits 3**, the router will forward the right-justified three digits (411, 611, or 911) and only strip the 9.

The **prefix** *<number>* command will add any specified digits to the front of the dialed number before routing the call. This is useful for dial peer 93 in Example 8.12. Because international numbers can be a variable length, it is impossible to tell what value to enter for the **forward-digits** command. By using the **prefix 011** command, the automatic digit stripping feature of POTS dial peers will strip the explicitly defined 9011 digits from the pattern, and the **prefix** command will then add the 011 back in its place.

Private Line Automatic Ringdown

Although not directly related to dial-peer configuration, Private Line Automatic Ringdown (PLAR) configurations rely heavily on existing dial peers to complete a call. Ports configured with PLAR capabilities automatically dial a number as soon as the port detects an off-hook signal. The most obvious use for PLAR configurations is emergency phones in locations such as company elevators or parking garages. The configuration in Example 8.13 designates x1101 (shown in Figure 8.8) as a PLAR extension that will immediately dial x1102 as soon as a user lifts the receiver.

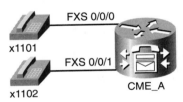

Figure 8.8 *PLAR Configuration Diagram*

Example 8.13 *FXS PLAR Configuration*

Key Topic

```
CME_A(config)# voice-port 0/0/0
CME_A(config-voiceport)# connection ?
  plar      Private Line Auto Ringdown
  tie-line  A tie line
  trunk     A Straight Tie Line
CME_A(config-voiceport)# connection plar ?
  WORD  A string of digits including wild cards
  tied  dedicated tie to this number
CME_A(config-voiceport)# connection plar 1102
```

The FXS voice port 0/0/0 is now hard-coded to dial the number 1102 as soon as a user lifts the handset.

PLAR can be useful in a variety of other circumstances as well. One common scenario is using FXO connections to the PSTN, as shown in Figure 8.9.

Figure 8.9   *FXO PSTN Connections*

Although the **destination-pattern** command from dial-peer configuration mode is very useful for dictating what is able to go *out* the PSTN FXO ports, it is not too useful for handling what comes *in* the FXO ports. When the CME_A router shown in Figure 8.9 receives an incoming call from the PSTN, the call information sent from the PSTN carrier does not include dialed number information (this is known as Dialed Number Identification Service [DNIS]). It *does* include caller ID information (known as Automatic Number Identification [ANI]), but this does not help the router to know where to send the call when it is received. As a result, calls into the CME_A router will hear a second dial tone played after they have dialed into the CME_A router from the PSTN. This is essentially the router saying, "Yes, I've received your call, please tell me what to do now." If the caller on the phone were to dial 1500, the CME_A router would forward them to the receptionist. However, the likelihood of a PSTN caller doing this is very slim. This is where PLAR comes to the rescue. Example 8.14 configures two analog FXO ports as PLAR connections for incoming calls.

Example 8.14   *FXO PLAR Configuration*

```
CME_A(config)# voice-port 2/0/0
CME_A(config-voiceport)# connection plar 1500
CME_A(config-voiceport)# exit
CME_A(config)# voice-port 2/0/1
CME_A(config-voiceport)# connection plar 1500
CME_A(config-voiceport)# exit
```

By entering the **connection plar 1500** command under both FXO ports, the router receives incoming calls from the PSTN and immediately forwards them to the receptionist phone rather than playing a second dial tone.

Note Keep in mind that configuring PLAR connections for incoming calls is something you would only need to do for analog FXO trunks. Digital PSTN connections (such as T1 or E1) receive DNIS information for incoming calls, which the router can use for Direct Inward Dial (DID) services.

Understanding Router Call Processing and Digit Manipulation

Understanding how the router processes dialed digits is critical to accurately implementing dial peers. There are two primary rules to guide you in your dial peer strategy:

- The most specific destination pattern always wins.

- Once a match is found, the router immediately processes the call.

This section presents examples of these rules in action. Example 8.15 shows the dial peers for a router.

Example 8.15 *Sample Dial-Peer Configuration 1*

```
dial-peer voice 1 voip
 destination-pattern 555[1-3]...
 session target ipv4:10.1.1.1
dial-peer voice 2 voip
 destination-pattern 5551...
 session target ipv4:10.1.1.2
```

If a user dials the number 5551234, both dial peers match, but the router will choose to use dial peer 2 because it is a more specific match (5551... matches 1000 numbers while 555[1-3]... matches 3000 numbers). Now, Example 8.16 shows what happens if you add a third dial peer to this configuration.

Example 8.16 *Sample Dial-Peer Configuration 2*

```
dial-peer voice 1 voip
 destination-pattern 555[1-3]...
 session target ipv4:10.1.1.1
dial-peer voice 2 voip
 destination-pattern 5551...
 session target ipv4:10.1.1.2
dial-peer voice 3 voip
 destination-pattern 5551
 session target ipv4:10.1.1.3
```

If the user again dials 5551234, the router will use dial peer 3 to route the call. Likewise, the router will process only the 5551 digits and drop the 234 digits. This can be useful for emergency patterns such as 911 or 9911 (in North America) because the call is immediately routed when a user dials this specific pattern.

Tip   If you ever have a question of which dial peer will match a specific string, Cisco routers include a handy testing feature. From privileged mode, enter the command **show dialplan number** *number*, where *number* is the number you would like to test. The router will display all matching dial peers in the order in which the router will use them. The router will list more specific matches first.

Because the router immediately routes the call after it makes a specific match, it is always best to avoid overlapping dial plans if possible.

Note   Avoiding overlapping dial plans may be impossible at times. In these cases, you need to get creative with your dial peers to accomplish your objectives. For example, if you were required to have a dial peer matching the destination pattern 5551 while a second dial peer had the destination pattern 5551..., you could use a configuration like this as a solution:

```
dial-peer voice 2 voip
 destination-pattern 5551...
 session target ipv4:10.1.1.2
dial-peer voice 3 voip
 destination-pattern 5551T
 session target ipv4:10.1.1.3
```

Notice the T wildcard after 5551, which matches 0–32 digits. Users dialing extension 5551 would now have to press the pound key (#) after they finished dialing or wait the 10-second interdigit timeout period.

You could also accomplish this objective using some fancy digit manipulation techniques, which you learn about in the upcoming section.

Matching Inbound and Outbound Dial Peers

When a router receives a voice call, it must always match a dial peer in some way in order for the router to process the call. While this may seem like a simplistic statement, there is actually quite a bit of strategy that must be in place to accomplish this in both the inbound and outbound direction. Take the scenario presented in Figure 8.10, which opened this section on dial peers.

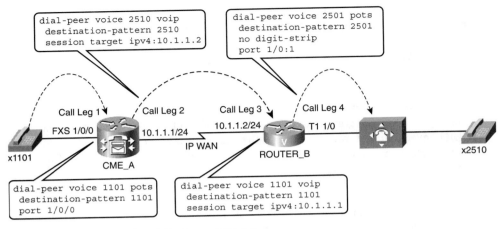

Figure 8.10 *Inbound and Outbound Dial Peers*

In addition to the call legs, Figure 8.10 displays the dial-peer configurations necessary to complete end-to-end calls from x1101 to x2510 and vice versa. Now, matching the outbound dial peers is easy: take the dialed digits and compare them to the destination patterns under the dial peers you have configured on the router to find the most specific match. For example, if x1101 dials x2510, the CME_A router looks at its dial peers and realizes there is a VoIP dial-peer match directing the call to the IP address 10.1.1.2. When ROUTER_B receives the call, it realizes the dialed digits are an exact match to the POTS dial peer 2501, which causes the router to send the call out the T1 interface to the attached PBX system. This process explains how the router matches the *outbound* dial peers (shown in Figure 8.10 as Call Leg 2 and Call Leg 4), but how does the route match the *inbound* dial peers? A router matches inbound dial peers through the following five methods:

**Key
Topic**

1. Match the dialed number (DNIS) using the **incoming called-number** dial-peer configuration command.

2. Match the caller ID information (ANI) using the **answer-address** dial-peer configuration command.

3. Match the caller ID information (ANI) using the **destination-pattern** dial-peer configuration command.

4. Match an incoming POTS dial peer by using the **port** dial-peer configuration command.

5. If no match has been found using the previous four methods, use dial peer 0.

Look at the diagram shown in Figure 8.10. Call legs 2 and 4 have been accounted for as *outbound* dial peers matched by using the dialed number (DNIS) information against the **destination-pattern** command under the dial peers. Here's how the router uses the previous list of five rules to match the inbound dial peers:

For Call Leg 1:

1. (*NO MATCH*) 2510 (the dialed number) did not match an **incoming called-number** dial-peer configuration command on the CME_A router because this command did not exist in the configuration.

2. (*NO MATCH*) x1101 caller ID information (ANI) did not match an **answer-address** dial-peer configuration command on the CME_A router because this command did not exist in the configuration.

3. (*NO MATCH*) x1101 caller ID information (ANI) did not match the **destination-pattern** dial-peer configuration command on the CME_A router because x1101 does not have any caller ID information. That is, the phone itself does not provide caller ID information to the router, because an analog phone does not know its own phone number.

4. (*MATCH*) x1101 did come in FXS port 1/0/0, which matched an incoming POTS dial peer on the CME_A router by using the **port** dial-peer configuration command (**port 1/0/0**).

Using the five-step matching process, the CME_A router was able to match an *inbound* dial peer using the incoming port value of the attached analog phone. The CME_A router then processes the *outbound* dial peer (Call Leg 2), and the call arrives at ROUTER_B. Once again, ROUTER_B works through the five-step process to match an inbound dial peer:

For Call Leg 3:

1. (*NO MATCH*) 2510 (the dialed number) did not match an **incoming called-number** dial-peer configuration command on ROUTER_B because this command did not exist in the configuration.

2. (*NO MATCH*) x1101 caller ID information (ANI) did not match an **answer-address** dial-peer configuration command on ROUTER_B because this command did not exist in the configuration.

3. (*MATCH*) x1101 caller ID information (ANI) does match the **destination-pattern** dial-peer configuration command for the VoIP dial peer 1101 on ROUTER_B.

In this case, the VoIP dial peer 1101 on ROUTER_B doubles as both the *outgoing* dial peer for calls placed to x1101, and as an *incoming* dial peer for calls coming from x1101.

Now, just to see the inbound matching process in its entirety, imagine that there was no VoIP dial peer 1101 on ROUTER_B, as shown in Figure 8.11.

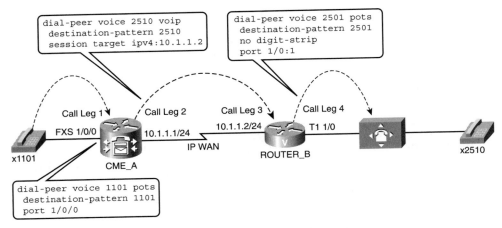

Figure 8.11   *Matching Inbound Dial Peers Using Dial Peer 0*

The first result is that you could not place calls to x1101 from ROUTER_B (or the PBX system attached to ROUTER_B). However, what if x1101 called x2510? The CME_A and ROUTER_B routers have enough information to match the outbound call legs. ROUTER_B is just missing the information for the inbound dial peer (Call Leg 3). Here's how the decision process would flow:

1. (*NO MATCH*) 2510 (the dialed number) did not match an **incoming called-number** dial-peer configuration command on ROUTER_B because this command did not exist in the configuration.

2. (*NO MATCH*) x1101 caller ID information (ANI) did not match an **answer-address** dial-peer configuration command on ROUTER_B because this command did not exist in the configuration.

3. (*NO MATCH*) x1101 caller ID information (ANI) does match the **destination-pattern** dial-peer configuration command because the VoIP dial peer 1101 was removed on ROUTER_B.

4. (*NO MATCH*) x1101 did not come in a POTS interface (FXS, FXO, E&M, Voice BRI/T1/E1 digital interface) that could be matched using the **port** command; rather, x1101 came across a VoIP connection.

5. (*MATCH*) Because ROUTER_B could not find a match using the previous four methods, it will use dial peer 0.

So this now begs the question, "What is dial peer 0?" Dial peer 0 is like a default gateway dial peer that appears when there is no dial-peer match (this applies only for *inbound* dial peers, not for *outbound* dial peers). Although this does allow the call to complete, you have no control over dial peer 0. You cannot configure it nor change any of its default settings. Dial peer 0 uses the following, unchangeable settings:

- **Any voice codec:** Dial peer 0 will handle any incoming voice codec; it is not hard-coded to any specific codec.

- **No DTMF relay:** DTMF relay sends dialed digits outside of the audio stream. This is useful because compressed codecs often distort dialed tones on the call.

- **IP Precedence 0:** This is probably the most painful default of dial peer 0. Setting the traffic to IP Precedence (IPP) 0 strips all QoS markings. The router now treats the voice traffic the same as the data traffic.

- **Voice Activity Detection (VAD) enabled:** VAD allows you to save bandwidth by eliminating voice traffic during periods of silence on the call.

- **No Resource Reservation Protocol (RSVP) support:** The lack of RSVP goes right along with the lack of any QoS for the voice calls. The router will not reserve any bandwidth specifically for dial peer 0 calls.

- **Fax-rate voice:** The router will limit the bandwidth available to fax signals to the maximum allowed by the VoIP codec. This could devastate fax calls if you are using a low-bandwidth compressed codec.

- **No application support:** Dial peer 0 cannot refer calls to outside applications, such as an Interactive Voice Response (IVR) system.

- **No Direct Inward Dial (DID) support:** Dial peer 0 cannot use the DID feature to automatically forward calls from an outside PSTN carrier to internal devices.

In light of this list of dial peer 0 features, it would be best to always match an inbound dial peer where you can control the configuration.

Using Digit Manipulation

Digit manipulation is the process of adding or removing digits from a dialed number to help a call reach an intended destination. You have already seen a few of the digit manipulation commands during the discussion of the automatic digit stripping feature of POTS dial peers (such as the **no digit-strip** and **forward-digit** commands). Before we look at some practical examples, Table 8.6 shows a list of common digit manipulation commands you can use on a Cisco router.

Table 8.6 *Common Digit Manipulation Methods on Cisco Routers*

Command	Mode	Description
prefix *digits*	POTS dial peer	Allows you to specify digits for the router to add before the dialed digits. Example: **prefix 011** adds the numbers 011 to the front of the originally dialed number.
forward-digits *number*	POTS dial peer	Allows you to specify the number of right-justified digits to forward. Example: **forward-digits 4** forwards only the right-most four digits from the dialed number.

continues

Table 8.6   *Common Digit Manipulation Methods on Cisco Routers*   *continued*

Command	Mode	Description
[no] **digit-strip**	POTS dial peer	Enables or disables the default digit stripping behavior of POTS dial peers. Example: **no digit-strip** turns off the automatic digit stripping behavior under a POTS dial peer.
num-exp *match digits set digits*	Global	Transforms any dialed number matching the *match* string into the digits specified in the *set* string. Example: **num-exp 4... 5...** matches any four-digit dialed number beginning with 4 into a four-digit number beginning with 5 (4123 becomes 5123). Example: **num-exp 0 5000** matches the dialed digit 0 and changes it to 5000.
voice translation-profile	Global and POTS or VoIP dial peer	Allows you to configure a translation profile consisting of up to 15 rules to transform numbers however you want. The translation profile is created globally and then applied to any number of dial peers (similar to an access list).

Following are four practical scenarios in which these digit manipulation commands can prove quite useful.

Practical Scenario 1: PSTN Failover Using the prefix Command

One of the benefits of using VoIP communication over traditional telephony is the ability to have more than one path to a destination. A common scenario encountered is that shown in Figure 8.12.

The organization shown in Figure 8.12 would prefer to use the IP WAN as its primary communication path between Arizona and Texas. However, if the IP WAN should fail, calls between the offices should use the PSTN as their communication path.

One of the benefits of using VoIP is the merging of voice networks into one, seamless communication path. Because calls are traveling over the IP WAN, users in the Arizona office can dial the users in the Texas office using their four-digit (6XXX) extension. Likewise, users in the Texas office can dial the users in the Arizona office using their four-digit (5XXX) extension. It would be quite inconvenient to require all the users in the Arizona office to dial the Texas office using the PSTN DID range rather than the four-digit extension (and vice versa).

Using a combination of the **preference** and **prefix** commands, you can allow this failover transformation to occur dynamically, as shown in Example 8.17.

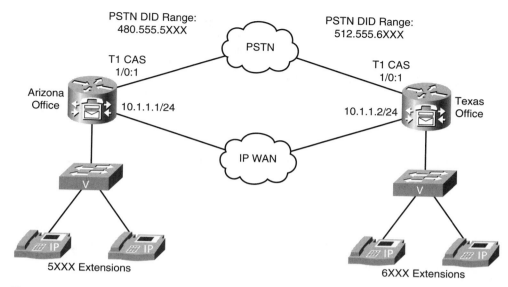

Figure 8.12   *Multiple Voice Paths*

Example 8.17   *Dynamic WAN to PSTN Failover Implementation*

```
Arizona(config)# dial-peer voice 10 voip
Arizona(config-dial-peer)# destination-pattern 6...
Arizona(config-dial-peer)# session target ipv4:10.1.1.2
Arizona(config-dial-peer)# preference 0
Arizona(config-dial-peer)# exit
Arizona(config)# dial-peer voice 11 pots
Arizona(config-dial-peer)# destination-pattern 6...
Arizona(config-dial-peer)# port 1/0:1
Arizona(config-dial-peer)# preference 1
Arizona(config-dial-peer)# no digit-strip
Arizona(config-dial-peer)# prefix 1512555
Texas(config)# dial-peer voice 10 voip
Texas(config-dial-peer)# destination-pattern 5...
Texas(config-dial-peer)# session target ipv4:10.1.1.1
Texas(config-dial-peer)# preference 0
Texas(config-dial-peer)# exit
Texas(config)# dial-peer voice 11 pots
Texas(config-dial-peer)# destination-pattern 5...
Texas(config-dial-peer)# port 1/0:1
Texas(config-dial-peer)# preference 1
Texas(config-dial-peer)# no digit-strip
Texas(config-dial-peer)# prefix 1480555
```

Key
Topic

The **preference** command allows the router to determine which dial peer it should use in the case where the destination patterns are identical. It may seem a little counterintuitive, but the router considers *lower* preferences to be better than higher preferences (the preference value can be any number from 0–10). The default preference for a dial peer is 0. Thus, the **preference 0** command in Example 8.17 under dial peer 10 on both routers is redundant.

Key Topic

Tip   If you create multiple dial peers with exactly equal destination patterns and preferences, the router will randomly choose a dial peer to use.

Looking at the Arizona router in Example 8.17, you can see that dial peer 10 is the more preferred path to the Texas router. Because the connection uses VoIP dial peers, no automatic digit stripping occurs, nor are any digit manipulation commands required (keep in mind that the **no digit-strip**, **forward-digits**, and **prefix** commands are only valid under POTS dial peers anyhow).

If the IP connection between Arizona and Texas fails, the Arizona router will begin using the next most preferred dial peer, which is dial peer 11. To overcome the automatic digit stripping feature of POTS dial peers, the **no digit-strip** command is used (otherwise, the router would strip the 6 digit from the dialed number). Because a four-digit number is invalid on the PSTN, the **prefix 1512555** command adds the necessary prefix information to get the call across the PSTN.

Note   If the IP WAN fails, all the active calls established during the WAN failure will disconnect and be required to redial. There is no "dynamic failover" mechanism for calls already established.

Practical Scenario 2: Directing Operator Calls to the Receptionist

This practical scenario is fairly simple. The organization shown in Figure 8.13 would like to direct all calls to the operator number 0 to the receptionist at extension 5000.

Because this is a "universal" transformation (you *always* want to change the dialed number 0 to 5000), you can accomplish this objective using the **num-exp** global configuration command, which is shown in Example 8.18.

Example 8.18   *Transforming Dialed Numbers Using* **num-exp**

```
Voice_RTR(config)# voice-port 1/0/1
Voice_RTR(config-voiceport)# connection plar 0
Voice_RTR(config-voiceport)# exit
Voice_RTR(config)# num-exp 0 5000
```

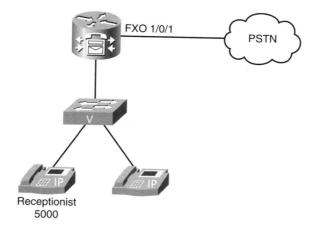

Figure 8.13   *Redirecting Operator Calls*

Now, anytime the number 0 is dialed from anywhere in the organization (could be an IP phone, FXS port, and so on), the voice router automatically transforms it to 5000 and then searches for a dial peer allowing it to reach the number 5000.

> **Note**   The router applies the **num-exp** command the instant it receives a dialed number, even before it attempts to match an inbound dial peer.

Practical Scenario 3: Specific POTS Lines for Emergency Calls

As organizations move more to VoIP connections, they are finding cost-saving benefits by eliminating traditional telephony connections at remote offices in favor of centralizing all PSTN calls (and toll charges) at a central site. Figure 8.14 illustrates this type of network design.

This type of call routing allows an organization to get higher call volume from a single location, which typically allows the organization to negotiate cheaper long-distance rates with its PSTN carrier.

> **Note**   Some countries restrict businesses from forwarding PSTN calls over the IP WAN. You should always check with the local government regulations before you do this. Thankfully, the United States is not one of those countries.

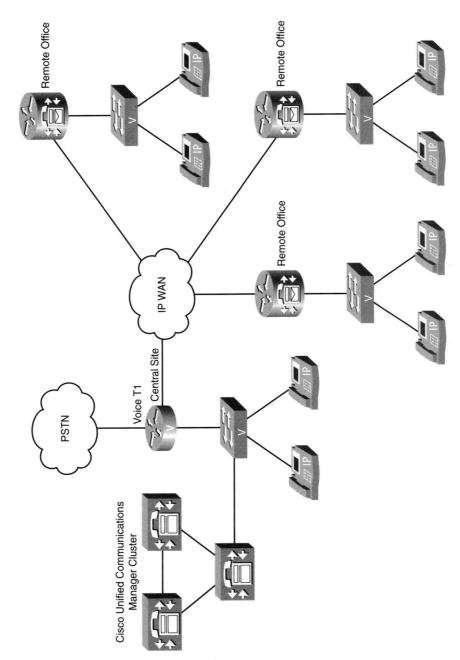

Figure 8.14   *Centralizing PSTN Access*

Although the centralization of PSTN calls offers significant cost savings, the remote sites will need to keep at least one local PSTN connection for emergency calling. This is because PSTN carriers provide location information to emergency service providers based on the POTS connection. If emergency calls from the remote offices were to traverse the IP WAN and leave the PSTN connection at the central site, the emergency service provider would receive location information for the central site.

Depending on the size of the remote office, you can typically dedicate one or two analog FXO ports for emergency calls. The configuration in Example 8.19 configures the necessary dial peers for dual FXO ports connected to the PSTN. This example assumes the FXO ports are 1/0/0 and 1/0/1.

Example 8.19   *Dynamic WAN to PSTN Failover Implementation*

```
REMOTE_RTR(config)# dial-peer voice 10 pots
REMOTE_RTR(config-dial-peer)# destination-pattern 911
REMOTE_RTR(config-dial-peer)# port 1/0/0
REMOTE_RTR(config-dial-peer)# no digit-strip
REMOTE_RTR(config-dial-peer)# exit
REMOTE_RTR(config)# dial-peer voice 11 pots
REMOTE_RTR(config-dial-peer)# destination-pattern 9911
REMOTE_RTR(config-dial-peer)# port 1/0/0
REMOTE_RTR(config-dial-peer)# forward-digits 3
REMOTE_RTR(config-dial-peer)# exit
REMOTE_RTR(config)# dial-peer voice 12 pots
REMOTE_RTR(config-dial-peer)# destination-pattern 911
REMOTE_RTR(config-dial-peer)# port 1/0/1
REMOTE_RTR(config-dial-peer)# no digit-strip
REMOTE_RTR(config-dial-peer)# exit
REMOTE_RTR(config)# dial-peer voice 13 pots
REMOTE_RTR(config-dial-peer)# destination-pattern 9911
REMOTE_RTR(config-dial-peer)# port 1/0/1
REMOTE_RTR(config-dial-peer)# forward-digits 3
```

This configuration creates two identical destination patterns for the two FXO ports. Because the **preference** command is not used to indicate a more preferred dial peer, the router will randomly choose one of the FXO ports as an exit point anytime a user dials 911 or 9911 (the additional 9 may be entered if users are accustomed to dialing 9 for an outside line). The dial peers created for the 911 destination pattern (dial peers 10 and 12) are also assigned the **no digit-strip** command. Otherwise, the automatic digit stripping rule of POTS dial peers would strip any explicitly defined digits (which are all of them in this case; the router would not send any digits to the PSTN). The dial peers created for the 9911 destination pattern (dial peers 11 and 13) are assigned the **forward-digits 3** command to send the right-justified three digits (911, in this case) to the PSTN and allow the automatic digit stripping rule to remove the initial 9 access code.

Practical Scenario 4: Using Translation Profiles

The digit manipulation commands discussed thus far allow you to perform "minor translations" to a number. For example, you could add some digits using the **prefix** command or ensure digits do or do not get stripped with the **forward-digit** command. The **num-exp** command allows you to make the biggest changes of all, but these changes are applied globally to the router, which may not give you the flexibility all situations require. Translation profiles are useful to address these needs. If you find yourself saying, "I want to change *this* dialed number to *that* dialed number, but only when it goes out *this* port," you are in need of translation profiles.

Working with translation profiles is definitely not as easy as working with the "simple" digit manipulation methods discussed earlier. Any implementation of translation profiles requires a three-step process:

Step 1.   Define the rules that dictate how the router will transform the number.

Step 2.   Associate the rules into a translation profile.

Step 3.   Assign the translation profile to a dial peer.

In a way, this is similar to access-list configuration on a router.

To demonstrate the configuration of translation profiles, consider the scenario illustrated in Figure 8.15.

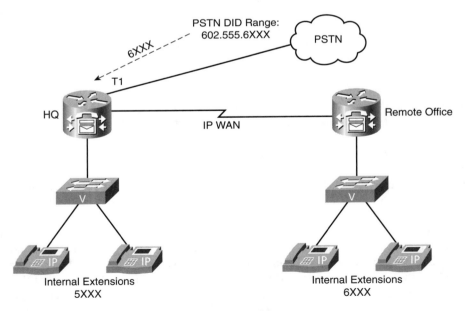

Figure 8.15   *Translating DID Ranges to Internal Extensions*

The headquarters of this organization uses the DID range from a PSTN provider of 602.555.6XXX. This allows PSTN callers to dial directly into the organization without being redirected by a receptionist. Typically, when you lease a block of DID numbers, the PSTN carrier will strip the numbers down to a four-digit extension. In this case, the DID block assigned to the organization (6XXX) does not match its internal extension range (5XXX). The administrator of this network would like to translate all 6XXX dialed numbers to 5XXX, but *only if these dialed numbers come in from the T1 PSTN interface*, so as to not interfere with the numbering scheme of the remote office. To accomplish this, you cannot use the **num-exp 6... 5...** global configuration command because it will interfere with dialing the 6XXX extensions at the remote office. This situation is ideal for translation profiles.

The first step to configure translation profiles is to create the translation rules. These use the general syntax shown in Example 8.20.

Example 8.20   *Translation Rule General Syntax*

```
Router(config)# voice translation-rule rule number
Router(cfg-translation-rule)# rule 1 /match/ /set/
Router(cfg-translation-rule)# rule 2 /match/ /set/
Router(cfg-translation-rule)# rule 3 /match/ /set/ ...and so on
```

Example 8.21 configures the necessary translation rule for the previous scenario.

Example 8.21   *Configuring Translation Rules*

```
HQ_RTR(config)# voice translation-rule 1
HQ_RTR(cfg-translation-rule)# rule 1 ?
  /WORD/  Matching pattern
  reject  Call block rule
HQ_RTR(cfg-translation-rule)# rule 1 /6/ ?
  /WORD/  Replacement pattern
HQ_RTR(cfg-translation-rule)# rule 1 /6/ /5/
```

The syntax in the **rule 1** command may look a little cryptic. The first entry between the set of forward slashes (/) is the match statement. This tells the router, "Look for the number 6." The entry between the second set of forward slashes is the set statement. This tells the router, "Replace the 6 you found from the match statement with a 5." In this case, the router will change the first 6 that is found to a 5.

Thankfully, Cisco does not leave you "hoping" that the translation rule will work properly once it is applied to the interface. You can use the **test voice translation-rule** command from privileged mode to test any rules you create before you apply them, as shown in Example 8.22.

Example 8.22   *Testing Translation Rules*

```
HQ_RTR# test voice translation-rule 1 6546
Matched with rule 1
Original number: 6546    Translated number: 5546
Original number type: none       Translated number type: none
Original number plan: none       Translated number plan: none
HQ_RTR# test voice translation-rule 1 6677
Matched with rule 1
Original number: 6677    Translated number: 5677
Original number type: none       Translated number type: none
Original number plan: none       Translated number plan: none
```

The Example 8.22 output indicates the translation rule tests successfully. 6546 is translated to 5546 and 6677 is translated to 5677.

Next, you need to take the voice translation rule and assign it to a translation profile. The translation profile designates whether the translation rule will change the calling (caller ID or ANI) or called (dialed number or DNIS) information. Example 8.23 assigns translation rule 1 to a translation profile called CHANGE_DID.

Example 8.23   *Assigning Translation Rules to a Translation Profile*

```
HQ_RTR(config)# voice translation-profile ?
  WORD   Translation profile name
HQ_RTR(config)# voice translation-profile CHANGE_DID
HQ_RTR(cfg-translation-profile)# translate ?
  called            Translation rule for the called-number
  calling           Translation rule for the calling-number
  redirect-called   Translation rule for the redirect-number
  redirect-target   Translation rule for the redirect-target
HQ_RTR(cfg-translation-profile)# translate called ?
  <1-2147483647>  Translation rule tag
HQ_RTR(cfg-translation-profile)# translate called 1
```

Example 8.23 assigns translation rule 1 as a called (dialed number) translation. Because the scenario requires you to change the DID information, this is the proper assignment. Assigning the translation rule as a calling translation would change the caller ID of a person calling into the organization.

The last step is to assign the translation profile. The following example assumes the router is using POTS dial peer 100 as the *inbound* dial peer for calls coming from the PSTN:

```
HQ_RTR(config)# dial-peer voice 100 pots
HQ_RTR(config-dial-peer)# translation-profile incoming CHANGE_DID
```

Notice that the example applies the translation profile in the *incoming* direction. This causes it to affect calls coming *in* from the PSTN rather than outgoing calls. The translation profile is now in effect, accomplishing the objective of the scenario.

Note   You can do far more with translation profiles (and far more complex patterns that you can match with translation rules). This is covered more in the CVOICE exam of the CCVP certification track.

If you are interested, I (Jeremy) have recorded a free video that explains translation rules in depth. You can download this video from http://streamer.cbtnuggets.com/ freevideos/cisco/cvoice6_18.wmv.

With all these various methods of digit manipulation, two questions can quickly arise: Which method gets applied first? Will the router remove added prefix digits because of the automatic digit stripping rule? Figure 8.16 answers these questions by displaying the order of operations for outgoing POTS dial peers. The order remains the same for VoIP dial peers; however, most digit manipulation commands only apply to POTS dial peers.

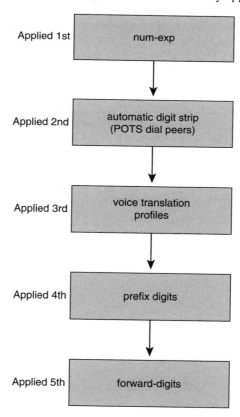

Figure 8.16   *Digit Manipulation Order of Operation for POTS Dial Peers*

Quality of Service

QoS is a topic that has been hinted at in nearly every chapter of this book. In order for a VoIP network to operate successfully, the voice traffic must have priority over the data traffic as it traverses its way from one end of the network to the other. The Cisco definition of QoS is as follows:

Quality of service is the ability of the network to provide better or special service to a set of users and applications at the expense of other users and applications.

That sounds like exactly what the voice traffic needs as it crosses the network: better or "special" service than the typical data traffic such as web browsing, FTP transfers, e-mail traffic, and so on. The voice traffic needs this not so much because of bandwidth requirements (VoIP uses very little bandwidth compared to most data applications), but rather delay requirements. Unlike data, the time it takes a voice packet to get from one end of the network to the other *matters*. If a data packet crossing the network experiences delay, a file transfer bar might take a couple more seconds to complete or a web page might take a half second longer to load. From a user's perspective, this is not a big deal. However, if voice traffic crossing the network experiences delay, conversations begin to overlap (a person begins speaking at the same time as another person), the conversation breaks up, and, in some extreme cases, the voice call drops.

To combat these issues, you need to ensure not only that there is bandwidth available for VoIP traffic, but that the VoIP traffic gets the *first* bandwidth available. This means if there is a bottleneck in the network where a router queues traffic before it is sent, the router will move the waiting voice traffic ahead of the data traffic to be sent at the first available interval. Accomplishing this is the job of QoS. QoS is not a tool in itself, but rather, a category of many tools aimed at giving you complete control over the traffic crossing your network. There may be times when you just use a single QoS tool aimed at decreasing the delay of traffic. Other times, you may employ multiple QoS tools to control delay, reserve bandwidth, and compress data that is heading over the WAN. How and when you use each of the QoS tools depends on the network requirements of your traffic and the characteristics (such as bandwidth, delay, and so on) of the network supporting the traffic.

Understanding the Enemy

Before you can deploy QoS successfully, you need to know what you are fighting against. The following are the three enemies of your VoIP traffic:

- **Lack of bandwidth:** Multiple streams of voice and data traffic are competing for a limited amount of bandwidth.

- **Delay:** The time it takes a packet to move from the original starting point to the final destination; delay comes in three forms:

    - **Fixed delay:** Delay values that you cannot change; for example, it takes a certain amount of time for a packet to travel specific geographical distances. This value is considered fixed. QoS cannot impact fixed delay issues.

- **Variable delay:** Delay values that you can change; for example, queuing delay (how long a packet waits in a router's interface queue) is variable because it depends on how many packets are currently in the queue. You can impact queuing delay by selectively moving voice packets ahead of data packets.

- **Jitter (delay variations):** Jitter describes packets that have different amounts of delay between them; for example, the first voice packet of a conversation might take 100 ms to reach a destination while the second voice packet might take 110 ms. There is 10 ms of delay variation (jitter) between these packets.

- **Packet loss:** Packets lost due to a congested or unreliable network connection.

These are enemies that plague every network environment; however, the stakes are much higher when you add VoIP traffic to an existing data network. Users are accustomed to a PBX-style environment in which there is a separate network and dedicated bandwidth assigned just for voice traffic. The tolerance for crackling, echoing, or dropped calls from a voice network is very low.

QoS is designed to keep voice traffic running smoothly during *temporary* moments of congestion on the network. It is not a "magic bullet" that can solve any network scenario. For example, if there is a network environment in which the WAN link is constantly lacking bandwidth, adding voice to the link and expecting QoS to take care of the situation is similar to rearranging the deck chairs on the sinking *Titanic*. QoS can only do so much; either your data applications will perform so slowly they are no longer functional or your voice traffic will experience quality issues. This also goes the other way; if you have a network environment in which fiber-optic cable is the norm and gigabit speeds abound, you may never experience network congestion. These environments will get little to no gain by using QoS because most QoS tools only engage during times of network congestion.

Your goal with QoS is to provide consistent bandwidth to voice traffic in such a way that there is low, steady delay from one end of the network to the other. To accomplish this, you need to have QoS in some form at *any point of the network where congestion exists*. This means doing an end-to-end audit of your network to determine the traffic types that exist and the service levels required for those traffic types.

Requirements for Voice, Video, and Data Traffic

The different traffic types that cross your network every day each have their own QoS requirements. Some of these requirements may be very loose; the network would essentially need to fail for the application to stop working. Other requirements may be very tight, requiring high-speed connectivity with low delay for the application to work successfully. This section describes general goals for voice, video, and data.

> **Tip**   There are a plethora of QoS software utilities available that will analyze your network traffic and report the bandwidth and delay each traffic type receives from the network. A popular tool in the Cisco realm is NetQoS (http://www.netqos.com).

Network Requirements for Voice and Video

Unlike data traffic, voice traffic is very predictable. Whereas data traffic may jump considerably if a large web download or file transfer is started, voice traffic remains a consistent value for each call entering and leaving the network. The actual amount of bandwidth required for voice is heavily dependent on the codec you are using. Chapter 7 has an entire section dedicated to calculating the amount of bandwidth required for each VoIP call.

In addition to bandwidth requirements, voice traffic has the following additional one-way requirements:

- **End-to-end delay:** 150 ms or less

- **Jitter:** 30 ms or less

- **Packet loss:** 1% or less

Video traffic has identical delay requirements as voice, but consumes quite a bit more bandwidth. In addition, the bandwidth can vary depending on how much movement is in the video (lots of movement increases the bandwidth required for video considerably).

Network Requirements for Data

It is impossible to give one sweeping guideline for all data applications, because every data application that exists has its own QoS requirement. When designing QoS for the data applications on your network, you should divide your applications into no more than four or five broad categories. For example:

- **Mission-critical applications:** These are applications that are critical to your organization, requiring dedicated bandwidth amounts.

- **Transactional applications:** These applications are typically interactive with users and require rapid response times. For example, a technical support employee might use a database application to retrieve caller information based on previous case ID values.

- **Best-effort applications:** These applications are noncritical or uncategorized. For example, web browsing, e-mail, and FTP file transfers would fall into this category.

- **Scavenger applications:** These nonproductive applications typically have no business need, but consume excessive amounts of bandwidth. For example, peer-to-peer file-sharing applications such as Kazaa, BitTorrent, and LimeWire would fall into this category.

You can assign each of these data application categories a specific level of QoS. You can then map the actual applications to these categories using a variety of methods (such as incoming interface, exit interface, access-lists, and so on).

Using Cisco AutoQoS

Deploying QoS can be complex (which is why there's a difficult CCVP exam dedicated just to the topic). To help ease the learning curve for QoS, Cisco created a mechanism called AutoQoS, which allows you to enable a variety of QoS mechanisms with very little QoS knowledge. AutoQoS ended up working so well out of the box that many network administrators who have full knowledge of the QoS capabilities and configuration on Cisco devices use it. AutoQoS has moved to this acclaimed status because it deploys a template QoS configuration in line with Cisco QoS best practices based on the bandwidth and encapsulation you have configured under each of your router or switch interfaces. This template-based QoS deployment offers multiple advantages to manual QoS configuration:

- **Reduces the time of deployment:** Entering a single command on a device is much less time consuming than the potentially complex QoS configurations.

- **Provides configuration consistency:** Using a single-command QoS template on each device ensures that all the devices use a similar QoS configuration that is not as prone to forgotten commands or mistypes.

- **Reduces deployment cost:** It takes quite a bit of time and training to get fully up to speed on everything QoS has to offer.

- **Allows manual tuning:** You can manually adjust and tune the template-based configuration deployed by AutoQoS to fit your specific network QoS requirements.

Before you can deploy AutoQoS on your network, you must first establish the trust boundary for your voice traffic. However, to understand the concept of a trust boundary, you must first have a basic understanding of QoS markings. As a device sends traffic, that traffic may or may not have QoS markings attached to it. These markings may or may not be trustworthy. For example, a Cisco IP phone marks all of its traffic with an extremely high priority. In this case, the markings are trustworthy because the audio traffic from the phone does indeed need high-priority service. However, a technology-savvy user might configure a computer to mark traffic from it with the same high-priority marking as the voice traffic. In this case, the marking is not trustworthy.

Now we can jump back to the concept of a trust boundary. The trust boundary is the point of the network where you begin trusting that the network traffic is accurately identified with the correct QoS marking. Depending on the capabilities of the devices on your network, you can you can begin applying QoS markings close to the user devices, as shown in Figure 8.17.

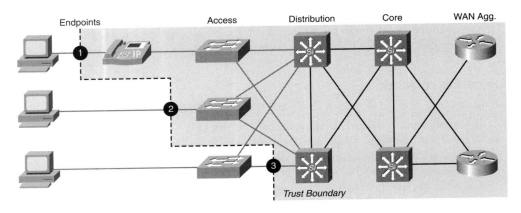

Figure 8.17   *Possible QoS Trust Boundaries*

Cisco IP phones have the ability to mark their own traffic as high priority and strip any high-priority markings from traffic sent by the attached PC. If you are using the Cisco IP phone to mark traffic, you have extended the trust boundary to point 1 shown in Figure 8.17. This is the ideal trust point because it distributes the QoS marking process to many Cisco IP phones rather than forcing the switches to apply QoS markings to a higher volume of traffic. If you have PCs attached to the network and you have access layer switches with QoS capabilities, you can begin marking at these devices (this is point 2 in Figure 8.17). If your access layer switches do not have QoS capabilities, then the first possible place you can apply QoS markings is at the distribution layer switches (shown as point 3 in Figure 8.17). This will work just fine; however, it adds an extra load to the distribution layer switches. Likewise, you will have network traffic passing through access layer switches without any QoS treatment. Although this is usually a safe bet—because access layer switches typically have higher-speed connections, on which congestion is rare—it is always best to apply QoS in as many places as possible where there is a potential bottleneck.

Note   AutoQoS uses CDP to detect Cisco IP phones on Cisco switches and properly configure the QoS settings. This ensures that a user cannot disconnect their IP phone and attach another device to receive high-priority network treatment. Be sure you do not disable CDP on switches supporting Cisco IP phones.

Now we have come to the point of configuring AutoQoS. Amazingly, by Cisco's design, enabling AutoQoS is accomplished through a single command applied under interface configuration mode. To enable AutoQoS in your network, you must first identify the interfaces to which applying AutoQoS makes sense. AutoQoS does not need to be applied under every switch and router interface in your network (although it probably won't hurt anything if you did this). It primarily should be applied to interfaces on which the devices or applications need special or preferred treatment over others. Figure 8.18 shows a typical network. The interfaces labeled A represent areas of the network where you would use AutoQoS.

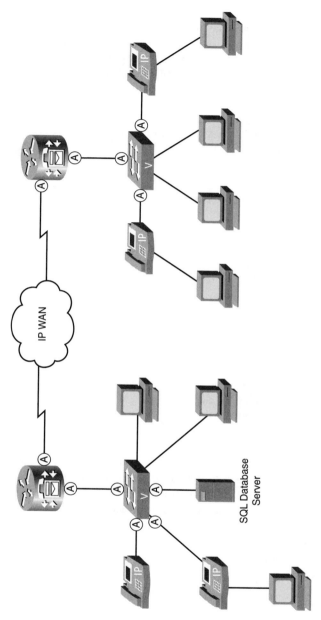

Figure 8.18   *AutoQoS Configuration Points*

As you can see from Figure 8.18, you'll be typing this one command quite a few times. Before you enter the AutoQoS command, always ensure that you have entered the correct bandwidth statement under the Serial interfaces of your routers, because a router cannot auto-detect the actual speed of a WAN connection. A router can detect all other interfaces without requiring the **bandwidth** command.

Note AutoQoS uses a sophisticated queuing method known as Low Latency Queuing (LLQ). This queuing method provisions a specific amount of bandwidth for the various types of network traffic, including voice. Using AutoQoS features with incorrectly configured **bandwidth** commands may cause substandard network service.

The AutoQoS command syntax may be slightly different depending on where you enter it. The syntax in Example 8.24 enables AutoQoS for the interfaces shown in Figure 8.18 that are connected to the Cisco IP phones.

Example 8.24 *Enabling AutoQoS on the Access Layer Switchports*

```
Voice_Switch# show run interface FastEthernet 0/3
Building configuration...
Current configuration : 169 bytes
!
interface FastEthernet0/3
 description CONNECTION TO IP PHONE
 switchport access vlan 10
 switchport mode access
 switchport voice vlan 5
 spanning-tree portfast
end
Voice_Switch# config term
Enter configuration commands, one per line.  End with CNTL/Z.
Voice_Switch(config)# interface fa0/3
Voice_Switch(config-if)# auto qos ?
  voip  Configure AutoQoS for VoIP
Voice_Switch(config-if)# auto qos voip ?
  cisco-phone      Trust the QoS marking of Cisco IP Phone
  cisco-softphone  Trust the QoS marking of Cisco IP SoftPhone
  trust            Trust the DSCP/CoS marking
Voice_Switch(config-if)# auto qos voip cisco-phone
Voice_Switch(config-if)# ^Z
Voice_Switch# show run interface FastEthernet 0/3
Building configuration...
Current configuration : 510 bytes
!
interface FastEthernet0/3
 description CONNECTION TO IP PHONE
 switchport access vlan 10
 switchport mode access
 switchport voice vlan 5
 mls qos trust device cisco-phone
 mls qos trust cos
 auto qos voip cisco-phone
```

```
wrr-queue bandwidth 10 20 70 1
wrr-queue min-reserve 1 5
wrr-queue min-reserve 2 6
wrr-queue min-reserve 3 7
wrr-queue min-reserve 4 8
wrr-queue cos-map 1 0 1
wrr-queue cos-map 2 2 4
wrr-queue cos-map 3 3 6 7
wrr-queue cos-map 4 5
priority-queue out
spanning-tree portfast
end
```

Notice the options given by the context-sensitive help when the **auto qos voip ?** command was entered. Entering the command **auto qos voip cisco-phone** or **auto qos voip cisco-softphone** will only enable the trust boundary if CDP detects a Cisco IP phone or Cisco IP Communicator (or equivalent Cisco IP SoftPhone device) attached to the port. If a user removes this device, the trust boundary is broken and will not be restored until the device is reattached. If you enter the command **auto qos voip trust**, the switch trusts the markings from the attached device regardless of what it is. You will need to use this command if you purchase non-Cisco IP phones. Keep in mind that using this command is susceptible to users removing the non-Cisco IP phone and attaching rogue devices.

Note   Before the **auto qos voip** command was entered under the FastEthernet 0/3 interface in Example 8.24, a **show run** command was performed so that you could see the current syntax entered under the interface. Notice how many commands were generated after entering the **auto qos voip** command. It is very beneficial that the Cisco switch (and router) shows you all the individual commands so that you can optionally tune the settings to fit your environment exactly.

If the configuration generated by the **auto qos voip** command is not desired, you can remove this configuration simply by entering **no auto qos voip**.

Example 8.25 shows the AutoQoS syntax to use on the switch for the interface connecting to the router.

Example 8.25   *Enabling AutoQoS on the Switch-Router Uplink*

```
Voice_Switch# show run interface FastEthernet 0/1
Building configuration...
Current configuration : 169 bytes
!
interface FastEthernet0/3
```

continues

Example 8.25   *Enabling AutoQoS on the Switch-Router Uplink   continued*

```
 description CONNECTION TO ROUTER
 switchport access vlan 10
 switchport mode access
 spanning-tree portfast
end
Voice_Switch# config term
Enter configuration commands, one per line.  End with CNTL/Z.
Voice_Switch(config)# interface fa0/1
Voice_Switch(config-if)# auto qos voip trust
Voice_Switch(config-if)# ^Z
Voice_Switch# show run int fa0/1
Building configuration...
Current configuration : 369 bytes
!
interface FastEthernet0/1
 description CONNECTION TO ROUTER
 switchport access vlan 10
 switchport mode access
 mls qos trust cos
 auto qos voip trust
 wrr-queue bandwidth 10 20 70 1
 wrr-queue min-reserve 1 5
 wrr-queue min-reserve 2 6
 wrr-queue min-reserve 3 7
 wrr-queue min-reserve 4 8
 wrr-queue cos-map 1 0 1
 wrr-queue cos-map 2 2 4
 wrr-queue cos-map 3 3 6 7
 wrr-queue cos-map 4 5
 priority-queue out
end
```

You can configure the interface between the switch and router with the **auto qos voip trust** command, because you would consider the QoS markings from the router as trusted.

Finally, you can enable AutoQoS on the router's FastEthernet and Serial interfaces with the syntax in Example 8.26.

Example 8.26   *Enabling AutoQoS on Router Interfaces*

```
CME_Voice# show run int fa0/0
Building configuration...
!
interface FastEthernet0/0
```

```
  ip address 172.30.4.3 255.255.255.0
  ip nat inside
  ip virtual-reassembly
  duplex auto
  speed auto
 end
CME_Voice# show run int s0/1/0
Building configuration...
 !
interface Serial0/1/0
 bandwidth 512
 ip address 10.1.1.1 255.255.255.0
 encapsulation ppp
 no fair-queue
 clock rate 2000000
end
CME_Voice# configure terminal
Enter configuration commands, one per line.  End with CNTL/Z.
CME_Voice(config)# interface FastEthernet 0/0
CME_Voice(config-if)# auto ?
  discovery  Configure Auto Discovery
  qos        Configure AutoQoS
CME_Voice(config-if)# auto qos voip trust
CME_Voice(config-if)# exit
CME_Voice(config)# interface Serial 0/1/0
CME_Voice(config-if)# auto qos voip trust
CME_Voice(config-if)# ^Z
CME_Voice# show run int fa0/0
Building configuration...
 !
interface FastEthernet0/0
 ip address 172.30.4.3 255.255.255.0
 ip nat inside
 ip virtual-reassembly
 duplex auto
 speed auto
 auto qos voip trust
 service-policy output AutoQoS-Policy-Trust
end
CME_Voice# show run int s0/1/0
Building configuration...
 !
interface Serial0/1/0
 bandwidth 512
```

continues

Example 8.26   *Enabling AutoQoS on Router Interfaces   continued*

```
no ip address
encapsulation ppp
auto qos voip trust
no fair-queue
clock rate 2000000
ppp multilink
ppp multilink group 2001100116
end
```

The changes to the router interfaces look relatively tame compared to the amount of syntax entered under the switch interfaces; however, what you are *not* seeing are the billion other commands (or perhaps slightly less than a billion) that were entered in other configuration modes of the router to create class maps, policy maps, multilink interfaces, and so on. The full explanation of those commands will be saved for the CCVP QoS material.

> **Note**   In Example 8.26, after entering the **auto ?** command under the FastEthernet interface, notice one of the options you are given is **auto discovery**. This enables a newer, ultra-incredible version of AutoQoS that allows the router to *monitor your network for an extended time* to discover known types of data, voice, and video traffic that are considered higher priority based on common high-priority application types. After the router has captured enough traffic, it will generate QoS policy recommendations that you can choose to apply or ignore.

Table 8.7 summarizes the different variations of AutoQoS commands you can enter on Cisco switch and router platforms.

Table 8.7   *AutoQoS Syntax Variations*

Command	Platform	Description
auto qos voip	Router or Layer 3 switch	Enables AutoQoS without trusting any existing markings on packets. The router will re-mark all traffic types using access lists or Network-Based Application Recognition (NBAR) to identify traffic (higher processor-utilization tasks).
auto qos voip trust	Router or switch	Enables AutoQoS, trusting any existing QoS markings that enter the interface.
auto qos voip cisco-phone	Switch	Enables AutoQoS, trusting any existing QoS markings that enter the interface only if the switch detects a Cisco IP phone attached through CDP.
auto qos voip cisco-softphone	Switch	Enables AutoQoS, trusting any existing QoS markings that enter the interface only if the switch detects a Cisco IP SoftPhone (such as Cisco IP Communicator) attached through CDP.

Note   QoS engineers identify what have been called QoS markings in the previous section as Class of Service (CoS) and Type of Service (ToS) markings. CoS is a marking that exists in the Layer 2 header of a frame, which a switch can identify. ToS is a marking that exists in the Layer 3 header of a packet, which a router can identify. This topic is explored in depth in the material for the QoS CCVP certification exam.

Exam Preparation Tasks

Review All the Key Topics

Review the most important topics in the chapter, noted with the key topics icon in the outer margin of the page. Table 8.8 lists and describes these key topics and identifies the page number on which each is found.

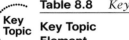

Table 8.8 *Key Topics for Chapter 8*

Key Topic Element	Description	Page Number
Figure 8.1	Illustrates the use of analog FXS ports	249
Figure 8.2	Illustrates the use of analog FXO ports	252
Note	Signaling channel information for T1 and E1 interfaces	258
List	Description of POTS and VoIP dial peers	259
Figure 8.5	Illustrates the use of call legs to design dial-peer configurations	260
Example 8.7	Basic POTS dial-peer configuration	262
Text	Highlights the automatic digit stripping rule of POTS dial peers	265
Example 8.11	Basic VoIP dial-peer configuration	266
Table 8.3	Summarizes dial-peer wildcards	267
Table 8.4	Provides examples of using the dial-peer bracket wildcard	268
Table 8.5	Provides a sample PSTN dialing plan for North America	269
Example 8.13	Basic PLAR configuration using FXS interfaces	270
List	Highlights the rules Cisco routers use to handle overlapping dial peers	272
List	The method a router uses to match inbound dial peers	274
List	Characteristics of dial peer 0	277
Table 8.6	Summarizes digit manipulation commands	277

Key Topic Element	Description	Page Number
Example 8.17	Implementing WAN to PSTN failover using **preference** and **prefix** commands	
Tip	Tip on how the router handles identical dial peers	
List	The three areas of concern when deploying QoS	
List	Key delay requirements for voice and video traffic	
Table 8.7	Reviews the variations of AutoQoS syntax	

Complete the Tables and Lists from Memory

Print a copy of Appendix C, "Memory Tables" (found on the CD), or at least the section for this chapter, and complete the tables and lists from memory. Appendix D, "Memory Tables Answer Key," also on the CD, includes completed tables and lists to check your work.

Definitions of Key Terms

Define the following key terms from this chapter, and check your answers in the glossary.

Dialed Number Identification Service (DNIS)

Automatic Number Identification (ANI)

dial peer

Foreign Exchange Station (FXS) ports

Foreign Exchange Office (FXO) ports

Private Line Automatic Ringdown (PLAR)

Direct Inward Dial (DID)

Exam topics covered in Part IV:

- Describe the Cisco Unity Express hardware platforms

- Configure the foundational elements required for Cisco Unified Communications Manager Express to support Cisco Unity Express

- Describe the features available in Cisco Unity Express

- Configure AutoAttendant services using Cisco Unity Express

- Configure basic voice mail features using Cisco Unity Express

Part IV: Voice Mail with Cisco Unity Express

What Is Cisco Unity Express?: This section introduces Cisco Unity Express. It discusses the hardware and software components that make up Cisco Unity Express and the role that Cisco Unity Express plays in Cisco Unified Communications solutions.

Features and Functions of Cisco Unity Express Voice Mail: This section describes the subscriber and caller voice-mail features that are available on the Cisco Unity Express platform.

Features and Functions of Cisco Unity Express Auto Attendant: This section describes the auto-attendant features available on the Cisco Unity Connection platform.

Cisco Unity Express Management: This section examines both the administrator and subscriber management capabilities of Cisco Unity Express.

CHAPTER 9

Cisco Unity Express Concepts

Cisco Unity Express is a compact hardware platform that provides a cost-effective solution for voice-mail and auto-attendant features to small and medium-sized businesses and enterprise branch sites. With Cisco Unity Express, smaller sites and remote branch offices can now deploy many of the features typically available only in larger sites or host sites. This chapter discusses these features.

"Do I Know This Already?" Quiz

The "Do I Know This Already?" quiz allows you to assess whether you should read this entire chapter or simply jump to the "Exam Preparation Tasks" section for review. If you are in doubt, read the entire chapter. Table 9.1 outlines the major headings in this chapter and the corresponding "Do I Know This Already?" quiz questions. You can find the answers in Appendix A, "Answers to the 'Do I Know This Already?' Quizzes."

Table 9.1   *"Do I Know This Already?" Foundation Topics Section-to-Question Mapping*

Foundation Topics Section	Questions Covered in This Section
What Is Cisco Unity Express?	1–5
Features and Functions of Cisco Unity Express Voice Mail	6–9
Features and Functions of Cisco Unity Express Auto Attendant	10–11
Cisco Unity Express Management	12–13

1. Identify the four Cisco Unity Express hardware platforms currently available.

   a. CUE1, CUE2, CUE3, and CUE4

   b. NM-CUE1, NM-CUE2, NMW-CUE, and AIM-CUE

   c. AIM-CUE, NM-CUE, NM-CUE-EC, and NME-CUE

   d. AIM-CUE, NM-CUE, CUE-EC, and NME-CUE-EC

2. Which Cisco Unity Express module(s) is/are installed inside of a Cisco router?

   a. The CUE2 and CUE4 modules

   b. The NM-CUE module

   c. The NM-CUE and AIM-CUE modules

   d. The AIM-CUE module

3. Which factor determines the maximum number of simultaneous sessions supported by Cisco Unity Express?

   a. The installed license

   b. The hardware platform

   c. The configuration

   d. The weather

4. Which factor determines the number of mailboxes supported by Cisco Unity Express?

   a. The installed license

   b. The hardware platform

   c. The configuration

   d. The weather

5. What operating system does Cisco Unity Express run on?

  a. Cisco IOS

  b. A Linux-based operating system

  c. Microsoft Windows Server 2000

  d. Microsoft Windows Server 2003

6. How are messages in a general delivery mailbox (GDM) accessed?

  a. By logging in to the GDM extension number via the telephony user interface (TUI)

  b. By logging in to a subscriber mailbox that is associated with the GDM

  c. By logging in to the GDM extension number via the GUI

  d. A GDM is not accessed. All messages are forward to a distribution list.

7. What is the difference between a password and a PIN in Cisco Unity Express?

  a. Nothing; they are two terms that mean the same thing.

  b. A password provides TUI authentication, whereas a PIN provides GUI authentication.

  c. A password provides GUI authentication, whereas a PIN provides TUI authentication.

  d. A password is used for both TUI and GUI authentication, whereas a PIN is used for application authentication.

8. Which two methods can the message notification function use to alert a subscriber of a new message?

  a. Place a phone call

  b. Red light

  c. Flashing envelope

  d. Send an e-mail

9. What does integrated messaging provide?

  a. Allows a subscriber's e-mail and voice-mail to be delivered to the same e-mail account

  b. Allows a subscriber to access both voice-mail and e-mail content from a single MAPI-capable e-mail client

  c. Allows a subscriber to access both voice-mail and e-mail content from a single MAPI-capable server

  d. Allows a subscriber's e-mail and voice-mail to be delivered to the same voice-mail account

10. Identify the default auto attendant (AA) greetings/prompts.

    a. Business open prompt

    b. Business closed prompt

    c. Alternate greeting

    d. Welcome prompt

    e. Holiday prompt

    f. Emergency prompt

11. How are AA prompts recorded/rerecorded?

    a. Using the administrator's mailbox

    b. Using a subscriber's mailbox

    c. Using the administrator GUI home page

    d. Using the administrator via telephone feature

12. How do you configure a Cisco Unity Express backup to run at 2 a.m.?

    a. Set the backup schedule to begin the backup process at 2 a.m.

    b. The administrator must click the **Start Backup** button at 2 a.m.

    c. Because 2 a.m. is generally outside of normal business hours, a backup cannot be scheduled for this time.

    d. Set the backup schedule to begin the backup process two hours past midnight.

    Starting a backup is a manual process for Cisco Unity Express. An administrator must log in to the GUI and click the Start Backup button to begin the process.

13. How do you keep configuration information synchronized between Cisco Unity Express and Cisco Unified CME?

    a. Use the synchronize feature in the Cisco Unity Express GUI.

    b. Use the synchronize feature in the CME CLI.

    c. Synchronization requires a reboot of both CME and Cisco Unity Express.

    d. CME and Cisco Unity Express both operate under the same operating system, so they cannot lose synchronization.

Foundation Topics

What Is Cisco Unity Express?

Cisco Unity Express is a small hardware appliance that is installed on a Cisco router. Unlike the Cisco Unified Communications Manager Express (CME) IOS-based operating system, the Cisco Unity Express operating system is Linux based. This means that Cisco Unified CME and Cisco Unity Express are two distinct systems that interoperate to provide voice mail, auto attendant, and other functions. This separation gives Cisco Unity Express the capability to integrate with both Cisco Unified CME and Cisco Unified Communications Manager.

Note   In the past, Cisco Unified Communications Manager was known as Cisco CallManager, often abbreviated CCM. This chapter uses the complete new name, Cisco Unified Communications Manager.

Where Does Cisco Unity Express Fit?

Cisco currently has two other product lines that provide voice-mail and auto-attendant functions, so why introduce another product? Table 9.2 compares the three current Cisco product lines in the messaging space.

Table 9.2   *Cisco Unity Product Comparison*

	Cisco Unity Express	Cisco Unity Connection	Cisco Unity
Mailboxes	Up to 250	Up to 7500	Up to 7500 per server
Messaging Type	Voice mail and integrated messaging	Voice mail and integrated messaging	Voice mail, integrated messaging, and unified messaging
Auto Attendant Capability	Yes	Yes	Yes
Platform	Linux router based	Windows or Linux server based	Windows server based
PBX/TDM Support	No	Yes	Yes
Redundancy	No	No	Yes

Key Topic

Each product line has the capability to provide voice-mail and auto-attendant functions. The main differences between the listed Cisco Unity product lines are the maximum number of mailboxes available per product and the platform the product is supported on. Currently, Cisco Unity Express is the only platform that is installed on a Cisco Integrated Services Router (ISR). This makes Cisco Unity Express attractive to small to medium-sized businesses that do not have the staff, or the desire, to support external servers. The scalability of up to 250 mailboxes also fits nicely into a small to medium-sized business. Finally, Cisco Unity Express is installed in a Cisco router that is local to the end users and provides messaging and auto-attendant functions for local Cisco IP phones. This means that WAN connectivity and QoS-enabled WAN circuits are not required to ensure the quality of voice-mail and auto-attendant services.

All these factors make Cisco Unity Express a good fit for small to medium-sized businesses and enterprise branch locations.

Hardware Flavors of Cisco Unity Express

Cisco Unity Express is a small hardware appliance that is installed on a Cisco ISR. Currently the Cisco Unity Express hardware platform comes in the following four flavors:

- Cisco Unity Express Advanced Integration Module (AIM-CUE)
- Cisco Unity Express Network Module (NM-CUE)
- Cisco Unity Express Network Module with Enhanced Capability (NM-CUE-EC)
- Cisco Unity Express Enhanced Network Module (NME-CUE)

Offering four platforms allows the Cisco Unity Express messaging solution to be tailored to the requirements of the site it will be serving.

Cisco Unity Express Advance Integration Module

The AIM-CUE is a module that is installed inside of a Cisco ISR. The module runs a Linux operating system and is controlled by the Intel Celeron 300-MHz CPU with 256 MB of synchronous dynamic random-access memory (SDRAM). 1 GB of flash memory is used to store the operating system, Cisco Unity Express configuration files, and voice-mail messages. This module is field replaceable.

This module is an entry-level hardware platform for Cisco Unity Express, providing up to 50 mailboxes, 14 hours of storage, and either four or six ports that can be used for simultaneous voice sessions, depending upon the model of Cisco ISR it is installed in.

Cisco Unity Express Network Module

The NM-CUE is a network module that is installed in an external network slot of a Cisco ISR. The module runs a Linux operating system and is controlled by a 500-MHz CPU with 256 MB of SDRAM. A 20-GB IDE hard drive is used to store the operating system, Cisco Unity Express configuration files, and voice-mail messages. This hard drive is not field replaceable.

This module is hot swappable on Cisco 3745 and 3845 routers; however, a proper shutdown of the Linux operating system is required before the unit is removed. Hot swapping of this module is not supported on the 3745 router or the 2800 series ISRs.

The Fast Ethernet port and Compact Flash slot available on the front of the NM-CUE module are not supported by the Cisco Unity Express application.

This module is the midlevel hardware platform for Cisco Unity Express, providing up to 100 mailboxes, 100 hours of storage, and eight ports that can be used for simultaneous voice sessions.

Cisco Unity Express Network Module with Enhanced Capability

The NM-CUE-EC is a network module that is installed in an external network slot of a Cisco ISR. The module runs a Linux operating system and is controlled by a 500-MHz CPU with 512 MB of SDRAM. A 20-GB IDE hard drive is used to store the operating system, Cisco Unity Express configuration files, and voice-mail messages. This hard drive is not field replaceable.

This module is hot swappable on Cisco 3745 and 3845 routers; however, a proper shutdown of the Linux operating system is required before the unit is removed. Hot swapping of this module is not supported on the 3745 router or the 2800 series ISRs.

The Fast Ethernet port and Compact Flash slot available on the front of the NM-CUE-EC module are not supported by the Cisco Unity Express application.

This module is a higher-end hardware platform for Cisco Unity Express, providing up to 250 mailboxes, 300 hours of storage, and 16 ports that can be used for simultaneous voice sessions.

Cisco Unity Express Enhanced Network Module

The NM-CUE is a network module that is installed in an external network slot of a Cisco ISR. The module runs a Linux operating system and is controlled by a 1-GHz CPU with 512 MB of SDRAM. A 40-GB IDE hard drive is used to store the operating system, Cisco Unity Express configuration files, and voice-mail messages. This hard drive is not field replaceable.

This module is hot swappable on Cisco 3845 routers; however, a proper shutdown of the Linux operating system is required before the unit is removed. Hot swapping of this module is not supported on the 2800 series ISRs.

The Fast Ethernet port and Compact Flash slot available on the front of the NME-CUE module are not supported by the Cisco Unity Express application.

This module is the high-end hardware platform for Cisco Unity Express, providing up to 250 mailboxes, 300 hours of storage, and 24 ports that can be used for simultaneous voice sessions.

Cisco Unity Express Module Comparison

Table 9.3 lists capacity differences between the four Cisco Unity Express hardware platforms.

Table 9.3   *Cisco Unity Modules and Capabilities*

	AIM-CUE	NM-CUE	NM-CUE-EC	NME-CUE
Mailboxes	Up to 50	Up to 100	Up to 250	Up to 250
Voice Ports/ Simultaneous Voice Sessions	6	8	16	24
Installation	In motherboard slot	In network module slot	In network module slot	In network module slot
Maximum Storage	14 hours	100 hours	300 hours	300 hours

Support for a Cisco Unity Express module is dependant upon the model of Cisco ISR it is installed in and the IOS version the router is running. Table 9.4 lists the router support and minimum IOS version for each module.

Table 9.4   *Router and Minimum IOS Required*

Router Model	AIM-CUE	NM-CUE	NM-CUE-EC	NME-CUE
Cisco 2600XM	12.3(7)T	12.3(11)T5 12.3(14)T1 12.4(1)	12.3(4)T	Not supported
Cisco 2650XM	12.3(7)T	12.3(11)T5	12.3(4)T	Not supported
Cisco 2651XM		12.3(14)T1 12.4(1)		
Cisco 2691	12.3(7)T	12.3(11)T5 12.3(14)T1 12.4(1)	12.3(4)T	Not supported
Cisco 2801	12.3(8)T4	Not supported	Not supported	Not supported
Cisco 2811	12.3(8)T4	12.3(11)T5	12.3(8)T4	12.4(9)T
Cisco 2821		12.3(14)T1		
Cisco 2851		12.4(1)		

Router Model	AIM-CUE	NM-CUE	NM-CUE-EC	NME-CUE
Cisco 3725	12.3(7)T	12.3(11)T5	12.3(4)T	Not supported
Cisco 3745[1]		12.3(14)T1		
		12.4(1)		
Cisco 3825	12.3(11)T	12.3(11)T5	12.3(11)T	12.4(9)T
Cisco 3845		12.3(14)T1		
		12.4(1)		

1. The AIM-CUE must go in the slot labeled AIM1 on a Cisco 3745 router. Installing the AIM-CUE in the slot labeled AIM0 can damage the AIM-CUE.

Note   The version of Cisco Unity Express software that a Cisco Unity Express hardware module can run is dependant upon the version of IOS on the supported router. Table 9.4 lists minimum IOS version requirements to support Cisco Unity Express. Note that an upgrade of the router's IOS may be necessary to support the desired version of Cisco Unity Express software.

Cisco Unity Express Software

The Cisco Unity Express module comes from Cisco preloaded with a Linux operating system and the currently shipping version of Cisco Unity Express software. The Linux operating system is not field configurable. The Cisco Unity Express software, on the other hand, can be upgraded in the field.

Cisco Unity Express software can be broken down into three different categories:

- Cisco Unity Express voice-mail and auto-attendant software

- Cisco Unity Express optional IVR software

- Cisco Unity Express PC application software

Table 9.5 lists the files that make up Cisco Unity Express voice-mail and auto-attendant software.

Table 9.5   *Cisco Unity Express Voice-Mail and Auto-Attendant Software*

Filename	Description
cue-vm-k9.nm-aim.3.1.x.pkg	The main software package file
cue-installer.nm-aim.3.1.x	Installer image (also known as the Helper image)
cue-vm-installer-k9.nm-aim.3.1.x.prt1	Installer payload file
cue-vm-full-k9.nm-aim.3.1.x.prt1	Voice-mail application
cue-vm-upgrade-k9.nm-aim.2.3.4_3.1.x.prt1	Package file to upgrade from version 2.3.4
cue-vm-langpack.nm-aim.3.1.x.pkg1	Language package file
cue-vm-en_US-langpack.nm-aim.3.1.x.prt1	English (US) language package

Note   At the time of this writing, version 3.1 is the latest version of Cisco Unity Express software, so this chapter and the next one will focus on version 3.1.

Note that each individual filename lists the version of Cisco Unity Express that it is it part of. In this example, each software component includes 3.1.x in the filename. This tells us that this software is for Cisco Unity Express 3.1.

The first four files listed in Table 9.5 are used to load the voice-mail and auto-attendant applications on the Cisco Unity Express hardware platform. These files make up the core of the Cisco Unity Express 3.1 software.

The fifth file is used to upgrade the core voice-mail and auto-attendant software on an existing Cisco Unity Express module from version 2.3.4 to version 3.1.

The last two files are used to install a language on the Cisco Unity Express module. The choice of language file(s) dictates what language is spoken when Cisco Unity Express plays a system prompt. In this example, American English was installed. Cisco Unity Express supports the following languages:

- American English (U.S.)
- British English (UK)
- Chinese
- Danish
- Dutch
- French (European)
- French (Canadian)

- German

- Italian

- Japanese

- Korean

- Portuguese (Brazilian)

- Spanish (European)

- Spanish (Latin American)

- Spanish (Mexico)

- Swedish

As of this writing, the NME-CUE, NM-CUE-EC, and NM-CUE support up to five languages, whereas the AIM-CUE supports two languages.

The next chapter will discuss how these files are installed and configured on the Cisco Unity Express hardware platform.

Table 9.6 lists the optional add-on software for Interactive Voice Response (IVR) support.

Table 9.6   *Optional Add-on Software Package for IVR Support*

Filename	Description
cue-ivr-jsp.3.1.x.tar	Installer for the Java Server pages, Servlet, and VoiceXML web application development kit for Cisco Unity Express applications using the IVR feature

Cisco Unity Express version 3.x introduced the capability of performing IVR functions. IVR can be defined as providing information to a caller without requiring human intervention. For example, a call to your local bank may ask for you to enter your account number. After entering the digits on the phone's keypad, the system plays your account balance back to you in spoken words. This task is performed in an interactive fashion without the need for human intervention.

Although IVR is a feature of Cisco Unity Express 3.x, installation and configuration of IVR functions are beyond the scope of this book.

Note   For detailed information about the capabilities and configuration of IVR on Cisco Unity Express, refer to *Cisco Unity Express 3.1 IVR CLI Administrator Guide*, which can be found on Cisco.com at the following URL:

http://www.cisco.com/en/US/docs/voice_ip_comm/unity_exp/rel3_1/administration/guide/ivr/ivrcliadmin.html

Table 9.7 lists the two external applications that support Cisco Unity Express functions. Both applications are installed and run from a computer, and cannot be installed or run from the Cisco Unity Express module itself.

Table 9.7   *PC Applications for Custom Scripting and Historical Reporting Support*

Filename	Description
CUEEditor3.1.x.exe	Installer for Cisco Unity Express Editor
CUCEHistoricalReportsInstall-3.1.x.exe	Installer for the Cisco Unified Communications Express Historical Reporting Client

Cisco Unity Express Editor is a software application that is used to create custom scripts that define the caller's experience once the call is routed to Cisco Unity Express. For example, a call to your local bank may ask for you to enter your account number. After entering the digits on the phone's keypad, the system plays your account balance back to you in spoken words. The process of answering the call, playing the prompt "Please enter your account number," collecting the digits dialed, and playing the prompt that states the balance is a sequence of steps programmed into a script. It is the custom script that performs the IVR function in the last example. Although scripting is an integral part of IVR, this is not the only use. Scripts also run prompt and collect features.

For example, a call to your local insurance agent asks you to press 1 for John Smith or press 2 for Jane Doe. After you enter your choice, your call is routed to John or Jane and then a conversation ensues. This is not an IVR function, because human intervention was required, but a script was still needed to prompt for action, collect the choice, and redirect the call. This is an example of a prompt-and-collect script.

Cisco Unity Express scripts are discussed again in the "Cisco Unity Express Custom Scripting" section; however, an in-depth discussion of script steps and scripting methods is beyond the scope of this book.

Note   For detailed information about the capabilities and configuration of custom scripting on Cisco Unity Express, refer to *Cisco Unity Express 3.1 Guide to Writing and Editing Scripts*, which can be found on Cisco.com at the following URL:

http://www.cisco.com/en/US/docs/voice_ip_comm/unity_exp/rel3_1/administration/guide/script/ScriptEditor.html

The Cisco Unified Communications Express Historical Reporting Client is an application that allows an administrator to schedule, view, print, and save call information gathered from Cisco Unity Express. Call information is defined as how a call is treated by the Cisco Unity Express script. For example, a call is answered by a Cisco Unity Express script and the first step plays a prompt to the caller. During the prompt, the user decides that they have dialed the wrong number and hangs up. This call will appear as an abandoned call in the Cisco Unity Express Historical Reporting Client because the call was never completed or marked as handled.

The Cisco Unity Express Historical Reporting Client is typically used in conjunction with IVR functionality. Like IVR, the Cisco Unity Express Historical Reporting Client is beyond the scope of this book.

> **Note**   For detailed information about the capabilities and configuration of the Cisco Unity Express Historical Reporting Client, refer to *Cisco Unified Communications Express Historical Reporting Client Configuration Guide*, which can be found on Cisco.com at the following URL:
>
> http://www.cisco.com/en/US/docs/voice_ip_comm/unity_exp/rel3_1/configuration/guide/hrc/HRC.pdf

Cisco Unity Express Licensing

Cisco Unity Express licensing is determined by three factors:

- The IP PBX type that will connect to Cisco Unity Express
- The Cisco Unity Express module type the license file will be loaded on
- The number of mailboxes required for the site that the Cisco Unity Express will be serving

Table 9.8 lists the Cisco Unity Express licensing available when connecting to Cisco Unified CME.

Table 9.8   *License Packages for Cisco Unified Communications Manager Express*

Filename	Mailbox License	Cisco Unity Express Modules
cue-vm-license_12mbx_cme_3.1.x.pkg	12 mailboxes	AIM-CUE
		NM-CUE
		NM-CUE-EC
		NME-CUE
cue-vm-license_25mbx_cme_3.1.x.pkg	25 mailboxes	AIM-CUE
		NM-CUE
		NM-CUE-EC
		NME-CUE

continues

Table 9.8   *License Packages for Cisco Unified Communications Manager Express continued*

Filename	Mailbox License	Cisco Unity Express Modules
cue-vm-license_50mbx_cme_3.1.x.pkg	50 mailboxes	AIM-CUE
		NM-CUE
		NM-CUE-EC
		NME-CUE
cue-vm-license_100mbx_cme_3.1.x.pkg	100 mailboxes	NM-CUE
		NM-CUE-EC
		NME-CUE
cue-vm-license_150mbx_cme_3.1.x.pkg	150 mailboxes	NM-CUE-EC
		NME-CUE
cue-vm-license_200mbx_cme_3.1.x.pkg	200 mailboxes	NM-CUE-EC
		NME-CUE
cue-vm-license_250mbx_cme_3.1.x.pkg	250 mailboxes	NM-CUE-EC
		NME-CUE

Table 9.9 lists the Cisco Unity Express licensing available when connecting to Cisco Unified Communications Manager.

Table 9.9   *Cisco Unity Express Licenses for Cisco Unified Communications Manager*

Filename	Mailbox License	Cisco Unity Express Modules
cue-vm-license_12mbx_ccm_3.1.x.pkg	12 mailboxes	AIM-CUE
		NM-CUE
		NM-CUE-EC
cue-vm-license_25mbx_ccm_3.1.x.pkg	25 mailboxes	AIM-CUE
		NM-CUE
		NM-CUE-EC
cue-vm-license_50mbx_ccm_3.1.x.pkg	50 mailboxes	AIM-CUE
		NM-CUE
		NM-CUE-EC

Filename	Mailbox License	Cisco Unity Express Modules
cue-vm-license_100mbx_ccm_3.1.x.pkg	100 mailboxes	NM-CUE
		NM-CUE-EC
cue-vm-license_150mbx_ccm_3.1.x.pkg	150 mailboxes	NM-CUE-EC
cue-vm-license_200mbx_ccm_3.1.x.pkg	200 mailboxes	NM-CUE-EC
cue-vm-license_250mbx_ccm_3.1.x.pkg	250 mailboxes	NM-CUE-EC

The Cisco Unity Express license to connect to a Cisco Unified Communications Manager is denoted by "ccm" in the filename, whereas the license to connect to a Cisco Unified CME uses "cme" in the filename.

Note that, regardless of the IP PBX type, the number of mailboxes dictates the Cisco Unity Express module required. For example, a 12-mailbox license can be loaded on any Cisco Unity Express module, but a 250-mailbox license cannot be installed on an AIM-CUE module. Chapter 10, "Cisco Unity Express Configuration," discusses how these license files are installed on the Cisco Unity Express hardware platform.

Although IVR functionality is beyond the scope of this book, it is important to understand that additional IVR licensing is needed to perform IVR functions. Table 9.10 lists licensing options for Cisco Unity Express IVR.

Table 9.10 *Cisco Unity Express IVR Licensing Options*

Filename	IVR License	Cisco Unity Express Modules
cue-vm-license_2port_ivr_3.1.x.pkg	2 IVR sessions	AIM-CUE
		NM-CUE
		NM-CUE-EC
cue-vm-license_4port_ivr_3.1.x.pkg	4 IVR sessions	AIM-CUE
		NM-CUE
		NM-CUE-EC
cue-vm-license_8port_ivr_3.1.x.pkg	8 IVR sessions	AIM-CUE
		NM-CUE
		NM-CUE-EC
cue-vm-license_16port_ivr_3.1.x.pkg	16 IVR sessions	AIM-CUE
		NM-CUE
		NM-CUE-EC

continues

Table 9.10   *Cisco Unity Express IVR Licensing Options, Continued*

Filename	IVR License	Cisco Unity Express Modules
cue-vm-license_20port_ivr_3.1.x.pkg	20 IVR sessions	AIM-CUE
		NM-CUE
		NM-CUE-EC
cue-vm-license_2port_ivr_inc_nme_3.1.x.pkg	Upgrade license to add 2 IVR sessions	AIM-CUE
		NM-CUE
		NM-CUE-EC

Cisco Unity Express to IP PBX Integrations

Currently Cisco Unity Express has the capability to provide voice-mail and auto-attendant functions for Cisco Unified CME and Cisco Unified Communications Manager.

Integration with Cisco Unified CME

When integrated with CME, Cisco Unity Express provides voice-mail and auto-attendant services to the phones registered to the local CME. Because both CME and Cisco Unity Express are local to the IP phone, a QoS-enabled WAN is not necessary to ensure the quality of voice-mail messages.

During the Cisco Unity Express installation process, CME users and their phone settings can be imported into Cisco Unity Express with very little administration work. After installation, the tight integration between CME and Cisco Unity Express allows for a single point of administration via a web page. All moves, adds, and changes (MACs) can now be performed in a single location and synchronized between CME and Cisco Unity Express.

The CME/Cisco Unity Express combination provides a cost-effective solution to deliver advanced IP-based communications capabilities to small and medium-sized businesses.

Integration with Cisco Unified Communications Manager

When integrated with Cisco Unified Communications Manager, Cisco Unity Express provides voice-mail and auto-attendant services to phones as dictated by Cisco Unified Communications Manager. In this scenario, Cisco Unity Express at a branch location becomes an extension of the corporate-wide unified communications solution. This allows a centralized administrative staff to perform adds, moves, and changes for each branch location, without requiring Cisco Unity Express support staff at each site.

Because Cisco Unified Communications Manager and Cisco Unity Express are separated by a WAN circuit in the deployment, Cisco Unity Express is typically configured to interoperate with the local PSTN gateway while it is in Survivable Remote Site Telephony (SRST) mode. This feature allows Cisco Unity Express to continue to provide voice-mail and auto-attendant services to local IP phones in the event of a WAN outage.

The Cisco Unified Communications Manager/Cisco Unity Express combination provides a scalable solution to deliver fault-tolerant communications capabilities to enterprise branch locations.

Features and Functions of Cisco Unity Express Voice Mail

This section discusses the following messaging capabilities of Cisco Unity Express:

- Users and groups

- Subscriber mailbox versus general delivery mailbox

- Mailbox subscriber features

- Mailbox caller features

- VoiceView Express

- Integrated messaging

- Voice Profile for Internet Mail (VPIM)

Users and Groups

Within Cisco Unity Express, users and groups are used to configure mailboxes and assign permissions.

User/Subscriber Accounts

A user, also called a subscriber, is an account that is intended for the exclusive use of one individual. This account dictates the extension number of the mailbox, how the user's messages are stored, how messages can be retrieved and retained, and what permission this subscriber has.

Groups

A group is a collection of subscriber accounts. Like a subscriber account, a group account dictates the extension number of the mailbox, how the group's messages are stored, and how messages can be retrieved and retained.

Assigning permission on a group level allows the administrator to easily manage permissions for several subscribers. The following groups are created during Cisco Unity Express installation:

- Administrators
- Broadcast

A member of the administrators group has the ability to configure all aspects of Cisco Unity Express.

A member of the broadcast group has the ability to send a broadcast message to all subscribers of the local Cisco Unity Express as well as all members of another networked Cisco Unity Express location.

Subscriber Mailbox Versus General Delivery Mailbox

A mailbox is defined as a storage facility to hold a recorded message. Cisco Unity Express has two distinct types of mailboxes, the subscriber mailbox and the group delivery mailbox.

Subscriber Mailboxes

A user mailbox, also referred to as a subscriber mailbox, is typically assigned to one individual. That person personalizes and customizes the user mailbox to meet their individual needs.

For example, a subscriber mailbox is created and assigned to John Smith. John's phone is configured to forward to this subscriber mailbox if his extension is busy or he does not answer. When a caller is redirected to John's subscriber mailbox, a greeting is played to the caller. This greeting, created by John, may state, "Thank you for calling John Smith. I am either on the phone or away from my desk. Please leave a message." Once the caller leaves a message in the user mailbox, it becomes accessible by John for retrieval. John uses his personal pin number to log in to his user mailbox and listen to the message left by the caller.

A subscriber mailbox is designed to serve an individual user on Cisco Unity Express.

General Delivery Mailboxes

Unlike the subscriber mailbox, a general delivery mailbox (GDM) is assigned to a group of people.

For example, a GDM is created and assigned to the customer service department. The delivery of a message to the GDM is similar to the delivery of a message to a subscriber mailbox. An extension number associated with the GDM is configured to forward to Cisco Unity Express if this extension is busy or is not answered. A caller is redirected to the GDM greeting. This greeting may state, "Thank you for calling the customer service department. All of our representatives are currently busy assisting other customers.

Please leave a message and one of our representatives will return your call within two hours." Once the caller leaves a message in the GDM, it becomes accessible by anyone in the customer service group for retrieval.

Unlike a subscriber mailbox, a GDM does not have a pin assigned to it for login. To retrieve messages left in the GDM, a group member must log in to their personal user mailbox. Once they have logged in, they will be prompted with the option to retrieve messages for any GDM they are associated with.

For example, assume that John Smith has been configured as a member of the customer service GDM discussed above. When John logs into his subscriber mailbox, he will hear the prompt "For general delivery mailboxes, press 9." By choosing 9, John can retrieve messages left in the customer service GDM.

Note   Although any member of the group can log in to the GDM to retrieve messages, only one person at a time can access the mailbox.

A GDM is designed to serve a group of users as a shared mailbox on Cisco Unity Express.

Mailbox Subscriber Features

This section discusses the following features available to the owner of a user mailbox or to a group member of a GDM:

- Mailbox login, passwords, and PINs
- Tutorial
- Greetings
- Message management and playback
- Message types
- Message waiting indicator
- Message notifications
- Live reply and live record
- Distribution lists
- Mailbox storage

Mailbox Login, Passwords, and PINs

A password and PIN are associated with a user during the user creation in Cisco Unity Express or during an import of CME users. The system administrator has the option to generate a random value, leave the value blank, or specify a value for both the password and PIN.

Both the system administrator and the user have the option of changing the password and PIN after the user has been created, as long as the change falls within the defined system defaults set by the administrator. Table 9.11 lists the password and PIN default options available to the administrator.

Table 9.11   *Password and PIN Settings*

Configuration Option	Password	PIN
Enable expiry (days)	3–365	3–365
History depth	1–10	1–10
Minimum length	3–32	3–16
Account lockout policy	Disable lockout Permanent Temporary	Disable lockout Permanent Temporary
Number of attempts for temporary lock	1–200	1–200
Temporary lockout duration (mins)	Default of 5 minutes	Default of 5 minutes
Maximum number of failed attempts	1–200	1–200

The account lockout policy can be configured to permanently lock out a user after a maximum number of failed authentication attempts, configured to temporarily lock out a user for a configurable number of minutes, or be disabled and not track failed login attempts.

It is important to understand the difference between the password and PIN. A password is used by the subscriber for access into the graphical user interface (GUI) of Cisco Unity Express, whereas the PIN is used for telephony user interface (TUI) access into Cisco Unity Express. For example, when a subscriber presses the Messages button on their IP phone, the PIN is the value they need to enter to gain access to their messages. However, if the subscriber opens a web page to Cisco Unity Express and attempts to log in, they need to enter their username and password to be authenticated.

Tutorial

The tutorial provides a quick, easy, and scalable way to personalize and update basic settings of a mailbox without administrator intervention.

The first time a person presses the Messages button on their IP phone and enters their PIN to log in to a mailbox, they are greeted by the tutorial feature of Cisco Unity

Express. The tutorial explains each step and prompts the user to take action on each of the following mailbox options:

- Recorded/spoken name

- Record standard greeting

- Change password

The recorded name, also called the spoken name, is used by Cisco Unity Express to identify this mailbox to other subscribers on the system.

The next step in the self-enrollment process is to record your personal greeting that will be played to callers that are transferred to your voice mail.

The final step for self-enrollment is to select a password that you will use to log in to Cisco Unity Express via the TUI.

Note   Although the tutorial prompts for a password, the PIN is the value that is actually being requested and recorded for future TUI login. Remember that the password is used for GUI access, whereas the PIN is used for TUI access.

After you complete the tutorial, your mailbox has been personalized and is ready for use.

Note   For security reasons, initial access and first-time setup of a subscriber mailbox can only be done from the subscriber's primary extension.

Greetings

A greeting is the message that a caller hears when reaching a voice mailbox. Cisco Unity Express mailboxes have two distinct types of greetings, a standard greeting and an alternate greeting.

A standard greeting is the message the caller receives under normal circumstances. For example, John Smith's standard greeting may state, "Thank you for calling John Smith. I am either on the phone or away from my desk. Please leave a message."

An alternate greeting is used for emergencies and extended absences such as holidays, vacations, and emergencies. For example, John Smith's alternate greeting may state, "Thank you for calling John Smith. I am on vacation this week."

The alternate greeting is disabled by default. When enabled, the alternate greeting will override the standard greeting. This means that all callers will hear the alternate greeting until it is disabled. At that point, the standard greeting is played once again. This allows John Smith to let callers know he is on vacation this week without having to rerecord his standard greeting when he returns to the office.

Message Management and Playback

After a message has been left in a subscriber's mailbox or a GDM, the recipient has several options on how to treat the message. The following list summarizes these options.

- **Play and restart:** Allows the subscriber to hear the message content and restart the playback from the beginning of the message at any time during playback.

- **Fast forward and rewind:** Allow the subscriber to quickly move ahead or backward though a message by 3-second intervals.

- **Skip:** Allows the subscriber to interrupt playback of a message and leave the message unheard.

- **Save:** Allows the subscriber to archive the read message for later retrieval.

- **Reply to original sender:** Allows the subscriber to immediately respond to a received message. The reply is sent to the originator's voice mailbox. For example, assume that Jane Doe leaves a message in John Smith's mailbox. John listens to the message and decides that he needs to reply. John records his response and follows the voice-mail prompts needed to send the message. The message is then placed in Jane's voice mailbox, awaiting retrieval by Jane.

Note   For Cisco Unity Express to deliver the reply, the original sender, Jane Doe in this case, must be a defined subscriber in Cisco Unity Express. Callers from the PSTN cannot be recipients of a reply voice-mail message because they do not have an internal extension defined on Cisco Unity Express.

- **Forward to another subscriber:** Allows the recipient of a message to forward the received message to another Cisco Unity Express subscriber. For example, assume that John Smith receives a voice-mail message and decides that Jane Doe needs to hear it as well. John records an introduction and forwards both the introduction and the received message to Jane's mailbox. (A forwarded message can be marked urgent. Urgent messages play back before any new messages are heard when a user calls into their voice mailbox via the TUI. Playback order of messages is covered in the "Message Types" section of this chapter.)

Note   For Cisco Unity Express to deliver a forwarded message, the recipient of the forwarded message, Jane Doe in this case, must be a defined subscriber in Cisco Unity Express. Callers from the PSTN cannot be recipients of a forwarded message because they do not have an internal extension defined on Cisco Unity Express.

- **Delete:** Allows the subscriber to delete any received message.

- **Undelete:** Allows the subscriber to restore a message back to the mailbox.

Note   If a subscriber deletes a message and logs out of the mailbox, the deleted message will not be available to the subscriber upon the next login.

Message Types

Five message types can be found in a subscriber mailbox or GDM:

■ **Broadcast message:** A message that is sent to all subscribers on the Cisco Unity Express and potentially all other Cisco Unity Express modules that have been networked together. To send a broadcast message, the subscriber must be a member of the broadcast group.

■ **Expired message:** A message that has been in a mailbox past the retention date. Cisco Unity Express will not delete this message, but will prompt the subscriber to delete or save the message. If the message is saved once again, the expiry timer is reset.

■ **Urgent message:** A message that the sender has tagged to indicate that the content is of high importance.

■ **New message:** A message that has not been played.

■ **Saved message:** A message that has been listened to but retained for future retrieval.

The message type determines both the order in which messages are presented to the subscriber and the options available to handle the message. Table 9.12 lists the order and options by message type.

Table 9.12   *Message Type Order and Options*

Message Type	Order Played	Play	Replay	Save	Delete	Skip	Reply	Forward
Broadcast	1	Yes	Yes	Yes	Yes	No	No	No
Expired	2	Yes	Yes	Yes	Yes	No	No	No
Urgent	3	Yes	Yes	Yes	Yes	Yes	Yes	Yes
New	4	Yes	Yes	Yes	Yes	Yes	Yes	Yes
Saved	5	Yes	Yes	Yes	Yes	Yes	Yes	Yes

Key Topic

Notice that the first two message types, broadcast and expired, will be presented to the subscriber before any other messages can be accessed. The subscriber cannot skip, reply to, or forward a broadcast message or an expired message.

Message Waiting Indicator

A message waiting indicator (MWI) provides a mechanism to alert a subscriber that a new message has arrived in a mailbox. To provide this alert, Cisco Unity Express, in conjunction with Cisco Unified CME or Cisco Unified Communications Manager, uses both a red light (located on the handset of an IP phone) and a flashing envelope that appears in the phone display window next to the line button.

When a new message arrives in a mailbox, Cisco Unity Express sends an alert to Cisco Unified CME or Cisco Unified Communications Manager. The configuration of Cisco Unified CME or Cisco Unified Communications Manager, as well as the phone type, determines how the MWI notification appears on the IP phone.

Note   All models of IP phone support the red light MWI, but only phones with displays support the flashing envelope.

When a mailbox is assigned to a subscriber or group, an extension number is explicitly defined for the associated mailbox. When a new message arrives, Cisco Unity Express uses this extension number to inform CME or CCM which phone should receive the MWI.

For example, assume that John Smith's mailbox is extension 1000 and John's phone is connecting to a CME. When a new message arrives for John, Cisco Unity Express sends an alert to CME stating that a new message has arrived for mailbox 1000. CME then activates the MWI for John's primary line.

A GDM also has an assigned extension, so the MWI operation of the GDM is the same as the MWI operation of the subscriber mailbox. To provide MWI alerts to the group, the GDM extension must appear on the IP phone of each group member. For example, assume that the customer service group's extension is 1010. To send MWI alerts to each member of the customer service group when a new message arrives, extension 1010 must be a line appearance on each group member's IP phone.

The administrator has the option to enable or disable MWI notifications for all broadcast messages.

Message Notifications

The message notification feature provides another way for Cisco Unity Express to alert a subscriber that a message has arrived in their mailbox. Unlike an MWI, which sends a signal to an IP phone, message notification has the capability to place a phone call or send an e-mail to the subscriber when a new message arrives.

Message Notifications: System Level

By default, message notification is disabled both globally and on a per-user basis in Cisco Unity Express. This means that the administrator must first enable and configure message notification options system wide and then enable message notification for a user, before that user has the option of using message notification.

The following list describes the options the administrator has to configure message notification on a system level:

- Enable message notifications for either urgent messages or all messages.

- If a subscriber is alerted of a new message via a phone call, the administrator has the option of allowing the subscriber to log in and retrieve the new message during the notification call. If this option is not chosen by the administrator, the subscriber is forced to drop the notification call and dial back into Cisco Unity Express to retrieve the new message.

- Attach messages to outgoing e-mail notifications.

- Enable cascading notifications.

- Set the ring no answer (RNA) timeout, in seconds.

- Use a restriction table.

Message notification must be enabled at the system level in order for a subscriber to use this feature. The administrator also has the option of which type of message is considered valid to trigger a notification, an urgent message, or all received messages.

When a phone call is generated to alert the subscriber of a new received message, the subscriber has the option of logging into the mailbox during the received notification call, if allowed by the administrator. Otherwise, the notification will alert the subscriber and then the subscriber will have to hang up and dial into Cisco Unity Express to retrieve the message.

The administrator has the option of including a copy of the recorded message as an attachment to an e-mail notification. This delivers the recorded message without requiring the subscriber to log in to the mailbox.

Note   In order for Cisco Unity Express to send an e-mail notification, the external SMTP server must be configured and functional.

Enabling cascading messages allows a Cisco Unity Express subscriber to send a message notification to another Cisco Unity Express subscriber, or a Cisco Unity Express group, if the new message remains unread for a specified period of time. When notification is configured to dial a phone number, there is the risk that a voice-mail system will answer that call. In this case, Cisco Unity Express would not be able to distinguish between the voice-mail system and a live person answering the call. To mitigate this risk, an administrator can configure the ring no answer (RNA) option to limit the amount of time the call will remain in a ringing state before Cisco Unity Express considers the notification attempt as unsuccessful.

Finally, a restriction table can be used to limit the phone numbers that Cisco Unity Express can dial. For example, the administrator may allow the local calling area to be used for message notification, but may restrict toll calls.

Message Notifications: User Level

After the administrator has enabled and configured message notification on a system-wide basis, all users that require this feature must be given permission to use this option. This requires that the administrator enable message notification for each user on a per-user and per-group basis.

At the user level, Cisco Unity Express can be configured to call a phone number or send an e-mail to alert the subscriber of the received message. Each subscriber mailbox supports six device types that can be called or e-mailed in this event.

Table 9.13 lists the device and destination types.

Table 9.13   *Message Notification Device Types*

Device Type	Destination Type
Home phone	Phone number
Work phone	Phone number
Cell phone	Phone number
Pager (numeric)	Phone number
Text pager	E-mail address
E-mail inbox	E-mail address

For the destination types of phone number, the subscriber may enter a number to be dialed as well as any extra digits that need to be dialed after the phone number. Extra digits can be 0 through 9, with * inserting a 1-second pause.

For the destination types of e-mail address, the subscriber may enter a valid e-mail address and a customized line of text.

Regardless of the destination type, the subscriber has the option to generate an alert for all messages or for urgent messages only. The subscriber can also specify the day and time that a notification will be generated. For example, John Smith can configure his message notification option to call his cell phone for any message received Monday through Friday from 8 a.m. to 5:30 p.m., while Jane Doe can configure her message notification option to send an e-mail to her text pager if an urgent message is received at any time.

Finally, a subscriber has the ability to configure up to two cascading subscribers or groups, with a time delay between each other. For example, assume John Smith has configured all urgent messages to send a notification to his cell phone. John has also configured a cascade to Jane Doe after 5 minutes and a cascade to the Customer Service group after 10 minutes. When an urgent message is received in John's mailbox, an alert is sent to his cell phone. If the attempt to contact John fails, Jane will be notified 5 minutes after the message has been received. If the attempt to contact Jane fails, the customer service group will be notified 10 minutes after the message was received in John's mailbox.

Live Reply and Live Record

The live reply feature allows a subscriber to use the received caller identification number (Automatic Number Identification [ANI]) and place a phone call to that caller during voice-mail message playback. For example, assume that John Smith receives a voice mail from his business associate Bill at 404-555-1212. During the call, John decides to invoke the live reply feature and call Bill back. The live reply feature will use Bill's ANI or originating number (404-555-1212) and generate a call to this number, ringing Bill's phone.

Note   Live reply requires that caller ID be enabled and configured such that Cisco Unity Express receives a number that can be dialed in order to generate the return call.

The live record feature enables a subscriber to record a live call and have that call delivered into the subscriber's mailbox. For example, John calls Bill and decides that he needs to record this conversation. John can invoke the live record feature and his conversation with Bill will be stored in John's mailbox. Once the message has been delivered to the mailbox, it can be played, replayed, saved, or forwarded to any subscriber or group of subscribers.

Distribution Lists

A distribution list is simply a list of subscribers who are grouped together under one name and number in order to send a single voice mail to each member of the group simultaneously. There are two types of distribution lists, public and private.

Public Distribution Lists

A public distribution list is a collection of subscribers that is available to all Cisco Unity Express subscribers to use as a distribution list. For example, a public distribution list called "everyone" is created upon Cisco Unity Express installation. This public distribution list contains all Cisco Unity Express subscribers. Once a message is addressed to this public distribution list, all subscribers defined in Cisco Unity Express will be able to access the message.

A public distribution list can be created by any subscriber. For example, suppose John Smith needs a way to send a voice mail to all members in the customer services group. John can create a public distribution list named "Customer Service" that includes each desired member of the customer service group. Because this distribution list is a pubic list, any subscriber defined in Cisco Unity Express can address a message to this list.

Private Distribution Lists

Each subscriber has the ability to create up to ten private distribution lists in Cisco Unity Express. A private distribution list is a collection of subscribers created by a single subscriber for exclusive use by that subscriber. In the previous example, if John Smith had created the "Customer Service" distribution list as a private list, John would be the only subscriber that could address a message to that distribution list.

Mailbox Storage

Mailbox storage defines how much of the Cisco Unity Express storage space can be used to hold received messages. Cisco Unity Express breaks storage down into two categories: overall storage space for Cisco Unity Express, and the space allocated on a per-user basis.

The overall Cisco Unity Express storage space is defined in minutes of recorded voice and is determined by the hardware platform of Cisco Unity Express. For example, an NM-CUE has 6000 minutes of storage space available to the sum of all subscribers. This number of minutes can be reduced; however, it cannot be increased without changing the hardware platform.

The per-user storage allocation is determined by the administrator during the subscriber's mailbox creation. The administrator can increase or decrease the storage available to that subscriber, both during or after subscriber creation. For example, assume John Smith's mailbox was just created on an NM-CUE. If the administrator used default values, John's mailbox is capable of storing 3000 seconds of recorded voice. The administrator has the option to decrease or increase this value.

Note   Increasing the per-user mailbox value assumes that enough of the overall space, 6000 minutes in the previous example, is unallocated to other subscribers.

When a subscriber presses the Message button or dials into their Cisco Unity Express voice mailbox, Cisco Unity Express compares the user storage allocated to the actual storage used. If the percentage is above 90 percent, the subscriber is greeted with an announcement explaining that their inbox is almost full and that if the inbox exceeds the storage limit, the subscriber will not be able to send or receive messages. The subscriber is then asked to delete messages. As the percentage nears 100 percent utilization, Cisco Unity Express announces to the subscriber that their inbox is now full and they will no longer receive new messages. The subscriber is once again asked to delete messages. A caller is told that the mailbox they are trying to call is full and to please try again later.

Mailbox Caller Features

This section discusses the features available to the caller while they are listening to a greeting or leaving a message in a user mailbox or a GDM:

- Record message options
- Operator assistance
- Mailbox login

Record Message Options

When a caller is routed to a subscriber's mailbox, they hear the active greeting of the mailbox. The caller has the option to bypass this greeting and proceed directly to leaving the message for the subscriber.

Note   A voice-mail message must be at least 2 seconds long to be considered valid and retained by Cisco Unity Express.

After the message has been recorded, the caller has the following options:

- Review the recorded message
- Re-record the message
- Set normal or urgent priority on the message
- Cancel the message

When the caller is satisfied with the recording and sends the message, they may either hang up or remain on the line and be transferred to the system operator.

Operator Assistance

Operator assistance, also referred to as zero out, allows a caller to reach an operator while in voice mail. Cisco Unity Express provides a default system operator and a specific operator defined per mailbox.

The specific operator is configured on an individual subscriber mailbox basis and is invoked when a caller is listening to the mailbox greeting. For example, a caller reaches John Smith's voice mail, hears John's alternate greeting, and realizes that John is on vacation. By pressing 0 during the greeting, the caller is redirected to the extension that has been defined as the operator of John's mailbox.

The system operator is used if operator assistance has not been configured on an individual subscriber mailbox, or if the caller is transferred to the operator by Cisco Unity Express, such as after leaving a message.

Mailbox Login

Mailbox login enables a subscriber to log in to their mailbox from outside the office or away from their IP phone. For example, assume that John is out of the office and needs to check his voice mail. John can call his office number and wait until the call is delivered to Cisco Unity Express. Once he hears his greeting, he presses * and is prompted for his extension and password. John can then enter his credentials and have access to his subscriber mailbox to play back his voice-mail messages.

Note   Although the TUI prompts for John's "password," it is really the PIN that he must enter to gain access.

Being prompted for an extension and password means that any Cisco Unity Express subscriber has the ability to log in to their mailbox and check messages from the greeting of any other mailbox.

VoiceView Express

VoiceView Express provides an alternative to TUI access. Unlike the TUI, which requires a subscriber to dial into his or her voice mailbox, VoiceView Express operates as an IP phone service. IP phone services are XML-based web pages that Cisco IP Phones are capable of rendering. If an IP phone has been configured to allow VoiceView Express, a subscriber can log in to their mailbox, check messages, administer messages, send messages, and configure mailbox options, all from the display screen of the IP phone.

VoiceView Express is an XML IP phone service that can be assigned to an IP phone in Cisco Unified CME or Cisco Unified Communications Manager. When the subscriber presses the Services button on the phone, the subscriber is prompted for their mailbox ID and PIN. Once a subscriber has authenticated, the subscriber can log in to their mailbox and check messages from any IP phone that has been configured for VoiceView Express.

VoiceView Express can be enabled or disabled on a systemwide basis by the administrator. A session idle timeout value can also be set by the administrator to free sessions that are no longer in use. The session idle timeout range is between 5 minutes and 30 minutes, with the default being 5 minutes.

Prior to Cisco Unity Express 3.x, VoiceView Express was only available on the NM-CUE, NM-CUE-EC, and NME-CUE platforms. With release 3.x, VoiceView Express is available on the CUE-AIM for up to three simultaneous sessions.

Integrated Messaging

With Cisco Unity Express, a subscriber has the option of using the TUI, VoiceView Express, or their e-mail client to retrieve messages. Integrated messaging provides access to voice-mail messages via an e-mail client and allows a subscriber to treat voice-mail messages similarly to e-mail messages.

Using an IMAP-capable e-mail client, a subscriber has the option of adding an IMAP e-mail account to their existing e-mail client. This allows the subscriber's e-mail client to access both the subscriber's normal e-mail and their voice mail.

For example, assume that John Smith has an IMAP-capable e-mail client that he uses to send and receive corporate e-mail. Because his client is IMAP capable, John can add his voice-mail account on Cisco Unity Express as an additional e-mail account in his client. Then, John can receive both e-mail and voice mail in the same client.

Note   Integrated messaging and unified messaging can both be retrieved from a single client; however, there is a distinct difference between the two. Unified messaging implies that both voice-mail and e-mail messages come to the same account, such as john.smith@mycompany.com, and are retrieved from the same inbox on the client. Integrated messaging implies that voice mail and e-mail have separate accounts, one e-mail account, such as john.smith@mycompany.com, and one voice-mail account, such as john.smith@cue.mycompany.com. Although both e-mail and voice mail can be retrieved with the same client, the messages will appear in different inboxes within the client.

Prior to Cisco Unity Express 3.x, integrated messaging was only available on the NM-CUE, NM-CUE-EC, and NME-CUE platforms. With release 3.x, integrated messaging is available on the CUE-AIM for up to 20 simultaneous IMAP sessions.

Voice Profile for Internet Mail

Voice Profile for Internet Mail (VPIM) is a feature that allows one voice-mail system to exchange messages with another voice-mail system.

In the past, if a subscriber of one voice-mail system wanted to forward a message to a subscriber of another voice-mail system, the sending system had to place a call to the receiving system and play the message in real time. This means that a real-time medium must be available between the two voice-mail systems, such as a public switched telephone network (PSTN) connection or a LAN/WAN connection with quality of service (QoS) guarantees.

As you learned in the "Integrated Messaging" section, Cisco Unity Express has the capability of treating a voice-mail message in a similar fashion as an e-mail message. This capability allows Cisco Unity Express to forward a voice-mail message as an e-mail message using the Simple Message Transport Protocol (SMTP), without the need for a real-time connection between the systems. VPIM is the standard format of this exchange.

Features and Functions of Cisco Unity Express Auto Attendant

This section discusses the following auto-attendant capabilities of Cisco Unity Express:

- Cisco Unity Express Automated Attendant
- Cisco Unity Express Custom Scripting

Cisco Unity Express Automated Attendant

An Automated Attendant (AA) enables a business to answer and direct incoming phone calls to the appropriate person within the business without requiring human intervention.

Default Auto Attendant Scripts

A call is routed from Cisco Unified CME or Cisco Unified Communications Manager to the Cisco Unity Express AA. When the call arrives at the Cisco Unity Express AA, a Cisco Unity Express script is activated. This script determines the treatment the caller will receive. For example, assume that a caller dials 404.555.1050 and is routed to a Cisco Unity Express AA. The caller hears "Welcome to the automated attendant. To enter the phone number of the person you are trying to reach, press 1. To enter the name of the person you are trying to reach, press 2. To transfer to the operator, press 0." The caller now has an option of how to reach a subscriber or the system operator. It is the Cisco Unity Express script that determines which greetings the caller hears, when the caller hears them, and what dialing options the caller has.

A default installation of Cisco Unity Express includes two AA scripts that can be implemented and personalized with minimal effort and without requiring a resource that has Cisco Unity Express Editor experience. The following are the default Cisco Unity Express AA scripts:

- Auto Attendant script
- Auto Attendant Simple script

Both AA scripts are preloaded on Cisco Unity Express during installation; however, the default script used by Cisco Unity Express is the Auto Attendant script. The Auto Attendant Simple script is comparable to the Auto Attendant script with a few features removed. The following sections discuss the features of these scripts and note where differences exist.

AA Greetings/Prompts

AA greetings, also referred to as AA prompts, are similar to voice-mail greetings, discussed earlier. AA prompts are the messages that a caller hears when they are routed to the AA. As with voice mail, administrators and subscribers with the proper permissions can record and personalize an AA greeting. Unlike a voice mailbox, AA offers the capability to change the greeting based upon the day or a specific time of day.

By changing the content of a prompt a business can personalize the AA script to suit the business's needs without requiring the script itself to be altered.

The following greetings are available within the default AA scripts:

- Welcome prompt

- Business Open prompt

- Business Closed prompt

- Holiday prompt

The Welcome prompt is the first prompt a caller hears when connected to the AA script. This is typically the message that the business wants the caller to hear regardless of the day or time the call is received. For example, this message may be personalized to state "Thank you for calling the ABC Company, the worldwide leader in widget manufacturing." By default, this prompt states "Welcome to the automated attendant."

After the Welcome prompt has been played, Cisco Unity Express consults the configured schedule and holiday list to determine which prompt to play next. Schedules determine open versus closed hours and day-of-week logic.

If the call arrives at the AA during normal business hours on a nonholiday, the Business Open prompt is played to the caller. This is typically a message that the business wishes to play to the caller only during normal business hours. For example, this message can be personalized to state "We are all hard at work making your next order of widgets." By default, this prompt is blank and silence is played for a brief instant.

If the call arrives at the AA outside normal business hours on a nonholiday, the Business Closed prompt is played to the caller. This is typically a message that the business wishes to play to the caller outside of normal business hours. For example, this message can be personalized to state "Sorry, even widgets need a rest, so we are currently closed. Please call us during normal business hours." By default, this prompt states "We are currently closed. Please call back later."

If a caller is routed to the AA during a holiday, the Holiday prompt is played to the caller. The Holiday prompt is used to announce company holidays. For example, the Holiday prompt can be customized to state "It is a holiday in widget land. Please call back after the holiday." By default, this prompt states "We are closed today. Please call back later."

Each of these prompts can be personalized to fit the business needs Cisco Unity Express is serving, without having to modify the AA scripts.

After the personalized prompts have been played, Cisco Unity Express prompts the caller for the caller's desired action by playing the following prompt, "To enter the phone number of the person you are trying to reach, press 1. To enter the name of the person you are trying to reach, press 2. To transfer to the operator, press 0." The caller then has the option to reach a subscriber by name or extension or to transfer to the operator.

Note   This message is played regardless of which personalized prompt is played. Cisco Unity Express Editor can be used to customize the default AA script to change this behavior.

Business Hours Settings

Business hours are determined by a schedule that is configured within Cisco Unity Express. This schedule is broken down into half-hour increments on a Monday through Sunday basis. To operate in the normal business mode, place a check on the half hour time slot. To operate in the closed business mode, clear the check from the time slot. For example, assume that business hours are Monday through Friday from 08:30 to 17:30 (5:30 p.m. in 12-hour time format). For Monday, you would place a check mark in the 08:30 time slot box, 09:00 time slot box, 09:30 time slot box, 10:00 time slot box, and so on, and end with the final time slot box of 17:30 checked. The 18:00 time slot box would be left unchecked. The same pattern follows suit for the other week days, while all time slot boxes during the weekend would remain unchecked.

Cisco Unity Express offers the capability to create a schedule for a day and copy that schedule to any other individual day, all weekdays, or the weekend. In the preceding example, you can copy the Monday schedule you created to all weekdays, and then create a schedule for Saturday, leaving all time slot boxes unchecked. Finally, you can copy the Saturday schedule to Sunday to complete your AA scheduled business hours of Monday through Friday from 08:30 to 17:30.

After you have created a schedule, you can save and apply it to the AA without the need to change the default AA script.

Note   If you require more granular control than half-hour increments for the open/closed settings, you need to change the AA script. You can use Cisco Unity Express Editor to customize the default AA script to provide more granular control.

Holidays Settings

A holiday setting is simply a list of dates that requires a Holiday prompt to be played to all AA callers. Dates can be entered by calendar date, specifying the day, month, and year; or dates can be entered as fixed dates, specifying only the month and day. A fixed date is valid for any year. For example, a fixed date of December 25 is valid to specify Christmas day for any year.

After holidays have been defined for a given year, Cisco Unity Express offers the capability to copy holiday settings for that year to the following year.

Note   If you require more granular control than full-day increments for the holiday settings, you need to change the AA script. You can use Cisco Unity Express Editor to customize the default AA script to provide more granular control.

AA Operator

The AA operator is similar to the voice-mail system operator in that this is the extension that will be dialed if a caller dials 0 during the playback of any prompt other than the welcome prompt. This allows a caller to reach a live person if they do not know the name or extension of the person they are trying to reach.

Note   The operator function is not available in the Auto Attendant Simple script.

Dial by Name and Dial by Extension

When a caller is redirected to the AA, they are given the option to be transferred to a subscriber. To identify the desired subscriber, the caller can choose to spell the subscriber's name or enter the subscriber's extension.

With the spell-by-name function, the administrator has the option to require callers to use either last name first or first name first. For example, a search for John Smith using the last-name-first configuration would result in the caller entering Smith John on the phone keypad, while the first-name-first configuration would require the caller to enter John Smith. This configuration is global, meaning that every caller must use the same method of spell by name. Typically, only a few letters need to be dialed in order to eliminate other candidate subscribers and transfer the caller to John Smith. The number of letters required depends on the number of subscriber matches that exist in Cisco Unity Express.

Note   The spell-by-name function can only be configured to use last name first with the Auto Attendant Simple script.

If the spell-by-name function cannot find the person the caller is looking for, the caller is given the option to retry a spell-by-name lookup or be transferred to the operator.

Administration via Telephone System

Administration via Telephone (AVT) gives an administrator an easy way to record custom prompts and to quickly record and enable the AA alternate greeting. When dialing into the AVT, the administrator is prompted to authenticate by entering their extension number and PIN.

Once authenticated, the administrator can quickly record and enable an alternate greeting to inform all callers of the current situation. For example, assume that severe weather conditions have forced the business to close. The administrator can override the normal AA greeting with a prompt that states "Thank you for calling. Due to severe weather conditions, we have been forced to close for the day. Please call back later."

Another benefit of AVT is that the administrator can record custom prompts. These custom prompts can then be used by the AA to personalize the caller's experience.

Cisco Unity Express Custom Scripting

With Cisco Unity Express Editor software, an administrator can fully customize the caller's experience when their call is routed into the Cisco Unity Express AA. Cisco Unity Express Editor is a collection of software steps that defines what treatment the caller will receive. For example, assume that you want to write a script that accomplishes the following common tasks:

- Answer the call

- Determine the time of day

- If open, play a prompt allowing the caller to choose which subscriber to be transferred to. "Press 1 to talk to John Smith. Press 2 to talk to Jane Doe."

- If closed, transfer the caller to an off-premises number.

This can be accomplished by using Cisco Unity Express Editor to create a custom script, with each task described previously performed by software steps in the script. Whereas this example demonstrates a very basic script, Cisco Unity Express Editor has the capability to create very complex and detailed call flows. Figure 9.1 shows Cisco Unity Express Editor.

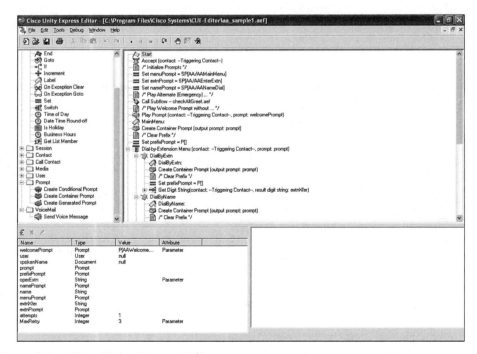

Figure 9.1   *Cisco Unity Express Editor*

Note   For detailed information about the capabilities and configuration of custom scripting on Cisco Unity Express, refer to *Cisco Unity Express 3.1 Guide to Writing and Editing Scripts* on Cisco.com at the following URL:

http://www.cisco.com/en/US/docs/voice_ip_comm/unity_exp/rel3_1/administration/guide/script/ScriptEditor.html

Sample Cisco Unity Express AA scripts can also be found on Cisco.com:

http://www.cisco.com/cgi-bin/tablebuild.pl/cue-311-aa-samples

Note that downloading software from Cisco.com requires a Cisco.com login.

Cisco Unity Express Management

Cisco Unity Express management can be thought of as the ongoing operation or upkeep of the system and the received messages. This section discusses the following types of management available on Cisco Unity Express:

- Administrator management
- Subscriber management
- Record message options for the caller

Administrator Management

Administrator management consists of the tasks required to handle the day-to-day operation of the overall Cisco Unity Express system. This can include adding users, unlocking user accounts, changing the AA greeting, and backing up the Cisco Unity Express system. This section illustrates where these types of administrator tasks can be configured.

Note   To perform administrator-level tasks, a subscriber must log in to the system using an ID that has administrative privileges.

Command-Line Interface Versus Graphical User Interface Administrator Management

Traditionally, the CLI has been the preferred method of accessing and configuring Cisco devices, such as Cisco routers and switches. However, Cisco Unity Express runs on a Linux-based operating system, so the CLI of Cisco Unity Express is vastly different from the CLI of traditional Cisco devices. To use the Cisco Unity Express CLI, the administrator must first open a Telnet session (using a Telnet client) to either the hostname or the IP address of the Cisco ISR router that houses Cisco Unity Express. Next, the administrator must open a session from the Cisco ISR router to Cisco Unity Express.

Example 9.1 shows the CLI for Cisco Unity Express.

Example 9.1   *Cisco Unity Express CLI*

```
CME# service-module service-Engine 1/0 session
Trying 10.100.1.1, 2066 ... Open
CUE >
CUE > enable
Password:
CUE #
```

Note   Configuration of Cisco Unity Express, and CLI commands used to access Cisco Unity Express, will be discussed in more detail in Chapter 10.

Cisco Unity Express also offers the option of configuration via a GUI. Figure 9.2 shows an example of the Cisco Unity Express GUI.

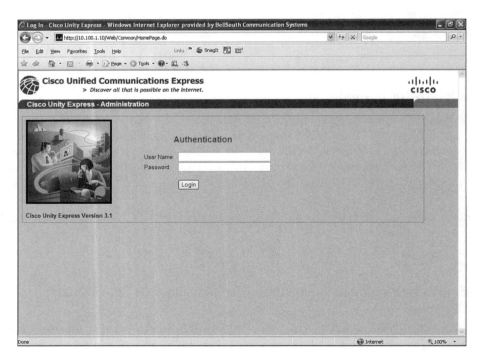

Figure 9.2   *Cisco Unity Express GUI*

To use the Cisco Unity Express GUI, open Microsoft Internet Explorer, version 6 or higher, and type **http://***CUE-Server* in the Address line, where *CUE-Server* is either the IP address of Cisco Unity Express or a hostname that can be resolved to an IP address.

The Cisco Unity Express GUI has the capability to administer all of the common Cisco Unity Express features via the web page, without requiring the administrator to use the CLI. The Cisco Unity Express GUI also offers the capability to administer many of the Cisco Unified CME functions from the same web page. Configuration changes can now be performed in a single common GUI and then synchronized between the CME and Cisco Unity Express. For the rest of this chapter, administrator management will focus on using the GUI to accomplish the tasks needed.

The administrator must provide login credentials to proceed. After the proper credentials have been supplied, the administrator has full access to all Cisco Unity Express menus. Figure 9.3 shows an example of the administrator GUI home page configuration options after login.

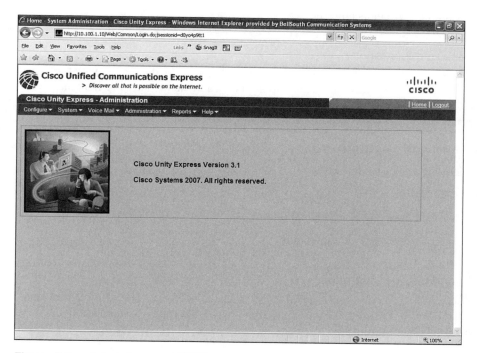

Figure 9.3   *Administrator GUI Home Page*

The menus at the top of the web page, Configure, System, Voice Mail, Administration, Reports, and Help, provide access to different configuration options within Cisco Unity Express. This section discusses the common options.

User and Group Administration

User and group administration options are located under the Configure menu along the top of the Cisco Unity Express GUI home page. These pages are used to configure attributes for a specific user or group. The following is a list of common administrator tasks that can be accomplished for subscriber accounts and groups:

- Reset passwords and PINs

- Configure name information

- Associate a phone

- Assign a primary extension

- Assign an E.164 address

- Assign a language

- Enable/configure message notification

- Configure mailbox settings

- Configure group membership

Voice Mail Administration

Both global and subscriber-specific voice-mail settings can be configured with the Cisco Unity Express GUI. Most voice-mail options are located under the Voice Mail menu of the Cisco Unity Express GUI home page. The following is a list of common administrator tasks that can be accomplished for voice-mail configuration:

- Mailbox size limitations

- Message size limitations

- MWI configuration

- Integrated messaging configuration

- VoiceView Express configuration

Auto Attendant Administration

Most Auto Attendant settings can be found by choosing **Voice Mail > Auto Attendant**. The following is a list of common administrator tasks that can be accomplished for Auto Attendant administration:

- Call-in number

- Script choice

- Language

- Prompt choices

- Dial by first or last name

- Operator extension

- Schedule choice

Backup and Restore

Backup and restore options can be found under the Administration menu of the Cisco Unity Express GUI home page.

Backing up Cisco Unity Express requires the administrator to configure an FTP server (to use as the target server on which the backup files will be stored) and login credentials to access the FTP server.

Note   The login credentials supplied must have permission to upload, download, and make directories on the FTP server.

After an FTP server has been configured, the administrator must define what is to be backed up. The following list shows the three options available for backup:

- **Configuration:** Back up system configuration information

- **Data:** Back up voice-mail message content

- **Historical reporting:** Back up historical reporting information

After the administrator has defined the backup options, they can begin the backup by clicking the **Start Backup** button. Starting a backup is a manual process for Cisco Unity Express.

To restore a backup, the administrator can choose a backup from a list of successful backups maintained by Cisco Unity Express. Cisco Unity Express will retrieve the previously stored files from the configured FTP server.

Note   During both the backup and restore processes, Cisco Unity Express is taken offline and all user sessions are terminated. After the backup or restore process has completed, Cisco Unity Express must be manually brought back online by the administrator.

Reports

Reports can be found under the Reports menu of the Cisco Unity Express GUI home page. Cisco Unity Express offers administrators several levels of reporting:

- Voice mail

- Mailboxes

- Backup history

- Restore history

- Network Time Protocol
- Call history
- Real-time reports

These reports allow the administrator to monitor Cisco Unity Express to determine the heath of the system. From these reports, the administrator can determine trending information, such as how many mailboxes are in use, how many mailboxes can be added, how much storage is used by each subscriber, what is the total free storage space on the system, when was the last time the system was backed up, and which subscribers have the most activity.

CME Configuration

Another benefit of the Cisco Unity Express GUI is the capability to configure most CME CLI features. To add a phone in CME, you must first use the CLI to configure an e-phone; next, you need to add and assign an ephone-dn to the configured e-phone. All this work is CLI based. An administrator can now perform these same tasks with the common interface into CME provided by the Cisco Unity Express GUI.

The CME configuration options are located under the Configure and System menus of the Cisco Unity Express GUI home page.

Synchronizing and Saving Information

Because changes can be made to either the Cisco Unified CME CLI or the Cisco Unity Express GUI, it is possible to lose synchronization between the two. For example, if a phone is added using the CME CLI, it is possible that the Cisco Unity Express GUI may not be aware of the new phone. To correct this type of situation, Cisco Unity Express offers the capability to synchronize the changes between the CME and Cisco Unity Express.

After the CME and Cisco Unity Express have been synchronized, the Cisco Unity Express GUI offers the capability to save the current configuration of CME and Cisco Unity Express independently and restart Cisco Unity Express.

These options can be found under the Administration menu of the Cisco Unity Express GUI home page.

Subscriber Management

An end user, or subscriber, has the ability to manage their own user account via either the GUI or the TUI. This section discusses the common management features available to subscribers.

Graphical User Interface Subscriber Management

Like the administrator's Cisco Unity Express GUI, subscribers can open Microsoft Internet Explorer, version 6 or higher, and type **http://CUE-Server**, where *CUE-Server* is either the IP address of Cisco Unity Express or a hostname that can be resolved to an IP address. The subscriber will enter their username and password to log in to the GUI.

Note   The password entered here is the password that is configured in Cisco Unity Express, *not* the PIN. The password is used for GUI authentication, while the PIN is used for TUI authentication.

Figure 9.4 shows an example of the subscriber GUI home page configuration options after login.

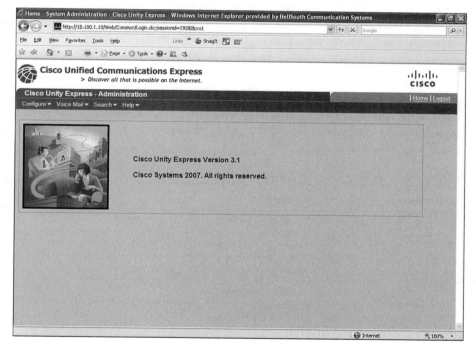

Figure 9.4   *Subscriber GUI Home Page*

Notice that the subscriber GUI home page is similar to the administrator GUI home page, but without as many configuration options. A subscriber (that is, someone who is not a member of the administrator's group) has permission to change only the configuration settings of their subscriber account. The common subscriber configuration options offered by Cisco Unity Express are as follows:

- Change password and PIN
- Configure zero-out extension
- Select language
- Enable alternate greeting
- View public distribution lists
- Configure private distribution lists
- Configure message notification
- Search local directory
- Obtain help

Telephony User Interface Subscriber Management

Cisco Unity Express offers subscribers a robust TUI to manage and customize their voice mailboxes. This section examines the typical subscriber TUI options.

Mailbox Options

Several options are available to the owner of a subscriber mailbox or a member of a GDM upon login. A greeting is played that announces the number of new and saved messages, after which the subscriber is prompted to choose the desired function. Table 9.14 lists these mailbox options.

Table 9.14   *Cisco Unity Express Mailbox Options*

Button Press	Option
1	Play new messages
2	Send a message
3	Play old messages
4	Setup options
9	Access GDM
0	Help
*	Exit

Note   If no new messages or old messages are present upon login, these options are not announced. If a GDM is not associated with this subscriber, this option is not announced.

Mailbox Setup Options

The mailbox setup options allow a subscriber to interact with the mailbox and customize the caller's experience when leaving a message. Table 9.15 lists the options available under the setup options menu (by pressing 4 in the mailbox options).

Table 9.15   *Mailbox Setup Options*

Button Press	Option
1	Greetings
2	Message settings
3	Personal settings
4	Language settings
0	Help
*	Exit

When the subscriber presses 1 to access the greetings options, the active greeting is identified and played to the subscriber. For example, if John Smith returns from vacation, logs in to his mailbox, and chooses setup options (button press 4) and then greetings (button press 1), he hears "Your current greeting is the alternate greeting... 'Thank you for calling John Smith. I am on vacation this week.'" John is then prompted to choose what he would like to do with his greeting. Table 9.16 lists the greeting options.

Table 9.16   *Greeting Options*

Button Press	Option
1	Re-record this greeting
2	Turn on/off alternate greeting
3	Edit greetings
4	Play all greetings
0	Help
*	Exit

The message settings options are found as button press 2 on the mailbox setup options menu. Table 9.17 lists the message settings options.

Table 9.17   *Message Settings*

Button Press	Option
1	Change message notification
4	Voice-mail distribution lists
0	Help
*	Exit

The personal settings options are found as button press 3 on the mailbox setup options menu. Table 9.18 lists the personal settings options.

Table 9.18   *Personal Settings*

Button Press	Option
1	Change password
2	Re-record the current recorded name
0	Help
*	Exit

Note   The change password option refers to the phone password (or PIN). It does not change the GUI password.

The language settings options are found as button press 4 on the mailbox setup options menu. Table 9.19 lists the language settings options.

Table 9.19   *Language Settings*

Button Press	Option
1	Select first installed language
2	Select second installed language
3	Select third installed language
4	Select fourth installed language
0	Help
*	Exit

Note   Language settings options 1 through 4 are available only if four languages are installed in Cisco Unity Express. If one language is installed, there will be only a single option, for the installed language. If two languages are installed on Cisco Unity Express, the subscriber will have a choice between the two installed languages. The number of languages installed is determined by the hardware platform Cisco Unity Express is installed on.

Notice that each menu has the option of button press 0 to obtain help and button press * to exit. By pressing 0 in any menu, the subscriber can receive instructions for configuring the options available in that specific menu. For example, pressing 0 in the language settings menu will provide language settings help, whereas pressing 0 in the message settings menu will provide message settings help. The button press * can be used in any menu to go back to the previous menu selection. For example, pressing the * key in the language setting menu returns the subscriber to the setup options menu.

Message Playback Options

The preceding section explored the options available that impact the presentation of the mailbox to a caller and how the subscriber can interact with a mailbox. This section discusses the options that a subscriber has after a message has been left in the subscriber's mailbox.

The receiver of a message has several options available to them to effectively handle the message. Some options dictate how the full message is treated, while other options affect the playback of the message content.

Table 9.20 lists the options available during playback of a received message.

Table 9.20   *Message Playback Options*

Button Press	Option
1	Restart message
2	Save message
3	Delete message
4	Reply to message
5	Forward message
6	Mark message new
7	Rewind message
8	Pause message
9	Fast-forward message
0	Help
*	Cancel

Record Message Options for the Caller

When a caller is routed to a subscriber's mailbox, they hear the active greeting of the mailbox. The caller has the option to bypass this greeting and proceed directly to leaving the message for the subscriber.

After the message has been left, the caller has the options defined in Table 9.21.

Table 9.21   *Record Message Options*

Button Press	Option
1	Send with normal priority
2	Send with urgent priority
3	Play recorded message
4	Re-record message
6	Cancel
#	Skip greeting

Exam Preparation Tasks

Review All the Key Topics

Review the most important topics in the chapter, noted with the key topics icon in the outer margin of the page. Table 9.22 lists and describes these key topics and identifies the page number on which each is found.

Table 9.22   *Key Topics for Chapter 9*

Key Topic Element	Description	Page Number
Table 9.2	Cisco Unity product comparison	309
List	Lists the four different Cisco Unity Express hardware platforms	310
Table 9.3	Cisco Unity Express modules and capabilities	312
Table 9.8	Cisco Unity Express licensing for CME	317
Table 9.11	Password and PIN settings	324
List	Message management and playback list	326
Table 9.12	Message type order and options	327
List	AA prompts list	336
Figure 9.3	Cisco Unity Express administrator GUI home page	343
List	User and group administration list	343–344
List	Voice-mail administration list	344
List	Auto Attendant administration list	344
Figure 9.4	Cisco Unity Express subscriber GUI home page	347
List	Subscriber configuration options list	347–349

Complete the Tables and Lists from Memory

Print a copy of Appendix C, "Memory Tables" (found on the CD), or at least the section for this chapter, and complete the tables and lists from memory. Appendix D, "Memory Tables Answer Key," also on the CD, includes completed tables and lists to check your work.

Definitions of Key Terms

Define the following key terms from this chapter, and check your answers in the glossary.

Cisco Unity Express

Automated Attendant (AA)

general delivery mailbox (GDM)

Cisco Unity Express greeting/prompt

Cisco Unity Express password/PIN

Cisco Unity Express administrator

Cisco Unity Express subscriber

Cisco Unity Express Advance Integration Module (AIM-CUE)

Cisco Unity Express Network Module (NM-CUE)

Cisco Unity Express Network Module with Enhanced Capability (NM-CUE-EC)

Cisco Unity Express Enhanced Network Module (NME-CUE)

message waiting indicator

message notifications

live reply and live record

public distribution list

private distribution list

integrated messaging

Voice Profile for Internet Mail (VPIM)

Cisco Unity Express Auto Attendant script

Cisco Unity Express custom scripting

Cisco Unity Express Editor

Administration via Telephone (AVT) system

Cisco Unity Express graphical user interface (GUI)

Cisco Unity Express telephony user interface (TUI)

VoiceView Express

mailbox subscriber features

mailbox caller features

Cisco Unity Express Installation and Upgrade: This section describes how the Cisco Unity Express software is loaded on the hardware platform.

Cisco Unity Express Configuration: This section discusses the configuration options available on Cisco Unity Express.

Cisco Unity Express Troubleshooting: This section explains basic troubleshooting methods for Cisco Unity Express.

CHAPTER 10

Cisco Unity Express Configuration

Chapter 9, "Cisco Unity Express Concepts," described and discussed the physical hardware of the Cisco Unity Express device as well as the features, functions, and benefits that Cisco Unity Express provides. This chapter focuses on how to configure the Cisco Unity Express module to provide these benefits.

"Do I Know This Already?" Quiz

The "Do I Know This Already?" quiz allows you to assess whether you should read this entire chapter or simply jump to the "Exam Preparation Tasks" section for review. If you are in doubt, read the entire chapter. Table 10.1 outlines the major headings in this chapter and the corresponding "Do I Know This Already?" quiz questions. You can find the answers in Appendix A, "Answers to the 'Do I Know This Already?' Quizzes."

Table 10.1 *"Do I Know This Already?" Foundation Topics Section-to-Question Mapping*

Foundation Topics Section	Questions Covered in This Section
Cisco Unity Express Installation and Upgrades	1–4
Cisco Unity Express Configuration	5–9
Cisco Unity Express Troubleshooting	10–12

1. How do you make a connection to the Cisco Unity Express CLI?

   a. Telnet to the IP address of Cisco Unity Express

   b. Connect a console cable to the console port of Cisco Unity Express

   c. Issue the **service-module service-engine** *module/port* **session** command from within Cisco Unified CME

   d. Issue the **cue** *module/port* **session** command from within Cisco Unified CME

2. What type of server does Cisco Unity Express require to download software?

   a. TFTP server

   b. FTP server

   c. Web server

   d. Cisco Unity Express does not require a server.

3. When would the **software download** upgrade command be used?

   a. When performing either a fresh install or an upgrade from Cisco Unity Express version 1.x and higher.

   b. Only when performing an upgrade from Cisco Unity Express version 1.x and higher.

   c. When performing an upgrade from Cisco Unity Express version 2.3.4 only.

   d. Never; Cisco Unity Express does not currently support upgrades.

4. Which features are enabled by Cisco Unity Express licenses? (Choose three.)

   a. Support for either Cisco Unified Communications Manager or Cisco Unified Communications Manager Express (CME)

   b. Number of recording hours supported

   c. Number of subscriber mailboxes supported

   d. Number of IVR ports supported

   e. Number of concurrent system ports

   f. Number of languages supported

5. Which of the following is not configured by the Cisco Unity Express post-installation configuration tool?

   a. Cisco Unity Express's IP address

   b. Cisco Unity Express's hostname

   c. Cisco Unity Express's DNS

   d. Cisco Unity Express's NTP

   e. Cisco Unity Express's time zone

   f. Cisco Unity Express's administrative credentials

6. Which server is curial to Cisco Unity Express?

   a. NTP

   b. DHCP

   c. DNS

   d. SMTP

7. Which of the following is not a Cisco Unified CME dial-peer configuration used by Cisco Unity Express applications? (*X* represents digits.)

   a. **destination-pattern** *XXXX*

   b. **session protocol sipv2**

   c. **session target ipv4:***X.X.X.X*

   d. **port** *module/port*

   e. **dtmf-relay sip-notify**

   f. **codec g711ulaw**

   g. **no vad**

8. How is MWI configured on Cisco Unified CME? (Choose two.)

   a. A single dial-peer is configured to turn MWI on and off.

   b. One dial-peer is configured to turn MWI on and a second dial-peer is configured to turn MWI off.

   c. A single ephone-dn is configured to turn MWI on and off.

   d. One ephone-dn is configured to turn MWI on and a second ephone-dn is configured to turn MWI off.

   e. A static string of digits is configured followed by a number of dots equal to the length of the CME extensions.

   f. A number of dots equal to the length of the CME extensions is configured followed by a static string of digits.

9. What is not configured in the Cisco Unity Express Initialization Wizard?

    a. Users

    b. Passwords

    c. Mailbox defaults

    d. Cisco Unity Express's administrative credentials

    e. Cisco Unified CME's administrative credentials

10. How can you tell if the Cisco Unity Express module is in a steady state?

    a. Issue the command **show cue** *module/port* **state** from the Cisco Unity Express CLI

    b. Issue the command **show service-module service-engine** *module/port* **status** from the Cisco Unity Express CLI

    c. Issue the command **show cue** *module/port* **state** from the CME CLI

    d. Issue the command **show service-module service-engine** *module/port* **status** from the CME CLI

11. Which **debug** command can be used in Cisco Unified CME to troubleshoot MWI problems?

    a. debug dial-peer mwi

    b. debug ephone mwi

    c. debug service-module service-engine mwi

    d. debug mwi

12. Which **debug** command can you use in Cisco Unity Express to troubleshoot MWI problems?

    a. debug cue mwi

    b. debug service-module service-engine mwi

    c. Cisco Unity Express CLI does not use the **debug** command; it uses the **trace** command instead.

    d. None of the options provided are correct.

Foundation Topics

Cisco Unity Express Installation and Upgrade

As discussed in Chapter 9, Cisco Unity Express is a hardware module that is installed in a Cisco router. Unlike the Cisco Unified Communications Manager Express (CME) IOS-based operating system, the Cisco Unity Express operating system is Linux based. This means that Cisco Unified CME and Cisco Unity Express are two distinct systems. Because of this separation, Cisco Unity Express software must be loaded and configured on the Cisco Unity Express module before it can provide voice-mail, auto-attendant, and other functions to Cisco Unified CME or Cisco Unified Communications Manager. This section examines what is needed to load Cisco Unity Express software on the Cisco Unity Express module.

Installing the Cisco Unity Express Module

The AIM-CUE module is the only Cisco Unity Express module that is installed inside a Cisco router. The NM-CUE, NM-CUE-EC, and NME-CUE modules are external hardware modules that are inserted into an external network module slot on a Cisco router.

Note   Refer to Chapter 9 for detailed information on router and IOS support for the different Cisco Unity Express modules as well as notes about hot swapping and slot placement.

Once the Cisco Unity Express module has been successfully installed in the router and power is applied, a service interface will appear. Example 10.1 shows abbreviated output from the **show run** command that illustrates the new interface.

Example 10.1   *Interface Service-Engine*

```
CME# show run
!
! Output omitted for brevity
!
interface Loopback0
ip address 10.100.1.1 255.255.255.0
!
interface FastEthernet0/1
 ip address 10.1.1.1 255.255.255.0
!
interface Service-Engine1/0
 !
```

In this example, the Cisco Unity Express module, a NM-CUE, is installed in slot 1, unit 0, creating the interface service-engine 1/0. Note that the slot number is dependant upon the physical network module slot that Cisco Unity Express is installed in. If Cisco Unity Express had been installed in slot 2 of a Cisco 2821, the service-engine would be assigned slot 2, unit 0. The AIM-CUE module, which is installed inside the Cisco router, not in a network module slot, is always assigned a service-engine of slot 0, unit 1.

First, the service-engine must be assigned an IP address. This can be accomplished using the **ip address** command on the service-engine interface; however, this approach requires the use of a new IP subnet that must be propagated to all routers in the network. The best practice is to assign an IP address to the service-engine using the **ip unnumbered** command, as shown in Example 10.2.

Example 10.2   ip unnumbered *Command*

```
CME# show run
!
! Output omitted for brevity
!
interface Loopback0
ip address 10.100.1.1 255.255.255.0
!
interface FastEthernet0/0
 ip address 10.1.1.1 255.255.255.0
!
interface Service-Engine1/0
 ip unnumbered Loopback0
!
```

The **ip unnumbered** command allows the service-engine to share the IP address of another interface, avoiding the issue of dedicating an IP subnet to the service-engine. In this example, the service engine is sharing an IP address with interface Loopback 0, which is configured to use 10.100.1.1. A loopback interface was chosen because this address is always in an up state even if other interfaces on the router are down because of circuit failures. This means that the service-engine will also remain in an up state. For this reason, using **ip unnumbered** and specifying a loopback interface is best practice.

Next, the service-module must be assigned an IP address and a default gateway. You can think of the service-module as the internal interface of Cisco Unity Express, while the service-engine is the external interface of Cisco Unity Express. Traffic from Cisco Unity Express to an endpoint, such as an IP phone, will originate from the service-module, pass to the service-engine, and then route to the endpoint. Traffic from the endpoint will be forwarded to the service-engine, pass to the service-module, and then route to the Cisco Unity Express application.

Example 10.3 shows abbreviated output from the **show run** command that illustrates the service-module configuration.

Example 10.3   *Displaying the Service Module Configuration*

```
CME# show run
!
! Output omitted for brevity
!
interface Loopback0
ip address 10.100.1.1 255.255.255.0
!
interface FastEthernet0/0
 ip address 10.1.1.1 255.255.255.0
!
interface Service-Engine1/0
ip unnumbered Loopback0
 service-module ip address 10.100.1.10 255.255.255.0
 service-module ip default-gateway 10.100.1.1
!
```

In this example, the service-module is assigned an IP address of 10.100.1.10 using the **service-module ip address** command. Notice that the service-module is on the same IP subnet as the IP address of the service-engine, which is Loopback 0 because the **ip unnumbered** command was used.

Next, the default gateway is configured using the **service-module ip default-gateway** command. The default gateway is the IP address configured for the service-engine, or 10.100.1.1 in this example. Remember that traffic from Cisco Unity Express uses the service-module as an originating point. There needs to be a way for this traffic to be passed to the service-engine in order for the traffic to be routed out to the endpoint. The way this is accomplished is by assigning the IP address of the service-engine as the default gateway to the service-module.

Finally, a path needs to be added for traffic sent to Cisco Unity Express. Because the service-module is the internal interface of Cisco Unity Express, endpoint traffic destined for Cisco Unity Express cannot access this interface directly without passing through the external interface, the service-engine. This requires that a static IP route be configured in the router to redirect all traffic destined for the service-module to the service-engine interface. Example 10.4 adds the IP route statement and shows all IOS configurations needed to provide IP connectivity to the Cisco Unity Express module.

Example 10.4   *Complete Cisco Unified CME Configuration for Cisco Unity Express IP Connectivity*

```
CME# show run
!
! Output omitted for brevity
!
interface Loopback0
```

continues

Example 10.4   *Complete Cisco Unified CME Configuration for Cisco Unity Express IP Connectivity   continued*

```
ip address 10.100.1.1 255.255.255.0
!
interface FastEthernet0/0
 ip address 10.1.1.1 255.255.255.0
!
interface Service-Engine1/0
ip unnumbered Loopback0
service-module ip address 10.100.1.10 255.255.255.0
 service-module ip default-gateway 10.100.1.1
!
ip route 10.100.1.10 255.255.255.255 Service-Engine1/0
!
```

Notice that this static route is a host route, because the subnet mask is 255.25.255.255. This means that packets destined for 10.100.1.10 alone are routed to the service-engine; no other addresses in this subnet will be routed to the service-engine.

At this point the Cisco Unity Express module has been installed and has IP connectivity.

To connect to the command-line interface (CLI) of the Cisco Unity Express module, use the **session** option on the **service-module service-engine** command. Example 10.5 shows the command syntax used to connect to the CLI of a Cisco Unity Express module installed in slot 1/0.

Example 10.5   *Connecting to the Cisco Unity Express CLI*

```
CME# service-module service-Engine 1/0 session
Trying 10.100.1.1, 2066 ... Open
CUE>
```

> **Note**   After issuing this command, the session may appear to hang or freeze and not return the CLI prompt. Press the Enter key to access the CLI prompt.

Installing and Upgrading the Cisco Unity Express Software

After you have installed the service-engine in the Cisco router, configured it for IP connectivity, and made a CLI connection, you can load the Cisco Unity Express software on the hardware module.

Table 10.2 lists the files that make up the Cisco Unity Express voice-mail and auto-attendant software.

Table 10.2 *Cisco Unity Express Voice-Mail and Auto-Attendant Software*

Filename	Description
cue-vm-k9.nm-aim.3.1.x.pkg	The main software package file
cue-installer.nm-aim.3.1.x	Installer image (also known as the Helper image)
cue-vm-installer-k9.nm-aim.3.1.x.prt1	Installer payload file
cue-vm-full-k9.nm-aim.3.1.x.prt1	Voice-mail application
cue-vm-upgrade-k9.nm-aim.2.3.4_3.1.x.prt1	Package file to upgrade from version 2.3.4
cue-vm-langpack.nm-aim.3.1.x.pkg1	Language package file
cue-vm-en_US-langpack.nm-aim.3.1.x.prt1	English (U.S.) language package

Note   Refer to Chapter 9 for more information about the Cisco Unity Express software files.

File Transfer Protocol (FTP) is used to load the Cisco Unity Express software on the Cisco Unity Express hardware platform. This means that you will need to copy the files to an FTP server that Cisco Unity Express can access. There are several freeware and shareware FTP server applications that can be used for this process.

Cisco Unity Express software can be loaded as an upgrade from version 2.3.4 to version 3.1. In an upgrade, messages and Cisco Unity Express configurations are retained; however, a full backup of Cisco Unity Express is recommended before the upgrade. To upgrade from any other versions of Cisco Unity Express to version 3.1, a clean install is required. A clean install will delete messages and Cisco Unity Express configuration, so a full backup is required prior to the clean install.

Once the Cisco Unity Express software files have been copied to an FTP server, you have two options for installing or upgrading Cisco Unity Express:

- Copy the software to the Cisco Unity Express hardware platform and run it locally

- Run the software from the FTP server

The **software download** command is used to copy the Cisco Unity Express files to the Cisco Unity Express hardware platform without performing a clean install or an upgrade. Table 10.3 lists the options of the **software download** [{*server*} | {*clean*} | {*upgrade*} | {*status*} | {*abort*}] command.

Table 10.3   software download *Command*

Option	Explanation
software download server url ftp://*server-ip-address*[/*dir*] [**username** *username* **password** *password*]	*server-ip-address*[/*dir*] refers to the IP address and the directory of the FTP server.
software download clean {*package-file-name* | **url ftp:**//*ftp-server-ip-address*/ *package-file-name*}	*package-file-name* refers to the name of the file to be downloaded, while *ftp-server-ip-address* refers to the IP address of the FTP server that contains the file to be loaded. If the **software download server** command has been previously configured, the **url ftp** option is not needed.
software download upgrade {*package-file-name* | **url ftp:**//*ftp-server-ip-address*/ *package-file-name*}	*package-file-name* refers to the name of the file to be downloaded, while *ftp-server-ip-address* refers to the IP address of the FTP server that contains the file to be loaded. If the **software download server** command has been previously configured, the **url ftp** option is not needed.
software download status	This command reports the status of a software download currently in progress.
software download abort	This command is used to cancel a software download that is currently in progress.

The following command syntax shows that 10.1.1.11 is the FTP server, cue-vm-k9.nm-aim.3.1.1.pkg is the main software package file, and the **upgrade** option is used, indicating that the current version of Cisco Unity Express is version 2.3.4 and Cisco Unity Express will be upgraded to version 3.1:

Key
Topic

```
CUE#
CUE# software download upgrade url ftp://10.1.1.11/cue-vm-k9.nm-aim.3.1.1.pkg
```

The following syntax shows the same command using the **clean** option, indicating that this will be a fresh install of Cisco Unity Express version 3.1. If a previous version of Cisco Unity Express resides on the hardware platform, the existing messages and configuration must be backed up and restored if they need to be retained.

```
CUE#
CUE# software download clean url ftp://10.1.1.11/cue-vm-k9.nm-aim.3.1.1.pkg
```

Running the **software download** command is useful if your FTP server is not local to Cisco Unity Express or if you need to upgrade after hours and want to have the software local to Cisco Unity Express, ready to implement at the designated time.

The **software download status** command can be used to verify that the Cisco Unity Express software has been copied to the Cisco Unity Express hardware module. Example 10.6 illustrates a successful software load.

Example 10.6   software download status *Command*

```
CUE# software download status
Download request completed successfully.
CUE#
```

The **software install** command is used to load or upgrade the Cisco Unity Express software. Similar to the **software download** command, the **software install** command can be used with the **upgrade** option to upgrade from version 2.3.4 to version 3.1, or with the **clean** option to perform a fresh install. Table 10.4 lists the options of the **software install** [{clean} | {upgrade}] command.

Table 10.4   software install *Command*

Command	Option and Function
software install clean {*package-file-name* | **url ftp:**//*ftp-server-ip-address*/package-file-name}	*package-file-name* refers to the name of the file to be installed, while *ftp-server-ip-address* refers to the IP address of the FTP server that contains the file to be loaded.
	If the **software download server** command has been previously configured, the **url ftp** option is not needed.
software install upgrade {*package-file-name* | **url ftp:**//*ftp-server-ip-address*/*package-file-name*}	*package-file-name* refers to the name of the file to be installed, while *ftp-server-ip-address* refers to the IP address of the FTP server that contains the file to be loaded.
	If the **software download server** command has been previously configured, the **url ftp** option is not needed.

Example 10.7 shows the **software install** syntax using the **clean** option, where the Cisco Unity Express software is being installed directly from the FTP server.

Example 10.7   software install clean *Command*

```
CUE# software install clean url ftp://10.1.1.11/cue-vm-k9.nm-aim.3.1.1.pkg

WARNING:: This command will download the necessary software to
WARNING:: complete a clean install.  It is recommended that a backup be done
WARNING:: before installing software.

WARNING:: The system will briefly be brought to an offline state
WARNING:: This will terminate any active call and prevent new calls
WARNING:: from being processed.

Would you like to continue? [n] y
```

Choosing **yes** at the prompt shown in Example 10.7 causes the Cisco Unity Express software to begin to load onto the hardware platform. The Cisco Unity Express files continue to be downloaded and validated until the installer is prompted to choose the appropriate language files. Example 10.8 shows the language file of U.S. English being installed.

Example 10.8   *Choosing Language Files*

```
Maximum 5 language add-ons allowed for this platform.
Please select language(s) to install from the following list:

Language Installation Menu:

 # Selected   SKU    Language Name (version)
-----------------------------------------------------------------------
 1            ITA    CUE Voicemail Italian (3.0.0.0)
 2            ESP    CUE Voicemail European Spanish (3.0.0.0)
 3            ENU    CUE Voicemail US English (3.0.0.0)
 4            FRA    CUE Voicemail European French (3.0.0.0)
 5            ESO    CUE Voicemail Latin American Spanish (3.0.0.0)
 6            ESM    CUE Voicemail Mexican Spanish (3.0.0.0)
 7            NLD    CUE Voicemail Dutch (3.0.0.19)
 8            SVE    CUE Voicemail Swedish (3.0.0.19)
 9            FRC    CUE Voicemail Canadian French (3.0.0.0)
10            ENG    CUE Voicemail UK English (3.0.0.0)
11            DEU    CUE Voicemail German (3.0.0.0)
12            DAN    CUE Voicemail Danish (3.0.0.0)
13            PTB    CUE Voicemail Brazilian Portuguese (3.0.0.0)
14            KOR    CUE Voicemail Korean (3.0.0.0)
15            CHS    CUE Voicemail Mandarin Chinese (3.0.0.0)
16            JPN    CUE Voicemail Japanese (3.0.0.0)
-----------------------------------------------------------------------
```

```
Available commands are:
# - enter the number for the language to select one
r # - remove the language for given #
i # - more information about the language for given #
x - Done with language selection

Enter Command:3

Language Installation Menu:

 #  Selected   SKU     Language Name (version)
----------------------------------------------------------------
 1             ITA     CUE Voicemail Italian (3.0.0.0)
 2             ESP     CUE Voicemail European Spanish (3.0.0.0)
 3      *      ENU     CUE Voicemail US English (3.0.0.0)
 4             FRA     CUE Voicemail European French (3.0.0.0)
 5             ESO     CUE Voicemail Latin American Spanish (3.0.0.0)
 6             ESM     CUE Voicemail Mexican Spanish (3.0.0.0)
 7             NLD     CUE Voicemail Dutch (3.0.0.19)
 8             SVE     CUE Voicemail Swedish (3.0.0.19)
 9             FRC     CUE Voicemail Canadian French (3.0.0.0)
10             ENG     CUE Voicemail UK English (3.0.0.0)
11             DEU     CUE Voicemail German (3.0.0.0)
12             DAN     CUE Voicemail Danish (3.0.0.0)
13             PTB     CUE Voicemail Brazilian Portuguese (3.0.0.0)
14             KOR     CUE Voicemail Korean (3.0.0.0)
15             CHS     CUE Voicemail Mandarin Chinese (3.0.0.0)
16             JPN     CUE Voicemail Japanese (3.0.0.0)
----------------------------------------------------------------

Available commands are:
# - enter the number for the language to select one
r # - remove the language for given #
i # - more information about the language for given #
x - Done with language selection

Enter Command:x
ui_install scripts executed successfully.
CUE#
```

Although U.S. English was the only language chosen in this example, the NM-CUE module used in the example supports up to five languages.

> **Note** Refer to Chapter 9 for the number of languages supported by each Cisco Unity Express hardware platform.

After you choose languages, enter an **x** to instruct Cisco Unity Express that all desired languages have been selected and to proceed with the installation.

At this point the system will be put back into an offline state as the Cisco Unity Express language files are installed. Upon completion of the installation, Cisco Unity Express will perform a cleanup of the downloaded installation files and automatically reboot the Cisco Unity Express module to bring the system into an online state, using the upgraded version.

Adding and Verifying Cisco Unity Express Licenses

The license file dictates the following options for Cisco Unity Express:

- Support for either Cisco Unified Communications Manager or Cisco Unified CME
- Number of general delivery mailboxes (GDM) supported
- Number of subscriber mailboxes supported
- Number of IVR ports supported

> **Note** As discussed in Chapter 9, the hardware platform that Cisco Unity Express resides on places a constraint of maximum supported ports and mailboxes as well. Therefore, the license file cannot exceed the limits of the hardware platform.

Installing a Cisco Unity Express license follows the same process as installing the Cisco Unity Express software. Example 10.9 shows a Cisco Unity Express license file being loaded on an FTP server. This license file enables support for CME and 100 mailboxes.

Example 10.9 *Installing Cisco Unity Express Licenses*

```
CUE# software install clean url ftp://10.1.1.11/cue-vm-license_100mbx_cme_3.1.1.pkg

WARNING:: This command will install the necessary software to
WARNING:: complete a clean install.  It is recommended that a backup be done
WARNING:: before installing software.

WARNING:: The system will briefly be brought to an offline state
WARNING:: This will terminate any active call and prevent new calls
WARNING:: from being processed.

Would you like to continue? [n] y
```

```
Downloading ftp cue-vm-license_100mbx_cme_3.1.1.pkg
Bytes downloaded :  5342


Validating package signature ... done
compatibility mode
 - Parsing package manifest files... complete.
Validating installed manifests ............complete.
 - Checking Package dependencies... complete.
 - Checking Manifest dependencies for subsystems in the install candidate list..
 .
complete
The system will be brought to offline state for a brief period
and will be brought back to online state automatically
No work order produced.
The system is back in online state
Performing Hot install ...starting_phase:
install-files.sh /dwnld/.hot_work_order
install_file  /dwnld/pkgdata/cue-vm-license_100mbx_cme_3.1.1.pkg 2 __LICENSE__ none
voicemail_lic.sig
Size of buff is: 65536
65536 bytes written
55296+0 records in
108+0 records out
901
Reading 901 from input stream ...


Check license policies:
max_mailboxes=100
max_ivr_ports=
ivr_incremental=
mailbox_incremental=


add_file /dwnld/pkgdata/cue-vm-license_100mbx_cme_3.1.1.pkg 1 / /sw/installed/
  manifest/lmanifest.signed none
Remove  //dwnld/pkgdata/cue-vm-license_100mbx_cme_3.1.1.pkg
Remove  //dwnld/.install_started
Size of buff is: 65536
65536 bytes written
Reading License... Parsing...
100 MAILBOX LICENSE
/tmp/license/voicemail_lic.sig
done
 complete.


 Important:: A Reload is required in order for the new License to take effect.
CUE#
```

Notice that the name of the license file in Example 10.9 is cue-vm-license_100mbx_cme_3.1.1.pkg. From this name you can deduce the number of mailboxes supported (100) and the type of IP PBX (Cisco Unified CME) supported. This means that Cisco Unity Express will support a CME installation with up to 100 mailboxes. If Cisco Unity Express needed to support 100 mailboxes on a Cisco Unified Communications Manager installation, the cue-vm-license_100mbx_ccm_3.1.1.pkg license file would have been installed. The two licenses are mutually exclusive, meaning that a single Cisco Unity Express cannot support both a Cisco Unified CME installation and a Cisco Unified Communications Manager installation simultaneously.

Note   After the Cisco Unity Express Initialization Wizard has been completed (as described later in this chapter), the license cannot be changed between CME and CCM support without a fresh install of the Cisco Unity Express software.

Once the license file has been installed on Cisco Unity Express, you can use the **show software** command to verify the number of licensed mailboxes and the IP PBX supported. Table 10.5 lists the options of the **show software** command.

Table 10.5   show software *Command*

Command	Option and Function
show software {directory | download server | licenses | packages | versions}	The **directory** option lists the contents of the software directory.
	The **download server** option displays the IP address of the download server if configured.
	The **licenses** option displays the installed license files.
	The **packages** option lists the configured Cisco Unity Express application packages.
	The **versions** option displays the current versions of all configured Cisco Unity Express applications.

Example 10.10 shows the output from the **show software license** command after the cue-vm-license_100mbx_cme_3.1.1.pkg license file has been loaded on an NM-CUE module.

Example 10.10   *Verifying Cisco Unified CME Support*

```
CUE# show software license
Installed license files:
 - voicemail_lic.sig : 100 MAILBOX LICENSE


Core:
 - Application mode: CCME
 - Total usable system ports: 8


Voicemail/Auto Attendant:
 - Max system mailbox capacity time: 6000
 - Default # of general delivery mailboxes: 20
 - Default # of personal mailboxes: 100

 - Max # of configurable mailboxes: 120


Interactive Voice Response:
 - Max # of IVR ports: Not Available


Languages:
 - Max installed languages: 5
 - Max enabled languages: 5
CUE#
```

Notice that Cisco Unity Express now has the capability of hosting 100 mailboxes and can be configured to support Cisco Unified CME. By default, an additional 20 mailboxes can be configured as GDMs. As discussed in Chapter 9, the NM-CUE module supports eight system ports, 100 hours of recording time, and five languages.

Example 10.11 shows the output from the **show software license** command after the cue-vm-license_100mbx_ccm_3.1.1.pkg license file has been loaded on an NM-CUE module.

Example 10.11   *Verifying Cisco Unified Communications Manager Support*

```
CUE# show software license
Installed license files:
 - voicemail_lic.sig : 100 MAILBOX LICENSE


Core:
 - Application mode: CCM
 - Total usable system ports: 8


Voicemail/Auto Attendant:
 - Max system mailbox capacity time: 6000
 - Default # of general delivery mailboxes: 20
 - Default # of personal mailboxes: 100
```

continues

Example 10.11   *Verifying Cisco Unified Communications Manager Support   continued*

```
- Max # of configurable mailboxes: 120

Interactive Voice Response:
- Max # of IVR ports: Not Available

Languages:
- Max installed languages: 5
- Max enabled languages: 5
CUE#
```

Notice that the only difference between Example 10.10 and 10.11 is the IP PBX that Cisco Unity Express will support. In Example 10.11, Cisco Unity Express will be configured to support Cisco Unified Communications Manager.

Cisco Unity Express Configuration

This section examines the configuration needed for Cisco Unity Express to communicate with Cisco Unified CME. This includes the final Cisco Unity Express CLI configurations and the Cisco Unity Express web initialization. The CME CLI configurations needed for interoperability between Cisco Unified CME and Cisco Unity Express are also discussed.

Cisco Unity Express Post-Installation Configuration

After an installation or upgrade of Cisco Unity Express software, the system will run the service-engine post-installation configuration tool. This tool allows the installer to implement the following Cisco Unity Express configurations:

- Hostname

- Domain name

- Primary and secondary Domain Name System (DNS) servers

- Primary and secondary Network Time Protocol (NTP) servers

- Time zone

- Administrative credentials

Example 10.12 shows modified output from the post-installation configuration tool (output not relevant to this example has been removed).

Example 10.12   *Post-Installation Configuration Tool*

```
IMPORTANT::

IMPORTANT::       Welcome to Cisco Systems Service Engine

IMPORTANT::        post installation configuration tool.

IMPORTANT::

IMPORTANT:: This is a one time process which will guide

IMPORTANT:: you through initial setup of your Service Engine.

IMPORTANT:: Once run, this process will have configured

IMPORTANT:: the system for your location.

IMPORTANT::

IMPORTANT:: If you do not wish to continue, the system will be halted

IMPORTANT:: so it can be safely removed from the router.

IMPORTANT::


Do you wish to start configuration now (y,n)? y

Are you sure (y,n)? y


Enter Hostname

  (my-hostname, or enter to use se-10-100-1-10): cue


Enter Domain Name

  (mydomain.com, or enter to use localdomain): cisco.com


Would you like to use DNS (y,n)?y


Enter IP Address of the Primary DNS Server

  (IP address): 10.1.1.15

Found server 10.1.1.15


Enter IP Address of the Secondary DNS Server (other than Primary)

  (IP address, or enter to bypass): 10.1.1.16

Found server 10.1.1.16


Enter Fully Qualified Domain Name(FQDN: e.g. myhost.mydomain.com)

or IP address of the Primary NTP server

  (FQDN or IP address, or enter for 10.100.1.1): 10.100.1.1

Found server 10.100.1.1


Enter Fully Qualified Domain Name(FQDN: e.g. myhost.mydomain.com)

or IP address of the Secondary NTP Server

  (FQDN or IP address, or enter to bypass):


Please identify a location so that time zone rules can be set correctly.
```

continues

Example 10.12   *Post-Installation Configuration Tool*   *continued*

```
Please select a continent or ocean.
1) Africa             4) Arctic Ocean     7) Australia       10) Pacific Ocean
2) Americas           5) Asia             8) Europe
3) Antarctica         6) Atlantic Ocean   9) Indian Ocean
#? 2


Please select a country.
 1) Anguilla              18) Ecuador            35) Paraguay
 2) Antigua & Barbuda     19) El Salvador        36) Peru
 3) Argentina             20) French Guiana      37) Puerto Rico
 4) Aruba                 21) Greenland          38) St Kitts & Nevis
 5) Bahamas               22) Grenada            39) St Lucia
 6) Barbados              23) Guadeloupe         40) St Pierre & Miquelon
 7) Belize                24) Guatemala          41) St Vincent
 8) Bolivia               25) Guyana             42) Suriname
 9) Brazil                26) Haiti              43) Trinidad & Tobago
10) Canada                27) Honduras           44) Turks & Caicos Is
11) Cayman Islands        28) Jamaica            45) United States
12) Chile                 29) Martinique         46) Uruguay
13) Colombia              30) Mexico             47) Venezuela
14) Costa Rica            31) Montserrat         48) Virgin Islands (UK)
15) Cuba                  32) Netherlands Antilles  49) Virgin Islands (US)
16) Dominica              33) Nicaragua
17) Dominican Republic    34) Panama
#? 45


Please select one of the following time zone regions.
 1) Eastern Time
 2) Eastern Time - Michigan - most locations
 3) Eastern Time - Kentucky - Louisville area
 4) Eastern Time - Kentucky - Wayne County
 5) Eastern Standard Time - Indiana - most locations
 6) Eastern Standard Time - Indiana - Crawford County
 7) Eastern Standard Time - Indiana - Starke County
 8) Eastern Standard Time - Indiana - Switzerland County
 9) Central Time
10) Central Time - Michigan - Wisconsin border
11) Central Time - North Dakota - Oliver County
12) Mountain Time
13) Mountain Time - south Idaho & east Oregon
14) Mountain Time - Navajo
15) Mountain Standard Time - Arizona
16) Pacific Time
```

```
17) Alaska Time
18) Alaska Time - Alaska panhandle
19) Alaska Time - Alaska panhandle neck
20) Alaska Time - west Alaska
21) Aleutian Islands
22) Hawaii
#? 1


The following information has been given:


        United States
        Eastern Time


Therefore TZ='America/New_York' will be used.
Is the above information OK?
1) Yes
2) No
#? 1


Configuring the system. Please wait...
Changing owners and file permissions.
Change owners and permissions complete.


IMPORTANT::
IMPORTANT::            Administrator Account Creation
IMPORTANT::
IMPORTANT:: Create an administrator account. With this account,
IMPORTANT:: you can log in to the Cisco Unity Express GUI and
IMPORTANT:: run the initialization wizard.
IMPORTANT::


Enter administrator user ID:
  (user ID): cueadmin
Enter password for admin:
  (password): cisco
Confirm password for admin by reentering it:
  (password): cisco


SYSTEM ONLINE
cue>
```

The service-engine post-installation configuration tool begins by prompting the installer to start the configuration, followed by a prompt confirming that the configuration process should proceed.

Next the installer is prompted to either enter a hostname for the Cisco Unity Express module or take the default hostname. The default hostname in this example is se-10-100-1-10, which is "se" followed by the IP address of the service-engine. In this example, the hostname of **cue** was specified over the default hostname.

A prompt for a domain name follows. The installer has the option of entering the company's domain name or using the default domain name of localdomain. In this example, the domain name is configured as cisco.com.

The installer is asked if DNS will be used by the Cisco Unity Express module. If yes, the installer is prompted to enter the primary and secondary DNS server IP addresses. If no, a message appears stating that IP addresses must be used for all configurations.

Note   Although Cisco Unity Express has the capability to use DNS to resolve IP addresses from hostnames, this means that the DNS server must be operational and accessible for Cisco Unity Express to interact with any host or endpoint that is defined by a hostname. For this reason, specifying IP addressing over hostnames is best practice.

Next the installer is prompted to enter the IP address of the primary and secondary NTP servers. If a DNS server has been configured in the previous step, the installer has the option of entering the fully qualified domain name (FQDN) of the NTP server. Unlike DNS, Cisco Unity Express assumes that an NTP server will be configured, because time is critical to the delivery and time-stamp information of voice-mail messages. In this example, Cisco Unity Express is configured to use Cisco Unified CME as the NTP server because CME is synchronized with an authoritative NTP server.

For Cisco Unity Express to be configured for the proper time zone, the installer is prompted to enter their location, country, and time zone. In this example, Americas, United States, and Eastern Time were chosen. This causes Cisco Unity Express to ask if it is in the same time zone as New York City.

Finally, administrative credentials are entered. These credentials will be used when accessing the Cisco Unity Express GUI later in this chapter. In Example 10.12, the administrative user ID is configured as cueadmin and the password is configured as cisco.

At this point, Cisco Unity Express has completed the post-installation configuration and the system is brought online.

Configuring Cisco Unified CME to Support Cisco Unity Express

This section focuses on the Cisco Unified CME configuration necessary to support Cisco Unity Express. This includes the HTTP server configuration, dial-peer configurations, message waiting indicator (MWI) configurations, and changes required in the telephone services configuration of Cisco Unified CME.

HTTP Server Options

Although Cisco Unity Express does support CLI configuration, most administration and management of Cisco Unity Express is accomplished via a web browser. Because Cisco Unity Express is a module inserted into a Cisco router, the router itself must have the capability to serve HTTP traffic. On a Cisco router, this capability is controlled with the **ip http** command. To turn on the HTTP server on a Cisco router, use the **ip http server** command. Once the HTTP server has been enabled, the server needs to be configured to host the proper files to the HTTP clients. The HTTP server is configured to point to the proper files using the **ip http path** command. Example 10.13 shows the configuration necessary to enable and configure HTTP support on a Cisco router.

Example 10.13   *Enabling the HTTP Server*

```
CME# show run
!
! Output omitted for brevity
!
ip http server
ip http path flash:
!
```

In this example, the HTTP server is enabled on the Cisco router, and the files being hosted by the server are located in the router's flash memory.

When the HTTP server is enabled on a Cisco router, the authentication method uses the enable password configured on the router. An authentication, authorization, and accounting (AAA) server or a locally configured username and password should be used to provide security to the HTTP server. This can be accomplished using the **ip http authentication** command with either the **aaa** or **local** option. Example 10.14 shows the HTTP server using AAA authentication.

Example 10.14   *HTTP Server Using AAA Authentication*

```
CME# show run
!
! Output omitted for brevity
!
ip http server
ip http path flash:
!
ip http authentication aaa
!
```

Dial Peers for Cisco Unity Express

A dial peer is used to route a telephony call based upon the number that is dialed. In the case of Cisco Unity Express, dial peers are used to route calls from Cisco Unified CME to Cisco Unity Express. Example 10.15 shows the dial-peer configuration needed to route calls inbound to Cisco Unity Express.

Example 10.15   *Dial Peer Configuration for Cisco Unity Express*

```
CME# show run
!
! Output omitted for brevity
!
dial-peer voice 7000 voip
 description VoiceMail
 destination-pattern 7000
 session protocol sipv2
 session target ipv4:10.100.1.10
 dtmf-relay sip-notify
 codec g711ulaw
 no vad
!
dial-peer voice 7001 voip
 description AutoAttendant
 destination-pattern 7001
 session protocol sipv2
 session target ipv4:10.100.1.10
 dtmf-relay sip-notify
 codec g711ulaw
 no vad
!
dial-peer voice 7002 voip
 description AVT
 destination-pattern 7002
 session protocol sipv2
 session target ipv4:10.100.1.10
 dtmf-relay sip-notify
 codec g711ulaw
 no vad
!
```

Example 10.15 shows three dial peers defined. Dial peer 7000 will be used to route calls to the voice-mail application, dial peer 7001 will route calls to the auto-attendant application, and dial peer 7002 will route calls to the Administration via Telephone (AVT) application. The **destination-pattern** command on the dial peer defines the dialed number that this dial peer will route. For example, a dialed number of 7000 will match the statement **destination-pattern 7000** in dial peer 7000 and therefore use that dial peer to route the call. Because each dial peer has a similar configuration, the dial peers can be condensed into a single dial peer using the statement **destination-pattern 700[0-2]**; however, defining each dial peer independently allows for more granular control over the routed calls and provides for easier troubleshooting.

Example 10.16 shows the dial-peer options that must be configured to properly route calls between Cisco Unified CME and Cisco Unity Express.

Example 10.16   *Dial-Peer Options*

```
CME# show run
!
! Output omitted for brevity
!
dial-peer voice 7000 voip
 description VoiceMail
 destination-pattern 7000
 session protocol sipv2
 session target ipv4:10.100.1.10
 dtmf-relay sip-notify
 codec g711ulaw
 no vad
!
```

Key
Topic

Cisco Unity Express uses the Session Initiation Protocol (SIP) to provide call control. Therefore, Cisco Unified CME must be configured to communicate with Cisco Unity Express using SIP. This is accomplished using the **session protocol sipv2** command on the dial peer.

Because a dial peer is used to route calls, the dial peer must have a target destination defined to route received calls. The definition of the target is configured using the **session target** command. In this example, received calls on this dial peer are being routed to the version 4 IP address of 10.100.1.10, which is the IP address of the service-module. The static IP route added earlier in this chapter will route the calls to the service-engine to be passed to the service-module.

Dual-tone multifrequency (DTMF) signals are the tones that are played when a key is pressed on a traditional phone or an IP phone. Because Cisco Unified CME and Cisco Unity Express are using IP to provide signaling, and not traditional audio paths, these tones are not played as audio tones between the two systems. In order for Cisco Unified CME to instruct Cisco Unity Express that a tone was received from a caller, CME must relay the tone in a format that Cisco Unity Express can interpret. This is done using the **dtmf-relay sip-notify** command on the dial peer.

The codec defined on a dial peer defines what type of encoding the voice stream will use as it traverses the dial peer. Although Cisco Unified CME can support multiple codecs, currently Cisco Unity Express supports only the G.711 codec specification for all voice streams. The command **codec g711ulaw** is used to instruct Cisco Unified CME to use only the G.711 codec. If no codec is configured, the dial peer will default to the G.729a codec specification.

Finally, Voice Activity Detection (VAD) is a feature that allows a dial peer to stop sending IP packets when silence is detected and to begin sending IP packets once again if speech, or voice, is detected. In order for the CME dial peer to interact with Cisco Unity Express, VAD must be disabled. This is accomplished by using the **no vad** command on the dial peer.

The CME dial peers are now ready to route calls to Cisco Unity Express.

Telephony Service Configurations for Cisco Unity Express

As discussed in previous chapters, the telephony service configuration defines how the IP phones will interact with Cisco Unified CME. If Cisco Unity Express is integrated with Cisco Unified CME, additional changes are needed in the telephony service configuration to support the integration. Example 10.17 shows abbreviated output from a **show run** command listing these changes.

Example 10.17   *Telephony Service Configurations for Cisco Unity Express*

```
CME# show run
!
! Output omitted for brevity
!
telephony-service
 max-ephones 10
 max-dn 20
 ip source-address 10.100.1.1 port 2000
 voicemail 7000
 web admin system name cmeadmin password cisco
 dn-webedit
 time-webedit
!
```

The **voicemail** option under the telephony service configuration defines the number that will be dialed when an IP phone user presses the voice-mail button on their IP phone. In this example, the voice-mail pilot number is 7000, matching the voice-mail dial peer defined earlier in this chapter.

The **web admin system** command defines the administrative credentials that Cisco Unity Express will use to access the CME GUI. This access allows for a single administrative portal to administer both Cisco Unity Express and Cisco Unified CME. You can use the **secret** option in place of the **password** option to prevent the password from displaying in clear text when a **show run** command is issued.

> **Note**   Although the Cisco Unity Express GUI provides a single administrative point for both Cisco Unified CME and Cisco Unity Express, CME administration and configuration through the Cisco Unity Express GUI is beyond the scope of this book. The *Cisco Unified CME GUI User Guide* can be found on Cisco.com at http://www.cisco.com/en/US/docs/ voice_ip_comm/cucme/gui/user/guide/ cmegui_user.pdf.

The **dn-webedit** command allows the system administrator to add CME directory numbers (DN) to IP phones using the Cisco Unity Express GUI.

The "Cisco Unity Express Post-Installation Configuration" section of this chapter discussed the importance of an NTP server. Using an authoritative NTP server is strongly recommended, but in rare circumstances, time may have to be configured locally without an authoritative NTP server. In these instances, using the **time-webedit** command permits the system administrator to change the system time using the Cisco Unity Express GUI.

MWI Configuration

A message waiting indicator (MWI) is sent from Cisco Unity Express to Cisco Unified CME to inform CME that a new message has arrived in a subscriber's mailbox. Cisco Unity Express does this by sending a static string of unique digits to CME and then appending the extension of the subscriber's mailbox. Example 10.18 shows the MWI configuration necessary.

Example 10.18   *MWI Configuration*

```
CME# show run
!
! Output omitted for brevity
!
ephone-dn  19
 number #40....
 mwi on
!
!
ephone-dn  20
 number #41....
 mwi off
!
```

Key Topic

As discussed in previous chapters, the **ephone-dn** command is used to create and customize a directory number. This is how Cisco Unified CME assigns a static string of digits to turn the MWI on or off. In this example, if Cisco Unity Express sends the digits #401000 to Cisco Unified CME, CME will match the digits to ephone-dn 19. This ephone-dn will strip the static digits #40, leaving the digits 1000, and then, because of the command **mwi on**, Cisco Unified CME will turn on the MWI light for extension 1000. If Cisco Unity Express sends the digits #411000 to CME, CME will match ephone-dn 20. Similarly, ephone-dn 20 will strip the static digits #41 and turn off the WMI light for extension 1000, because of the **mwi off** option configured on ephone-20.

> **Note**   The digits #40 and #41 can be dialed from any phone. This means that dialing
> #401000 from a Cisco IP phone will turn the MWI light on for extension 1000. To prevent
> this from occurring, a nondialable number can be used. For example, A40*xxxx* could be
> assigned to ephone-dn 19 to turn the MWI light on and A41*xxxx* could be assigned to
> ephone-dn 20 to turn the MWI light off. In this case, Cisco Unity Express would send the
> digits A401000 to turn on the MWI light for extension 1000, but the keypad of a Cisco IP
> phone cannot dial A401000.

Cisco Unity Express GUI

As mentioned earlier in this chapter, using the Cisco Unity Express GUI is the most common method of configuring and administering the Cisco Unity Express module. To
access the Cisco Unity Express GUI, open Microsoft Internet Explorer version 6 or later,
and point the browser to http://*CUE Server*, where *CUE Server* is either the IP address
assigned to the service-module or a hostname that can be resolved to the IP address of
the service-module. Figure 10.1 shows the initial login screen of the Cisco Unity Express
GUI.

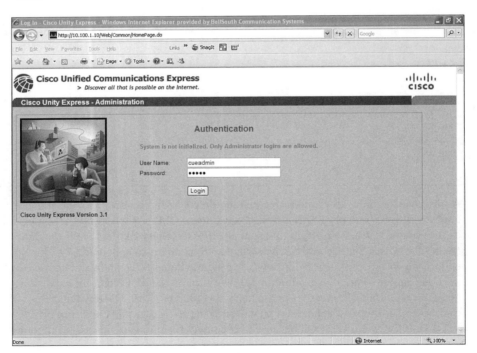

Figure 10.1   *Cisco Unity Express GUI Initial Login*

Notice that the system states that only administrators can log in because the system has
not yet been initialized. You must log in using the credentials configured in the post-
installation configuration tool. In this example, the username is cueadmin and the password is cisco.

The following sections discuss the final configurations necessary to import the CME settings and bring Cisco Unity Express online, and describe how to use the Cisco Unity Express CLI to verify proper configuration.

Cisco Unity Express Initialization Wizard

After you have successfully logged into the Cisco Unity Express module, you can complete the Cisco Unity Express installation process. You have the option of using the Cisco Unity Express GUI or the Cisco Unity Express CLI to complete the installation, as shown in Figure 10.2.

Key Topic

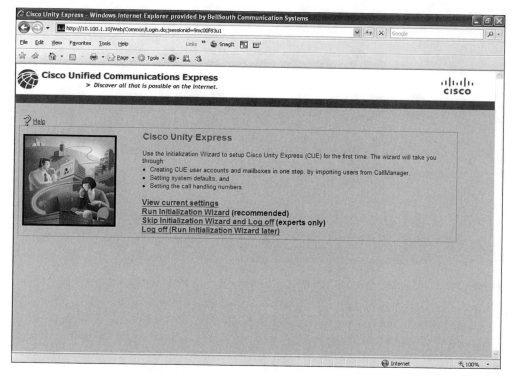

Figure 10.2 *Cisco Unity Express Initialization Wizard*

Note   Although it is possible to configure Cisco Unity Express through the CLI, it is a complex process compared to the GUI option; therefore, the GUI method is recommended.

After you click the Run Initialization Wizard link, the first page of the Cisco Unity Express Initialization Wizard asks for the IP address and login credentials that Cisco Unity Express will use to access Cisco Unified CME. Note that these login credentials are not the administrative credentials configured in Cisco Unity Express, but rather the login credentials that were configured in Cisco Unified CME using the **web admin system** command. In the present example, the username is cmeadmin and the password is cisco. Figure 10.3 shows the login configuration needed for this example.

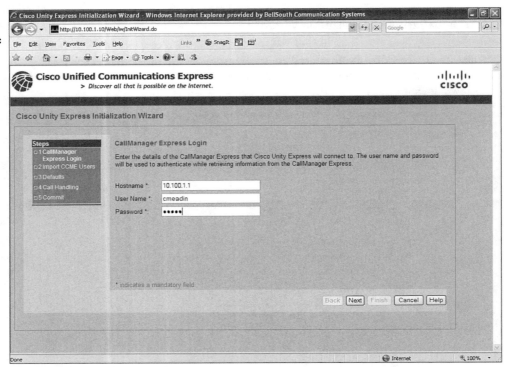

Figure 10.3 *Cisco Unified CME IP Address and Login Credentials*

Next, the Initialization Wizard lists the currently configured users in Cisco Unified CME. You can then import the desired users into Cisco Unity Express. Upon import, you can choose a primary extension for the user, create a mailbox for the user's primary extension, place the user's ID in the Cisco Unity Express administrator's group, and set the call forward busy (CFB) and call forward no answer (CFNA) treatment of the primary extension to be forwarded to the voice-mail application. Figure 10.4 shows the Import Cisco Unified CME Users page.

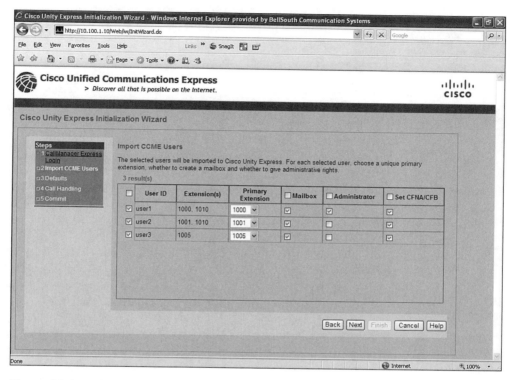

Figure 10.4 *Importing Cisco Unified CME Users*

In this example, user1, user2, and user3 will be imported into Cisco Unity Express. User1's primary extension will be configured as 1000, user2's as 1001, and user3's as 1005. Each user will have a Cisco Unity Express mailbox created for their respective primary extensions, and each primary extension will be configured in Cisco Unified CME to forward all busy and unanswered calls to Cisco Unity Express. User1 will be imported as an administrator.

After the users have been identified, you need to define the defaults that will be used for the imported users. Figure 10.5 shows the Defaults page of the Initialization Wizard.

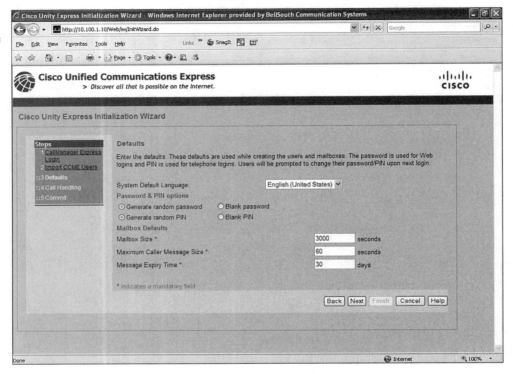

Figure 10.5 *Imported Cisco Unified CME Users Defaults Page*

In this example, all users will be configured with English as their system language. Cisco Unity Express will assign a random password and PIN for each user. Each mailbox will hold 3000 seconds of recorded voice, with a maximum message size of 60 seconds, and messages older than 30 days will be marked as expired.

Figure 10.6 shows how Cisco Unity Express will route calls.

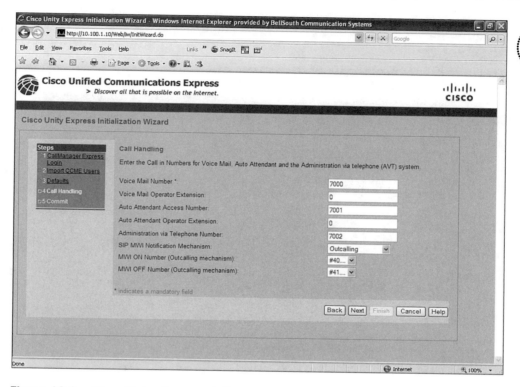

Figure 10.6 *Cisco Unity Express Call Handling*

This page mirrors the configuration performed in Cisco Unified CME to prepare for Cisco Unity Express integration. Notice that the voice-mail number, auto-attendant number, and AVT number entered on this page match the SIP dial peers created in the "Dial Peers for Cisco Unity Express" section of this chapter.

The voice-mail and auto-attendant operator extensions are the directory numbers that will ring if a caller presses the 0 key on their phone while listening to a voice-mail greeting and auto-attendant prompt, respectively. In this example, Cisco Unity Express will send a 0 digit to Cisco Unified CME if either of these conditions occurs.

During the initialization, Cisco Unity Express was able to identify the **mwi on** command configured on ephone-dn 19 and the **mwi off** command configured on ephone-dn 20. Because of this, Cisco Unity Express automatically populates the MWI fields with the correct values.

The Commit page, shown in Figure 10.7, gives you one last chance to review and change your selections before committing the configurations to memory.

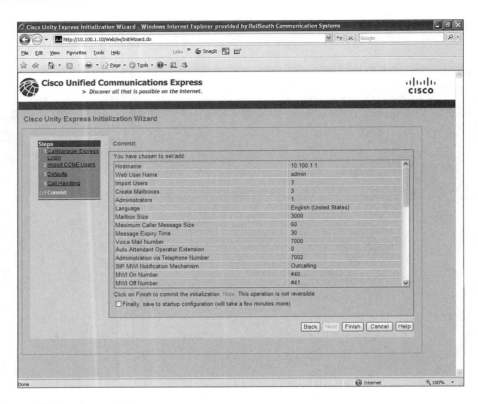

Figure 10.7 *Commit Page*

Notice that all configuration options selected during the Initialization Wizard are listed on the Commit page. Use the Back button to change any selection, or check the Finally, Save to Startup Configuration box and click Finish to commit the selections to memory. As noted on this page, after you click Finish, all changes become permanent.

The final page lists the success or failure of each process within the Cisco Unity Express Initialization Wizard. Figure 10.8 shows that each process was successful in this example.

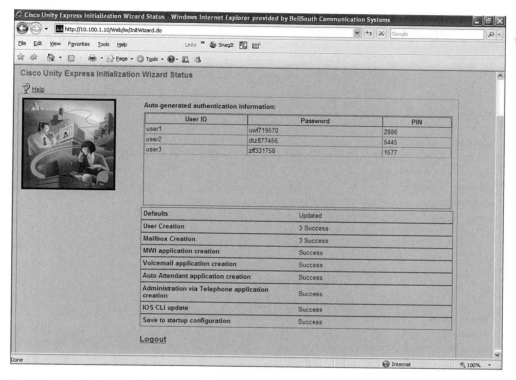

Figure 10.8   *Initialization Wizard Completion Page*

While configuring the imported user defaults in Figure 10.5, the Cisco Unity Express was configured to generate a random password and PIN for each imported user. This page lists the password and PIN values that were generated for each user. You can record these values and deliver them to the appropriate user.

Note   In case the auto-generated password and PIN are not recorded during this step, the auto-generated value will appear on the appropriate user's configuration page within the Cisco Unity Express GUI. Once the user performs their initial login, the system forces a password and PIN change. The user-defined passwords and PINs are not displayed on the user's configuration page.

CLI Verification

Saving the configuration to startup configuration means that all selections chosen during the Initialization Wizard are written to the Cisco Unity Express CLI. Example 10.19 shows abbreviated output from a **show run** command in the Cisco Unity Express CLI.

Example 10.19   *Cisco Unity Express CLI* show run *Command Output*

```
cue# show run

 Output omitted for brevity


Generating configuration:

username cueadmin create
username user1 create
username user2 create
username user3 create
username user1 phonenumber "1000"
username user2 phonenumber "1001"
username user3 phonenumber "1005"

groupname Administrators member cueadmin
groupname Administrators member user1

ccn application ciscomwiapplication aa
 description "ciscomwiapplication"
 parameter "strMWI_OFF_DN" "#41"
 parameter "strMWI_ON_DN" "#40"

ccn subsystem sip
 gateway address "10.100.1.1"

ccn trigger sip phonenumber 7000
 application "voicemail"
 maxsessions 8

ccn trigger sip phonenumber 7001
 application "autoattendant"
 maxsessions 8

ccn trigger sip phonenumber 7002
 application "promptmgmt"
 maxsessions 1

voicemail default mailboxsize 3000
voicemail operator telephone 0

voicemail mailbox owner "user1" size 3000

voicemail mailbox owner "user2" size 3000

voicemail mailbox owner "user3" size 3000

cue#
```

Notice that the configuration entered into the Initialization Wizard is now saved as part of the Cisco Unity Express configuration.

Cisco Unity Express Troubleshooting

For Cisco Unity Express to provide voice-mail and auto-attendant services, several pieces need to work together. For this reason, troubleshooting requires that you isolate where the problem exists by asking the questions, "What is working?" and "What is not working?" Asking these questions will help to determine if the root problem exists in one of the following areas:

■ Compatibility

■ Cisco Unity Express configuration

■ IP connectivity

■ Call routing

■ MWI

This section asks these questions and examines some of the most common issues and troubleshooting methods for Cisco Unity Express.

Compatibility

When troubleshooting issues with Cisco Unity Express, first verify compatibility: is Cisco Unity Express recognized by Cisco Unified CME? The **show version** command can answer this question, as illustrated in Example 10.20.

Example 10.20   *Determining the Cisco Unified CME Version*

```
CME# show version
Cisco IOS Software, 2800 Software (C2800NM-ADVIPSERVICESK9-M), Version 12.4(15)T
4, RELEASE SOFTWARE (fc2)
Cisco 2811 (revision 53.50) with 507904K/16384K bytes of memory.
Processor board ID FTX1030A1SF
11 FastEthernet interfaces
1 Serial interface
1 terminal line
2 Channelized T1/PRI ports
1 Virtual Private Network (VPN) Module
1 cisco service engine(s)
DRAM configuration is 64 bits wide with parity enabled.
239K bytes of non-volatile configuration memory.
1957536K bytes of ATA CompactFlash (Read/Write)
CME#
```

Does the service-engine appear in the output of the **show version** command? If not, check the compatibility list for Cisco Unity Express and verify that the model of Cisco router and IOS version are supported.

Cisco Unity Express Configuration

This section lists questions to help you troubleshoot Cisco Unity Express configuration. First ask, is Cisco Unity Express up and running in Cisco Unified CME? The **show interface service-engine** command, shown in Example 10.21, can answer that question.

Example 10.21   show interface service-engine 1/0 *Command Output*

```
CME# show interface service-Engine 1/0
service-engine1/0 is up, line protocol is up
  Interface is unnumbered. Using address of FastEthernet0/1 (10.100.1.1)
CME#
```

Are both the service-engine and line protocol in an up state? If not, check the configuration of the service-engine against the steps described in the "Installing the Cisco Unity Express Module" section of this chapter.

Next ask, is the service-module in a steady state? In the present example, the Cisco Unity Express module is installed in port 1/0 so you can use the **service-module service-engine 1/0 status** command to display the current state, as shown in Example 10.22.

Key Topic

Example 10.22   service-module service-engine 1/0 *status Command Output*

```
CME# service-module service-engine 1/0 status
Service Module is Cisco Service-Engine1/0
Service Module supports session via TTY line 66
Service Module is in Steady state
Getting status from the Service Module, please wait..
Cisco Unity Express 3.1.1
CUE Running on NM
CME#
```

If the service-engine is not in a steady state, and the configuration appears to be correct, you can reload the module with the **service-module service-engine 1/0 reload** command. If the system is in a failed state and will not recover after a reload, you can use the **service-module service-engine 1/0 reset** command to force a hard boot of Cisco Unity Express. Note that this method of reboot may result in data loss.

IP Connectivity

This section describes several questions to help you troubleshoot IP connectivity. First ask, can I ping the IP address of the service-engine (as shown in Example 10.23)?

Example 10.23   *Pinging the Service Engine*

```
CME# ping 10.100.1.10
Sending 5, 100-byte ICMP Echos to 10.100.1.10, timeout is 2 seconds:
!!!!!
Success rate is 100 percent (5/5), round-trip min/avg/max = 1/1/1 ms
CME#
```

If the service-engine does not respond to a ping, ask the question, is there a route to the IP address of the service-engine. The **show ip route** command can answer this question, as shown in Example 10.24.

Example 10.24   *The* show ip route *Command*

```
CME# show ip route 10.100.1.10
Routing entry for 10.100.1.10/32
  Known via "static", distance 1, metric 0 (connected)
  Routing Descriptor Blocks:
  * directly connected, via Service-Engine1/0
      Route metric is 0, traffic share count is 1
CME#
```

Is there a route in Cisco Unified CME's routing table for the IP address of the service-engine? If not, check the configuration for the **ip route** statement and verify that IP routing has been enabled on Cisco Unified CME.

Call Routing

This section asks several questions and uses **show** and **debug** commands to assess call routing issues. Ask the question, are calls to the voice-mail, auto-attendant, and AVT pilot numbers answered by Cisco Unity Express? If not, verify that the dial peers are configured correctly in Cisco Unified CME and that they match the pilot numbers configured in Cisco Unity Express. You can use the **show dial-peer voice** command to look for clues, as shown in Example 10.25.

Example 10.25   show dial-peer voice *Command Output*

```
CME# show dial-peer voice 7000
VoiceOverIpPeer7000
        description = `Voicemail',
        tag = 7000, destination-pattern = `7000',
        group = 7000, Admin state is up, Operation state is up,
        DTMF Relay = enabled,
        session-protocol = sipv2, session-transport = system,
        codec = g711ulaw,   payload size =  160 bytes,
        VAD = disabled, Poor QOV Trap = disabled,
```

continues

Example 10.25 show voice dial-peer *Command Output   continued*

```
        Last Disconnect Cause is "10  ",
        Last Disconnect Text is "normal call clearing (16)",
        Last Setup Time = 1051131.
        Last Disconnect Time = 1051026.
CME#
```

Verify that the dial-peer is up and reflects the correct configuration. See the last disconnect cause and the last disconnect text to find out what happened to the last call presented to this dial peer.

To examine call routing across the dial peer in real time, you can enable debugging on Cisco Unified CME. A debug is simply a command that instructs Cisco Unified CME to show all selected processes in real time. For example, the dial peers in CME use SIP to communicate to Cisco Unity Express, so you can debug a SIP process to see what is happening on the dial peers in real time. Example 10.26 shows the SIP processes that can be debugged.

Example 10.26 *Determining Processes That Can Be Debugged with the* debug ccsip
Command

```
CME# debug ccsip ?
  all        Enable all SIP debugging traces
  calls      Enable CCSIP SPI calls debugging trace
  error      Enable SIP error debugging trace
  events     Enable SIP events debugging trace
  info       Enable SIP info debugging trace
  media      Enable SIP media debugging trace
  messages   Enable CCSIP SPI messages debugging trace
  preauth    Enable SIP preauth debugging traces
  states     Enable CCSIP SPI states debugging trace
  transport  Enable SIP transport debugging traces
```

Note   Some debugs, such as **debug ccsip all**, can severely impact system performance and should be used only after normal business hours and on an as-needed basis. Debugs should be turned off after troubleshooting has been completed, by using the **undebug all** command.

Example 10.27 shows abbreviated output from the **debug ccsip calls** command.

Example 10.27   debug ccsip calls *Command Output*

```
CME# debug ccsip calls
Jun 24 16:08:17.339: //31/973F77918054/SIP/Call/sipSPICallInfo:
The Call Setup Information is:
Call Control Block (CCB) : 0x48851A30
State of The Call        : STATE_ACTIVE
TCP Sockets Used         : NO
Calling Number           : 1000
Called Number            : 7000
Source IP Address (Sig ): 10.100.1.1
Destn SIP Req Addr:Port  : 10.100.1.10:5060
Destn SIP Resp Addr:Port : 10.100.1.10:5060
Destination Name         : 10.100.1.10

Jun 24 16:08:17.339: //31/973F77918054/SIP/Call/sipSPIMediaCallInfo:
Number of Media Streams: 1
Media Stream             : 1
Negotiated Codec         : g711ulaw
Negotiated Codec Bytes   : 160
Nego. Codec payload      : 0 (tx), 0 (rx)
Negotiated Dtmf-relay    : 8
Dtmf-relay Payload       : 0 (tx), 0 (rx)
Source IP Address (Media): 10.100.1.1
Source IP Port     (Media): 17568
Destn  IP Address (Media): 10.100.1.10
Destn  IP Port     (Media): 16904
Orig Destn IP Address:Port (Media): 0.0.0.0:0

Jun 24 16:08:44.195: //31/973F77918054/SIP/Call/sipSPICallInfo:
Disconnect Cause (CC)    : 16
Disconnect Cause (SIP)   : 200

CME#
```

Verify that these values reflect the correct configuration. If not, check the configuration in both Cisco Unity Express and Cisco Unified CME. Investigate the disconnect cause received to help isolate why a call is failing. In this example, the SIP disconnect cause of 200 and the CC disconnect cause of 16 both reflect a normal call clearing.

MWI

When assessing the MWI issues, ask the following questions: Does the MWI light turn on when a message is left? Does it turn off when all messages are heard? If not, verify that the ephone-dn configuration for the MWI in Cisco Unified CME matches the MWI configuration within Cisco Unity Express. To see the MWI process in real time, use the **debug ephone mwi** command as shown in Example 10.28.

Example 10.28   debug ephone mwi *Command Output*

```
CME# debug ephone mwi
EPHONE mwi debugging is enabled
CME#
Jun 24 16:54:42.011: SetCallInfo MODE 1 calling dn -1 chan 1 dn 19 chan 1
Jun 24 16:54:42.011: calling [7000] called [#401000]
Jun 24 16:54:42.011: SkinnyTryCall to 1000 instance 1 start at 0SkinnyTryCall to
 1000 instance 1 match DN 1
Jun 24 16:54:42.011: ephone-2[2]:Set MWI line 1 to ON count 0
CME#
CME#
Jun 24 16:55:17.283: SetCallInfo MODE 2 calling dn -1 chan 1 dn 20 chan 1
Jun 24 16:55:17.283: alling [7000] called [#411000]
Jun 24 16:55:17.283: SkinnyTryCall to 1000 instance 1 start at 0SkinnyTryCall to
 1000 instance 1 match DN 1
Jun 24 16:55:17.283: ephone-2[2]:Set MWI line 1 to OFF
CME#
```

Notice that the output from this **debug** command follows the call flow described in the "MWI Configuration" section of this chapter.

Cisco Unity Express Trace Files

While debugs are an excellent way to find clues to the root of problems on Cisco Unified CME, debugs are not supported on Cisco Unity Express. In place of the **debug** command, Cisco Unity Express offers the **trace** command. The **trace** command can be used to view real-time information about Cisco Unity Express activity and to collect trace information in files named atrace.log and messages.log.

> **Note**   The atrace.log file is a binary file and cannot be read by the Cisco Unity Express administrator. You must send it to the Cisco Technical Assistance Center (TAC) to decipher.

Because the **trace** command is specific to Cisco Unity Express, all commands specific to collecting and viewing trace files exist inside the Cisco Unity Express CLI. From the Cisco Unity Express CLI, issue the **show trace** command to display the traces currently running. Example 10.29 shows abbreviated output of the **show trace** command.

Example 10.29   show trace *Command Output*

```
cue# show trace


!Output omitted for brevity


MODULE              ENTITY              SETTING
ccn                 Engine              00000001
config-ccn          sip-subsystem       00000001
voicemail           mailbox             0000003f
voicemail           message             0000002f


LOG NAME                                STATUS
atrace.log                              enabled


cue#
```

To enable a specific Cisco Unity Express trace, use the **trace** command followed by the
module, entry, and activity of the trace. For example, to enable a trace for all activity on
the SIP subsystem, you would use the command **trace ccn subsystemsip all**, where **ccn** is
the module, **subsystemsip** is the entity, and **all** is the activity. Example 10.30 shows that
you can use **?** to view each category.

Example 10.30   *Starting a Trace*

```
cue# trace ?


!Output omitted for brevity


  BackupRestore Module
  all           Every module, entity and activity
  ccn           Module
  dns           Module
  management    Module
  networking    Module
  ntp           Module
  snmp          Module
  voicemail     Module
  voiceview     Module
  webInterface  Module
  webapp        Module
```

continues

Example 10.30   *Starting a Trace   continued*

```
cue# trace ccn ?
  Admn          Entity
  Engine        Entity
  SubsystemEmail Entity
  SubsystemHttp Entity
  SubsystemJtapi Entity
  SubsystemSip Entity
  all           Every entity and activity

cue# trace ccn Subsystemsip ?
  DBUG          Activity
  XDBG          Activity
  all           Every activity

cue# trace ccn subsystemsip all
```

When the desired trace has been enabled, you can view real-time information about Cisco Unity Express's activities by using the **show trace buffer tail** command, as shown in Example 10.31.

Example 10.31   *Viewing a Trace in Real Time*

```
cue# show trace buffer tail

!Output omitted for brevity

Press <CTRL-C> to exit...
4434 07/18 17:08:58.020 ACCN SIPS 0 ... Cisco SIP Channel Recovery #0.1216415338
019 done.
4441 07/18 17:09:46.601 DSSP LWRE 0 Received UDP packet on 10.100.1.10:5060 ,source
  10.100.1.1:64069
INVITE sip:7000@10.100.1.10:5060 SIP/2.0
Via: SIP/2.0/UDP 10.100.1.1:5060;branch=z9hG4bK34510
Remote-Party-ID: <sip:1000@10.100.1.1>;party=calling;screen=no;privacy=off
From: <sip:1000@10.100.1.1>;tag=6E5818-2322
To: <sip:7000@10.100.1.10>
Date: Fri, 18 Jul 2008 21:09:46 GMT
Call-ID: AF4348F3-544411DD-8023CA6D-3E10A904@10.100.1.1
Supported: 100rel,timer,resource-priority,replaces
Min-SE:  1800
Cisco-Guid: 2940142402-1413747165-2149501549-1041279236
User-Agent: Cisco-SIPGateway/IOS-12.x
Allow: INVITE, OPTIONS, BYE, CANCEL, ACK, PRACK, UPDATE, REFER, SUBSCRIBE, NOTIFY,
  INFO, REGISTER
CSeq: 101 INVITE
```

```
Max-Forwards: 70
Timestamp: 1216415386
Contact: <sip:1000@10.100.1.1:5060>
Call-Info: <sip:10.100.1.1:5060>;method="NOTIFY;Event=telephone-event;
  Duration=2000"
Expires: 180
Allow-Events: telephone-event
Content-Type: application/sdp
Content-Disposition: session;handling=required
Content-Length: 184
```

To view trace information stored in the buffer, use the **show trace buffer long** command. The **paged** option can be added to make the output easier to read, as shown in Example 10.32.

Example 10.32   *Showing the Cisco Unity Express Trace Buffer*

```
cue# show trace buffer long paged
4340 07/18 15:13:39.071 ACCN APPS 0 Application Manager is not instantiated yet
 - state = OUT_OF_SERVICE
4340 07/18 15:13:39.072 ACCN APPS 0 Application Subsystem: INITIALIZING ->
  OUT_OF_SERVICE
4340 07/18 15:13:39.072 ACCN APPS 0 SS_OUT_OF_SERVICE:Application subsystem in
out of service
4340 07/18 15:13:39.172 ACCN LLDA 0 getLDAPFailProofOperations has been called
4340 07/18 15:13:39.172 ACCN LLDA 0 iniLDAPCfg in LDAPFailProofOoperations was
different from the stored one OR static instance of LDAPFailProofOperations is
null
4340 07/18 15:13:39.173 ACCN LLDA 0 Constructor for LDAPFailProofOperations called
4340 07/18 15:13:39.175 ACCN LLDA 0 getLDAPFailProofOperations has been called
4340 07/18 15:13:39.175 ACCN LLDA 0 the iniLDAPCfg passed to
  getLDAPFailProofOperations was null
4340 07/18 15:13:39.175 ACCN LLDA 0 This is the file name which is used to create
  INILDAPConfiguration /usr/wfavvid/ccndir.ini
4340 07/18 15:13:39.200 ACCN LLDA 0 Constructor for LDAPFailProofOperations called
4340 07/18 15:13:39.201 ACCN LLDA 0 ENTER: setIdentity(null)
4340 07/18 15:13:39.201 ACCN LLDA 0  EXIT: setIdentity()
4340 07/18 15:13:39.201 ACCN LLDA 0 ENTER: setCredentials(null)
4340 07/18 15:13:39.201 ACCN LLDA 0  EXIT: setCredentials()
4340 07/18 15:13:39.201 ACCN LLDA 0 ENTER: setObjectSchemaSource()
 -- More –
```

To view the contents of the messages.log file, use the **show log name messages.log** command, as shown in Example 10.33.

Example 10.33   *Displaying Contents of the* **messages.log** *File*

```
cue# show log name messages.log
Press <CTRL-C> to exit...
#!/bin/cat
19:59:09 logmgr: BEGIN FILE
07/16/08 19:59:09 install_file  /dwnld/pkgdata/cue-vm-license_100mbx_cme_3.1.1.p
kg 2 __LICENSE__ none
07/16/08 19:59:10 voicemail_lic.sig
07/16/08 19:59:14 add_file /dwnld/pkgdata/cue-vm-license_100mbx_cme_3.1.1.pkg 1
/ /sw/installed/manifest/lmanifest.signed none
07/16/08 19:59:14 Remove  //dwnld/pkgdata/cue-vm-license_100mbx_cme_3.1.1.pkg
07/16/08 19:59:14 Remove  //dwnld/.install_started
19:59:06 logmgr: START
<45>Jul 16 19:59:06 localhost syslog-ng[1467]: syslog-ng version 1.6.8-cisco
  starting
<197>Jul 16 19:59:06 localhost syslog_ng:     INFO startup.sync syslog-ng arrived
 phase online
<6>Jul 16 19:59:08 localhost kernel: klogd 1.4.1, log source = /proc/kmsg started.
<4>Jul 16 19:59:08 localhost kernel: Cannot find map file.
<6>Jul 16 19:59:08 localhost kernel: No module symbols loaded - kernel modules not
  enabled.
<4>Jul 16 19:59:08 localhost kernel: Linux version 2.6.11.11cisco
  (ealyon@fndn-bld-system9) (gcc version 3.4.3) #1 Thu Oct 25 14:58:17 PDT 2007
```

The current atrace.log and messages.log files can be viewed by issuing the **show logs** command, as shown in Example 10.34.

Example 10.34   *Showing the Cisco Unity Express Logs*

```
cue# show logs
    SIZE             LAST_MODIFIED_TIME                              NAME
       0     Tue Jul 15 17:34:06 EDT 2008               CiscoJtapi1.log
       0     Wed Jul 16 13:23:15 EDT 2008               CiscoJtapi2.log
    4608     Wed Jul 16 19:59:37 EDT 2008                   install.log
    6320     Thu Jul 17 16:11:00 EDT 2008                         dmesg
      39     Wed Jul 16 19:59:09 EDT 2008             messages.log.prev
    7638     Thu Jul 17 16:11:06 EDT 2008                    syslog.log
  123933     Tue Jun 24 23:10:51 EDT 2008                  shutdown.log
 1522175     Fri Jul 18 17:10:28 EDT 2008                    atrace.log
   10337     Sat Jun 21 14:23:47 EDT 2008             postgres.log.prev
104857717    Tue Jun 24 15:58:08 EDT 2008               atrace.log.prev
    3212     Thu Jul 17 16:12:18 EDT 2008                  postgres.log
    3354     Thu Jul 17 16:11:08 EDT 2008                      klog.log
 2888459     Fri Jul 18 17:10:28 EDT 2008                  messages.log
   12484     Sat Jun 21 14:15:13 EDT 2008         shutdown_installer.log
cue#
```

The atrace.log file can be copied from the Cisco Unity Express module to an FTP server and then provided to TAC. This is accomplished with the command **copy log atrace.log url ftp://** followed by the FTP server name or IP address, as shown in Example 10.35.

Example 10.35   *Copying the* atrace.log *File*

```
cue# copy log atrace.log url ftp://10.1.1.11/atrace.log
  % Total    % Received % Xferd  Average Speed   Time    Time     Time  Current
                                 Dload  Upload   Total   Spent    Left  Speed
100 1486k    0     0   100 1486k     0    920k  0:00:01  0:00:01 --:--:-- 1034k
cue#
```

Restoring Cisco Unity Express to the Factory Defaults

At times it is necessary to restore the Cisco Unity Express module back to factory defaults. You can accomplish this by placing the Cisco Unity Express module in an offline state and issuing the command **restore factory default**, as shown in Example 10.36.

Example 10.36   *Restoring Factory Defaults*

```
CME# service-module service-Engine 1/0 session
Trying 10.100.1.1, 2066 ... Open
cue>
cue> offline
!!!WARNING!!!: If you are going offline to do a backup, it is recommended
that you save the current running configuration using the 'write' command,
prior to going to the offline state.

Putting the system offline will terminate all end user sessions.

Are you sure you want to go offline[n]? : y
cue(offline)> restore factory default
!!!WARNING!!!: This operation will cause all configuration and data
on the system to be erased. This operation is not reversible.

Do you wish to continue[n]? : y
Restoring the system. Please wait .....done
System will be restored to factory default when it reloads.
```

After the system restarts, Cisco Unity Express will run the post-installation configuration tool.

Note   All data and configuration on Cisco Unity Express will be lost when the factory defaults are restored. Backing up the system is highly recommended before you attempt this procedure.

Exam Preparation Tasks

Review All the Key Topics

Review the most important topics in the chapter, noted with the key topics icon in the outer margin of the page. Table 10.6 lists and describes these key topics and identifies the page number on which each is found.

Key Topic

Table 10.6 *Key Topics for Chapter 10*

Key Topic Element	Description	Page Number
Example 10.4	Complete Cisco Unified CME configuration for Cisco Unity Express IP connectivity	363-364
Example 10.5	Command syntax used to connect to the Cisco Unity Express CLI	364
Syntax	Shows the **upgrade** option	366
Syntax	Shows the **clean** option	367
Example 10.7	Command syntax used to perform a clean install of Cisco Unity Express	368
Example 10.8	Choosing language files	368
Example 10.11	**show software license** output	373–374
Example 10.12	Post-installation configuration tool	375–377
Example 10.16	Dial-peer options	381
Example 10.17	Telephony service configurations for Cisco Unity Express	382
Example 10.18	MWI configuration	383
Figure 10.1	Cisco Unity Express GUI initial login	384
Figure 10.2	Cisco Unity Express Initialization Wizard	385
Figure 10.3	Cisco Unified CME IP address and login credentials	386
Figure 10.4	Importing Cisco Unified CME users	387
Figure 10.5	Imported Cisco Unified CME users Defaults page	388

Key Topic Element	Description	Page Number
Figure 10.6	Cisco Unity Express call handling	
Figure 10.7	Commit Page	
Figure 10.8	Initialization Wizard completion page	
Example 10.22	**service-module service-engine 1/0 status** command output	

Complete the Tables and Lists from Memory

Print a copy of Appendix C, "Memory Tables" (found on the CD), or at least the section for this chapter, and complete the tables and lists from memory. Appendix D, "Memory Tables Answer Key," also on the CD, includes completed tables and lists to check your work.

Definitions of Key Terms

Define the following key terms from this chapter, and check your answers in the glossary.

service-engine

service-module

Cisco Unity Express CLI

Cisco Unity Express GUI

MWI

Exam topics covered in Part V:

- Describe the function and operation of Cisco Configuration Assistant

- Configure UC500 device parameters

- Configure UC500 network parameters

- Configure UC500 dial plan and voice mail parameters

- Configure UC500 SIP trunk parameters

- Configure UC500 voice system features

- Configure UC500 user parameters

Part V: The Smart Business Communications System Suite

Unified Communications and the Smart Business Communications System: This section provides an introduction to the concept of Unified Communications and explains how the Smart Business Communications System (SBCS) is positioned to deliver it to the small-medium business (SMB) market.

Components of the Smart Business Communications System: This section introduces the components of the Smart Business Communications System.

Common Deployment Scenarios: This section closes out the chapter with a discussion on how the Smart Business Communications System would be deployed in various scenarios.

CHAPTER 11

Introducing the Smart Business Communications System

The Cisco Smart Business Communications System (SBCS) is a secure and intuitive communications platform designed specifically for the needs of the small-medium business (SMB) market. It was introduced to bring the power of Cisco Unified Communications to a realm where simplicity and affordability are of utmost importance. Simplicity is delivered in this suite through its ease of installation and maintenance. It provides to smaller organizations that lack the benefit of a dedicated IT staff the capability to implement Cisco Unified Architecture at a fraction of the cost once associated with SMB projects. Affordability is delivered in this suite because its systems offer increased return on investment (ROI) to business owners. SBCS is inexpensive to install and maintain over time.

The first section of this chapter begins with a discussion of Unified Communications (UC) and explains how the SBCS family of UC500 products is positioned to deliver its value to the small business. The chapter then moves into a discussion of the individual UC500 components that comprise the SBCS family. Finally, the chapter explores the most common ways this platform is deployed.

"Do I Know This Already?" Quiz

The "Do I Know This Already?" quiz allows you to assess whether you should read this entire chapter or simply jump to the "Exam Preparation Tasks" section for review. If you are in doubt, read the entire chapter. Table 11.1 outlines the major headings in this chapter and the corresponding "Do I Know This Already?" quiz questions. You can find the answers in Appendix A, "Answers to the 'Do I Know This Already?' Quizzes."

Table 11.1   *"Do I Know This Already?" Foundation Topics Section-to-Question Mapping*

Foundation Topics Section	Questions
Unified Communications and the Smart Business Communications System	1–2
Components of the Smart Business Communications System	3–6
Common Deployment Scenarios	7–8

1. Which of the following items is *not* currently part of Cisco's design for the Smart Business Communications System strategy?

    a. Make it simple to deploy

    b. Make it affordable

    c. Make it upgradeable to work with larger enterprise systems like Cisco Unified Communications Manager

    d. Make it secure

    e. Make it expandable through the integration of third-party products

2. Which three of the following items did Cisco use to simplify the deployment of the Smart Business Communications System?

    a. Assume a typical use case for the system and then preconfigure the system settings following Cisco recommended best practices.

    b. Assume a specific user count in each product SKU and then bundle in the appropriate licensing to support that user count.

    c. Remove the portions of the Cisco Unified Communications suite that require more engineering expertise.

    d. Provide several options for PSTN connectivity and then engineer the correct amount of Digital Signal Processor (DSP) resources appropriate for that design.

    e. Remove the ability to customize the solution and therefore provide a template-based configuration.

3. Which statement best describes the MoH port on the Cisco Unified Communications 500 Series Router?

    a. An RJ45 uplink that provides an interface to monitor the Music on Hold being played in the SBCS system

    b. A standard audio jack that facilitates the integration of an external Music on Hold audio source

    c. A special port that connects to the last FXS port

    d. A special port that provides emergency dial tone during a power outage

    e. The link through which the MoH RTP stream from the Cisco Media Server arrives

4. Which device is required to support more than three wireless APs?

   a. Cisco 521 Wireless Express Access Point

   b. Cisco 526 Wireless Express Mobility Controller

   c. Cisco Catalyst Express Switch

   d. Cisco Unified Communications 500 Series Router with Built-in Controller

5. Which of the following is *not* supported as part of a Smart Business Communications System deployment?

   a. Easy VPN Remote and Server Support

   b. Network Address Translation

   c. Routing protocols such as OSPF, EIGRP, and BGP

   d. Cisco IOS Firewall

6. Why do you need to consider the type and distribution of phones deployed in an SBCS solution when using the PoE switch ports built into the UC520 system?

   a. Administrators and executives should be deployed with higher-end phones than those used by typical users.

   b. The integrated switch in the UC520 system has a maximum inline power distribution of 80 watts. Class 3 handsets such as the 7965G require 12 watts of power each. Plugging eight Class 3 devices into the integrated switch would oversubscribe the power capabilities of that switch and would result in some of the phones being unable to power up.

   c. Class 3 phones will not work in the UC520's integrated switch.

   d. Deploying too many Class 3 phones within the UC520's integrated switch will lead to unsafe operating temperatures within the chassis.

7. Which model of Cisco Catalyst Express switch would you use in a 48-user deployment?

   a. Two Cisco Catalyst Express 520-24PC switch

   b. One Cisco Catalyst Express 520-48LC switch

   c. One Cisco Catalyst Express 520-24PC switch

   d. One Cisco Catalyst Express 520-48PC switch

   e. Two Cisco Catalyst Express 520-24LC switch

8. Why does projected growth need to be considered when choosing the correct UC520 product SKU for a deployment?

  a. Undersizing your initial deployment will result in deployment delays and extra shipping costs.

  b. Because the UC520 is a fixed configuration device and is not field serviceable, there is no hardware migration plan for moving from a smaller 8/16-user chassis to a larger 24/32/48-user chassis.

  c. Large deployments cannot be managed with the CCA tool. If expected growth of the system leads to an elaborate network design, another product line should be selected.

  d. Projected growth does not need to be considered when designing a network that includes the UC520 system.

Foundation Topics

Unified Communications and the Smart Business Communications System

In April 2007, Cisco introduced a new solution designed to bring the power of Unified Communications to small businesses. Introduced under the name Smart Business Communications System (SBCS), the UC500 product family makes up a fully featured and economical solution that provides voice, data, video, security, and wireless in a manner that is simple, affordable, manageable, and complete.

To understand the importance of the individual components of the SBCS suite and their unique value to the small business world, it is important to first develop an understanding of the concept of Unified Communications (UC) and its value to business. A technical understanding of each of the suite's components and their respective speeds, interface options, and configurations is important. Understanding them and developing a seasoned engineer who is familiar with their respective implementations is one of the reasons for the CCNA certification process. With that said, grasping the technical aspects of the suite without an understanding of the business value that its components deliver to a business is a short-sighted venture. A well-rounded engineer will seek to understand not only the technical components of the SBCS suite but also the business reasons for implementing it.

To that end, before discussing the technical components of the suite, the first part of the chapter works to develop your understanding of the concept of UC.

With that understanding, you will begin to grasp how UC tools positively affect the small business's ability to attract, service, and maintain its customers and how you, as an engineer, play a part in that.

So just what is this ever-evolving concept referred to as Unified Communications?

In 1999, Cisco introduced the concept of the Architecture for Voice, Video, and Integrated Data (AVVID). This architecture was the first step in a plan to develop an all-encompassing blueprint for converged networks. AVVID was Cisco's initial framework for a network where voice, data, and video could coexist on a single IP-based network. At its outset, IP telephony was the architecture's primary focus, but its long-range vision included the concepts of security and mobility as well. As the concept of convergence began to be understood by the IT community, Cisco began to demonstrate the power in delivering secure and mobile communications without barriers. By 2003, early adopters of IP telephony began to realize that AVVID encompassed much more than the ability to save on long-distance phone bills and that it was a platform for business rather than simply a dial-tone replacement. As wireless communications in the form of wireless data LANs (WLANs) and cellular networks became more and more a standard offering in corporate communications, Cisco's initial AVVID framework, with ideals of convergence, mobility, and security, grew into what has become the industry term Unified Communications.

The concept of Unified Communications has now evolved from what was a visionary framework for convergence in AVVID into a communications architecture that automates and ties together both human and device communications. It has become an architecture that seeks to minimize the differences between the way we would like to communicate and the way we must communicate given time, device, and location constraints. But what does that mean? A discussion about Unified Communications as it is today and its practical uses will clarify its modern definition.

When learning about Cisco Unified Communications, keep the following important points in mind:

- Cisco UC-based communications are effective.

- Communications that use Cisco Unified Communications are more personal than simplistic key systems and unresponsive voice mail.

Unified Communications systems facilitate more effective communications by connecting someone seeking feedback or information with the proper source of that information on first contact. A person with knowledge is connected with a person in need without delay. In a traditional office setting, it is common to hear someone leaving a voice mail and uttering the proverbial line, "phone tag, you're it." This conversation comes after two parties trying to relay some form of information continue to miss each other and are relegated to communicating through a recording. Hours and, in some cases, days pass while a decision is postponed waiting for two parties to communicate. In business, where time to market and reaction time to customers can make or break a deal, phone tag can be fatal. In a call center environment where a business's productivity and ultimate success is measured in a call's time to resolution, time wasted trying to track down the person that can address the customer's issue has a cost in terms of staffing and customer satisfaction. Getting to the right person with the right answer, on the first attempt, is crucial to keeping call resolution times at a minimum. A call center often measures its customer response in what is known as a service-level goal (SLG). A successful business's expended effort should be directed at obtaining, serving, and maintaining customers instead of at facilitating a discussion. With Unified Communications tools, decisions can be made in real time and a customer's problem can be brought to resolution quickly, because the barriers to communication have been mitigated.

Consider a scenario in which a help desk engineer takes a call and is trying to resolve a customer issue. Unknown to the help desk engineer, the person with the information relevant to diagnosing and solving a desperate customer's issue is on vacation. Traditional communications tools might lead to a message sitting in a mailbox for a week while a decision maker vacations in the Caribbean, unaware of the need for his input. Unified communications tools such as Unified Messaging, Single Number Reach, VPN, Presence, and Collaboration provide the help desk engineer with not only the availability status of the person they are trying to contact, but also the information about whether another person who is able to answer his question is currently available via her cell phone in Australia. The help desk engineer calls his resource in Australia and is able to obtain the information needed to aid his customer immediately. This series of communications was effective because the help desk engineer was able to respond to his customer's business need quickly.

In a competitive scenario, the business using UC is able to provide an answer to its customers before a competitor has the chance to return an initial call. The ability to react effectively to a customer's need directly affects both sales and profitability.

Communications platforms that use UC tools are more personal because a business can react to its customers at any time and any place. This ability creates a feeling of relationship with a customer. The small business is able to treat every customer as a top priority. Personally answering calls outside typical business hours is easier with the mobility tools that UC brings. As mentioned earlier, the ability to react quickly to customers not only makes a business effective but also affords the business the time to be more intimate with its customers. Time that would have ordinarily been spent tracking down people and information can now be directed at keeping a customer feeling like part of the family. Faster reaction time to a problem enables a business to concentrate on a business relationship rather than on the problem.

With the introduction of the SBCS suite of products, Cisco delivered the power of Unified Communications to the small business world, a world where its innovation has been desired but has up until now remained elusive. By making the SBCS suite simple and affordable, Cisco has given the small business the opportunity to increase its own productivity and its capability to deliver unparalleled value to its customers. Having such tools, previously only available to much larger businesses, the small business can facilitate communications that are more personal. The resulting more intimate style of communications builds relationships that are conducive to attracting new customers. It makes easy the task of keeping existing customers loyal. Increased communications among the small business's staff enables the business to respond quickly to its customers' needs. The ability to take communications on the road—to be able to communicate anywhere via VPN or Mobility, at any time, on any device—makes the small business extremely nimble and highly available.

Unified Communications brings the capacity for business transformation, and the ramifications are immense. For the small business, introducing the power of Unified Communications means that it can compete with large enterprises. For small businesses, Unified Communications tools can level the business playing field; however, to be feasible, those tools have to be simple, affordable, manageable, and complete. It is here where the SBCS suite hits its mark.

Simplicity

Cisco began the design of its small business–focused UC suite with an overarching principle—simplicity. One of the best parts of working with Cisco products is the fact that they are both feature rich and powerfully flexible. Because Cisco provides a handful of ways to accomplish any given task, its products are able to meet its customers' needs where other vendors cannot. While flexibility is an asset, there are times when the overworked and underappreciated IT pro has too many options and too little time. Incomplete and confusing configurations are the result. In situations where an IT pro has more work than time, simplicity is required. With the breadth of the Cisco Unified Communications product line and its ever-deepening list of features, the process of designing, installing, and maintaining a system can be difficult to simplify. Those engineers that are tasked with designing a Cisco UC solution can appreciate the fact that a thorough design requires a lot of thought and attention to detail.

Suffice it to say, configuring Cisco's UC suite can be nontrivial; however, in the SBCS suite, Cisco took what has traditionally been a lot of work and made it simple by creating preconfigured UC platform packages based on commonly used configurations. Because the number of users in a system often determines both the type of hardware in a design and the way in which it is implemented, Cisco based those packages on user count.

Predefined Hardware and Licensing Configuration

Cisco simplified the implementation of the SBCS suite by pre-engineering the most challenging aspects of a UC design. Arguably, the two most difficult items to engineer correctly in a Cisco UC project are Digital Signal Processors (DSPs) and licensing. Engineering for the correct placement, implementation, and quantity of DSPs requires a solid understanding of how they work and how they are implemented in hardware. Implementing and maintaining the correct licensing for a solution requires the engineer to be up to date with the latest licensing requirements of the UC portfolio and conscientious about keeping that license up to date in terms of upgrades and new users. To be frank, those tasks are difficult. In keeping with the principle of making the SBCS suite simple, those difficult tasks have been pre-engineered.

Because the products that make up the SBCS suite have been designed especially for the small business, the type and quantity of hardware required and the way that hardware will be used can be assumed. The UC520 comes in predetermined configurations that are suitable for small business. It comes in configurations for 8 users, 16 users, 32 users, and 48 users. Embedded in those configurations are the appropriate licensing and DSPs necessary to run those systems in an average-use scenario. By focusing the products and their respective use cases within the solution, two of the most difficult aspects of working with the Cisco UC portfolio have already been handled. The engineer responsible for implementing the system is freed up to spend time and energy on other tasks.

Plug and Play in a Feature-Rich Suite

Cisco simplified the implementation and management of the SBCS suite by taking the best UC solutions in its portfolio and building them into a new suite of products designed to work together with minimal configuration. Each member of the SBCS suite has been designed to be recognized by and managed with the Cisco Configuration Assistant (CCA, a GUI-based tool used for configuration of the UC5XX platform), which applies a default, best-practice configuration to each device. If the SBCS system needs to be expanded, perhaps to add a new wireless infrastructure, the Cisco 526 Wireless Express Mobility Controller is simply plugged into a switch port and powered on. The CCA is then used to automatically integrate the new device into the suite's configuration. The CCA adds the new device to all its topology maps, monitoring graphs and tables, and configuration screens.

Because each of the products in the SBCS suite has been designed to work with one another, the CCA is able to recommend changes that can optimize the system's setup. In a series of clicks via the suite's configuration GUI, the system is able to integrate additional value and power.

Predefined Use Case Assumptions

Cisco simplified the SBCS suite by preconfiguring each of the system components in a manner that addresses the needs of small business in a majority of system deployments. Best-practice configurations for QoS, security, and VLAN segmentation are included in the system's default configuration. The system is preconfigured with typical IOS firewall feature set commands that protect the system from unauthorized external access. As a result, and without any conscious security configuration, the system can be plugged into a public Internet connection via the system's Fast Ethernet WAN port and immediately provide protected access for all the devices in the system. When wireless is part of the system's configuration, a best-practice security policy is applied. Deploying a wireless network with guest access takes minutes, not days. Out of the box there is a VLAN for data and a VLAN for voice. Along with this best-practice VLAN design, a QoS policy that is appropriate for a voice-grade network is applied. This QoS policy allows voice traffic to be placed at a higher priority than data traffic, which is crucial in a UC environment.

Years of Cisco engineering best practices and experience is realized by simply providing power to the system. To have a fully functional key system, you need only supply the UC520 chassis with power, plug a telephone line into one of the standard PSTN ports (the port type varies by model), and then plug an IP telephone handset into one of the onboard Power-over-Ethernet (PoE) switch ports. The system is so powerful in its out-of-the-box configuration that if all you want is basic key system functionality and voice mail, you never have to log in to the configuration utility. If you need another phone, sim-ply plug it in and the system will auto-configure it—a process called auto-registration. The system delivers powerful tools without effort. That is elegant simplicity.

Cisco Configuration Assistant Tool

Cisco simplified the management of the SBCS suite by designing a management interface that is powerful, intuitive, and complete. The Cisco Configuration Assistant (CCA) is a GUI configuration tool that simplifies the customization of any preconfigured system parameters that cannot be left to system defaults. The CCA is aware of the components that make up the SBCS suite and will poll a new system to determine which of the components have been applied to a particular setup. The CCA facilitates drag-and-drop software updates, provides built-in system management graphs and charts, and enables point-and-click configuration.

Affordability

On top of making the SBCS suite simple, Cisco focused on making it affordable. Affordable not only in the cost to purchase the solution, but also affordable to deploy, monitor, and maintain.

When discussing the subject of affordability, one naturally initially thinks in terms of price. While Cisco certainly lowered the overall cost of the SBCS hardware suite by packaging a full-featured solution of components that typically require a substantial investment in servers, routers, switches, and other peripherals into a few purpose-built chassis, the real reason the SBCS suite can be termed affordable is that it has been engineered to be easy to deploy, monitor, and maintain. The SBCS suite is affordable because it has been designed to deliver powerful tools that add value to a business's bottom line without having to dedicate a lot of time and effort to keeping it running. Small business owners will be happy to note that SBCS systems do not require a full-time IT staff to operate and maintain; they are self-sustaining.

Manageability

Building a powerful Unified Communications platform that is both simple and affordable requires a focus on manageability. Manageability is intricately tied to simplicity and affordability. Simply put, a system is neither simple nor affordable if managing the system is difficult and time-consuming. To a small business, the simplicity and affordability of the SBCS suite is directly related to the business's ability to manage the suite without a full-time IT staff. With this in mind, Cisco developed the CCA, which has already been briefly discussed. Because of the power that the CCA tool delivers to the SBCS suite, it warrants further discussion. The CCA delivers streamlined provisioning and a powerful way to perform ongoing management of the SBCS suite.

The CCA contains a list of features coined "Cisco Smart Assist" that enables such things as auto-discovery of supported devices and auto-configuration of those devices. The Cisco Smart Assist features recommend optimization settings and, upon system initialization, implement such things as the following:

- Automatic assignment of phone extensions

- Dial plan setup

- Voice and data VLAN settings

- Firewall policy setup and activation

- Cisco best-practice QoS policies

In addition to aiding in the system's initial setup, the CCA provides an interactive topology view of the SBCS implementation, front-panel views of the devices integrated into the system, system monitoring and reporting tools that facilitate troubleshooting, and time-saving drag-and-drop Cisco IOS system software upgrades.

Complete

Cisco finalized its design of the SBCS suite by ensuring that it was not only simple, affordable, and manageable but also complete. Although you might be tempted to lump the term "complete" into a pile of other convenient marketing terms, it is important to understand that in developing the SBCS suite, Cisco sacrificed neither functionality nor the ability to extend the system when it designed it to be simple.

The tools in the Cisco Unified Communications portfolio that deliver the most value to a business's bottom line have been powerfully integrated into this suite; integrated in a manner focused on small business. Simplicity in the SBCS suite comes from a calculated focus on small business and not by cutting functionality.

The SBCS suite deserves the designation of "complete" because it has been designed to be extendable to include additional business productivity applications. Application developers such as Stonevoice (with its Skype Gateway functionality), varied customer relationship management (CRM) package developers, voice mail integrators, calendar integrators, and countless other partners have delivered applications that continue to accentuate the value a small business derives by using Cisco Unified Communications.

Components of the Smart Business Communications System

Armed with an understanding of UC and how Cisco brought its power to the small business with the SBCS suite, this section presents a technical discussion of the suite's components.

The SBCS suite delivers the power of Unified Communications to the small business with several key components, as listed and described in Table 11.2.

Table 11.2   *Smart Business Communications System Suite Components*

Component	Key Function
UC500 Series for Small Business (UC520)	Suite's central point of connection, IP routing, security policy enforcement, VPN server and endpoint, central call processing, and voice mail.
Catalyst Express Family of Switches (CE520)	Endpoint connectivity and system expansion.
Cisco 521 Wireless Express Access Point	System expansion via 802.11b/g wireless data and voice communications. Runs in standalone and controller-based modes.
Cisco 526 Wireless Express Mobility Controller	Centralized control of Cisco 521 Wireless Express Access Points.
Cisco Configuration Assistant (CCA)	Windows-based application suite provisioning, maintenance, and monitoring.

UC500 Series for Small Business

The UC500 Series for Small Business (UC520) is the key component in the SBCS system. If you were to compare the SBCS suite to the human body, the UC520 would be the heart. This chassis performs several functions within the SBCS suite and is a central point of connection. As the SBCS suite's heart, the UC520 provides inter-VLAN routing, sophisticated security and policy enforcement features via IOS firewall features (referred to as the firewall feature set), and Easy VPN Remote and Server support for remote connectivity. The UC520 provides central call processing for the SBCS suite via CUCME version 4.3 (including SIP trunk support), and voice-mail services via CUE 3.03. It supports the full portfolio of Cisco Unified IP phones via eight built-in PoE (802.3af or Cisco pre-standard) switch ports, and contains the voice ports necessary to attach the system to the PSTN.

Although the UC520 device is based on, and is similar in function to, the Integrated Services Router platform, it does not support dynamic routing protocols such as EIGRP or OSPF, Survivable Remote Site Telephony (SRST), Communications Manager integration, or WAN interface cards for remote office data connectivity.

The UC520 chassis is not field upgradeable. The form factor purchased limits the number of users supported in terms of both licensing and hardware and cannot be physically upgraded. When integrating the SBCS suite, anticipated growth plans should be taken into account. If growth plans indicate that there is a potential for more than 16 users at some point in the future, it is wise to invest in a larger system when initially deploying the system.

As has been discussed previously, one of the ways Cisco was able to bring the power of Unified Communications to small business was by simplifying the platform and its configuration based on common use-case scenarios. Because the number of users in an installation is the most variable aspect of the system design, and the number of users plays a major part in determining the quantity and type of hardware within a system, this is where Cisco segmented the SBCS product offerings. A majority of the product SKUs available in the SBCS suite are different variations of the UC520 chassis. All UC520 product SKUs have the following:

- A console port

- A 3.5mm Music on Hold (MoH) audio jack

- An integrated eight-port 10/100BASE-TX PoE switch

- Four FXS ports

- A 10/100BASE-TX WAN port

- A 10/100BASE-TX LAN expansion port

SKUs that support 8 or 16 users come in a desktop chassis with external power and the option for an integrated wireless access point. The SKUs that support up to 32 or 48 users come in a rack-mount form factor and do not offer an integrated wireless option but can incorporate an external wireless infrastructure.

Tip   The integrated 10/100BASE-TX switch provides a total of 80W of 802.3af or Cisco prestandard PoE. Administrators should be careful not to oversubscribe the inline power available. With the recent support of the 7945/7965/7975 generation of Class 3 802.3af IP handsets, oversubscription is possible with the internal switch. The integration of an external Catalyst Express switch can be used to get around this potential limitation.

UC520 8- and 16-User Use Case

The UC520 chassis for 8 and 16 users is a 1.5U device with an external power module. This device comes in desktop form factor but can be mounted in a standard 19-inch rack with an add-on rack-mount kit for the chassis and its external power supply. It is orderable in several configurations based on the user count supported (either 8 or 16), whether an integrated wireless AP is desired, and the type of PSTN connectivity desired (either Basic Rate Interface [BRI] or Foreign Exchange Office [FXO]). The 8- and 16-user models come with a fixed packet voice data module, type 2 (PVDM2), the PVDM2-32, which is used for voice termination, conferencing, and transcoding.

Figure 11.1 depicts the front panel of the 8-user model with the FXO and integrated wireless options. The 16-user model with similar options has the same port configuration, because licensing is the key difference between the 8- and 16-user models. The 16-user models require an additional Catalyst Express switch to support the requirements for an additional eight data and PoE ports.

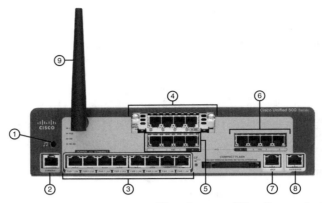

Figure 11.1   *UC520 8- and 16-User Chassis with 4 FXO Ports*

Moving from left to right in Figure 11.1, the ports are as follows:

1. **Music on Hold (MoH) audio jack:** This port is a 3.5-mm audio port for live audio feeds. The system passes audio feeds from this port into the small business network as a multicast stream. Although the system comes preconfigured with an MoH file that resides in compact flash, this file is not played when a live audio stream is connected to the MoH jack. MoH can fail back and forth between the live MoH audio jack and the file in compact flash. This failover typically takes about 30 seconds.

2. **Console/Aux port:** This port is usually used for system recovery or direct access to the UC520 IOS command line. This port can detect modems and can switch between Console and Aux port functionality. This port can be used for remote management when connected to a modem.

3. **Power over Ethernet (PoE) ports:** These ports are 10/100BASE-TX ports that can supply up to 15.4W of 802.3af or Cisco prestandard PoE power to any PoE device. The switch integrated into the UC520 chassis can support a maximum of 80W over its eight PoE ports. Port designations in IOS are FastEthernet 0/1/0–7.

4. **Voice expansion port:** This port is a traditional VWIC slot that enables PSTN connectivity to be expanded. This port supports the following interface cards: VIC-4FXS/DID, VIC2-2FXO, VIC2-4FXO, VIC2-2BRI-NT/TE, VIC2-FXS, VIC3-2FXS/DID, VIC3-4FXS/DID, and VWIC2-1MFT-T1/E1.

5. **FXO ports:** These four integrated Foreign Exchange Office ports are unique to the FXO version of the UC520 and are used for basic PSTN connectivity. Port designations in IOS are voice-port 0/1/0–3. These ports would be replaced by two BRI ports in the 8- and 16-user BRI model.

6. **FXS ports:** These four Foreign Exchange Station ports are found in every model of the UC520. These ports are used for integrating analog phone devices such as a fax machine, modem, or a traditional analog phone. Port designations in IOS are voice-port 0/0/1–3.

7. **WAN port:** This port is a 10/100BASE-TX port used to connect the UC520 to an external uplink. Typically this port would be used to connect to a cable modem or a DSL router for Internet access. By default, this port is configured to receive its IP address via DHCP and is considered an outside interface by the firewall feature set. This port is designated as FastEthernet 0/0 in IOS.

8. **LAN expansion port:** This port is a 10/100BASE-TX port used to uplink a Catalyst Express switch to support system expansion.

9. **Integrated wireless AP:** This integrated wireless access point is an 802.11b/g AP and is available only in the 8- and 16-user UC520 models.

Figure 11.2 illustrates the two-port BRI model of the 8- and 16-user UC520 chassis and highlights the fact that the integrated wireless access point is a factory-installable option. In this figure, the wireless option has not been selected.

Figure 11.2   *UC520 8- and 16-User Chassis with Two BRI Ports*

UC520 24-, 32-, and 48-User Use Case

In comparison to the 8- and 16-user UC520 models, which are 1.5U in height, come in a desktop form factor, and utilize an external power supply, the UC520 chassis for 24, 32, and 48 users is a rack-mountable 2U device with an integrated power supply. This chassis is orderable in several preconfigured options based on the number of users to be supported and the PSTN interfaces required. The PSTN options available in these models are scaled for a denser user deployment and include options for FXO densities as high as 12 ports, an optional integrated T1/E1 interface, and optional BRI densities as high as 6 ports. Product SKUs are very descriptive and describe the built-in PSTN options available in each model. It is important to note that the integrated wireless option is not available in the 24-, 32-, or 48-user models.

Similar to the requirements in the 16-user desktop model, to support a user count greater than 8 users, a separate Catalyst Express switch is required for data and PoE.

Figure 11.3 depicts the front panel of the 24-, 32-, and 48-user model with an integrated T1/E1 port.

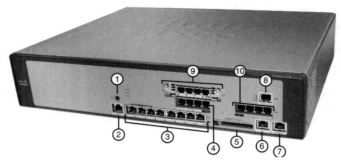

(Photo Courtesy of Cisco Systems, Inc. Unauthorized use not permitted.)

Figure 11.3   *UC520 24-, 32-, and 48-User Chassis with Integrated T1/E1 Port*

Starting from the left and running generally counterclockwise in Figure 11.3, the ports are as follows:

1. Music on Hold (MoH) port

2. Console/Aux port

3. Power over Ethernet (PoE) ports

4. FXO ports

5. Compact Flash slot

6. WAN port (10/100BASE-TX)

7. LAN expansion port (10/100BASE-TX)

8. T1/E1 port

9. Voice expansion port

10. FXS ports

Catalyst Express Family of SBCS Switches

The Cisco Catalyst Express 520 (CE520) Series Switches are a family of fixed-configuration switches specifically engineered for the SBCS suite of products. If the UC520 models can be considered the heart of the SBCS suite, the CE520 switches would be considered its backbone. The CE520 switches are a feature-rich and scalable platform with which Cisco extends the capacity of the SBCS system from 8 users up to 48. The CE520 switches provide wire-speed Fast Ethernet to Gigabit Ethernet connectivity, provide PoE (802.3af or Cisco prestandard), and come preconfigured with the QoS and security policies that deliver Cisco's documented best practices for IP communications and wireless deployments. The CE520 family is managed exclusively via the CCA GUI and therefore does not come with a console/aux port as does the UC520 chassis.

Note   Switches outside the CE520 family can be incorporated into an SBCS design but cannot be configured, managed, monitored, or maintained by the CCA. Administration and configuration of these switches would need to be coordinated with the SBCS suite and would be done with each device's native configuration interface.

Cisco has engineered several different models within the CE520 family to meet the diverse needs found in small business. Table 11.3 lists the models relevant to the CE520 family.

Table 11.3   *Catalyst Express 520 Switches*

Model	Port Type Configuration	PoE Ports (Yes or No)	Ideal Use Case
CE520-8PC	8 10/100BASE-TX access ports	Yes	Low-density IP phone, wireless AP, or IP video networks
	1 10/100/1000BASE-TX or SFP uplink port	No	
CE520-24TT	24 10/100BASE-TX access ports	No	Basic desktop installation with need for integrated QoS and VLAN configuration
	2 10/100/1000BASE-TX uplink ports	No	
CE520-24LC	20 10/100BASE-TX access ports	No	Basic desktop connectivity needs with limited PoE requirements
	4 10/100BASE-TX access ports	Yes	
	2 10/100/1000BASE-TX of SFP uplink ports	No	
CE520-24PC	24 10/100BASE-TX access ports	Yes	Full-scale IP phone systems or larger wireless networks
	2 10/100/1000BASE-TX or SFP uplink ports	No	

continues

Table 11.3   *Catalyst Express 520 Switches   continued*

Model	Port Type Configuration	PoE Ports (Yes or No)	Ideal Use Case
CE520G-24TC	24 10/100/1000BASE-TX access ports	No	High-speed backbone switch for server connectivity or high-speed desktop connectivity requirements
	2 10/100/1000BASE-TX or SFP uplink ports	No	

The Cisco Mobility Express System

In the SBCS suite, the needs for wireless voice and for wireless data connectivity are addressed with the Cisco 521 Wireless Express Access Point. Depending on the wireless coverage and manageability requirements of a particular design, the system can be managed and extended with the Cisco 526 Wireless Express Mobility Controller. As indicated earlier in this chapter, basic wireless requirements in the SBCS suite can be addressed by ordering the integrated wireless option in the UC520 8- and-16 user models. In the 32- and 48-user models of the UC520, the integrated option is not available. In cases where a 32- or 48-user UC520 model has been deployed or additional wireless coverage is required above and beyond the single AP integrated in the UC520 chassis, the Cisco 521 Wireless AP can be added to design to scale the solution.

The Cisco 521 Wireless Express 802.11b/g AP operates in one of two modes:

- **Standalone mode (mode one):** The CCA is used to manage up to three independent Cisco 521 APs.

- **Controller-based mode (mode two):** Used in cases where four or more wireless APs are required or where this mode is a better fit for a particular implementation. In this mode, the CCA requires the introduction of the Cisco 526 Wireless Express Mobility Controller. Each Cisco 526 Mobility Controller can manage up to six APs, and a maximum of two Controllers can be added to a single SBCS system. In mode two, the CCA can control (via the Cisco 526 Wireless Express Mobility Controller) up to as many as 12 APs in a single SBCS deployment.

It is important to mention that, in keeping with the SBCS suite's design tenets of affordability, simplicity, and power, a robust wireless security policy has been pre-engineered into the system. The Cisco 521 Wireless APs support AES encryption and are both 802.11i-compliant and WPA/WPA2 certified. Best-practice security policies are automatically implemented by the CCA, which saves time, ensures configuration accuracy, and keeps the management of the system simple.

Common Deployment Scenarios

This final section of the chapter first briefly discusses the planning that should be done to correctly implement the SBCS suite and then closes by discussing the most common ways in which the components of the SBCS suite are deployed.

SBCS Network Design Planning

Network architects will tell you that when designing a new data and voice infrastructure, several items are typically considered:

- What business issues is this design trying to address?

- What tools do I have to address those issues?

- What are the budget constraints?

- How much growth is anticipated and will this design scale?

- How many users will this design have to support?

- How will this design be supported and managed?

With this information, an engineer can begin to assemble a design that addresses business issues. A well-engineered system does not start with unpacking boxes of network equipment; it starts with planning. In the case of the SBCS, a lot of the network planning and design has been engineered directly into the system. Cisco, by pre-engineering and prepackaging the SBCS suite, has presented its customers with a simplified way to enjoy the benefits of Unified Communications. What is left for the customer and his technology integration partner to decide is which of the SBCS suite of products are needed and how they should fit into the small business environment.

Assuming for a moment that the decision has been made to pursue the integration of Unified Communications with the SBCS suite, consideration has already been given to business issues, tools, and budget constraints. To a large extent, the design management decisions have also been made, given that management tools for the SBCS suite are so intimately ingrained. What needs to be discussed moving forward, then, are growth projections and the number of users to be supported.

When implementing the SBCS suite of products, it is imperative to give thought to the number of users that are expected to be supported, including growth projections, prior to purchasing the system. The reason it is so important to determine the maximum users that might ultimately be supported lies in the fact that the UC520, the heart of the SBCS suite, is prepackaged based on the number of users each chassis will support. Prepackaging the UC520 is part of what makes the SBCS suite so easy to deploy; however, not considering the ramifications of prepackaging can be problematic. The UC520 is not field upgradeable, so if growth is not taken into account, the small business may be forced to rip out an existing installation and replace it with one that can scale to the new growth requirements. Although it has already been mentioned in this chapter, the following bears repeating—the UC520 chassis should be engineered for the maximum number of users that *could* be supported in the small business.

After considering the number of users that will ultimately be supported with the SBCS suite, the next step is to lay out the final configuration of the system.

Deploying the SBCS Suite for Eight Users

Deploying the SBCS suite for eight or fewer users is extremely simple. Because the heart of the system, the UC520, already has eight built-in PoE switch ports, an expansion switch from the CE520 family of switches is typically not needed. In this very small use case, the single integrated wireless AP will generally be sufficient for wireless needs. The 8- and 16-user models of the UC520 come in a desktop form factor, so if the system will be installed in a standard 19-inch rack, a special rack-mount kit must be added to the bill of materials. Figure 11.4 depicts the most common configuration for an office in which eight or fewer users are to be supported.

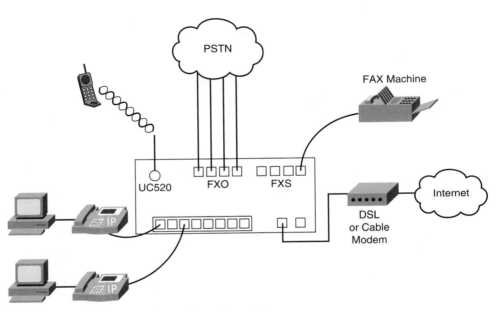

Figure 11.4   *SBCS Suite for Eight or Fewer Users*

Deploying the SBCS Suite for Up to 16 Users

Deploying the SBCS suite for up to 16 users is typically very much like the eight-user case with the exception of licensing and the requirement for additional PoE ports. Additional PoE ports are supplied by adding a Catalyst Express CE520-8PC to an appropriately licensed UC520 chassis as depicted in Figure 11.5. The AP integrated into the UC520 is typically sufficient in this small design, but if additional access points are required because of data throughput or wireless propagation issues, the Cisco 521 Wireless Express APs can be integrated into the design. Pay close attention to the number of switch ports required to support all the design's phones, PCs, APs, and servers.

If more than 16 data ports are required in the design, the CE520-8PC switch should be replaced with the CE520-24PC switch.

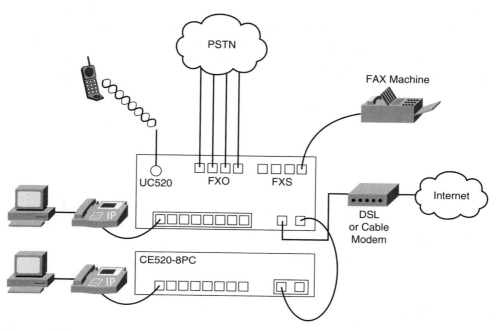

Figure 11.5   *SBCS Suite for Up to 16 Users*

Deploying the SBCS Suite for Up to 48 Users

Although no more difficult than deploying the SBCS suite for 8 or 16 users, the design for a system that supports up to 48 users is a bit different. As is the case in the deployment of every SBCS design, the UC520 is the heart of the design. The UC520 chassis that supports 32 or 48 users comes in a rack-mount form factor and does not come with an integrated wireless option. Typically, PSTN connectivity for an office of this size will be a channelized T1/E1; however, high-density FXO models of the UC520 are available. If the small business has a need for wireless communications, one or more Cisco 521 Wireless Express APs should be added to the design. In this scale of deployment, it is common to need more than just one AP. The CCA can manage up to three Cisco 521 Wireless Express APs in standalone mode. If more than three APs are required in the implementation, the Cisco 526 Mobility Express Wireless Controller should be added to the design. As is shown in Figure 11.6, this is generally the case in a 32-user deployment. Switch ports for 32 users and the required uplinks for servers and APs will require the addition of PoE ports. The CE520-24PC is added to the design in the 32-user scenario. If more than 32 data ports are required or if Gigabit Ethernet is required, any of the other members of the Catalyst Express family, such as the CE520G-24TC or the CE520-8PC, may be integrated into the solution.

Tip   A network design centered on the SBCS platform can be extended by adding additional equipment as necessary. It is not mandatory that all the equipment in your design be a member of the SBCS suite but you should be aware that you will lose the ability to manage non-SBCS equipment with the CCA GUI. If adding a switch such as the Cisco Catalyst 3560E-48PD, a switch commonly found in UC installations, makes sense in your particular design, then it is technically sound to do so. You must be aware, however, that it must be managed separately from the rest of the SBCS platform.

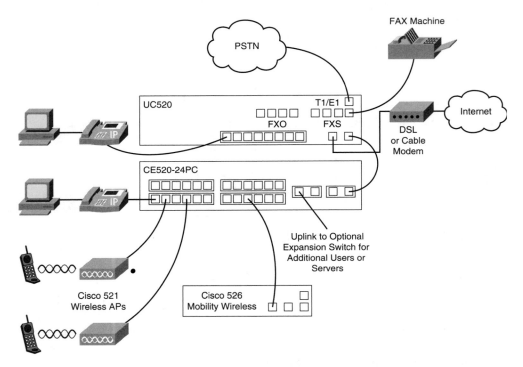

Figure 11.6   *SBCS Suite for Up to 32 to 48 Users*

Deploying the SBCS Suite as a WAN Branch Office

Although this type of SBCS deployment is likely to be uncommon, it is mentioned here to point out a few design caveats that should be taken into consideration when integrating the suite with a larger data infrastructure. The UC520 is engineered to use an upstream Ethernet connection, typical in a DSL or cable modem Internet service provider scenario. This connection is via the WAN port (refer to item 8 in Figure 11.1). If this office is a branch office and the overall system design requires the use of WAN protocols such as T1 or Frame Relay, a separate router is required to perform this function. It is tempting to want to install the supported VWIC2-1MFT-T1/E1 module in the voice expansion module of the UC520 and expect it to perform WAN termination.

Unfortunately, although this VWIC is supported in the voice expansion slot of the UC520, it is only supported in its voice capacity. Data termination in this slot is not supported. A second caveat that should be considered when implementing this design is that the UC520 does not support SRST or any form of Unified Communications Manager integration. Figure 11.7 depicts the most common WAN branch office type of deployment.

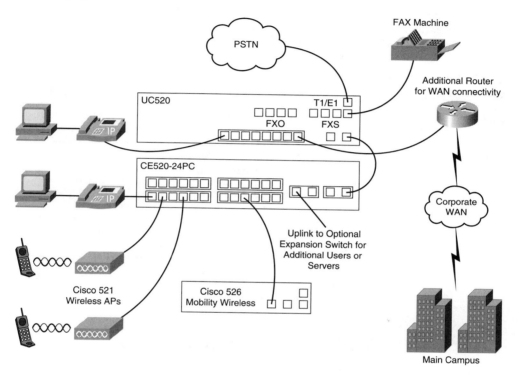

Figure 11.7   *SBCS Suite as a WAN Branch Office*

Exam Preparation Tasks

Review All the Key Topics

Review the most important topics in the chapter, noted with the key topics icon in the outer margin of the page. Table 11.4 lists and describes these key topics and identifies the page number on which each is found.

Table 11.4 *Key Topics for Chapter 11*

Key Topic Element	Description	Page Number
Paragraph	The SBCS suite brings the power of UC to small business	413
Definition	Key components of the Cisco Configuration Assistant (CCA)	418
Table 11.2	The SBCS suite's components and key functions	420
Paragraph	Understand the difference between the UC520 chassis and a Cisco ISR router	420
Paragraph	Understand that the UC520 is not field upgradeable	420

Complete the Tables and Lists from Memory

Print a copy of Appendix C, "Memory Tables" (found on the CD), or at least the section for this chapter, and complete the tables and lists from memory. Appendix D, "Memory Tables Answer Key," also on the CD, includes completed tables and lists to check your work.

Definitions of Key Terms

Define the following key terms from this chapter, and check your answers in the glossary.

Unified Communications

CCA

Cisco Smart Assist

voice expansion port

LAN expansion port

Foundation Topics: This section provides a quick review of how the UC500 Series for Small Business (UC520) fits into the overall design of the Smart Business Communications System (SBCS) and reviews the purpose of the Cisco Configuration Assistant (CCA).

Cisco Configuration Assistant: This section discusses the installation, function, and operation of the CCA and how it relates to operating the SBCS.

Configuring the UC520 for Voice: This section is the primary focus of this chapter and details the process of preparing a UC520 chassis to provide telephony and voice-mail services.

Using CCA for System Maintenance and Troubleshooting: This section introduces the CCA tools with which a system administrator would maintain and troubleshoot the SBCS platform.

CHAPTER 12

Configuring and Maintaining the UC500 Series for Voice

Armed with the knowledge of how IP phones are configured in Cisco Unified CME from Chapter 5 and having been introduced to the UC500 Series for Small Business in Chapter 11, you are now going to delve into the implementation, configuration, and maintenance of the voice components of the UC520 chassis. Chapter 11 introduced you to the SBCS suite and the fact that it was put together with simplicity in mind. This chapter walks you through the simple menus of the Cisco Configuration Assistant (CCA) tool and demonstrates that a fully functional Cisco Unified CME and Cisco Unity Express telephony system can be implemented in a matter of minutes and powerfully managed with a simple yet feature rich GUI.

"Do I Know This Already?" Quiz

The "Do I Know This Already?" quiz allows you to assess whether you should read this entire chapter or simply jump to the "Exam Preparation Tasks" section for review. If you are in doubt, read the entire chapter. Table 12.1 outlines the major headings in this chapter and the corresponding "Do I Know This Already?" quiz questions. You can find the answers in Appendix A, "Answers to the 'Do I Know This Already?' Quizzes."

Table 12.1   *"Do I Know This Already?" Foundation Topics Section-to-Question Mapping*

Foundation Topics Section	Questions Covered in This Section
Ensuring the Foundation	1
Cisco Configuration Assistant	2–6
Configuring the UC520 for Voice	7–10
Using CCA for System Maintenance and Troubleshooting	11

1. Which of the following best describes the power failover (PFO) feature implemented in the UC520?

   a. When power is lost, a Foreign Exchange Office (FXO) PSTN trunk is directly connected to a Foreign Exchange Station (FXS) analog port, allowing for calls to be placed during a power failure.

   b. The UC520, configured with dual power supplies, is able to fail from a primary power supply to a backup power supply in the event of a primary power supply hardware failure.

   c. When implemented in hot-standby pairs, call control fails over to a backup chassis in the event power is interrupted to the primary UC520 chassis.

   d. When the UC520 is implemented with an auxiliary PoE switch and loses power, the auxiliary switch can maintain power to phones.

2. Which of the following best describes the CCA tool?

   a. The CCA tool is a snap-in to a web browser that enables configuration and management of Cisco Unified Communications Manager Express.

   b. The CCA tool is a powerful and intuitive GUI that is used to manage, monitor, and customize the components of the Smart Business Communications System, including the UC500.

   c. The CCA tool is a command-line-based bulk-administration tool used to mass provision IP handsets in a CME environment.

   d. The CCA is a tool that is used exclusively for monitoring the SBCS suite once it has been deployed.

3. For a device to join a community, a candidate must have which three of the following items?

  a. An IP address

  b. Zero configuration

  c. HTTP or HTTPS enabled on the default ports

  d. Be supported by the CCA tool

  e. The console port set to 19200 baud

4. Out of the box, what is the default IP address assigned to the UC520 and used for seeding community discovery?

  a. 172.16.10.1

  b. 192.168.100.1

  c. 192.168.10.1

  d. 10.1.1.1

5. Which of the following protocols plays a key part in determining the initial topology view created by the CCA?

  a. SMTP

  b. NTP

  c. CDP

  d. Telnet

6. What is the default username and password combination to initially access the UC520 for device discovery?

  a. admin/password

  b. Cisco/password

  c. cisco/cisco

  d. admin/Cisco

7. What IP address range is assigned by default to the voice VLAN in an out-of-the-box configuration?

  a. 10.1.1.0/24

  b. 192.168.101.0/24

  c. 172.16.0.0/16

  d. 192.168.100.0/24

8. In an out-of-the-box installation, which of the following components requires the use of the Cisco Configuration Agent (CCA) prior to its first use?

   a. Music on Hold port

   b. Cisco Unity Express Voice Mail

   c. Power over Ethernet (PoE)

   d. Power failover (PFO)

9. If the UC520 system is deployed with all the system defaults, what extension will be assigned to the first IP handset to register with the system?

   a. 1001

   b. 100

   c. 201

   d. 500

10. On which tab of the Voice dialog box is call park enabled?

   a. Voice Features tab

   b. Dial Plan tab

   c. AA & Voicemail tab

   d. System tab

11. Which of the following tasks is not managed via the Maintenance menu on the CCA feature bar?

   a. Upgrading software within the suite

   b. Managing file systems

   c. Backing up and restoring suite component configurations

   d. Restarting and resetting devices

   e. All the provided options are managed in the GUI under the Maintenance menu.

Foundation Topics

To fully understand the concepts that will be discussed in this chapter and to better understand the steps required to configure the UC500 Series for voice, it is important to first understand what the system can do out of the box. It is important to understand:

■ The UC500 Series for Small Business, also known as the UC520, can deliver full-featured data, best-practice security, and remote VPN access with very little configuration.

■ The UC520 chassis can provide basic phone service without any user configuration.

To that end, a foundational discussion of the UC520 is in order. Your journey toward configuring the UC520 for voice begins with a high-level discussion of the data, security, and VPN architecture that the UC520 builds its Unified Communications capabilities upon.

Preconfigured Data, Security, and VPN Templates

The UC520 chassis, also known as the UC500 Series for Small Business, delivers tremendous value to small businesses right out of the box. The engineering might of an enterprise business is delivered to the small business by simply attaching the UC520 chassis to the small business's network. Many of the features found in enterprise class network equipment and the engineering know-how of large IT organizations have been rolled into this product out of the box. Starting with the system's delivery of an industry best-practice security and QoS configuration, and delivering all the way to providing basic dial tone without any configuration, the UC520 is a powerhouse.

The UC520 provides the core data infrastructure for a small office and comes preconfigured with the routing and switching configuration required to open a small branch office. The system's default configuration includes a native VLAN1 for data, and comes preconfigured with an auxiliary VLAN100 for the inclusion of voice. The WAN interface is preconfigured to receive its IP address from an Internet service provider (ISP) via DHCP. The internal switch ports are configured to receive private addressing via preconfigured private DHCP scopes served directly out of the UC520. In the default configuration, the data VLAN (VLAN1) receives addresses in the 192.168.10.0/24 network and the auxiliary VLAN (VLAN100) receives addresses in the 10.1.1.0/24 network. The routing to facilitate IP connectivity in and out of the system has been preconfigured.

Integrated with the network configuration that delivers data services to the small office is a well-thought-out security configuration. The UC520, built and configured with the Cisco IOS Firewall feature set, is designed to protect a small office connected to the Internet. The system has been designed to connect to the Internet via a DSL or cable modem and comes preconfigured to provide the security required to do so. The preconfigured security policy includes NAT, best-practice ACL filtering, and the foundation for an IPsec-based VPN network. The security policy automatically protects the voice VLAN from the data VLAN—a policy that is recommended to ensure quality voice in a converged network. In cases where the factory data network is expanded with the Cisco Configuration Assistant (CCA) to provide additional network coverage (new subnets and VLANs), the system is smart enough to apply the best-practice security policy to the newly introduced networks.

Carrying the system's native security abilities forward, the system is capable of delivering site-to-site EZ-VPNs between disparate UC520 systems and is able to deliver secured network access to remote users who use the Cisco VPN client. To deploy a secure VPN for remote users, the system will require an administrator to do some basic configuration. The creation of user accounts and secure password strings is required. Although not completely functional out of the box, you should walk away with the idea that a powerful remote-access network can be provided with very little intervention.

Note   Although having preconfigured users and password strings might have been convenient, Cisco did not configure them for security reasons. The VPN aspect of the UC520 has been simplified for ease of management but only as much as is prudent in a comprehensive security policy.

Preconfigured Basic Voice Platform

Built on top of the system's strong out-of-the-box foundation is a preconfigured phone switch with basic services. Without any configuration, a small business can be up and running with a basic phone system in minutes. Simply plugging in telephones and connecting a telephone line to the system's built-in FXO ports will provide a business with all that is necessary to make and receive calls. Even more impressive is the fact that the UC520's out-of-the-box phone configuration can provide basic phone services without power.

With the system's power failover (PFO) feature, the system can deliver emergency dial tone to an analog handset in the case of a power failure. This feature works by electrically connecting one of the system's Foreign Exchange Office (FXO) ports to a Foreign Exchange Station (FXS) port when power is removed from the chassis. This feature allows a designated analog handset to place calls through the system even in a power outage.

Although the UC500 Series for Small Business requires little effort from the network administrator to be useful, it can do even more. You can tailor the UC500 to your business's specific requirements by using the Cisco Configuration Assistant (CCA).

Cisco Configuration Assistant

CCA, an application that is downloadable from Cisco.com free of charge, is the tool you use to configure, manage, and maintain the SBCS suite. In Chapter 11 you were introduced to the Smart Business Communications System. In that introduction, the UC520 was likened to the human heart. As the central part of the suite, the UC520 is the heart of the SBCS platform. All voice and data traffic throughout the suite is processed and pumped out to the platform's peripherals through the UC520. If the SBCS suite can be likened to the human body and the UC520 is at its heart, the CCA tool is what breathes life and personality into the suite.

Obtaining and Installing the CCA Software

The CCA tool is a windows executable that you can download from Cisco.com.

Note   Access to most software downloads require a Cisco.com login, which you can obtain by clicking the Register link in the top-right corner of the web page.

To run the CCA tool, your computer must meet the following requirements:

- **Processor speed:** 1 GHz

- **DRAM:** 512 MB minimum; 1024 MB recommended for better performance

- **Hard-disk space:** 150 MB for Cisco Configuration Assistant alone; 300 MB recommended

- **Number of colors:** 65,536

- **Resolution:** 1024 x 768

- **Font size:** small

- **Windows version:** Windows XP SP1 or later, or Windows Vista Ultimate

You can obtain the CCA software from the following URL: http://tinyurl.com/5cn884. You will be asked to provide your Cisco.com login.

Note   The preceding URL is actually substantially longer but was shortened for your convenience. This URL directs you to version 1.6 of the CCA tool—the latest version available as of the time of this writing.

For those reading this book that may be a bit more adventurous, it is well worth your time to explore the Cisco.com website and drill down to the actual link. On your journey to the correct page within Cisco.com, you will find many valuable tools in your quest for Cisco certification. Figure 12.1 depicts the final CCA download page where you select the software revision appropriate to your needs.

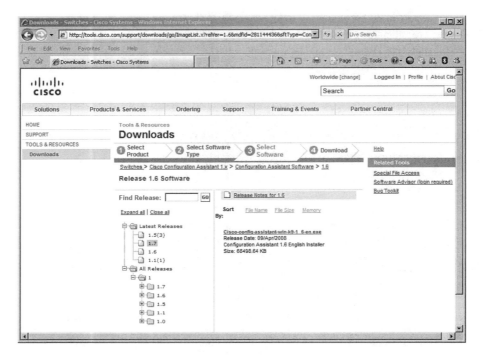

Figure 12.1   *CCA Download Page on Cisco.com*

After you download and install the software, you are ready to begin your adventure into the depths of the CCA tool.

Preparing CCA for System Management

To begin managing the SBCS suite, the CCA must first be made aware of the environment in which it will be operating. The system needs to know what devices it will be working with and how the suite is set up. Upon starting the CCA application for the first time, you will be presented with the window and dialog box shown in Figure 12.2.

At this point you are given the opportunity to create a new community or to connect to an existing community. The question you should ask yourself at this point is, "What is a community?" Before moving forward in the CCA GUI, a discussion about CCA communities is appropriate.

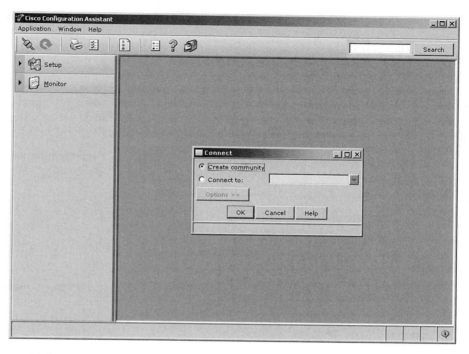

Figure 12.2   *Creating a CCA Community*

Understanding Communities

The concept of communities is an important topic to master in the context of the CCA tool. A CCA community is a "family" of SBCS suite devices knitted together to provide a UC solution for a particular location. Generally speaking, a CCA community is composed of the components of the SBCS suite. At the heart of the community there is a UC520 chassis. Adjoined to the UC520 is likely to be one or more Cisco Catalyst Express 520 Series Switches, several IP phones, and perhaps other SBCS suite components such as the Cisco Wireless Express 521 AP. This community of devices is managed via a common console and can be configured, monitored, and maintained as a single group rather than a bunch of disparate devices. Community device configurations will be backed up as a package and can be upgraded and patched as such. Network performance monitoring and error notification is treated as an integrated reporting solution rather than as a series of individual unrelated items.

In a social sphere, a community might be defined as a group of people who live in close proximity and share common interests, work, and resources. This social definition of a community lends itself nicely to describing the function of a CCA community. The SBCS suite of devices at a particular location (for example, devices in a close proximity) share a common design framework (common interests) and work as a suite to provide a well-rounded and powerful UC solution for a small business.

From a technical perspective, a CCA community is best likened to the community of devices that comprises a local-area network (LAN). The CCA community will represent all of those devices whose common purpose is to serve the voice and data requirements within a specific location and share a common backbone and management platform.

In addition to understanding the concept of a CCA community, it is important to understand the technical aspects of a community. To join a community, a device must meet the following criteria:

■   Have an IP address

■   Be supported by the CCA tool

■   Have either HTTP or HTTPS enabled on the default ports

The scope, or reach, of the community is limited by the following (the combined number of the following device types cannot exceed 25):

■   Catalyst Express Switches

■   800 Series Routers

■   UC 500 Series platforms (UC520)

■   WLAN controllers

■   Aironet Autonomous APs (individually managed APs that do not require a controller to operate)

■   HWIC Access Points

In addition, note the following restrictions:

■   No more than 15 of the maximum 25 devices are Catalyst Express Switches

■   The sum of 800 Series Routers Plus UC500 Series platforms is no more than five

■   No more than two WLAN controllers

■   The sum of Autonomous APs and HWIC APs is no more than three

Finally, it should be noted that non-SBCS devices can be recognized in a topology view of the community but they cannot be configured, monitored, and maintained with the CCA tool.

Note   For the purposes of this book, you will only look at managing one community at a time, although it is important to note that it is not out of the realm of possibility that multiple communities could be managed from a single CCA console. The CCA tool is capable of managing several communities through one console—it is just uncommon. In an enterprise network, it is entirely feasible that a centralized enterprise IT department, an outsourced consultant, or engineers from a Cisco Partner could manage a series of completely self-contained SBCS communities with a single console interface, if business requirements dictated the need.

Creating Communities

Now, with a preliminary understanding of the concept of a CCA community, you are poised to create your own. Creating your own community will go a long way toward cementing your understanding of the concept and its parameters.

To create a new CCA community, you must seed the new community discovery process. In that process, you need to decide how you will detect the members of your new CCA community. The default method involves selecting a central seed device, usually your UC520, and using its Cisco Discovery Protocol (CDP) tables to determine its neighbors. The process extends through the network by logging into the neighbors that were found in the seed device's CDP tables and then looking at their respective CDP tables. This process iterates up to four hops from the initial seed device. You should be aware that because this discovery method relies on CDP, non-Cisco devices in your topology or devices on which CDP has been disabled can lead to an abbreviated topology discovery. If a specific device is not automatically discovered, it can still be added in one of two other ways: either through a static discovery based on a specific IP address or a static discovery based on an entire subnet search.

Note   The term *seed device* may be new to you. This term comes from the network management field and is a reference to a device that is used as a launching point for network discovery. A seed device is usually at the center of a network, which is a useful place to begin discovery because it is likely to be closely connected to a majority of the devices in your network.

Follow these steps to create a new CCA community:

Step 1.   Select the **Create Community** radio button in the Connect dialog box (refer to Figure 12.3) and click **OK**.

Step 2.   In the Create Community window, shown in Figure 12.3, enter a name for your new community and, optionally, a company name. In the Discover Devices area, click the **Discover** drop-down arrow and choose **Devices Using a Seed IP Address**. Enter the default IP address of the UC520, which is **192.168.10.1**. Click **Start**.

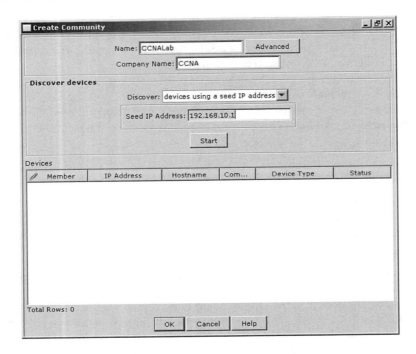

Figure 12.3   *Create Community Window*

Step 3.   A Security Certificate Alert appears, as shown in Figure 12.4. Click **Always.**

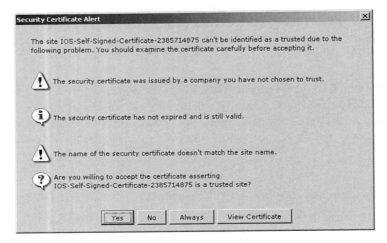

Figure 12.4   *Security Certificate Alert*

Step 4.   The CCA discovery process asks you for the UC520's authentication credentials, as shown in Figure 12.5. Out of the box, the UC520's default username is **cisco.** The default password is **cisco.** Passwords are case sensitive. Click OK.

Figure 12.5 *Device Authentication*

Step 5.   The CCA goes through a discovery process with CDP and identifies the devices in your CCA community. When the discovery process is completed, click **OK** and you will be presented with a view of your topology similar that shown in Figure 12.6.

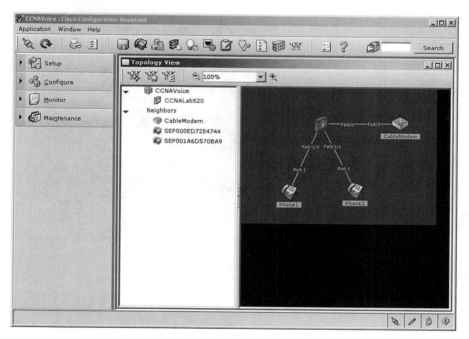

Figure 12.6 *CCA Topology View*

When the CCA tool presents you with the topology view of the network it discovered, you are finally ready to begin customizing it. To customize and manage the SBCS suite, you need to become familiar with the CCA interface.

Understanding the CCA Interface

Becoming familiar with the CCA interface is a key step toward mastering the configuration of the UC500 series. With that in mind, it is necessary to introduce you to the layout of the GUI and its diverse menus and icons. This section first presents the overall layout of the CCA interface at a high level and then briefly introduces the icons and options available to you in the CCA toolbar and feature bar.

The best way to get a feel for the way a geographic area is laid out is to go up to a high point and view the "lay of the land." You can do something similar to get a better understanding of the CCA interface. Looking at the layout of the CCA GUI from a "high level" and then drilling into the details will help you develop a strong understanding of how the tool is laid out. Figure 12.7 shows you how the GUI looks after creating a community.

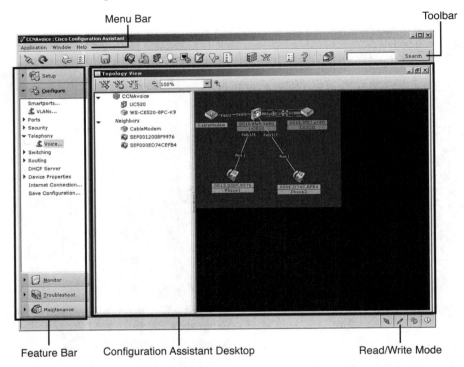

Figure 12.7   *CCA User Interface*

At the top of the screen is the menu bar. In the Application menu, you configure the application preferences, add and remove communities, and perform other high-level activities. The Window and Help menus are self-explanatory. It is worth mentioning, however, that the Help menu is extensive and is a good place to dig around while you are in the process of getting used to the GUI.

Just below the menu bar is the toolbar. This toolbar is where you will find yourself clicking most of the time while you are managing the SBCS suite. Which icons are visible in the toolbar will depend on whether you are physically connected to a live community. Figure 12.8 was captured while connected to a simple community and thus the toolbar is fully populated. Once you are familiar with each of the buttons on the toolbar, you will find that they are intuitive and easy to remember. Figure 12.8 shows the toolbar up close, with the most commonly used buttons labeled.

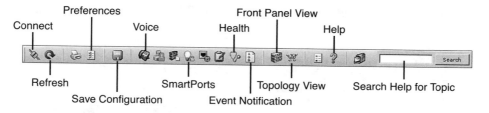

Figure 12.8 *CCA Toolbar*

The buttons that are relevant to configuring voice, troubleshooting the suite, and getting contextual based help are as follows:

- **Connect:** Opens the Connect window, in which you identify what you want to manage with the CCA, either a community or an individual device.

- **Refresh:** Refreshes the view in the Configuration Assistant window by requerying the community members. Any new members to the community are displayed.

- **Preferences:** Opens the Preferences window, where you can set user preferences.

- **Save Configuration:** Saves the changes you make to a device configuration.

- **Voice:** This is the primary button you will be using when configuring the UC520 for voice. Clicking this button is a shortcut for choosing Configure > Telephony > Voice in the feature bar.

- **SmartPorts:** Opens the SmartPorts window, in which you configure ports and devices by assigning roles. A SmartPort is how a port is assigned its role as a trunk or an access port and its native 802.1q VLAN.

- **Health:** Opens the Health window, in which you can monitor a number of devices' health measurements. This button is used extensively in maintaining and troubleshooting the SBCS suite.

- **Event Notification:** Opens a window that displays network conditions that an administrator should be aware of and that might require action.

- **Front Panel View:** Opens the Front Panel view of the devices managed in the community.

- **Topology View:** Opens a network map of the community. Topology view is depicted in Figure 12.7.

- **Help:** Opens the online help for the current window.

Note To keep the focus of this chapter on configuring the UC520 for voice, several of the icons that are visible are not described. If you would like additional information about any of the buttons and their respective features, the extensive Help menu is a great resource. Another helpful source of information is *Getting Started with Cisco Configuration Assistant*, available at Cisco.com, which provides the latest documentation for and screen shots of this tool.

Figure 12.9 shows the next major component of the CCA interface, the feature bar, located on the left side of the CCA desktop.

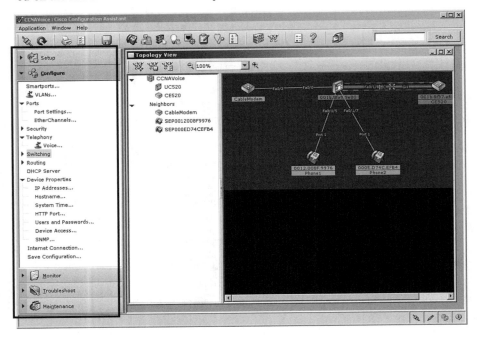

Figure 12.9   *CCA Feature Bar*

The five main menus in the feature bar, listed next, group together related tasks that you, as an administrator, will perform in your day-to-day activities:

- **Setup:** This set of features is used to do basic configuration for the members of the SBCS family and to enable them to be managed by the CCA tool.

- **Configure:** This set of features is used to manage individual ports and devices.

- **Monitor:** This feature set includes most of the tools to monitor the utilization and health of the system.

- **Troubleshooting:** This feature set is used to do basic system troubleshooting in the event of a system issue.

- **Maintain:** This feature set is used to perform basic system maintenance within the SBCS suite. The most common task you will perform from this menu is system backup.

When you click one of the five menu buttons on the feature bar, it expands to reveal the tasks that can be performed from that menu. Clicking an expanded section collapses the menu to hide the tasks associated with that menu.

Now that you have been briefly introduced to the CCA tool, it would be beneficial for you to take some time to get more familiar with it on your own. Once you are confident with the way the CCA tool is laid out, you will be ready to take on the task of configuring the UC520 for voice.

Configuring the UC520 for Voice

In Chapters 3 and 4 you spent a good deal of time building a foundation from which you would configure your first IP phone in Cisco Unified CME. In Chapter 11 and the first half of this chapter, you have been building a foundational knowledge of the SBCS suite, the components that go into that suite, and the CCA tool that manages it. In this final section of the chapter, you will build on that foundation by provisioning the voice features of the UC520 chassis.

CCA Telephony Smart Assist Features

Interwoven throughout the CCA tool are several macros that walk you through the process of provisioning devices in an SBCS community. There are macros that assist in deciding several questions: What type of roles should a given switch port be assigned. Should spanning tree be turned on or off on this port? What should the native VLAN be? To someone new to the field of networking, these questions might be a challenge to answer. There are macros for a brand-new wireless SSID and others that help administrators provision the voice portions of the suite. Collectively the macros are referred to as Cisco Smart Assist features and they are what make the SBCS suite so easy to manage.

The extent to which the Smart Assist features offer configuration guidance is dependant on whether or not the CCA tool is in Expert mode (the default) or Guide mode. Features in the feature bar with an icon that resembles a road sign can offer additional guided configuration help when the Guide mode option is selected. To enable Guide mode for those portions of the CCA tool that offer it, you must click Guide under the Application menu on the menu bar. To return to Expert mode simply click Expert under the same menu.

> **Note**   Clicking the road sign icon on the feature bar will not change the configuration mode that is to be used. To toggle between Expert and Guide modes you must select the mode under the Application menu on the menu bar.

The most powerful of the Cisco Smart Assist macros in the SBCS suite is the macro implemented in the Voice dialog box. Clicking the Telephony icon in the CCA toolbar or drilling down to **Configure > Telephony > Voice** in the feature bar will activate the Voice dialog box. Figure 12.10 shows the initial output of the Voice dialog box after going through what is typically a 30-second internal setup routine during which the UC520's configuration is polled.

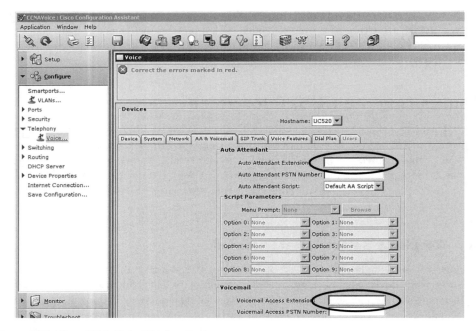

Figure 12.10 *CCA Voice Dialog Box*

Notice that there are sections of the CCA tool that are highlighted (outlined in Figure 12.10). These items need your attention to complete the initial deployment of the telephony features of the SBCS suite. Tabs within the Voice dialog box that have incomplete information will remain red. The text on tabs that have been successfully configured will turn green when the information provided is correct.

While the tabs would generally lend themselves to being configured from left to right, it is best to configure them in a manner in which tab interdependencies are satisfied without the Smart Assist features squawking at you because something isn't quite right. When all the tabs that you have changed information on are outlined in green, you are cleared to save your configuration and bring your new UC system to life.

You might have noticed that the Smart Assist macro running in the Voice dialog box jumped directly to the AA & Voicemail tab. This is the auto-attendant and voice-mail configuration screen that must be filled out—even in a default system. The macro is telling you that the tab needs your attention. Now that you have the Voice dialog box open, walk through the following process:

Step 1.   Begin by filling out the AA & Voicemail tab that comes up automatically:

    a.   In the **Auto Attendant Extension** field, enter **6001**. The field will remain outlined in red because you have filled in a four-digit extension and the Dial Plan tab still indicates that the default extension length is three digits.

    b.   In the **Auto Attendant PSTN Number** field, enter the auto attendant's full E.164 number—in this case **4445556001**.

c. Observe that the Auto Attendant Script drop-down list box has another script that could be selected by clicking on the drop-down box (aa_transfer.aef). This script can be used to create a menu tree for direct access to end users. Ignore this option for now but be aware of its existence.

d. In the **Voicemail Access Extension** filed, enter **6000**. This number will be the voice-mail pilot number for the phone system. Dialing this number directly or pressing the Voicemail button on an IP phone will call your voice-mail system. This field will also remain outlined in red because the extension length has not been changed yet on the Dial Plan tab.

e. In the **Voicemail Access PSTN Number** field, enter the full E.164 number of the voice-mail pilot—in this case **4445556000**.

Figure 12.11 shows how the AA & Voicemail tab should appear after you have completed this step.

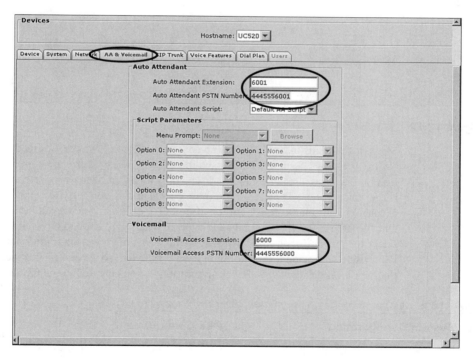

Figure 12.11   *AA & Voicemail Tab*

Step 2.   Click the **Device** tab, shown in Figure 12.12.

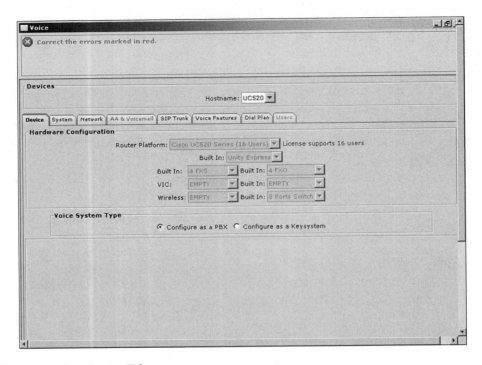

Figure 12.12   *Device Tab*

Most of the fields on this tab are grayed out. Because of the prepackaged nature of the SBCS suite (as discussed in Chapter 11), the hardware configuration in this tab is already established. The only area that needs your attention is the Voice System Type area. You must decide at this point if you would like to fashion your phone configuration after a PBX or after a traditional key system. What appears on other tabs in the voice macro will depend on what you select for this option. In the telephony world, the line between a traditional key system setup and a PBX configuration is blurring, so Table 12.2 outlines the high-level differences in the configuration as implemented in the UC520.

Table 12.2   *Comparing Key System and PBX Configurations*

Key System Configuration	PBX Configuration
No classes of restriction (COR); all phones are limited by PSTN capability.	COR is enforced on a phone-by-phone basis.
Inbound calls are always directed to an auto attendant.	Inbound calls can be directed directly to an extension with DID or by implementing a custom FXO-to-DN mapping.
Outbound calls are dialed by first selecting an open CO line.	Outbound trunk selection is determined by the system and not by the end user.

Step 3.   Click the **Configure as a PBX** radio button.

Step 4.   Click the **Dial Plan** tab.

If you had selected to configure the system as a key system, the Dial Plan tab would appear similar to what is shown in Figure 12.13. Instead, you see the Dial Plan tab shown in Figure 12.14.

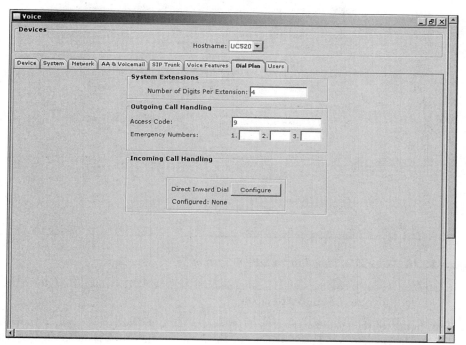

Figure 12.13 *Voice Dial Plan Tab for a Key System*

Step 5.   On the Dial Plan tab, enter **4** in the **Number of Digits Per Extension** field.

Notice that when you change the number of digits from the default of 3 to 4, the Users tab turns red and the AA & Voicemail tab turns green. This is because the value for auto-defined extensions listed in the Users tab is configured for only three digits. The Smart Assist macro in the Voice dialog box is letting you know that the Users tab now needs attention. Based on the fields that are filled in on this page, the Smart Assist macro will go out and create the required dial peers for PSTN access. Note that in both Figures 12.13 and 12.14, there is a field for emergency numbers. Do not manually prepend your emergency number (for example, 911) with your access code in this field (for example, 9911), because when the macro builds the appropriate dial peers for your emergency numbers, it will already prefix the number you put in the Access Code field.

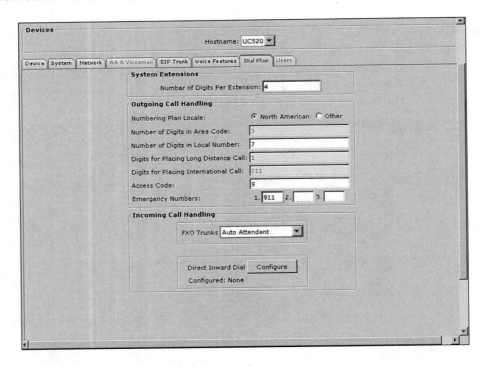

Figure 12.14 *Voice Dial Plan Tab for a PBX System*

Step 6.   In the Incoming Call Handling section, for the **FXO Trunks** drop-down list box, choose **Auto Attendant**.

This section of the Dial Plan tab tells the system what to do with calls inbound from the PSTN. The UC520 model used to generate the figures in this book is preconfigured with four FXO lines and does not have any digital connections to the PSTN. If a PRI, E1, or T1 is included in your UC520, you also need to configure settings for Direct Inward Dial (DID). For this example, you will leave the DID fields alone, but you will revisit this portion of the configuration when creating a SIP trunk. This portion of the Dial Plan tab is used to configure where the system sends a call when its FXO lines ring in. You have three FXO Trunks options to select from at this point:

- **Operator:** If you choose Operator, another field appears on the tab, asking you to enter the extension of the operator.

- **Custom Configuration:** Custom Configuration allows you to manually map each FXO line to a separate number.

- **Auto Attendant:** Choosing Auto Attendant sends the call to the number you designate as the auto attendant under the AA & Voicemail tab.

For this configuration, choose **Auto Attendant**.

Note   It is important to remember that the auto-attendant configuration on this tab is required to implement full auto-attendant functionality. With the AA & Voicemail tab as a prominent part of the Voice dialog box, it is easy to overlook this portion of the auto-attendant configuration.

Step 7.   Click the **Voice Features** tab, shown in Figure 12.15. Enable the voice features that you wish to enable and make sure that the DNs you enter conform to a four-digit dial plan.

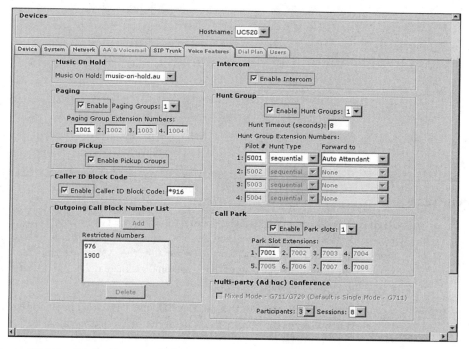

Figure 12.15   *Voice Features Tab*

The Voice Features tab is a busy tab. It is used to configure all sorts of options, from the Music on Hold (MoH) file you wish to play to hunt groups. Fortunately, the tab is laid out such that you click to enable any features you want and enter the appropriate DN.

Note   If you selected to configure the system as a key system, some of the features shown in Figure 12.15 will not appear in this window.

Step 8.   Click on the **User** tab, shown in Figure 12.16.

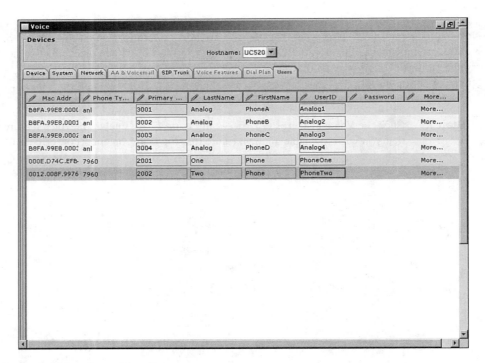

Figure 12.16   *Voice User Tab*

Because you already changed the default value for the Number of Digits Per Extension field under the Dial Plan tab, you need to correct the default extensions assigned for each phone device. By default, the system assigns extensions in the 200 range starting with extension 201. Instead, assign a four-digit extension to each phone.

Step 9.   Complete the **LastName**, **FirstName**, **UserID**, and **Password** fields for each phone. When you have correctly filled in all the fields on this tab, all of its fields will be outlined in green.

Step 10.   Click **More** in the row for your first phone. This opens a dialog box (see Figure 12.17) in which you can customize the configuration of your handsets.

Many of the settings for the phone are actually configured in this dialog box. In the top-right corner is a box that shows line configuration. By default, PhoneOne is configured based on the settings you entered in the User tab. If you would like to assign additional buttons to this phone, this is where you do it. In Figure 12.17, a second line has been applied to this phone.

Additional Line Configured

Figure 12.17 *More Options Dialog Box*

Step 11. To add an additional line to this phone, in the top-right corner of the More Options dialog box, click the button number you wish to configure. In the **Type** column, choose **Normal**. In the **Extension** column, enter a four-digit DN, in this case **2005**.

If you needed to create an overlay button rather than the default type of normal, you would choose Overlay in the Type column. Selecting Overlay as the button type enables the Overlay dialog box, which is brought up by clicking in the button's extension field. The Overlay dialog box is shown in Figure 12.18. As you can see in this figure, a properly configured overlay button requires that you choose at least two extensions. To create the overlay button, choose the extensions you wish to add to the overlay by clicking them in the Available Extensions list and then move them to the Selected Extensions list by clicking Add. When you are creating an overlay button, the extension that will show up on the phone line label is the extension that is highest in the Selected Extensions list. To rearrange the extensions on the overlay button to your liking, select the extension in the Selected Extensions list and then click the up and down arrows on the right side of the window as appropriate. When you are finished with the Overlay window, click OK or cancel to return to the More Options dialog box.

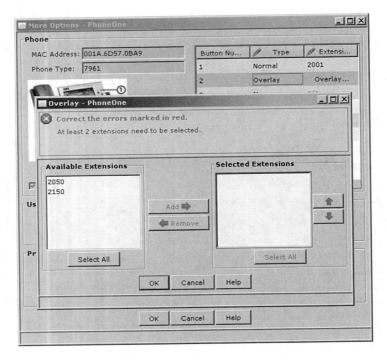

Figure 12.18   Configuring Overlay Extensions

The lower half of the More Options window is where you set the class of restrictions (COR) for this phone and where you associate the phone with pickup and hunt groups. The UC520 predefines several COR lists by default:

■ **Internal:** Gives access to internal DNs only.

■ **Local:** Gives access to internal DNs and the local PSTN.

■ **Domestic:** Gives access to internal DNs and the local and long-distance PSTN.

■ **International:** Gives access to internal DNs, the local and long-distance PSTN, and the international PSTN. This COR is functionally the same as Unrestricted because it has access to all route patterns.

■ **Unrestricted:** Gives unrestricted access. Phones assigned to this COR group do not have any COR lists associated with them. This is the functional equivalent of the International COR because no COR assignment is the technical equivalent of assigning access to all COR list members.

Step 12. Click **OK** in the More Options dialog box when you are done configuring the phone. This takes you back to the Users tab.

Notice that all the tabs under the Voice dialog box are now green. This indicates that you can save your configuration at this point if you have nothing else to change.

Step 13. Before you click Apply at the bottom of the Voice dialog box (the Apply button might be hidden, and you will need to scroll down to see it depending on your screen resolution), click the **Network** tab. On this tab, you can modify the settings automatically applied to the system default voice VLAN and its associated DHCP scope if you so desire. By default, the voice VLAN is VLAN100 and the IP range associated with it is 10.1.1.0/24. If you make changes to these settings, the UC520 system is smart enough to apply the appropriate changes to the system security policy, routing tables, and switch ports to maintain a uniform and complete configuration.

Step 14. Click **Apply** at the bottom of the page to complete your telephone system customization.

SIP Trunking on the UC520

The UC520 is capable of supporting SIP trunks for PSTN connectivity. SIP trunking is configured via the Voice dialog box, similar to configuring FXO ports as you did in the prior section.

If you have ever had to configure SIP trunks with a PSTN carrier, you know that in many cases it can be challenging. Although SIP is a standard, the configuration from one carrier to the next can vary widely. From differences in authentication to methods for negotiating codecs, there is a long list of items that need to be considered when configuring a system for SIP trunking. Despite the fact that SIP trunks can be challenging, Cisco has maintained its commitment to making the SBCS suite easy to configure—it has included the configurations required to implement with a few of the top SIP providers.

To configure SIP on the UC520, you must first verify that your UC520 system has a valid DNS server and domain name configured. To do so, in the CCA feature bar, choose **Configure > Device Properties > IP Addresses** and click the **Device Configuration** tab. If there are any incorrect settings in this window, fix them before proceeding to the SIP trunk configuration. This will save you a lot of trouble in the long run. When you have verified that your DNS configuration is accurate, click the **SIP Trunk** tab, shown in Figure 12.19.

In the Service Provider drop-down list, Cisco provides options to choose the backend configuration required to implement SIP trunking with AT&T and CBeyond Communications. When you select either of these providers, several carrier-specific configurations are added to the base UC520 configuration behind the scenes. If you select the option for Generic SIP Trunk Provider, successful configuration of the SIP trunk may require configuration to the UC520 via the command line. The configurations required will vary from carrier to carrier.

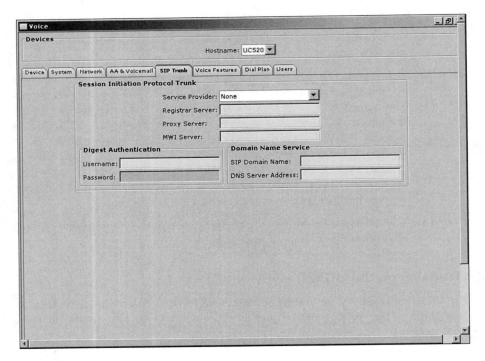

Figure 12.19   *SIP Trunk Configuration*

> **Note**   There is a process for other carriers to add their carrier-specific settings, as have AT&T and CBeyond Communications. Other vendors will publish their required configurations and be applied to this menu via future updates to the Configuration Assistant. Do not despair if your SIP carrier is not in this list; it might be in the process of getting added.

Key
Topic

At a minimum, the following steps are required to configure a SIP trunk on the UC520:

Step 1.   In the Session Initiation Protocol Trunk area of the SIP Trunk tab, select the appropriate provider from the **Service Provider** drop-down list.

Step 2.   Fill out the fields on the SIP Trunk tab as required by your provider. Proxy Server is the only field on this tab that is mandatory, although your SIP provider will most likely give you additional information for the Registrar Server field and the Digest Authentication fields.

Step 3.   Click the **Dial Plan** tab.

Step 4.   Click the **Configure** button next to Direct Inward Dial at the bottom of the tab.

Step 5.   The DID Configuration dialog box appears, in which you will configure a mapping of PSTN DID numbers to internal extensions. Click **Add** in the One-to-One DID Translation section to input the DID mappings appropriate for your installation. If a Many-To-One Mapping is appropriate for your installation, the following steps are relevant in that window as well.

Step 6.   Enter your DID mappings by entering a description, the DID number range assigned by your service provider, and the Internal Number that should be translated. Finally, click in the trunk portion of the row and select **SIP Trunk**.

Step 7.   Click **OK** at the bottom of the DID Configuration dialog box.

Step 8.   Click **Apply** at the bottom of the Voice dialog box to complete the configuration.

Using CCA for System Maintenance and Troubleshooting

Any network administrator will tell you that the two most common day-to-day tasks that they perform are system maintenance (tasks like patching and backups) and troubleshooting. The CCA tool provides an interface for both of those tasks.

System Maintenance with the CCA Tool

The CCA tool has been designed to make the task of maintaining the SBCS suite a trivial task. With the click of a few buttons under the Maintenance menu of the CCA feature bar, an administrator can perform the following tasks:

- Upgrade software within the suite

- Manage file systems

- Back up and restore suite component configurations

- Restart and reset devices

Figure 12.20 shows an example of the Configuration Archive dialog box that opens when you choose Configuration Archive under the Maintenance menu of the feature bar.

As you can see from Figure 12.20, backing up and restoring the system is as simple as pointing and clicking. An archive file for each of the devices backed up will be maintained in the directory you specify in this dialog box.

All the management features of the CCA tool are found under the Maintenance menu of the feature bar.

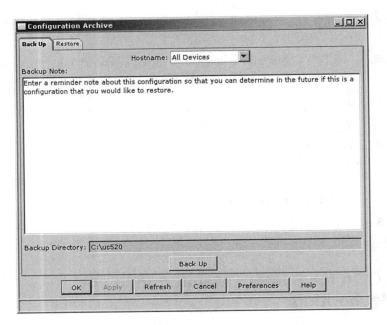

Figure 12.20   *CCA SBCS Suite Backup*

Network Troubleshooting with the CCA Tool

From time to time, a network will experience problems. The CCA tool provides the means for you to troubleshoot such problems. The tools available are found in one of three places within the CCA interface: the Event Notification dialog box, the Health dialog box, or the Troubleshoot menu of the feature bar.

Most commonly, your process of troubleshooting will take you to the Event Notification dialog box first. This dialog box is activated by clicking the **Event Notification** icon in the toolbar (shown earlier in Figure 12.8) or by clicking **Monitor > Event Notification** under the Feature bar. The screen that pops up will alert you to obvious system conditions that have occurred in the system. You can acknowledge all the events with a click of a button and, in many cases, resolve the issue right from this screen.

The second place you will look in the process of troubleshooting with the CCA tool is under the Health dialog box. The Health dialog box can be reached by clicking the stethoscope icon in the toolbar or by clicking **Monitor > Health** on the feature bar. In this handy tool, you can view system statistics in both graph and chart forms, as pictured in Figure 12.21. Figure 12.21 depicts the screen after clicking the Details button on the Health dialog box.

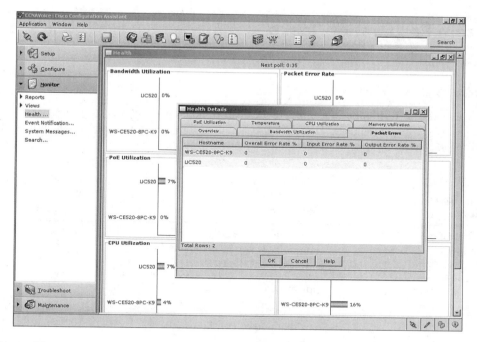

Figure 12.21   *System Menus*

The third place within the CCA tool that you will find useful troubleshooting information is under the Troubleshoot menu of the feature bar. Under this menu, you find the Links and Connectivity tool, which allows you to generate ICMP pings between devices for simple troubleshooting. This tool also enables you to do diagnostics on a port-by-port basis for members of the Catalyst Express family and will give you a simple message offering advice in correcting any issues that may be discovered.

Exam Preparation Tasks

Review All the Key Topics

Review the most important topics in the chapter, noted with the key topics icon in the outer margin of the page. Table 12.3 lists and describes these key topics and identifies the page number on which each is found.

Key
Topic

Table 12.3   *Key Topics for Chapter 12*

Key Topic Element	Description	Page Number
"Understanding Communities" section	Understanding the concept of a CCA community is key to understanding the function of the CCA tool.	443–445
List	Steps required to configure the UC520 for voice.	452–461
List	Steps required to configure SIP trunking on the UC520.	462–463

Definitions of Key Terms

Define the following key terms from this chapter, and check your answers in the glossary.

community

Cisco Discovery Protocol (CDP)

Smartports

key system

Direct Inward Dial (DID)

Power failover (PFO)

CHAPTER 13

Final Preparation

The first 12 chapters of this book cover the technologies, protocols, commands, and features you need to understand to pass the CCNA Voice exam. Although these chapters supply the detailed information, most people need more preparation than simply reading the first 12 chapters. This chapter details a set of tools and a study plan to help you complete your preparation for the exams.

If you are preparing for the CCNA Voice exam, be sure that you have already passed the CCNA level exams, either the CCNA Exam or the ICND1 and ICND2 exams, respectively. For information on passing the CCNA exams, refer to the *CCENT/CCNA ICND1 Official Exam Certification Guide* and the *CCNA ICND2 Official Exam Certification Guide.*

This short chapter has two main sections. The first section lists the exam preparation tools that are useful at this point in the study process. The second section lists a suggested study plan now that you have completed all the earlier chapters in this book.

Tools for Final Preparation

This section lists some information about the available tools and how to access them.

Exam Engine and Questions on the CD-ROM

The CD in the back of the book includes an exam engine—software that displays and grades a set of exam-realistic questions. These include drag-and-drop and many scenario-based questions that require the same level of analysis as the questions on the CCNA Voice exam. Using the exam engine, you can either practice using the questions in Study Mode or take a simulated (timed) CCNA Voice exam.

The installation process requires two major steps. The CD has a recent copy of the exam engine software, supplied by Boson Software (http://www.boson.com). The practice exam—the database of CCNA Voice exam questions—is not on the CD. Instead, the practice exam resides on the www.boson.com web server, so the second major step is to activate and download the practice exam.

Note   The cardboard CD case in the back of this book includes the CD and a piece of paper. The paper lists the activation key for the practice exam associated with this book. *Do not lose the activation key*.

Install the Software from the CD

The software installation process is fairly routine as compared with other software installation processes. To be complete, the following steps outline the installation process:

Step 1.   Insert the CD into your PC.

Step 2.   The software that automatically runs is the Cisco Press software to access and use all CD-based features, including the exam engine, viewing a PDF of this book, and viewing the CD-only appendixes. From the main menu, click the option to **Install the Exam Engine**.

Step 3.   Respond to prompt windows as with any typical software installation process.

The installation process might give you the option to register the software. This process requires that you establish a login at the www.boson.com website. You will need this login in order to activate the exam, so feel free to register when prompted.

Activate and Download the Practice Exam

Once the exam engine is installed, you should then activate the exam associated with this book, as follows:

Step 1.   Start the **Boson Exam Engine (BEE)** software from the **Start** menu.

Step 2.   The first time you start the software, it should ask you to either log in or register an account. If you do not already have an account with Boson, select the option to register a new account. (You must register in order to download and use the exam.)

Step 3.   Once you are registered, the software might prompt you to download the latest version of the software, which you should do. Note that this process updates the exam engine software (formally called the Boson Exam Environment), not the practice exam.

Step 4. To activate and download the exam associated with this book, from the exam engine main window, click the **Exam Wizard** button.

Step 5. In the Exam Wizard pop-up window, select **Activate a purchased exam** and click the **Next** button. (Although you did not directly purchase the exam, you did indirectly purchase the exam when you purchased the book.)

Step 6. Enter the Activation Key (from the paper inside the cardboard CD holder in the back of the book). Once you have entered it, click the **Next** button.

Step 7. The activation process will download the practice exam. Once completed, the main exam engine menu should list a new exam, with a name like "ExSim for Cisco Press CCNA Voice ECG." If you do not see the exam, make sure you have selected the My Exams tab on the menu. You may need to click the plus sign icon (+) to expand the menu in order to see the exam.

At this point, the software and practice exam are ready to use.

Activating Other Exams

The exam software installation process, and the registration process, only has to happen once. Then, for each new exam, only a few steps are required. For instance, if you also bought the *CCENT/CCNA ICND1 Official Exam Certification Guide* and the *CCNA ICND2 Official Exam Certification Guide*, you could follow the steps listed in the last page or so to install the software and activate the exam associated with this book. Then, for the practice exam associated with the ICND1 book and ICND2 book, you only need to do a few more steps. Simply start the exam engine (if it is not still up and running) and perform Steps 4 and 5 from the previous list. In fact, if you purchase other Cisco Press books, or purchase a practice exam from Boson, you just need to activate each new exam as described in Steps 4 and 5.

You can also purchase additional practice exams from Boson directly from its website. When you purchase an exam, you receive an activation key, and then you can activate and download the exam—again without requiring any additional software installation.

The Cisco Learning Network

Cisco provides a wide variety of CCNA Voice preparation tools at a Cisco Systems website called the Cisco Learning Network. The Cisco Learning Network includes Quick Learning Modules, interviews with Cisco's Portfolio Manager for Voice Certifications, documents that give you a sneak peek at what's included in the Instructor Lead Training Course, and blogs and discussion forums to help you on your way.

To use the Cisco Learning Network, you do not need to have a registered login at Cisco.com but you can register as a member of the Learning Network. This will give you access to additional content. To register, simply go to http://tinyurl.com/66l8qv and supply the required information. (You do not need to work for Cisco or a Cisco partner to get a login.)

After you have registered, proceed to the Certifications area and look for the link to the CCNA Voice pages.

Study Plan

You could simply study using all the available tools, as mentioned earlier in this chapter. However, this section suggests a particular study plan, with a sequence of tasks that may work better than just using the tools randomly. However, feel free to use the tools in any way and at any time that helps you get fully prepared for the exam.

The suggested study plan separates the tasks into four categories:

- **Recall the Facts:** Activities that help you remember all the details from the first 12 chapters of the book.

- **Practice Configurations:** You must master configurations on various devices to pass the CCNA Voice exam. This category lists the items you can use to master configuration skills.

- **Build Troubleshooting Skills Using Scenarios:** To answer some exam questions that present a scenario, you may need to recall facts, find log information, and verify configurations. This plan section suggests activities that help you pull these different skills together.

- **Use the Exam Engine to Practice Realistic Questions:** The exam engine on the CD can be used to study using a bank of unique exam-realistic questions available only with this book.

Recall the Facts

As with most exams, there are many facts, concepts, and definitions that you must recall to do well on the test. This section suggests a couple of tasks that should help you complete your work to remember all the details:

Step 1. Review and repeat, as needed, the activities in the "Exam Preparation Tasks" section at the end of each chapter. Most of these activities help refine your knowledge of a topic while also helping you to memorize the facts.

Step 2. Using the exam engine, answer all the questions in the Book database. This question database includes all the questions printed in the beginning of each chapter. Although some of the questions may be familiar, repeating the questions will help you to improve your recall of the topics covered in the questions.

Practice Configurations

A large part of what a CCNA Voice exam involves is performing configurations on various devices. You may need to work on a CME router or UC500 device. Understanding these interfaces and various configurations is a must. This means that hands-on experience is going to take you over the edge to confidently and accurately build or verify configurations.

There are a number of sources for lab access. Some of these sources include rack rentals from trusted Cisco Partners, and if you are a Cisco Partner, you may even have access to the Partner E-Learning Connection (PEC). If you have access to a lab provided by your company, then take advantage of it. Nothing beats hands-on experience.

Additionally, you can review the key topics in each chapter. These often refer to key configuration elements.

Build Troubleshooting Skills Using Scenarios

Just as a real problem in a real network may be caused by a variety of issues—maybe a VLAN mismatch, bad cable, Spanning Tree, an incorrect TFTP configuration, or even errors in your documentation about the internetwork—the exam makes you apply a wide range of knowledge to answer individual questions. The one activity for this section is as follows:

> **Review the scenarios discussed in each chapter:** These scenarios make you think about issues covered in multiple chapters in the book and require more abstract thought to solve the problem.

Use the Exam Engine

The exam engine includes two basic modes:

- **Study mode:** Study mode is most useful when you want to use the practice exam questions for learning and practicing rather than simulating an actual testing environment. In study mode, you can select options such as whether you want to randomize the order of the questions, randomize the order of the answers, automatically see answers to the questions, and so forth.

- **Simulation mode:** Simulation mode simulates an actual CCNA Voice exam by requiring a set number of questions and a set time period. These timed exams not only allow you to study for the actual exam, but also help you simulate the time pressure that occurs on the actual exam.

Choosing Study or Simulation Mode

Both study mode and simulation mode are useful for preparation for the exams. Picking the correct mode from the exam engine's user interface is pretty obvious but you should still spend some time becoming familiar with the exam engine interface.

Passing Scores for the Cisco CCNA Voice Exams

When scoring your simulated exam using this book's exam engine, you should strive to get a score of 85 percent or better. However, the scoring on the book's exam engine does not match how Cisco scores the actual CCNA Voice exam. As it turns out, Cisco does not publish a lot of details about how it scores the actual exam, with the result being that you cannot reasonably deduce which questions you got right or wrong, and how many points are assigned to each question.

Cisco does publish some specific guidance about how it scores the exam, while other details have been mentioned by Cisco personnel during public presentations about the CCNA Voice exam. Some of the key facts about scoring follow:

■ Cisco gives partial credit on simulation questions, so complete as much of a simulation question as you can.

■ Some questions on the exam are weighted heavier than other questions. Some questions may not have any point value at all. However, you will not know the number of points assigned to each question, so always give each question your best shot.

■ The test does not adapt based on your answers to early questions in the test; for example, if you miss a RIP question as question 1, the test does not start giving you more RIP questions.

■ Cisco scores range from 300 to 1000, with a passing grade usually (but not always) around 800 for the CCNA Voice exam.

■ Scoring 800 out of 1000 does not necessarily mean that you got 80 percent of the questions correct.

Part VI: Appendixes

Answers to the "Do I Know This Already?" Quizzes and Q&A Sections

Chapter 1

1. A
2. B
3. A
4. B and C
5. B
6. C
7. D
8. D
9. C and E
10. B

Chapter 2

1. A, C, D
2. A and D
3. C
4. B
5. D
6. A
7. B
8. C
9. D and E
10. C

Chapter 3

1. A, C, and D
2. B
3. A and C
4. C
5. A
6. B
7. B
8. D
9. A
10. C
11. B

Chapter 4

1. B
2. A, D, and E
3. C
4. D
5. A and D
6. A
7. B
8. A, B, and D
9. A and C
10. D

Chapter 5

1. B
2. B
3. D
4. A
5. C

6. B
7. C
8. C
9. B
10. D

Chapter 6

1. B
2. C
3. A
4. D
5. D
6. C
7. D
8. B
9. A
10. A
11. B and C
12. A and C

Chapter 7

1. C
2. D
3. C
4. A
5. B
6. B
7. B and D
8. C
9. B
10. A

Chapter 8

1. A
2. D
3. C
4. E
5. D
6. A and C
7. B
8. C
9. B
10. C

Chapter 9

1. C
2. D
3. B
4. A and B. Both the hardware platform and the license come into play here. The hardware platform has a maximum mailbox limit and the license determines the number of mailboxes that can be configured within the platform's maximum limit.
5. B
6. B
7. C
8. A and D
9. B
10. A, B, D, and E
11. D
12. B. Starting a backup is a manual process for Cisco Unity Express. An administrator must log in to the GUI and click the Start Backup button to begin the process.
13. A

Chapter 10

1. C

2. B

3. C

4. A, C, and D

5. A

6. A

7. D. While port *module/port* is a valid dial-peer configuration, it is used for routing over a time-division multiplexing (TDM) connection. Cisco Unity Express uses IP, not TDM, to communicate with CME.

8. D and E

9. D. Cisco Unity Express's administrative credentials are used to gain access to the Initialization Wizard, but the Cisco Unity Express credentials are configured by the post-installation configuration tool.

10. D

11. B

12. C

Chapter 11

1. C

2. A, B, and D

3. B. The MOH port is a standard audio jack through which an external music source such as a radio, CD player, or an Apple iPod can be connected to provide a dynamic MOH audio stream. When this port is supplying audio, any file in flash designated as the MOH audio source is supplanted. Once the MOH port is disconnected, the flash-based MOH selection will resume playing.

4. A

5. C. Although the UC520 device is based on, and is similar in function to, the Integrated Services Router platform, it does not support dynamic routing protocols, Survivable Remote Site Telephony (SRST) and Communications Manager integration, or WAN interface cards for remote office data connectivity.

6. B

7. A. There are no 48-port switches in this family and only the Catalyst Express 520-24PC provides PoE on each of its 24 10/100 access ports.

8. B. If projected growth exceeds 16 users, the larger 24/32/48 SKUs should be selected in an initial design.

Chapter 12

1. A

2. B

3. A, C, and D

4. C

5. C. Cisco Discovery Protocol is used to determine device adjacencies. Once a device is selected as a seed device for a community, its CDP table is consulted and is the basis for network topology discovery.

6. C. The default username is cisco and the default password is cisco. The password is case sensitive.

7. A

8. B. While the system comes with many preconfigured settings, voice mail will not operate until an auto-attendant and pilot number are configured for the CUE module.

9. C

10. A. Call park slots must be configured and enabled on the Voice Features tab in the voice configuration portion of the CCA.

11. E

CCNA Voice Exam Updates: Version 1.0

Over time, reader feedback allows Cisco Press to gauge which topics give our readers the most problems when taking the exams. Additionally, Cisco may make small changes in the breadth of exam topics or in emphasis of certain topics. To assist readers with those topics, the author creates new materials clarifying and expanding upon those troublesome exam topics. As mentioned in the introduction, the additional content about the exam is contained in a PDF document on this book's companion website at http://www.ciscopress.com/title/1587202077. The document you are reading here is Version 1.0 of this appendix.

This appendix presents all of the latest update information available at the time of this book's printing. To make sure you have the latest version of this document, you should be sure to visit the companion website to see if any more-recent versions have been posted since this book went to press.

This appendix attempts to fill in a void that occurs with any print book. In particular, this appendix does the following:

- Mentions technical items that might not have been mentioned elsewhere in the book
- Covers new topics when Cisco adds topics to the CCNA Voice exam blueprint
- Provides a way to get up-to-the-minute current information about content for the exam

Always Get the Latest at the Companion Website

Given that the main purpose of this appendix is to be a living, changing document, it is very important that you look for the latest version online at the book's companion website. The document you are reading right now was downloaded from the website. To check for a later version since the time you downloaded this file, do the following:

1. Browse to http://www.ciscopress.com/title/1587202077.

2. Select the **Appendix** option under the **More Information** box.

3. Download the latest "Appendix B" document.

Note that the downloaded document has a version number. The latest version is the only version available from the companion website. The document is Version 1.0.

Technical Content

The current version of this appendix does not contain any additional technical coverage. This appendix is here simply to provide the instructions to check online for a later version of this appendix.

Memory Tables

Chapter 5

Table 5.2 *Separators for Use with the* button *Command*

Separator Character	Function
:	
b	
f	
m	
o	
c	
x	
s	
w	

Table 5.3   restart *Versus* reset *Commands*

Command	Used For
	Phone line changes
	Speed dial changes
	DHCP scope changes
	Date and time changes
	Firmware changes
	Locale changes
	Changes to button (services, messages, directories) URLs
	Voice mail number changes

Chapter 7

Table 7.2   *Audio Codec Bandwidth and MOS Values*

Codec	Bandwidth Consumed	MOS
G.711		4.1
Internet Low Bitrate Codec (iLBC)		4.1
G.729		3.92
G.726	32 kbps	3.85
G.729a		3.7
G.728	16 kbps	3.61

Table 7.7   *Protocol Summary*

Standards Body	Industry Support	Used on Gateways	Used on Cisco IP Phones	Architecture
ITU	Excellent	Yes	No	Peer-to-peer
IETF	Fair	Yes	Yes, limited	Client/server
IETF	Very good	Yes	Yes	Peer-to-peer
None	Proprietary	Yes, very limited	Yes	Client/server

Chapter 8

Table 8.3   *Wildcards You Can Use with the* **destination-pattern** *Command*

Wildcard	Description
	Matches any dialed digit from 0–9 or the * key on the telephone keypad. For example, 20.. matches any number from 2000 through 2099.
	Matches one or more instances of the preceding digit. For example, 5+23 matches 5523, 55523, 555523, and so on. This trend continues up to 32 digits, which is the maximum length of a dialable number.
	Matches a range of digits. For example, [1-3]22 matches 122, 222, and 322. You can include a caret (^) before the entered numbers to designate a "does not match" range. For example, [^1-3]22 matches 022, 422, 522, 622, 722, 822, 922, and *22.
	Matches any number of dialed digits (from 0–32 digits).
	Inserts a one-second pause between dialed digits.

Table 8.4   *Destination-Pattern Brackets Wildcard Examples*

Pattern	Description
	Matches dialed numbers beginning with 555, having 1, 2, or 3 as the fourth digit, and ending in any three digits
	Matches dialed numbers where the first digit is 1, 4, 5, or 6 and the last three digits are 555
	Matches dialed numbers where the first two digits are 55, the third digit is 5 or 9, and the last two digits are 12
	Matches dialed numbers where the first digit is *not* 1–7, the second and third digits are any number, and the last digit is 1, 3, or 5

Table 8.5   *Sample PSTN Destination Patterns for North America*

Pattern	Description
	Used for 7-digit dialing areas
	Used for 10-digit dialing areas
	Used for 11-digit long-distance dialing
	Used for service numbers such as 411, 611, and 911
	Used for international dialing

Table 8.6   *Common Digit Manipulation Methods on Cisco Routers*

Command	Mode	Description
	POTS dial peer	Allows you to specify digits for the router to add before the dialed digits. Example: **prefix 011** adds the numbers 011 to the front of the originally dialed number.
	POTS dial peer	Allows you to specify the number of right-justified digits to forward. Example: **forward-digits 4** forwards only the rightmost four digits from the dialed number.
	POTS dial peer	Enables or disables the default digit stripping behavior of POTS dial peers. Example: **no digit-strip** turns off the automatic digit stripping behavior under a POTS dial peer.
	Global	Transforms any dialed number matching the *match* string into the digits specified in the *set* string. Example: **num-exp 4... 5...** matches any four-digit dialed number beginning with 4 into a four-digit number beginning with 5 (4123 becomes 5123). Example: **num-exp 0 5000** matches the dialed digit 0 and changes it to 5000.
voice translation-profile	Global and POTS or VoIP dial peer	Allows you to configure a translation profile consisting of up to 15 rules to transform numbers however you want. The translation profile is created globally and then applied to any number of dial peers (similar to an access list).

Chapter 9

Table 9.2 *Cisco Unity Product Comparison*

	Cisco Unity Express	Cisco Unity Connection	Cisco Unity
Mailboxes server		Up to 7500	Up to 7500 per
Messaging Type		Voice mail and integrated messaging	Voice mail, integrated messaging, and unified messaging
Auto Attendant Capability		Yes	Yes
Platform		Windows or Linux server based	Windows server based
PBX/TDM Support		Yes	Yes
Redundancy		No	Yes

Table 9.3 *Cisco Unity Modules and Capabilities*

	AIM-CUE	NM-CUE	NM-CUE-EC	NME-CUE
Mailboxes				
Voice Ports/ Simultaneous Voice Sessions				
Installation				
Maximum Storage				

Table 9.11 *Password and PIN Settings*

Configuration Option	Password	PIN
Enable expiry (days)		
History depth		
Minimum length		
Account lockout policy		
Number of attempts for temporary lock		
Temporary lockout duration (mins)		
Maximum number of failed attempts		

Table 9.12   *Message Type Order and Options*

Message Type	Order Played	Play	Replay	Save	Delete	Skip	Reply	Forward
Broadcast								
Expired								
Urgent								
New								
Saved								

Chapter 10

Table 10.3   software download *Command*

Option	Explanation
software download server url ftp://*server-ip-address* [/*dir*] [username *username* password *password*]	
software download clean {*package-file-name* | url ftp://*ftp-server-ip-address*/*package-file-name*}	
software download upgrade {*package-file-name* | url ftp://*ftp-server-ip-address*/ *package-file-name*}	
software download status	
software download abort	

Table 10.4   software install *Command*

Command	Option and Function
software install clean {package-file-name | url ftp://ftp-server-ip-address/package-file-name}	
software install upgrade {*package-file-name* | url ftp://*ftp-server-ip-address*/*package-file-name*}	

Table 10.5   *show software Command*

Command	Option and Function
show software {directory	download server	licenses	packages	versions}	The **directory** option lists _____.
	The **download server** option displays _____.
	The **licenses** option displays _____.
	The **packages** option lists _____.
	The **versions** option displays _____.

Chapter 11

Table 11.2   *Smart Business Communications System Suite Components*

Component	Key Function
UC500 Series for Small Business (UC520)	
	Endpoint connectivity and system expansion.
	System expansion via 802.11b/g wireless data and voice communications. Runs in standalone and controller-based modes.
Cisco 526 Wireless Express Mobility Controller	
Cisco Configuration Assistant (CCA)	

Table 11.3   *Catalyst Express 520 Switches*

Model	Port Type Configuration	PoE Ports (Yes or No)	Ideal Use Case
CE520-8PC	8 10/100BASE-TX access ports		Low-density IP phone, wireless AP, or IP video networks
	1 10/100/1000BASE-TX or SFP uplink port		
CE520-24TT	24 10/100BASE-TX access ports		Basic desktop installation with need for integrated QoS and VLAN configuration
	2 10/100/1000BASE-TX uplink ports		
CE520-24LC	20 10/100BASE-TX access ports		Basic desktop connectivity needs with limited PoE requirements
	4 10/100BASE-TX access ports		
	2 10/100/1000BASE-TX of SFP uplink ports		
CE520-24PC	24 10/100BASE-TX access ports		Full-scale IP phone systems or larger wireless networks
	2 10/100/1000BASE-TX or SFP uplink ports		Full-scale IP
CE520G-24TC	24 10/100/1000BASE-TX access ports		Full-scale IP backbone switch for server connectivity or high-speed desktop connectivity requirements
	2 10/100/1000BASE-TX or SFP uplink ports		

Memory Tables Answer Key

Chapter 5

Table 5.2 *Separators for Use with the* **button** *Command*

Separator Character	Function
:	**Normal ring:** Line rings normally on incoming call and handset light flashes as phone rings.
b	**Call waiting beep, no ring:** The line ringer is suppressed on incoming call, but the handset light still flashes. Call waiting beeps are allowed during active calls.
f	**Feature ring:** The line performs a triple ring on incoming calls. This can be useful as a distinctive ring feature.
m	**Monitor mode:** The line does not ring for incoming calls and is unable to place outgoing calls. This mode simply monitors the status of a shared line. For example, if DN 1001 was assigned to ephone 1, you might also assign DN 1001 to the receptionist ephone 2 in monitor mode. This allows the receptionist to see if DN 1001 is currently in use, but not make or receive calls using the line.
o	**Overlay line (no call waiting):** Overlay lines are used to create a shared-line experience between multiple ephones. Overlay lines will be discussed later in this chapter.
c	**Overlay line (with call waiting):** Same idea as the prior separator, but adds call waiting functionality. Overlay lines will be discussed later in this chapter.
x	**Overlay expansion/rollover:** Allows calls to roll over to additional lines of the IP phone when a call is received on an overlay line on which there is already an active call established.

continues

Table 5.2   *Separators for Use with the* **button** *Command (Continued)*

Separator Character	Function
s	**Silent ring:** Disables ring and call waiting beep for incoming calls. The visual lights and onscreen indicators remain active.
w	**Watch mode:** Performs the same function as monitor mode (**m**), but watches *all* the lines on the phone for which the watched line is the primary. For example, if you configured a receptionist to watch DN 1001, which was the primary extension for ephone 1, the receptionist would see that ephone 1 was busy if DN 1001 was in use or if *any of the other lines* on the ephone using DN 1001 as its primary extension were in use. Again, this is primarily for receptionist use; a line in watch mode cannot receive or make phone calls.

Table 5.3   **restart** *Versus* **reset** *Commands*

Command	Used For
restart	Phone line changes
	Speed dial changes
reset	DHCP scope changes
	Date and time changes
	Firmware changes
	Locale changes
	Changes to button (services, messages, directories) URLs
	Voice mail number changes

Chapter 7

Table 7.2   *Audio Codec Bandwidth and MOS Values*

Codec	Bandwidth Consumed	MOS
G.711	64 kbps	4.1
Internet Low Bitrate Codec (iLBC)	15.2 kbps	4.1
G.729	8 kbps	3.92
G.726	32 kbps	3.85
G.729a	8 kbps	3.7
G.728	16 kbps	3.61

Table 7.7   *Protocol Summary*

	Standards Body	Industry Support	Used on Gateways	Used on Cisco IP Phones	Architecture
H.323	ITU	Excellent	Yes	No	Peer-to-peer
MGCP	IETF	Fair	Yes	Yes, limited	Client/server
SIP	IETF	Very good	Yes	Yes	Peer-to-peer
SCCP	None	Proprietary	Yes, very limited	Yes	Client/server

Chapter 8

Table 8.3   *Wildcards You Can Use with the* **destination-pattern** *Command*

Wildcard	Description
Period (.)	Matches any dialed digit from 0–9 or the * key on the telephone keypad. For example, 20.. matches any number from 2000 through 2099.
Plus (+)	Matches one or more instances of the preceding digit. For example, 5+23 matches 5523, 55523, 555523, and so on. This trend continues up to 32 digits, which is the maximum length of a dialable number.
Brackets ([])	Matches a range of digits. For example, [1-3]22 matches 122, 222, and 322. You can include a caret (^) before the entered numbers to designate a "does not match" range. For example, [^1-3]22 matches 022, 422, 522, 622, 722, 822, 922, and *22.
T	Matches any number of dialed digits (from 0–32 digits).
Comma (,)	Inserts a one-second pause between dialed digits.

Table 8.4 *Destination-Pattern Brackets Wildcard Examples*

Pattern	Description
555[1-3]...	Matches dialed numbers beginning with 555, having 1, 2, or 3 as the fourth digit, and ending in any three digits
[14-6]555	Matches dialed numbers where the first digit is 1, 4, 5, or 6 and the last three digits are 555
55[59]12	Matches dialed numbers where the first two digits are 55, the third digit is 5 or 9, and the last two digits are 12
[^1-7]..[135]	Matches dialed numbers where the first digit is *not* 1–7, the second and third digits are any number, and the last digit is 1, 3, or 5

Table 8.5 *Sample PSTN Destination Patterns for North America*

Pattern	Description
[2-9]......	Used for 7-digit dialing areas
[2-9]..[2-9]......	Used for 10-digit dialing areas
1[2-9]..[2-9]......	Used for 11-digit long-distance dialing
[469]11	Used for service numbers such as 411, 611, and 911
011T	Used for international dialing

Table 8.6 *Common Digit Manipulation Methods on Cisco Routers*

Command	Mode	Description
prefix *digits*	POTS dial peer	Allows you to specify digits for the router to add before the dialed digits. Example: **prefix 011** adds the numbers 011 to the front of the originally dialed number.
forward-digits *number*	POTS dial peer	Allows you to specify the number of right-justified digits to forward. Example: **forward-digits 4** forwards only the rightmost four digits from the dialed number.
[no] **digit-strip**	POTS dial peer	Enables or disables the default digit stripping behavior of POTS dial peers. Example: **no digit-strip** turns off the automatic digit stripping behavior under a POTS dial peer.

Command	Mode	Description
num-exp *match digits set digits*	Global	Transforms any dialed number matching the *match* string into the digits specified in the *set* string. Example: **num-exp 4... 5...** matches any four-digit dialed number beginning with 4 into a four-digit number beginning with 5 (4123 becomes 5123). Example: **num-exp 0 5000** matches the dialed digit 0 and changes it to 5000.
voice translation-profile	Global and POTS or VoIP dial peer	Allows you to configure a translation profile consisting of up to 15 rules to transform numbers however you want. The translation profile is created globally and then applied to any number of dial peers (similar to an access list).

Chapter 9

Table 9.2   *Cisco Unity Product Comparison*

	Cisco Unity Express	Cisco Unity Connection	Cisco Unity
Mailboxes	Up to 250	Up to 7500	Up to 7500 per server
Messaging Type	Voice mail and integrated messaging	Voice mail and integrated messaging	Voice mail, integrated messaging and unified messaging
Auto Attendant Capability	Yes	Yes	Yes
Platform	Linux router based	Windows or Linux server based	Windows server based
PBX/TDM Support	No	Yes	Yes
Redundancy	No	No	Yes

Table 9.3   *Cisco Unity Modules and Capabilities*

	AIM-CUE	NM-CUE	NM-CUE-EC	NME-CUE
Mailboxes	Up to 50	Up to 100	Up to 250	Up to 250
Voice Ports/ Simultaneous Voice Sessions	6	8	16	24
Installation	In motherboard slot	In network module slot	In network module slot	In network module slot
Maximum Storage	14 hours	100 hours	300 hours	300 hours

Table 9.11   *Password and PIN Settings*

Configuration Option	Password	PIN
Enable expiry (days)	3–365	3–365
History depth	1–10	1–10
Minimum length	3–32	3–16
Account lockout policy	Disable lockout Permanent Temporary	Disable lockout Permanent Temporary
Number of attempts for temporary lock	1–200	1–200
Temporary lockout duration (mins)	Default of 5 minutes	Default of 5 minutes
Maximum number of failed attempts	1–200	1–200

Table 9.12 *Message Type Order and Options*

Message Type	Order Played	Play	Replay	Save	Delete	Skip	Reply	Forward
Broadcast	1	Yes	Yes	Yes	Yes	No	No	No
Expired	2	Yes	Yes	Yes	Yes	No	No	No
Urgent	3	Yes	Yes	Yes	Yes	Yes	Yes	Yes
New	4	Yes	Yes	Yes	Yes	Yes	Yes	Yes
Saved	5	Yes	Yes	Yes	Yes	Yes	Yes	Yes

Chapter 10

Table 10.3   software download *Command*

Option	Explanation
software download server url ftp://server-ip-address[/dir] [**username** username **password** password]	server-ip-address[/dir] refers to the IP address and the directory of the FTP server.
software download clean {package-file-name | **url ftp://**ftp-server-ip-address/ package-file-name}	package-file-name refers to the name of the file to be downloaded, while ftp-server-ip-address refers to the IP address of the FTP server that contains the file to be loaded. If the **software download server** command has been previously configured, the **url ftp** option is not needed.
software download upgrade {package-file-name | **url ftp://**ftp-server-ip-address/ package-file-name}	package-file-name refers to the name of the file to be downloaded, while ftp-server-ip-address refers to the IP address of the FTP server that contains the file to be loaded. If the **software download server** command has been previously configured, the **url ftp** option is not needed.
software download status	This command reports the status of a software download currently in progress.
software download abort	This command is used to cancel a software download that is currently in progress.

Table 10.4   software install *Command*

Command	Option and Function
software install clean {package-file-name | url ftp://ftp-server-ip-address/ package-file-name}	*package-file-name* refers to the name of the file to be installed, while *ftp-server-ip-address* refers to the IP address of the FTP server that contains the file to be loaded.
	If the **software download server** command has been previously configured, the **url ftp** option is not needed.
software install upgrade {*package-file-name* | url ftp://*ftp-server-ip-address*/ *package-file-name*}	*package-file-name* refers to the name of the file to be installed, while *ftp-server-ip-address* refers to the IP address of the FTP server that contains the file to be loaded.
	If the **software download server** command has been previously configured, the **url ftp** option is not needed.

Table 10.5   show software *Command*

Command	Option and Function
show software {directory | download server | licenses | packages | versions}	The **directory** option lists the contents of the software directory.
	The **download server** option displays the IP address of the download server if configured.
	The **licenses** option displays the installed license files.
	The **packages** option lists the configured Cisco Unity Express application packages.
	The **versions** option displays the current versions of all configured Cisco Unity Express applications.

Chapter 11

Table 11.2   *Smart Business Communications System Suite Components*

Component	Key Function
UC500 Series for Small Business (UC520)	Suite's central point of connection, IP routing, security policy enforcement, VPN server and endpoint, central call processing, and voice mail.
Catalyst Express Family of Switches (CE520)	Endpoint connectivity and system expansion.
Cisco 521 Wireless Express Access Point	System expansion via 802.11b/g wireless data and voice communications. Runs in standalone and controller-based modes.
Cisco 526 Wireless Express Mobility Controller	Centralized control of Cisco 521 Wireless Express Access Points.
Cisco Configuration Assistant (CCA)	Windows-based application suite provisioning, maintenance, and monitoring.

Table 11.3   *Catalyst Express 520 Switches*

Model	Port Type Configuration	PoE Ports (Yes or No)	Ideal Use Case
CE520-8PC	8 10/100TX access ports wireless AP, or IP video networks	Yes	Low-density IP Phone,
	1 10/100/1000TX or SFP uplink port	No	
CE520-24TT	24 10/100TX access ports	No	Basic desktop installation with need for integrated QoS and VLAN configuration
	2 10/100/1000TX uplink ports	No	
CE520-24LC	20 10/100TX access ports	No	Basic desktop connectivity needs with limited PoE requirements
	4 10/100TX access ports	Yes	
	2 10/100/1000TX of SFP uplink ports	No	

continues

Table 11.3 *Catalyst Express 520 Switches (Continued)*

Model	Port Type Configuration	PoE Ports (Yes or No)	Ideal Use Case
CE520-24PC	24 10/100TX access ports	Yes	Full-scale IP phone systems or larger wireless networks
	2 10/100/1000TX or SFP uplink ports	No	
CE520G-24TC	24 10/100/1000TX access ports	No	High-speed backbone switch for server connectivity or high-speed desktop connectivity requirements
	2 10/100/1000TX or SFP uplink ports	No	

GLOSSARY

802.1Q   An industry-standard trunking protocol that allows traffic for multiple VLANs to be sent between switches.

802.3af Power over Ethernet (PoE)   Industry-standard method of supplying power over an Ethernet cable to attached devices.

administration via telephone (AVT) system   Gives an administrator an easy way to record custom prompts and to quickly record and enable the AA alternate greeting via a telephone connection.

analog signal   A method of signaling that uses properties of the transmission medium to convey sound characteristics, such as using electrical properties to convey the characteristics of voice.

auto-assignment   A feature that allows the Cisco Unified CME router to distribute ephone-dns to auto-registered IP phones.

auto attendant   A common application of Interactive Voice Response (IVR) to allow callers to use automated menus to navigate to specific areas of your company.

auto-registration   A Cisco Unified CME feature that allows Cisco IP phones to register with the CME router without an existing ephone configuration; auto-registration is turned on by default.

Automated Attendant (AA)   Provides a business with the ability to answer and direct incoming phone calls to the appropriate person within the business without requiring human intervention.

Automatic Number Identification (ANI)   The term used to describe caller ID information delivered to a voice processing device. Closely related to Dialed Number Identification Service (DNIS), which identifies dialed number information.

call park   A Cisco Unified CME feature that allows you to park a call on hold in a virtual "parking spot" until it can be retrieved.

call pickup   A Cisco Unified CME feature that allows you to answer another ringing phone in the network.

channel associated signaling (CAS)   A method of digital signaling in which signaling information is transmitted using the same bandwidth as the voice.

Cisco Configuration Assistant (CCA)   The GUI tool created by Cisco to provision, manage, troubleshoot, and maintain the Smart Business Communications System.

Cisco Discovery Protocol (CDP)   Protocol that allows Cisco devices to discover other, directly attached Cisco devices. Switches also use CDP to send voice VLAN information to attached IP phones.

Cisco Emergency Responder   Dynamically updates location information for a user based on the current position in the network and feeds that information to the emergency service provider if an emergency call is placed.

Cisco Inline Power   Cisco-proprietary, prestandard method of supplying power over an Ethernet cable to attached devices.

Cisco IOS License   A license from Cisco that allows a router to run the IOS software; most newly purchased routers come with an IOS license.

Cisco Smart Assist   The name commonly associated with the group of wizard-like features integrated into the Cisco Configuration Assistant that simplifies the provisioning and maintenance of the SBCS suite.

Cisco Unified Communications   An architecture that seeks to minimize the differences between the way we would *like* to communicate and the way we *have* to communicate given time, device, and location constraints.

Cisco Unified Communications 500 (UC500)   The small business call processing platform that is able to support up to 48 users.

Cisco Unified Communications Manager   The multiserver call processing platform that is able to support up to 30,000 users per cluster.

Cisco Unified Communications Manager Business Edition   The single-server call processing platform that is able to support up to 500 users and includes integrated voice mail.

Cisco Unified Communications Manager Express (CME)   The call processing platform that is able to support up to 250 users (depending on router hardware).

Cisco Unified Contact Center Express   A call center application that is able to support up to 300 agents.

Cisco Unified MeetingPlace   Provides a multimedia conference solution that gives you the capability to conference voice, video, and data into a single conference call.

Cisco Unified Mobility   Allows users to have a single contact phone number that they can link to multiple devices.

Cisco Unified Presence   Provides status and reachability information for the users of the voice network.

Cisco Unity   The unified messaging platform that is capable of supporting up to 7500 users per server and redundant server configurations.

Cisco Unity Connection   The single-server unified messaging platform that is capable of supporting up to 7500 users.

Cisco Unity Express   The unified messaging platform that is integrated into a Cisco Unified CME router; capable of supporting up to 250 users.

Cisco Unity Express administrator   A subscriber that is a member of the administrators group.

Cisco Unity Express Advance Integration Module (AIM-CUE)   An entry-level hardware platform for Cisco Unity Express, providing up to 50 mailboxes, 14 hours of storage, and either four or six ports that can be used for simultaneous voice sessions, depending upon the model of Cisco ISR router it is installed in.

Cisco Unity Express Auto Attendant (AA) script   A collection of software steps that defines each action to be performed on a received call.

Cisco Unity Express CLI   The command-line interface used to configure and administer Cisco Unity Express.

Cisco Unity Express custom scripting   The act of modifying the default Cisco Unity Express AA script to match a business need.

Cisco Unity Express Editor   A PC software application that is used to create Cisco Unity Express custom scripts.

Cisco Unity Express Enhanced Network Module (NME-CUE)   The high-end hardware platform for Cisco Unity Express, providing up to 250 mailboxes, 300 hours of storage, and 24 ports that can be used for simultaneous voice sessions.

Cisco Unity Express graphical user interface (GUI)   Provides subscribers and administrators with a web interface to use and manage Cisco Unity Express features and functions.

Cisco Unity Express greeting/prompt   A recoded message played to a caller.

Cisco Unity Express Network Module (NM-CUE)   The lower-midlevel hardware platform for Cisco Unity Express, providing up to 100 mailboxes, 100 hours of storage, and eight ports that can be used for simultaneous voice sessions.

Cisco Unity Express Network Module with Enhanced Capability (NM-CUE-EC)   The upper-midlevel hardware platform for Cisco Unity Express, providing up to 250 mailboxes, 300 hours of storage, and 16 ports that can be used for simultaneous voice sessions.

Cisco Unity Express password   Used to authenticate subscribers via the GUI.

Cisco Unity Express PIN   Used to authenticate subscribers via the TUI.

Cisco Unity Express subscriber   A user account configured in Cisco Unity Express.

Cisco Unity Express telephony user interface (TUI)   Provides subscribers and administrators with a telephone interface to use and manage Cisco Unity Express features and functions.

common channel signaling (CCS)   A method of signaling in which information is transmitted using a separate, dedicated signaling channel.

community   A group of devices managed by the Cisco Configuration Assistant via its IP address.

dial peer   Logical configuration used to define dial plan information on a Cisco router.

Dialed Number Identification Service (DNIS)   The term used to describe dialed number information delivered to a voice processing device. Closely related to Automatic Number Identification (ANI), which identifies caller ID information.

Direct Inward Dial (DID)   A voice configuration that allows users from the PSTN to dial directly into an individual phone at an organization without passing through a receptionist or automated attendant application.

directed pickup   A method used with call pickup to answer a phone directly by dialing the extension number of the ringing phone.

dual-tone multifrequency (DTMF)   A type of address signaling in which the buttons on a telephone keypad use a pair of high and low electrical frequencies to generate a signal each time a caller presses a digit.

Dynamic Trunking Protocol (DTP)   Allows switches to dynamically negotiate trunk links.

E.164   An international numbering plan created by the ITU and adopted for use on the PSTN.

Ear and Mouth (E&M)   Analog interface type that acts as a trunk to a PBX system.

ephone   A configuration in the CME router that represents a single IP phone (or IP telephony device).

ephone-dn   A configuration in the CME router that represents a single directory number (DN).

Extended Super Frame (ESF)   A modern T1 signaling method that sends 24 T1 frames at a time.

feature license   A license dictating the number of IP phones a Cisco Unified CME router is able to support.

feature ring   Causes an IP phone to ring with three consecutive pulses; configured by using the f button separator.

Foreign Exchange Office (FXO)   Analog interface type that connects to a telephone carrier central office (CO) or PBX system; FXO ports receive dial tone from the attached device.

Foreign Exchange Office (FXO) ports   Analog interfaces that allow you to connect a VoIP network to legacy telephony networks such as the PSTN or a PBX system.

Foreign Exchange Station (FXS)   Analog interface type that connects to a legacy, analog device (station); FXS ports provide dial tone to the attached device.

Foreign Exchange Station (FXS) ports   Analog interfaces that allow you to connect a legacy analog telephony device to a VoIP network.

G.711   Uncompressed audio codec consuming 64 kbps of bandwidth.

G.726   Compressed audio codec consuming 32 kbps of bandwidth.

G.728   Compressed audio codec consuming 16 kbps of bandwidth.

G.729   Compressed audio codec consuming 8 kbps of bandwidth.

general delivery mailbox (GDM)   A mailbox that is shared by a group of subscribers.

glare   An instance in which a user picks up a phone and connects unexpectedly to an incoming call.

ground start signaling   A method of signaling that relies on grounding wires connecting to a device to signal a new call; typically used in PBX systems to avoid glare.

H.323   Protocol suite created by the ITU-T to allow multimedia communication over network-based environments.

H.450.2   Industry-standard method of transferring calls without hairpinning.

H.450.3   Industry-standard method of forwarding calls without hairpinning.

hairpinning   A problem that occurs when a call is transferred or forwarded from one IP phone to another that keeps the audio path established (or hairpinned) through the original IP phone; this tends to cause QoS issues with the call.

integrated messaging   Provides access to voice-mail message via an e-mail client and allows a subscriber to treat voice-mail messages similarly to e-mail messages.

Interactive Voice Response (IVR)   An automated system that provides a recorded, automated process to callers accessing your voice network.

Internet Low Bitrate Codec (iLBC)   Compressed audio codec consuming 15.2 kbps of bandwidth.

Internet telephony service provider (ITSP)   Provides VoIP trunk connectivity to the PSTN to provide a cost savings over traditional telephony service providers (TSPs).

Inter-Switch Link (ISL)   A Cisco-proprietary trunking protocol, which has been replaced by the industry-standard 802.1Q.

key system   A system that allows a company to run a private, internal voice network; key systems are usually used in smaller companies and provide shared-line extensions to all devices (although many key systems now provide unique extensions to all devices).

LAN expansion port   The 10/100BASE-TX port in the UC520 that is automatically configured in the security configuration as the external system interface. This port is used to connect to a DSL or cable router for Internet access.

live record   Enables a subscriber to record a live call and have that call delivered into the subscriber's mailbox.

live reply   Enables a subscriber to use the received caller identification number (ANI) and place a phone call to that caller during voice-mail message playback.

local directory   The directory that is built automatically by the CME router as you define caller ID information for the ephone-dns.

local group pickup   A method used with call pickup to answer a ringing phone from within the local group of an IP phone.

local loop   The PSTN link between the customer premises (such as a home or business) and the telecommunications service provider.

loop start signaling   A method of signaling that relies on connecting the tip and ring wires connecting to a device to complete an electrical circuit; typically used in devices connecting to the PSTN.

mailbox caller features   Mailbox features that Cisco Unity Express offers to a caller, where the caller may or may not be a subscriber configured on Cisco Unity Express.

mailbox subscriber features   Mailbox features that Cisco Unity Express offers to a configured subscriber.

Mean Opinion Score (MOS)   A subjective method of determining voice quality; listeners hear a phrase read over a voice network and rate the quality of the audio on a scale of 1 to 5.

Media Convergence Server (MCS)   The server hardware platforms that support Cisco Unified Communications Manager software.

Media Gateway Control Protocol (MGCP)   Voice signaling protocol created by the IETF; allows voice gateways to be controlled by a centralized call agent in client/server fashion.

message notification   Feature used to generate a call, send an e-mail, or send a page to the subscriber when a new message has arrived in their mailbox.

message waiting indicator (MWI)   Provides a mechanism to alert a subscriber that a new message has arrived in a mailbox. This is typically achieved by turning on a light on the subscriber's IP phone.

Monitor Mode/Watch Mode   Line configuration that allows you to assign line instances to a Cisco IP phone that cannot be used for incoming or outgoing calls; rather, they can simply be used to check line status.

Network Time Protocol (NTP)   Synchronizes the clock of a network device to a more accurate NTP server.

Nyquist theorem   Describes the method of converting analog audio signals into digital format by sampling at twice the highest frequency of the audio.

other group pickup   A method used with call pickup to answer a ringing phone from another group number, which must be specified after pressing the GPickUp softkey.

overlay line   Allows shared line configurations by assigning multiple line instances to a single physical line button (overlay) on a Cisco IP phone; configured by using the o, c, or x separator.

phone user license   A license belonging to each Cisco IP phone that allows it to communicate with a Cisco Unified CME router or Cisco Unified Communications Manager server; most newly purchased IP phones come with a phone user license.

power failover (PFO)   The feature that allows the UC520 to complete calls out to the PSTN from a designated analog phone in the event of a power failure.

private branch exchange (PBX)   A system that allows a company to run an internal, private voice network; PBX systems are usually used in larger companies and provide unique extensions to all devices.

private distribution lists   A collection of subscribers created by a single subscriber for exclusive use by that subscriber.

Private Line Automatic Ringdown (PLAR)   A configuration used to enable "immediate dial" applications, such as a phone that immediately dials an emergency number when a user lifts the handset.

public distribution list   A collection of subscribers that is available to all Cisco Unity Express subscribers to use as a distribution list.

pulse-amplitude modulation (PAM)   The process of sampling an analog waveform many times to determine numeric electric amplitude values for digital conversion; PAM is typically combined with pulse-code modulation (PCM).

pulse-code modulation (PCM)   The process of converting pulse-amplitude modulation (PAM) values into binary number equivalents that voice equipment can transmit over digital circuits.

pulse dialing   A type of address signaling in which the rotary-dial wheel of a phone connects and disconnects the local loop circuit as it rotates around to signal specific digits.

Q.931   A signaling protocol used by ISDN CCS implementations.

quantization   The process of assigning analog signals a numeric value that can be transported over a digital network.

Real-time Transport Control Protocol (RTCP)   The UDP-based protocol responsible for transporting audio statistics; uses random, odd-numbered UDP ports from 16,384 to 32,767 for communication.

Real-time Transport Protocol (RTP)   The UDP-based protocol responsible for transporting audio packets; uses random, even-numbered UDP ports from 16,384 to 32,767 for communication.

robbed bit signaling (RBS)   An implementation of channel associated signaling (CAS) that steals the eighth bit of every sixth frame of a digital T1 circuit for signaling information.

router-on-a-stick   An inter-VLAN routing configuration that allows a single router to move data between VLANs by using a FastEthernet or greater interface broken into subinterfaces connected to a switch trunk port.

service engine   The interface that is created on Cisco Unified CME after the Cisco Unity Express hardware platform is installed and recognized by the router. CME will route calls through this interface to the service module for Cisco Unity Express to process.

service module   The internal interface of Cisco Unity Express. Cisco Unity Express will route calls through this interface to the service engine for Cisco Unified CME to process.

Session Initiation Protocol (SIP)   Voice signaling protocol created by the IETF as a lightweight alternative to H.323.

Signaling System 7 (SS7)   The protocol used within the telephony service provider network to provide inter-CO communication and call routing.

Skinny Client Control Protocol (SCCP)   Cisco-proprietary voice signaling protocol used to control Cisco IP phones.

Smartports   A CCA macro that aids in configuration of roles for individual ports.

Spanning Tree Protocol (STP)   A method designed to prevent loops in switched networks due to redundant inter-switch connections.

Super Frame (SF)   An early T1 signaling method that sent 12 T1 frames at a time.

Survivable Remote Site Telephony (SRST)   A configuration that allows a router to act as a failover device if an IP phone is unable to reach a Cisco Unified Communications Manager server.

switched virtual interface (SVI)   A routed interface on a switch.

time-division multiplexing (TDM)   A method of transmitting multiple channels of voice or data over a single digital connection by sending data in specific time slots.

trunk port   A port on a Cisco switch specifically configured to transmit multiple VLANs. Trunks are typically used between switch devices and in router-on-a-stick configurations.

virtual LAN (VLAN)   A configuration used to break a switch into multiple broadcast domains and IP subnets.

VLAN Trunking Protocol (VTP)   A Cisco-proprietary protocol that replicates VLAN database information to all switches participating in the same VTP domain.

voice expansion port   The integrated Voice/WAN Interface Card (VWIC) port in all models of the UC520 that allows for PSTN voice expansion. This port does not support WAN connectivity.

Voice Profile for Internet Mail (VPIM)   A feature that allows one voice-mail system to exchange messages with another voice-mail system.

VoiceView Express   An XML application that provides to subscribers GUI access to their voice-mail messages via the Services button on an IP phone.

Index

R

S

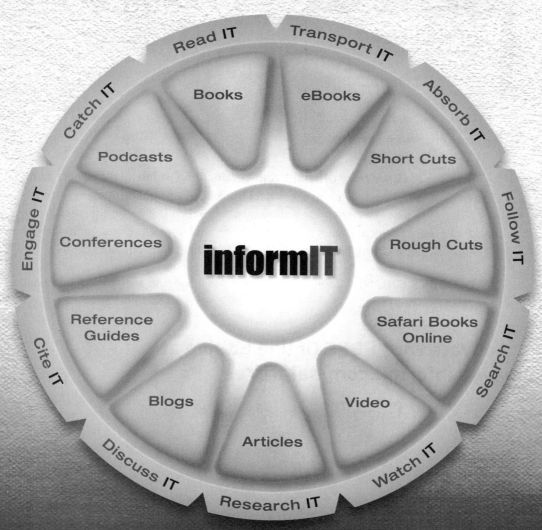

Your purchase of **CCNA Voice Official Exam Certification Guide** includes access to a free online edition for 45 days through the Safari Books Online subscription service. Nearly every Cisco Press book is available online through Safari Books Online, along with over 5,000 other technical books and videos from publishers such as Addison-Wesley Professional, Exam Cram, IBM Press, O'Reilly, Prentice Hall, Que, and Sams.

SAFARI BOOKS ONLINE allows you to search for a specific answer, cut and paste code, download chapters, and stay current with emerging technologies.

Activate your FREE Online Edition at www.informit.com/safarifree

> **STEP 1:** Enter the coupon code: RVTZPWA.

> **STEP 2:** New Safari users, complete the brief registration form.
> Safari subscribers, just login.

If you have difficulty registering on Safari or accessing the online edition, please e-mail customer-service@safaribooksonline.com